Theological Reflection

Elaine Graham is Samuel Ferguson Professor of Social and Pastoral Theology at the University of Manchester. She is the author of *Making the Difference: Gender, Personhood and Theology* (Mowbray, 1995), *Transforming Practice* (Mowbray, 1996, 2nd Edition, 2002) and *Representations of the Post/Human* (Manchester, 2002).

Heather Walton is Lecturer in Practical Theology at the University of Glasgow. She is co-editor, with Susan Durber, of *Silence in Heaven: a Book of Women's Preaching* (SCM Press, 1994) and co-editor, with Elizabeth Stuart, of the journal *Theology and Sexuality* (Sage).

Frances Ward is Residentiary Canon at Bradford Cathedral, West Yorkshire. She is author of *Lifelong Learning: Theological Education and Supervision* (SCM Press, 2005) and co-editor of *Studying Local Churches: A Handbook* (SCM Press 2005).

Theological Reflection:

Sources

Elaine Graham, Heather Walton
and Frances Ward

scm press

© Elaine Graham, Heather Walton and Frances Ward 2007

British Library Cataloguing in Publication data

A catalogue record for this book is available
from the British Library

ISBN 978-0-334-02977-9

First published in 2007 by SCM Press
13–17 Long Lane,
London EC1A 9PN

www.scm-canterburypress.co.uk

SCM Press is a division of
SCM-Canterbury Press Ltd

Typeset by Rowland Phototypesetting Ltd,
Bury St Edmunds, Suffolk
Printed and bound in Great Britain by
MPG Books Ltd, Bodmin, Cornwall

Contents

Editors' Preface

This volume is the companion to our earlier book, *Theological Reflection: Methods* (SCM Press, 2005) which set out seven types of theological reflection, highlighting their biblical, classical, modern and contemporary expressions. In this companion volume, we have assembled a selection of primary sources in order to demonstrate each method in greater detail and to indicate the versatility of each approach.

Each chapter contains a mixture of classic or foundational texts, plus a number of more contemporary selections, which are designed to show current examples of each method. A brief reiteration of the method in question is followed by extracts in roughly chronological order, preceded by some introductory paragraphs that highlight the critical significance of each text.

Readers will note that we have also assembled a set of texts for 'Theological Reflection' as a generic category. As we indicated in the Introduction to *Theological Reflection: Methods*, the literature in this area has expanded greatly over the past decade, and so it seemed appropriate to devote a separate section to some of the implications of this. The primary texts have therefore been selected to explore some of the underlying issues inherent in the turn to theological reflection in adult theological education, such as the nature of revelation, the relationship between 'tradition' and 'experience', and the locus of theological reflection in church, academy and society.

As with any collection of this kind, practical considerations have restricted our choice of texts. In addition to our primary selections, therefore, we have included a short bibliography of further references that we were unable to include in the chapters themselves. We hope that this will encourage readers to undertake literature searches for themselves, and to find further sources and resources for the activity of theological reflection.

Finally, we gratefully acknowledge the help and support of our colleagues, students, families and friends; but above all our thanks go to Beth Lintin and Andrew Wilshere, who helped with the copyright and the production of the manuscript, and to staff at SCM Press, especially Barbara Laing, Christine Smith, Jenny Willis and Michael Addison.

Elaine Graham
Heather Walton
Frances Ward

Introduction

Theological Reflection

Over the past 25 years, the identity of practical theology has been subject to considerable revision. This period has seen a shift from a discipline that regarded itself as supplying practical training for the ordained ministry, often within a clinical or therapeutic context, to one that understands (practical) theology as critical reflection on faithful practice in a variety of settings. This is about a move, therefore, from 'applied theology' to a 'theology of practice' – or as Pattison and Lynch have put it recently, 'from hints and helps to hermeneutics' (2005, p. 408) – with the activity of 'theological reflection' at its very heart.

Yet *Theological Reflection: Methods* also argued that the vogue within many parts of adult theological education for encouraging students to 'reflect theologically' has suffered from lack of rigour. In its emphasis on the immediate imperatives of ministry, it proceeds with no clear idea of how traditional Christian sources such as Scripture are to be handled; it lacks proper integration with other fields of scholarship such as biblical studies, systematic theology and the history of Christianity; and it does not equate its own contemporary practice of reflection with similar processes that have given rise to theological discourse throughout Christian history.

The aim of the companion volume to this one, *Theological Reflection: Methods* (SCM Press, 2005), was to address some of these deficiencies and attempt a new approach to the activity of theological reflection. Behind that book, and this volume, is a contention that 'theological reflection' is a perennial feature of Christian tradition. We argued that theological reflection has developed out of specific circumstances and historically came to birth in order to resolve particular demands experienced by the earliest Christian communities. The threefold task of facilitating Christian nurture, of describing the normative ethos and contours of the faithful community, and of engaging in dialogue and apologetics to the wider world constitutes theology as a form of 'practical wisdom' within which faithful discipleship is shaped. Addressing the three practical questions of nurture, identity and mission, Christians have turned to the sources of their faith, such as Scripture, experience, Church practice and cultural information, in order to sketch the normative horizons by which authentic living can be guided.

Theological Reflection: Methods set out seven different 'models' or exemplary methods of reflection. While these were necessarily heuristic devices, or 'ideal types', it was nevertheless our underlying conviction that each occupied a legitimate and significant place in the spectrum of Christian theology. Perhaps in this respect there is an analogy to be drawn between the science of genetics and theological reflection. The complex sequence of molecules known as deoxyribonucleic acid (DNA) is comprised of four base molecules – adenine, cytosine, guanine and thymine – which combine into many different sequences that carry the information necessary for the construction of cells and proteins. Similarly, many theological traditions talk of a 'quadrilateral' of sources – namely Scripture, tradition, culture or experience, and reason – which combine and interact in a variety of ways; and if the information encoded in DNA functions as the blueprint of life itself, so too the 'base elements' of Christian theology can be configured into many legitimate styles of doing theology that are capable of bestowing life and vitality upon the values of faith. Yet fundamentally, theological reflection arises from practical discipleship: in articulating the nature of faithful identity, in the search for theological foundations to moral reasoning and the importance of being able to engage with those who hold different world-views.

James N. Poling and Lewis S. Mudge, 'Editors' Introduction'

in *Formation and Reflection*, Philadelphia: Fortress Press, 1987, pp. xiii–xiv; xvi–xix; xx–xxiii.

This editorial introduction signals one of the earliest examples in contemporary practical theology of the turn from a discipline concerned with the applied or clerical skills for ministry towards a deeper and more intellectually rigorous attention to the practice of what is called 'theological reflection'.

One of the authors' central premises is that of the lack of clarity and rigour surrounding the activity of 'theological reflection' in adult theological education, clerical and lay. A vast gulf exists between the two worlds of academic theology and adult theological education as practised in ecclesial contexts, whereby any mutuality or interplay between the two is non-existent. Anticipating Ellen Charry's thesis (1997) concerning the centrality of Christian doctrine for the proper articulation of faithful virtue, Poling and Mudge argue that theological reflection is vital for the facilitation of Christian formation. This is a manifesto for the importance of 'doing theology in the community of faith', urging Christians, individually and corporately, to regard theological reflection as a vital part of the life of faith and as the wellspring of effective and authentic Christian discipleship.

Theology ultimately takes root in the life of the Church – a difficult prospect for those impatient with its conservatism or timidity. The Church may be 'a culture in its own right' (p. 10) but its theological reflection is not a discourse for its own preservation but in order that its members engage with the realities of the 'real world'.

What is the relation between 'theology' as an academic discipline and living, worshiping, serving communities of faith? Despite good intentions that it should be otherwise, many today would say that little relationship exists. On the one hand, the academic theological world seems preoccupied with its own problems of methodological coherence and reality reference. On the other, faith communities – whether oriented to the center, the left, or the right – function with scant attention to theology of the scholarly, critical kind. Nuances and qualifications aside, traditional Western assumptions about the relation between church and theology, between faith lived and faith thought-through, seem by and large to be evaporating before our eyes.

This does not bode well for the Christian faith. It is not that academicism is necessary to discipleship: far from it. But if faith by its nature seeks understanding, if conviction must stand up to critical, publicly responsible reflection, then the canons of critical inquiry as they have grown up in the West are indispensable until we have something better. Yet the professional theological community – located in institutions and faculties that see themselves as part of the academic world of doctoral programs, tenure, and all the rest – is now under attack from every side. Never entirely trusted by secularly minded colleagues, the theologians seem even less trusted today by congregations of believers. Although center, left, and right are distrustful for different reasons, the effect is the same. At the 'mainline' center, there is a loss of ecclesial and cultural identity and also a slide toward intellectual decay. 'Main-line' congregations want to be told who they are in a world that seems to have passed them by. They believe that seminary professors either do not understand them or deliberately make matters more complex than they need to be. The religious right believes this last point too, but also tends to think that many theologians are not believers in a sense which simple Christians can understand. The left, on the other hand, sees the theological community as unduly privileged: isolated in a position of relative power remote from the battles for justice and peace which faith communities must fight.

In this volume, eight theologians from various sectors of the academic world acknowledge these criticisms yet seek to reaffirm their responsibility to, and within, the community of faith. The vehicle of this reaffirmation is a convergence of concerns, variously identified by different observers, which may soon deserve to be called a movement. The editors have chosen to use the term 'practical theology', not because the expression is without drawbacks (some of our writers in fact are uncomfortable with it), but because for better or for worse it indicates a direction, and may suggest a genre.

By 'practical theology' we mean that movement among seminary and university and divinity-school faculty which makes the process of *formation* of Christian community and personhood in the world thematic for critical *reflection*. Reflection can be *about* the formation of the community of faith, and it can also be, in another form, an element *within* this process of formation. There are other ways in which the practical theology movement can be described. Our reasons for describing the movement in these particular terms will become evident in what follows.

This book eschews the current romanticism that theology simply is 'the work of the people of God'. Of course it is. But any pastor knows that if a typical congregation of Christian people is simply told to go and 'do theology', what will come out will be a mishmash of favorite scripture verses quoted out of context, superstitions, fragments of civil religion, vague memories of poorly taught Sunday-school lessons of long ago, and the like. Not an inspiring picture. The polls of 'religious beliefs' indicate enormous confusion among professed Christians about the content and implications of their faith. If the people are to be the theologians, as they must be, theology as a fully responsible enterprise must teach them what it is to do theology in the community of faith. They must be taught, so that they can then surpass their teachers.

. . .

Finding Leverage on the Problem

Given that we wish to close the gap between theological 'academics' and the shared life of faith, how may we gain leverage on the problem? The usual means have not worked very well. As Thomas Ogletree puts it in *Practical Theology*, 'We encourage the academically oriented to venture some practical life applications of the knowledge they have gained, and we urge the practically minded to draw more widely on the resources of the academic disciplines in "reflecting" on the meaning of concrete human involvements.'[1] But this, as the editors of the present book know from personal experience as theological educators, asks the student to perform feats of intellectual and practical integration that no one on the faculty seems prepared to demonstrate. The sense dawns that there are underlying questions here that have to do with our very conception of the theological task, with the conceptual equipment the church uses in thinking, and in thinking *about* its thinking. As Ogletree puts it, 'What we need is a reconstruction of our understandings of the relation between theory and practice in our theological work, and of the distinctions and connections between theoretical and practical knowledge that figure in that relation.'[2]

Any approach to such a reconstruction must begin with some frame of reference, some knot in the thread. This makes the work possible and simultaneously limits its scope. The terms 'formation' and 'reflection' taken together serve this purpose for us. What do these words mean? How are they related?

The word 'formation' is widely used of course, particularly in Roman Catholic circles, to refer to the training in disciplined spirituality received by a future priest or member of an order. But it has further meanings. One may speak of intellectual formation, ethical formation, personal formation, community formation, and so on. Formation may mean the *act* of giving shape to something, or the manner in which it *is* formed: by its past, its circumstances, its inherent structure. Thus formation may be a conscious process, as in a religious community, or the word may point to personal or cultural depth structure: present and powerful although we do not know it. As used in this book (and also where the notion is implied although different words are used) 'formation' is the total process by which a given expression of Christian faith – as a company of persons in community in a given setting – comes to be and perdures in the world. Formation is partly under conscious control as an exercise in leadership, but it is also partly a matter of materials, assumptions, tendencies already present in the situation. To be grasped, the complex elements in any given case of Christian formation must be teased out by use of the appropriate images, models, and concepts.

Hence, the element of 'reflection'. This word is at least as multivalent as 'formation'. The notion, naturally, has a history. The word may simply mean deliberation, a conscious standing aside from the march of events to pass alternative possibilities in review. Or it may mean, in a more sophisticated sense, an act by which we objectify our own processes of thought in order to examine their logical validity or their claim to generate knowledge. Taken to a still further stage, reflection may mean thinking designed to grasp symbolically the force or desire that comes to expression in the self. Or reflection may be transcendental (asking, say, on what conditions a world like this is possible), or metaphysical (asking what fundamental reality lies behind the world of flux and change). The essays in this book nowhere offer a philosophical reflection on reflection, for which the reader may be duly thankful. But all are *examples* of reflection in that they seek ways of sorting out what happens as the community of faith takes its shape in the world. To talk *about* this is to be engaged in a reflective process. Reflection necessarily means putting some kind of a grid over the material in order to get it into manageable categories. One may choose various conceptual means for doing this, thereby producing different descriptive characterizations. One may say, for example, that the process of formation is best thought of in 'praxis' terms, or that it is, in essence, a 'hermeneutic of situations'. Or one may argue that it should be treated as a form of ethical deliberation in which one may distinguish different levels. Or that it is essentially correlative, or essentially emancipatory. Ultimately, theology must ask what lies behind the witness of the people of God as such, reaching toward what Schubert Ogden calls 'fully reflective understanding'.[3]

This variety of possibilities, both in the definition of our terms and in our understanding of their relationship, offers rich resources for understanding the essays in this book. It does so, we trust, without limiting or distorting what the writers seek to say.

Potential Agreements and Emerging Questions

If issues are to be defined there must be agreement sufficient to permit meaningful questions to be posed. A certain consensus is beginning to appear about the terrain we are seeking to map. Our authors would probably agree in general to the following three propositions although each would wish to put each point in his or her own way: (1) that the contexts and ways in which Christian community and personhood are formed today have become almost unmanageably diverse: to the extent that one may doubt that any single style of theological reflection can hold them together, much less defend rationally the proposition that they represent one faith; (2) that today's academic theological disciplines are ill-equipped even to begin the needed reflection on formation: they have lost their grounding in the thought and experience of contemporary faith communities and in consequence have also lost clarity about their methods and reasons for being; and (3) that the traditionally conceived relationships between theory and practice, tradition and faith-enactment, need to be radically rethought in the light of the ways in which these polarities are transformed in actual communities of worship and service. Let us examine each of these propositions more closely.

. . .

Pluralism of one sort or another has long been with us, of course. The New Testament itself is a collection of documents from different contexts displaying important differences of presupposition, perception, and rhetorical method. The reality has been around for millennia, but the *concept* of pluralism is of recent vintage. The appearance of a concept means that it has become important to *mark* the reality: to insist that it be taken into account. 'Pluralism' now means something different from its older cousins 'indifferentism' and 'toleration'. It does not say that differences of religious belief and practice are unimportant, or that we may permit what we do not necessarily endorse or approve. 'Pluralism' says that something important has happened to society such that the perennial reality of fundamental difference among human beings and cultures has become salient, and thus claims our attention.[4]

What is this claim on our attention? Some are saying that it is a moral claim. Our planet has become a 'multicultural global village'. The easy communications we enjoy appear to have intensified the themes of individuality and group identification. At the moment at which the sense of the whole planet Earth and the whole human race is more evident to us than ever before, we are coming to realize that humanity is many communities, self-identified and discerned on the basis of many different rationales, each legitimately insisting on the right to be on its own terms, to be heard by others, to take its part in the councils of the human race. No longer may the dominant groups in society define reality so as to deny the identity of others and make their own ordering of the world seem equivalent to natural law. Reality itself is many things, depending on the angle from which we view it. And we feel moral pressure, not merely intellectual fascination, in these demands.[5]

This new recognition of pluralism has made its companion theme 'contextuality' a matter to be reckoned with as well. If one can no longer take for granted that the formative interaction between tradition and one's own context is simply normative, one must ask *how* such interactions take place and how 'other' interactions are to be regarded. The copious evidence of pluralism and contextuality throughout Scripture and church history begins to be seen in a new light. Above all, we want to know how radical the reality of pluralism is, how total the dependence of faith-formation upon context. On the one hand, we may hold to the view that tradition and faith are one despite their many forms. On this showing, all that is needed is skill in adapting the *depositum fidei* (tradition of faith) to the conditions that obtain in any given case. At the other extreme, we may conclude that we are faced with what amounts to an irreducible diversity of forms of Christian faith and life. If so, there may be no 'one gospel for the whole world', or at least not one that can be articulated or conceptualized as a single, identifiable entity.

Perhaps the truth lies somewhere in between. Still the intellectual and spiritual challenge is formidable. The church faces life-or-death issues, issues around which cluster questions of basic integrity and faithfulness to the gospel. But the issues in different parts of the world, in different cultures, are not the same. In the West, the 'crisis of cognitive claims' continues to be very real. But in Latin America, the issue is between the Christianity of the rich and the Christianity of the poor. And what of South Africa, Eastern Europe, or Asia? It is not merely a question of adaptation or application of the gospel to circumstances, but rather fundamental differences of perspective, divergent ways of conceiving what the gospel is about. When pluralism reaches a certain point, contextuality begins to become more important than tradition, more important than any ideal or essential unity the faith may possess. How far along this path is it legitimate to go?

The Rootlessness and Ineffectuality of 'Theology'

'Theology', as we know it, is not ready to deal with the situation described. Just at the moment in time when clarifying, unifying reflection on the myriad forms of the church is most needed, the theological community has reached a point of confusion about its own methodological coherence and sense of direction.

By 'theology' here we mean not merely 'systematic theology' but the entire academic enterprise within which critical reflection is carried on and pastors are trained: that is, theology in the sense of 'faculty of theology' or 'theological seminary'. Complaints about 'theology', as Edward Farley notes, are as old as the theological disciplines themselves. The critics have more often than not contended 'that theology effects a distanciation from the experientiality and activity of faith',[6] Theology is seen as 'intrinsically problematic because it fails to address the primacy and integrity of the individual human self, the church's actual situation, the concreteness of living language, the minister's pathos, the world's politics and oppressions'.[7]

These critical allegations are justified in varying degrees, depending on the type and social location of the institutions and persons concerned. On the one hand, today's seminary faculties are probably more involved in and knowledgeable about the life of the church than their predecessors of a generation ago. But at the same time, a very impressive proportion of today's theological scholarship is being produced in university and college departments of religious studies which have no formal connection with the church and, for the most part, little concern about it. In neither case has the relation between scholarship and the community of faith really been thought through. The 'guild mentality', with its powerful hold on the mechanisms of professional advancement, tends to inhibit the thought that is needed.

Yet, particularly in Protestantism, it is precisely these academic theologians in their isolated and alienated disciplines who are primary transmitters and interpreters of tradition. Protestant pastors, at least, tend to look back to seminary for their theological orientations rather than to ecclesiastical authority *per se*. Of course, Christians who are members of communions whose 'teaching authorities' are effectively separate from the academic world, or for whom liturgy is a primary carrier of tradition, are in a different situation, as may be members of evangelical groups that maintain a powerful, organizationally sustained, ethos. Still, the historical memory of the church is heavily dependent upon generation after generation of scholars. What happens if these scholars are essentially alienated from the communities of faith they nominally serve? What understanding of the church's deposit of faith is conveyed to new generations of seminarians when they receive it chopped into the arbitrary categories of the curriculum and squeezed into the methodological categories of the 'guilds'? 'Incoherence' and 'fragmentation' are words often heard when seminary education is the topic. Even where professors seek to transcend the narrow demands of their scholarly guilds, they find enormous difficulty building curricula in which the different subjects of study meaningfully interact, much less add up to articulated wholes.

The separation of academic theology from the practice of faith may also have something to do with what has been called the 'crisis of cognitive claims': the sense inside and outside the academy that we cannot account for the 'reality reference' of theological language. Charles Winquist, another of our contributors, refers to what has happened in the last several decades as 'a widening separation between descriptive theological language and the world that it claimed to describe'.[8] Winquist goes on to say, 'Theology questioned its own possibility. It talked less about God and more about the possibility of talking about God.'[9] Hence there has been a move toward acknowledgment that the theological use of language is metaphorical: in no way a mirror or replication of nature. 'The question that most theologians had to address was not if their statements were true but if they were meaningful.'[10]

This 'crisis of cognitive claims', which has really been with us in various forms since the Enlightenment, has led theologians to search for forms of reality reference suitable to the received content of the tradition. The so-called liberal movement sought the needed point of contact in a variety of different, allegedly inherent human capacities, each deemed universal to the species: religious feeling (Schleiermacher), moral experience (Kant, Ritschl), or existential anxiety (Bultmann). For this 'liberal' strategy, specific religious traditions were understood to give symbolic expression to one or another of these experiential possibilities. But today we are much less certain of the existence of moral and experiential universals as such and much more aware of the shaping power of particular environments and cultures. We begin to see that the church, or even the particular congregation, functions very much like a culture in its own right and must be studied as such without assuming from the start that the reality categories that apply to one instance also apply to another. The church must be the living, reflecting, social reality inside which the theological task is carried on. If theology is to recover its reality reference, it must be meaningfully resituated in the *ekklesia* as that discipline which grasps the constants of the faith community's thought and action. Theology on this reading ceases to be a discipline that seeks to articulate by intellectual means the nature of reality as such and becomes the ministry of reflection within the community which *is* the historical locus of the reality to which it refers.

. . .

Notes

1. Thomas Ogletree, 'Dimensions of a Practical Theology: Meaning, Action, Self,' in *Practical Theology: The Emerging Field in Theology, Church, and World*, ed. Don S. Browning (San Franscisco: Harper & Row, 1983), 84.

2. Ibid.

3. See Schubert M. Ogden, *On Theology* (San Francisco: Harper & Row, 1986), 1 and passim.

4. This discussion owes much to the suggestions of Edward C. Hobbs, 'Pluralism in the Biblical Context,' in *Hermeneutics and Pluralism Reader*, ed. William Wuellner and Marvin Brown (Berkeley: Center for Hermeneutical Studies, 1983), 53–81.

5. See Philip Hefner, 'Theology in the Context of Science, Liberation, and Christian Tradition,' in *World Views and Warrants* (Lanham, Md.: University Press of America, 1987).

6. Edward Farley, 'Interpreting Situations: An Inquiry into the Nature of Practical Theology,' in *Formation and Reflection*, ed. James N. Poling and Lewis S. Mudge (Philadelphia, Pa.: Fortress Press, 1987), 8.

7. Ibid.

8. Charles E. Winquist, 'Re-visioning Ministry: Postmodern Reflections,' in *Formation and Reflection*, ed. James N. Poling and Lewis S. Mudge (Philadelphia, Pa.: Fortress Press, 1987), 29.

9. Ibid.

10. Ibid.

Patricia O'Connell Killen and John de Beer, 'Searching for a Way to be faithful'

in *The Art of Theological Reflection* 2nd edition, New York: Gosspad, 2004, 1–4; 13–16, 18–19.

In this extract, Patricia Killen and John de Beer introduce one of the most frequently used styles of theological reflection, namely a conversational model. This essentially characterizes Christian decision-making as a mediation between the sources of 'tradition' and 'experience'. In a memorable metaphor, Killen and de Beer argue that those seeking to reflect theologically must 'befriend' these sources, drawing them in as conversation partners.

In keeping with one of the central premises of our approach to theological reflection, the practice of doing theology has a practical goal. The 'need for theological reflection' is rooted in practical discipleship; of the search for theological foundations to moral reasoning; and the importance of being able to engage with those who hold different world-views (p. 13). Yet the demands of pluralism mean that no one can simply cling to taken-for-granted or inherited beliefs without subjecting them to critical scrutiny. But does this mean that everyone is left to themselves to find their own values? Essentially, Killen and de Beer elaborate their theological method on this tension between the inherited tradition and the contemporary challenges of current experience (p. 16). This is the process by which Christians can have 'authentic lives' and 'integrated values' (p. 14).

Yet both these categories, 'tradition' and 'experience', need further elaboration. Neither is monolithic or self-evident; and while Killen and de Beer are describing a familiar and much-applied model of 'conversation' in their proposed art of theological reflection, it is perhaps more accurate to think of it as a conversation between two sets of pluriform, sometimes dissonant, sources.

Later in the book from which this is an extract, Killen and de Beer concentrate on practical exercises by which the interaction between them can be facilitated, although this is at the expense of exploring further the complexities of how the sources themselves are chosen. Nevertheless, Killen and de Beer's insistence, exemplified in this extract, upon the need to maintain a balance between the two, is also important: the process of theological reflection is, in part, a question of ensuring that neither side in the conversation comes to dominate, and that the two dimensions of the process exercise a moderating and dialogical influence on one another. Killen and de Beer argue for a sensibility of 'exploration' in which tradition and experience are allowed mutually to interrogate one another. 'Exploration' is contrasted on the one hand with the standpoint of 'certitude' – in which theological or other pre-existing world-views form absolute principles that are never allowed to be challenged or changed by new information. On the other hand, however, 'self-assurance' refuses either to acknowledge how far experience is conditioned by external factors or neglects to listen to the wisdom of the past. Both represent a failure to allow experience and tradition to interact fully and respond to situations in a spirit of exploration rather than resistance.

Without explicitly invoking the notion of praxis, Killen and de Beer suggest that the verification of the process of theological reflection, and the purpose of 'befriending' the strands of heritage, experience and faith community, will come in the capacity of the theological vision thus engendered to foster 'liberating, challenging, and life-giving' discipleship (p. 14). As with Ellen Charry, therefore, the authentication of theological reflection comes in its ability to nurture Christian virtue, or practical wisdom.

The Need for Theological Reflection

What path should I choose to live today? How can I discern a direction? How can I ground my decisions in the values that are important to me? Can I do so without coming to hate those who do not share those values, or is intolerance proof of conviction? Is there a way to find meaning in my life so that my choices do not seem random but reflect an integral pattern? Is the meaning of my life only my private possession or is it connected to others?

Sooner or later life confronts all of us with situations that raise questions like these, questions about the meaning, purpose, and value of our lives. Life experience invites us to reflect. In earlier times, before mass communication, easy travel, and extensive literacy, individuals received answers to such questions from the local community where they lived and from their religious tradition. Most often an individual's community and religious tradition were coextensive. Rarely did individuals face choices about either.

Our situation is different. We live in a global village, capable of watching victims of famine and war die on our television screens as we eat our dinner. Ease of transportation, communication technologies, extensive education, the mass media – these and more bring us regularly into contact with diverse cultures and religious traditions. The contours of our world do not allow us simply to accept answers to our questions handed down to us by communal or religious authorities. The challenges confronting us and the pluralistic world in which we live demand that we reflect on questions of meaning and value. We are called thoughtfully and carefully to make our own the answers we receive from our communities and religious traditions. This is what it means to appropriate our religious heritage critically and consciously.

Today, living on the verge of a new millennium and faced with personal, social, geopolitical and environmental choices and challenges not even imagined thirty years ago, let alone a hundred years ago, the consequences of our reflection on questions of meaning and value are momentous. The choices we make about how to live have significant impact not only for ourselves but for future generations and the planet on which we walk. Because so much is at stake, we need to pay attention to the character and quality of our reflective processes.

Traditionally, human beings asked questions of meaning and value in relationship to a religious tradition; for Christians, their Christian religious heritage. Today our pluralistic situation and the political and communal activities of certain Christian groups raise an additional question: Does the Christian tradition have anything to offer in finding the answers? Is Christianity a viable wisdom tradition as the twenty-first century dawns?

The answer is yes. It is possible to have authentic lives that reflect integral patterns grounded in values and religious wisdom. And it is possible to have such lives without using the Christian tradition as a weapon to overwhelm any and all who do not share a particular version of Christian living. This option is open to Christians who are willing to take their religious heritage seriously enough to grapple with it and their own lived experience religiously enough to entertain the possibility that God reaches out to them through it.

Authentic lives reflecting integral patterns grounded in religious wisdom and values result from seeking God's presence, not apart from the world, but in the midst of it. Seeking God's presence involves theological reflection, the artful discipline of putting our experience into conversation with the heritage of the Christian tradition. In this conversation we can be surprised and transformed by new angles of vision on our experience and acquire a deepened understanding and appreciation of our tradition. In this conversation we can find ourselves called to act in new, courageous, and compassionate ways. We are called to transformation.

Searching for meaning through theological reflection is not easy, because it does not yield the security of absolute answers. Rather, the search invites us to befriend our Christian heritage, our lived experience, our culture, and our contemporary faith community as conversation partners on the journey of faith. It asks us to hold our heritage, our culture, our community, and our own experience as companions in a conversation, a conversation where the questions and the exchange of discourse reveal new insights. Such conversation is the stuff of theological reflection. It invites us to bring our lives to the Christian heritage in a way that is liberating, challenging, and life-giving for us and for the Christian heritage.

Genuine conversation with our religious heritage is possible but not easy. Tendencies in the religious and wider culture of the United

States pull us away from such interaction in two directions. The first direction, evident in growing conservative evangelical Christianity and traditionalist Catholicism, is to equate Christian faith with certitude. The second direction, evident in secular culture and some forms of liberal Christianity, is to prefer current experience to all other sources of wisdom. Neither allows for a genuine conversation with the Christian heritage. In genuine conversation participants can invest without being controlling, can wonder without needing to judge, can disagree and still appreciate the other, and can be surprised and challenged by new insights or deepened understandings and appreciations of things already known. Profound and long-lasting transformations come from this kind of reflective process.

Relating to our own experience, our culture, our faith community, and our Christian heritage in a way that allows for genuine conversation leading to wisdom connects us deeply and creatively to God's presence and purposes for us. Before looking more closely at how to do that, however, we need to consider the general standpoints from which we approach our lives and our Christian heritage. Not every standpoint – a way of acting and thinking about life – contributes equally to making genuine theological reflection possible.

. . .

Cost of Certitude and Self-Assurance

The standpoint of certitude costs us our experience in order to possess the tradition. The standpoint of self-assurance costs us the richer meaning and understanding that the Christian tradition has to offer in order to make our current thoughts, feelings, and desires primary.

The problem with both certitude and self-assurance as exclusive standpoints is that they diminish our ability to relate to ourselves, our experience, our world, and our religious heritage. They lead us to deny or exaggerate our capacities as individuals and communities and to idolize or deny the reality of the traditions in which we come to awareness as human beings. From the standpoint of certitude alone we deny ourselves and our present experience in obeisance to an idealized past that we tell ourselves will save us if we simply submit. From the standpoint of self-assurance alone we deny the limits of much of our lives, our embeddedness in family, culture, and traditions and act as if we can construct our lives in their entirety.

The exclusive standpoints of certitude and self-assurance do not empower reflective, committed, compassionate lives. They lead us to repeat some of the tradition's teachings out of context in order to support particular arrangements of power, values, and roles that we hold dear and from which we benefit. They lead us to ignore other aspects of the tradition for the same purpose. Repetition and dismissal leave us deaf and blind to the resources of the Christian tradition and to the content of our current experience. Both act as a barrier between us and God's presence, power, and purpose. They block the ability of we who call ourselves Christians to mediate the compassion, love, justice, healing, forgiveness, and reconciliation of Jesus Christ for others. They seduce us into believing that life will not call into question our most cherished certainties. They obstruct growth in wisdom or understanding. Neither standpoint alone leads to a liberating encounter with God's Word in the tradition or in human experience.

Precisely because these two ways of understanding dominate discussions of individual and corporate values and spirituality in our culture and in our churches, we are in desperate need of authentic theological reflection. Without theological reflection, faith becomes something that belonged to the forebears of the tradition and currently is protected by the sanctioned theological experts. Faith is reduced to a possession. Faith serves as a justification for what we already think, religious code language to legitimate whatever psychological, sociological, economic, or political theory that we hold.

In the standpoint of certitude we protect fiercely the memory of the experience of God handed down from our religious forebears. All too frequently, however, we have not a clue what our religious forebears experienced and intended to convey to us because we are not aware of it in our own experience. In the standpoint of self-assurance we pay attention to our experience but miss many of its elements and its richer meaning because we do not trust that our forebears' wisdom adds anything to our experience.

Without authentic theological reflection we Christians cannot achieve the personal maturity and integrity appropriate to us. Theological reflection that involves heart and mind, consciousness and activity, provides a discipline in the life of faith. It enables us to integrate seemingly irreconcilable realms of activity and knowledge in our lives. As adult Christians we are called to more than mindless obedience to authority or totally self-determined thought and action.

Without authentic theological reflection we cannot exercise fully the ministry appropriate to us as baptized Christians. As the values of First World cultures increasingly undercut both humanistic and Christian visions it is crucial that we claim and present our faith in a manner that has integrity and is intelligible. Our presentation must be faithful to the fullest reading of the tradition, including the experience of the present community of faith. This gives it integrity. It also must make sense to any who, for the sake of discussion, will grant the presuppositions of faith. This makes it intelligible. The alternatives to presenting the faith in an intelligible fashion and with integrity are a certitude that turns gospel bread into stone or a self-assurance that reduces the individual to an isolated, self-contained, diminished being.

The complexity of our present situation makes it urgent that adult Christians learn to think, to feel, and to perceive faithfully. We must be able to engage the tradition in conversation so that we can bring its wisdom to bear powerfully in our lives and our worlds.

If authentic theological reflection cannot happen, if the Christian tradition's only value is to bolster and baptize social, economic, and political conventions, then it is dead or, worse, demonic. To ignore or actively to oppose the tradition when it is used in this way may seem to be the only options. But they can be costly ones. Ignoring or opposing the tradition can lead us to miss the wellspring of life in the Christian heritage. There is a continuing creative and faithful vitality within the Christian heritage that can renew the tradition and fund the lives of communities and individuals. This vitality can be tapped when people engage the tradition in genuine conversation, when they practise theological reflection.

Heather A. Warren, Joan L. Murray, and Mildred M. Best, 'The Discipline and Habit of Theological Reflection'

Journal of Religion and Health, Vol. 41, No. 4, Winter 2002, pp. 325; 327–30.

This text connects us with literature on the 'reflective practitioner' and theological reflection as an integral part of all professional development. Theological reflection is presented as contributing to professional self-understanding and enhancing practical efficacy. This locates practical theology as a kind of action-research: rooted in practical problematics and generating new knowledge that facilitates change and transformation, not only intellectual but practical too.

Yet many questions remain: the authors speculate whether theological reflection is a 'discipline' or 'habit' – or equally, whether it can be taught, and how. To take Edward Farley's notion of 'habitus' (1983) however, might encourage us to see that to immerse oneself in the lived experience of faith – its regular patterns of reading the Bible, liturgy and practices of ministry – represents a significant strand of formation in the discipline of theological reflection itself, as greater familiarity with the tradition in all its aspects from the inside facilitates an ability to make connections and to work creatively and constructively with the sources and resources of theology.

A final critical comment on this extract might be its lack of precision on the nature and content of 'tradition', and how that might be interpreted. As with many other evocations of 'tradition' in methods of theological reflection, the category remains essentially static and monolithic. By contrast, the articulation of seven different methods in Theological Reflection: Methods *demonstrates the plurality of understandings of culture, tradition and experience, as well as the interactions between them.*

Some Resources for Theological Reflection

Many resources are available for use in theological reflection ranging from emotion to one's personal history, to doctrine, to liturgy, to scripture. To foster the integration between the scholarly, ecclesiastical, and personal elements, we have identified clusters of such resources that the care giver can bring to bear in reflecting theologically on the clinical-pastoral encounter. The result is a typology of approaches with common elements.[1] Common to all the types is an interactive view of reality – the interplay between one's own history (personal story), his or her knowledge however cursory of at least one religious tradition, and an orientation to the future.

. . .

Our work with chaplains and CPE students has presented us with three principal ways of engaging in theological reflection: a distinctly Wesleyan approach, a dogmatic-doctrinal approach, and approaches through other distinct schools of theology (e.g. existentialist, Thomist, liberationist). We view these methods as portals into theological reflection. The first, often referred to as the Wesley Quadrilateral, asserts that the pursuit of Christian meaning occurs within the framework of the interplay between scripture, tradition, reason and experience. Scripture, the primary element, refers to the Old and New Testaments. Tradition pertains to the wisdom of the church transmitted in the writings, worship, and sayings of the faithful from the earliest days of the church to the present day, including scholarly texts (essays, sermons, commentaries), hymns, prayers, creeds, history, and

communities' particular legacies. Reason concerns the rational apprehension of reality. Experience is understood as the affective way of
engaging with and apprehending reality. The second method, the
dogmatic-doctrinal approach, seeks to understand the meaning of
events in terms of traditional Christian teachings on such subjects
generated by creedal and confessional sources as God, creation,
humankind, sin, the Trinity (Father, Son, Holy Spirit), salvation, revelation, the Blessed Virgin Mary, and the saints. The third approach
involves selecting one theological view from among the many
scholarly types – for example, existentialist, Thomist, liberationist.
Entrance into theological reflection through any one of these principal
ways need not exclude the others. Rather, associations may be made
among them.

Process for Theological Reflection

From our teaching, we have identified eight steps for engaging in
theological reflection. Though not a necessary step in this process, we
have often introduced our students to the process by discussing three
questions: 1) What is theology? 2) What is reflection (cf. meditation,
contemplation, analysis)? 3) What is theological reflection (cf. prayer,
systematic theology)?

The care giver begins his or her theological reflection by selecting
a clinical encounter he or she wants to explore. The care giver needs
to ask why he or she chose this particular encounter or why he or she
believes God is poignantly calling attention to Godself in this event.
The answer may not and probably will not be arrived at until the end
of the reflection. In some ways the proximate aim of theological
reflection is to determine why that particular encounter has such
immediate relevance to the care giver. Questions the care giver might
raise at this point are: Of all the recent encounters I have had, what
is it about this one that demands my attention? Am I thinking that
further engagement with the people involved is appropriate on my
part as the care giver? Do I sense that attention to this encounter has
something fundamental to do with my vocational identity?

The second step is for the care giver to narrate the clinical encounter. This can take the form of a verbatim, case study, critical incident
report, chart notes, or any other narrative form accessible to the care
giver.

Next, the care giver selects a theological approach from the typology. A few factors should be considered when making this choice.

What in the care giver's own story predisposes him or her to a particular theological method? Does he or she associate a particular doctrine with the encounter (e.g., sin, creation, atonement)? Does he or she associate a particular subject with the encounter (e.g., oppression, meaninglessness, hope, faith)? Does a particular passage from scripture, a hymn verse, a section of liturgy, or recited prayer come to mind? Answering these questions will help direct the care giver to an element in one of the three primary approaches identified above. At this point the care giver can recognize which of the theological approaches is most compelling.

The fourth step sees the care giver analyzing the encounter in terms of the typology. For example, if the care giver chooses the liberationist avenue of access, he or she will explore where and why oppression and powerlessness have occurred by asking such questions as, Who is or are the oppressors? Is it limited to an individual or does it involve family, community, institutions, corporations, or larger systems? What would freedom look like in this instance? What is the divine message to the oppressed? To the oppressor(s)? If the care giver uses the Wesley Quadrilateral, he or she will examine such questions as: What scripture is relevant? What does the church say historically about such a situation? What schools of thought speak to the encounter and what do they say? What feelings and moods did I, the care giver, experience? How does this data impact my relationship to God, others, and the natural world?

In the fifth step the care giver notes surprises – unexpected thoughts and feelings – that arose in the preceding analysis. The surprises may take the form of 'ah-ha's', 'oh-no's', or perplexity.

With these surprises in mind the care giver takes step six by making a statement about God both in relation to him or herself and the others in the encounter. The care giver seeks to understand who God is for the others in the encounter as well as for him or herself. At times these understandings may conflict, but even then the care giver will have a better idea of how next to proceed with the patient, family, or staff member without having to impose his or her particular presuppositions. Because theology is most often articulated in one's prayers, if the patient wants prayer, exploring the request and perhaps inviting the patient to pray will help elucidate that person's theology and relationship with God.

The seventh step involves crafting a pastoral care plan for the people served while the care giver is aware of his or her experience in the encounter. This entails a final assessment taking into account the person's history (physical, communal, social, religious, and psychological), his or her present condition, and future prognosis.[2] It will include a diagnosis, a weighing of psychological risk and gain versus maintenance and cost, and an appreciation for what will foster the person's ongoing spiritual formation. This does not necessarily require the care giver to have perceived the divine in the same way as those served.

The final step is for the care giver to articulate what has happened in his or her relationship with God in the process of serving others while being attentive to the theological realities in which they have been drawn together.[3] Such articulation might take the form of spoken prayer preferably in the presence of others or as an oral presentation to a peer group, whether chaplains or other pastoral care givers. The care giver should also offer a pastoral care plan for the people served when the opportunity for continued care on the care giver's part is possible. (See Table 1 for a summary of these eight steps.)

In our practice and teaching, we have learned that by intentionally and frequently engaging in theological reflection it becomes integrated into one's ministry of pastoral care. As a result the care giver develops a distinctive way of being in the health care environment that differs significantly from other health care professionals. The human desire for a conscious relationship with God, which is often masked by the popular term 'spirituality', requires the integration of body, mind, and spirit for its deepest engagement. In the discipline and habit of theological reflection, we find a framework and a cognitively integrating process available to chaplains and other pastoral care givers for developing their pastoral identity and practice, whether in institutional or congregational settings. Because theological reflection is a way of seeking truthfulness with integrity, it can be adapted and used by pastoral care givers in any religious tradition for their ongoing review of self and ministry. Finally, although we have presented theological reflection in terms of one-on-one pastoral encounter, the model we developed may be used in care givers' relations to groups and organizational systems.[4]

References

1. The classification of theological approaches for use in pastoral care was initially developed by the Rev. Mildred M. Best and the Rev. Dr John P. Oliver at the Duke University Medical Center, 1994.

2. For different frameworks used in making such assessments see: Fitchett, G., *Assessing Spiritual Needs: A Guide for Caregivers*, Minneapolis: Augsburg Fortress, 1993; Murray, J. L., 'Spiritual Assessment Guide', *Department of*

Chaplaincy Services and Clinical Pastoral Education Program Manual and Handbook, Charlottesville: University of Virginia Health System, 1997; rpt. 2000–2001, p. 63.

3. A model process for the care giver to use in exploring his or her relationship with God can be found in Murray, J. L., 'Relationship with God as a Dimension of Pastoral Supervision', *Journal of Supervision and Training in Ministry*, 1997, 18, p. 82.

4. Lebacqz, K, *Ethics and Spiritual Care: A Guide for Pastors, Chaplains, and Spiritual Directors*, Nashville: Abingdon Press, 2000.

TABLE 1

Summary of a Process for Theological Reflection

The Steps	Guiding Questions
1. Select the encounter	Which encounter will I choose for reflection? What is it about this encounter that attracts my attention? Do I sense that attention to this encounter has something to do with my identity?
2. Narrate the encounter	Who said what and to whom? What non-verbal communication was used?
3. Select a theological approach for the reflection	Do you associate a specific doctrine with the encounter (e.g. sin, creation, atonement)? Does a portion of scripture, a hymn, a section of liturgy, or a recited prayer come to your mind? Do you associate a particular subject with the encounter (e.g. oppression, freedom, meaninglessness, hope)?
4. Analyze the encounter in terms of the chosen approach	For a liberationist analysis: Who is or are the oppressors? What would liberation be in this instance? For a Wesleyan analysis: What does scripture say about the situation? What is the historical Christian witness to such a situation? What school(s) of thought pertains to the encounter? What feelings did you have? Others
5. Note surprises	What unexpected thoughts and feelings arose while doing the doing the analysis? Any perplexities?

6. Make a theological statement	What of God's nature is now known to you in a clearer or enriched way? How and in what way(s) is this different from what you believed before?
7. Design a pastoral care plan	What will foster the patient's, family member's, or staff member's spiritual formation?
8. Articulate in an oral presentation, written statement, or prayer (preferably to a peer group) what happened between you and God in the theological reflection	How does this change or modify my relation to God? What did I perceive about God's perception of me in relation to the God and the person(s) I served?

Rowan Williams, 'Trinity and Revelation'
in *On Christian Theology*, Oxford: Blackwell, 2000, pp. 131–5; 142–3; 145.

What is the meaning of 'revelation' in the context of theological reflection? Is the practice of theological reflection merely a human exercise, a kind of phenomenology or study of human knowledge, or is it possible to speak of 'God' and 'revelation' independent (or 'heteronomous') of human construction? Williams' response is that it is possible to speak of revelation without elevating theology beyond human experience or abstracting it into an ineffable realm of religious subjectivity.

People may suppose that the language of theology, and the efficacy of theological reflection, must entail the 'delivery of non-worldly truth ... in ways that cannot be confused with human discourse' (p. 24), and that revelation can only claim the necessary authority by manifesting itself in ways that are clearly independent of human construction. Yet for Williams this is unacceptable, not least because it defies any critical attention to the way in which humans do come to know and verify anything.

An alternative model of revelation, as knowledge that is capable of transcending the containment of human discourse, enables us to locate a source of authority that can be recognized as subverting or disrupting human certainties in the name of a reality that is not reducible to a purely anthropocentric frame of reference. From this, Williams sketches an alternative understanding of revelation: it represents an invitation, an invocation to a new way of thinking and acting. Revelation is what takes us out of ourselves, disrupts and disturbs the taken-for-grantedness of everyday knowledge, and points to a world that surpasses anything we could have created out of our own self-interest.

Rather than breaking into human consciousness from nowhere, 'revelation' is more like a paradigm shift, opening up new realizations, stimulating the imagination rather than delivering pre-packaged certainties. Although it is also a new way of knowing, but not so much a question of propositional facts as an understanding that one lives in a world of infinite possibilities, 'a sense of belonging in a new world' (p. 26). Thus Williams stresses, as we have done, the practical function of revelation and theological reflection: how does a new insight foster creative living? And is that consistent with established ways of engaging with the sources of faith in such a way as to enable the community to be open to the future?

In spite of everything, we go on saying 'God'. And, since 'God' is not the name of any particular thing available for inspection, it seems that we must as believers assume that we talk about God on the basis of 'revelation' – of what has been shown to us by God's will and action. If the word occurs in our speech and is not obviously vacuous, we are driven to conclude that we are – so to speak – *authorized* to use it. Yet this idea of being 'authorized' to speak of God is fraught with risk, and has frequently been put to deeply corrupt use. If revelation is seen as the delivery of non-worldly truth to human beings in pretty well unambiguous terms, discourse about God cannot be said to have roots in the ordinary events on which we depend for the 'authorizing' of our usual speech. It is possible to see the Incarnation itself simply as a sophisticated technique for ensuring that such non-worldly truth is accurately communicated: that God became human was a regrettable necessity which we may safely ignore after we have reached a certain stage of theological expertise.

Theology, in short, is perennially liable to be seduced by the prospect of bypassing the question of how it *learns* its own language. We can only talk intelligently about 'authorization' if we attend to this question; otherwise, authorization simply becomes an appeal to unchallengeable authority, and theological language is thought of as essentially heteronomous, determined from an elusive 'elsewhere'.

This is true not only of the kind of propositional account of revelation which very few contemporary theologians would accept, but which was once characteristic of wide areas of Protestant and Catholic theology alike; it is also (paradoxically) true of a liberal theology which appeals to some isolable core of encounter, unmediated awareness of the transcendent, buried beneath the accidental forms of historical givenness, a trans-cultural, pre-linguistic, inter-religious phenomenon. This may not result in quite the same intellectual totalitarianism as the 'propositional' approach; yet it still operates with a model of truth as something ultimately separable in our minds from the dialectical process of its historical reflection and appropriation. The impatience of some modern Anglo-Saxon theologians with the dogmatic tradition sometimes seems in part an impatience with debate, conflict, ambivalence, polysemy, paradox. And this is at heart an impatience with learning, and with learning about our learning.[1]

The danger of glib talk about 'authorization' and the authority linked with it is of theologizing what is 'given' as if the given represented the finished, the fixed.

. . .

The notion of faith as a healing or life-giving *project*, a proposal made in hope, looking towards a future of shared life and shared struggle, is liable to recede in such a perspective. 'Learning about learning' is learning how we develop meaningful constructs out of historical process and decision: in other words, it is (or can be) equally a learning about *doing*. To begin from a sense of achievedness, consummation, inevitably pushes such learning into the background; and thus it undermines its own claim to be able to speak with authority to an experience of conflict and fragmentation, to the historical aspiration and work of men and women.

The uncomfortable question with which we are left is: 'How do we speak of revelation or authorization without taking the obvious ideological shortcut?' Barth attempts, in the early volumes of his *Church Dogmatics*, to sketch a model of revelation which, because it never permits the revealed Word to be a human possession, avoids at first sight the danger of confusing authorization with ecclesiastical, or even scriptural, authority in the narrow sense. And he is careful to guard against the suggestion of a crude heteronomy.[2] Yet precisely because of the absolute isolation of the revelatory event from any historical condition (it occurs *in*, but not *as part* of history), the question of 'learning about learning' is again circumvented. Revelation interrupts the uncertainties of history with a summons to absolute knowledge, God's knowledge of and interpretation of himself.

How else, then, do we speak of revelation? The point of introducing the notion at all seems to be to give some ground for the sense in our religious and theological language that the initiative does not ultimately lie with us; before we speak, we are addressed or called. Paul Ricoeur, in an important essay on the hermeneutics of the idea of revelation,[3] has attempted to link the concept with a project for a 'poetics', which will spell out the way in which a poetic text, by offering a frame of linguistic reference other than the normal descriptive/referential function of language, 'restores to us that participation-in or belonging-to an order of things which precedes our capacity to oppose ourselves to things taken as objects opposed to a subject'.[4] The truth with which the poetic text is concerned is not verification, but manifestation.[5] That is to say that the text displays or even embodies the reality with which it is concerned simply by witness or 'testimony' (to use Ricoeur's favoured word).[6] It displays a 'possible world', a reality in which my human reality can also find itself: and in inviting me into its world, the text breaks open and extends my own possibilities.[7] All this, Ricoeur suggests, points to poetry as exercising a *revelatory* function – or, to rephrase this in the terms proposed at the beginning of this paragraph, it manifests an initiative that is not ours in inviting us to a world we did not make. This function is a challenge to the naive aspiration of human consciousness to autonomy ('the pretension of consciousness to constitute itself'[8]); yet it does not impose a simple heteronomy instead, it does not insist that meaning is delivered to us from a normative 'elsewhere'.

Revelation, on such an account, is essentially to do with what is *generative* in our experience – events or transactions in our language that break existing frames of reference and initiate new possibilities of life. Returning to some earlier remarks, we could say that revelation decisively advances or extends debate, extends rather than limits the range of ambiguity and conflict in language. It poses fresh questions rather than answering old ones. And to recognize a text, a tradition or an event as revelatory is to witness to its generative power. It is to speak from the standpoint of a new form of life and understanding whose roots can be traced to the initiating phenomenon. And we might add that – as an obvious corollary – when there is no longer a felt need to use the category of revelation, this can be attributed to an atrophying of the sense of belonging in a *new* world. Put in directly religious terms, it is the withering of anything that might be called an experience of grace, and a loss of confidence in the human worth-whileness or hopefulness of life in grace.

Thus 'revelation' is a concept which emerges from a questioning attention to our present life in the light of a particular past – a past seen as 'generative'. In terms of the scriptural history of Israel, the events of the Exodus were revelatory insofar as they were generative of the community of Israel itself; and Torah was revelatory because it was what specified the form of life of that community. In an exhaustive study,[9] Norman Gottwald has argued that if we are attempting to isolate an 'Old Testament doctrine of God', the only serious way in which this can be done is by attention to the social structures of Israel: the distinctiveness of YHWH does not lie in any theological attribute peculiar to him, but in the simple fact that he is the God of a people who live 'thus-and-not-otherwise' – the sort of God who can be the God of *this* community with its particular, socially distinctive features. For Gottwald, the salient features are the anti-authoritarian elements in Israel;[10] so that it should be possible to say of Israel's God that he cannot be the God of uncritical and authoritarian societies. But the main point is that Gottwald points us towards a concept of revelation dovetailing with Ricoeur's: the 'revelation' of YHWH occurs as part of the process whereby a community takes cognizance of its own distinctive identity. It constitutes a concept of God for itself by asking what it is that constitutes *itself*. To be able to answer the question about our roots, our context, what it is that has formed us, is at least to begin to deal with the question of the meaning of 'God'.

So it is right to say (with R. L. Hart, in his immensely important, if hermetic, essay on revelation[11]) that revelation is bound up with memory and yet not simply specified by reference to a sealed-off past occurrence. ' "Revelation" embraces (a) that which incites the hermeneutical spiral and also (b) this "that which" taken into human understanding, the movement of the hermeneutical spiral itself'[12] – or, in the terms I have already used, 'revelation' includes, necessarily, 'learning about learning'. Any theology of revelation is committed to attending to event and interpretation together, to the generative point and to the debate generated. And, if this is a correct analysis, the model of revelation as a straightforward 'lifting of a veil' by divine agency has to be treated with caution. 'Revelation' is certainly more than a mythologically slanted metaphor for the emergence of striking new ideas: the whole of our discussion so far presupposes that the language of revelation is used to express the sense of an initiative that does not lie with us and to challenge the myth of the self-constitution of consciousness. But the language of veil-lifting assumes a kind of passivity on the part of the finite consciousness which abstracts entirely from the issue of the newness of the form of life which first prompts the question about revelation. 'Is this event revelation?' is only a question that can be asked on the basis of the wider question: 'If we live like this, has revelation occurred?' And the problem of how to distinguish true from false 'revelations' can only be resolved in such a wider perspective – as Catholic theology has always recognized where alleged visions or locutions are concerned.[13]

. . .

Hart proposed that 'revelation' be taken to include both the event generating a hermeneutical enterprise and 'the movement of the hermeneutical spiral itself'. What I have so far suggested is that the Christian doctrine of God as Trinity permits us to see 'revelation' occurring in this way – through Son and Spirit together – and to see the structure of revelation itself as in a manner corresponding to God's own being. In fact, this last statement brings us back to something very close to Barth's insistence that the doctrine is simply an exegesis of the statement that 'God reveals himself'.[14] However, for Barth revelation is fundamentally the impartation of God's self-knowledge: we participate by revelation in this ultimate epistemological security. If we come at revelation from the more modest – if finally more demanding – position of Ricoeur's 'hermeneutics of testimony', the correspondence between the hermeneutical process and the divine act is of another kind. Revelation, from this perspective, is nothing to do with absolute knowledge. It both is and is not completed, 'over'; *what* we are interpreting is unquestionably this historical narrative and not another; we are not waiting for a more comprehensive or adequate story, because precisely of the comprehensiveness of the questioning provoked by this story. Yet this is not to say that there is an end to questioning or unclarity. The claims of our foundational story to universal relevance and significance mean that it must constantly be *shown* to be 'at home' with all the varying enterprises of giving meaning to the human condition. Thus the 'hermeneutical spiral' never reaches a plateau. For the event of Christ to be authentically revelatory, it must be capable of both 'fitting' and 'extending' any human circumstance; it must be re-presentable, and the form and character of its re-presentation are not necessarily describable in advance. The work continues, for the theologian and the Church at large, of discerning and naming the Christ-like events of liberation and humanization in the world *as* Christ-like, and, at the level of action, expressing this hermeneutical engagement in terms of concrete practical solidarity. And this unending re-discovery of Christ or representation of Christ, the revelatory aspect of the 'hermeneutical spiral', is, in Trinitarian perspective, what we mean by the illuminating or transforming operation of the Spirit. 'He will take what is mine and give it to you.'[15]

We also noted in the previous section that the generative significance of Jesus was 'learned' in the early communities in connection with the problems which they faced in grasping their distinctive identity as communities over against Judaism and the world of Hellenistic cults – problems to do with limits, relations to the 'outside', and mutual relations within the group. In recognizing these problems as *theological*, the Church admitted that the task of relating its present social reality to the events of Jesus' life, death and resurrection was basic to its self-understanding. To ask questions (of the kind arising at Corinth) about gifts of ministry and their interrelation was to ask what the fact of being in a community acknowledging Jesus as Lord *meant* in the organizing of life together. The 'lordship' of Jesus generates a communal life increasingly distinct from other contemporary options: the asking of fundamental theological questions represents the Church's movement from relatively unreflective to self-aware allegiance to Jesus. His lordship has to be theologized in gospel and worship, and the way in which he 'specifies' the new humanity has to be explored and articulated. This is how, over the protracted period during which the New Testament was composed, the Spirit may be said to have prompted the confession 'Jesus is Lord', in ever-greater richness and inclusiveness of meaning – the Spirit at work in the community's puzzlement at its own existence and character.

. . .

If, then, we follow something like Ricoeur's analysis of revelation, a statement like 'God reveals himself' will mean that God invites us into his 'world': new life is manifested historically, in event, speech, and memory restoring to us a 'participation-in or belonging-to an order of things which precedes our capacity to oppose ourselves to things taken as objects opposed to a subject'.[16] And in this case, the 'order of things' in question is the primary order of all things, the creative liberty of God. Further, because that liberty is both freely shown and freely given to us, it is manifested as inseparable from care, love, grace: creativity is gift and nurture, not abstract power and capacity-to-effect. If creativity is revealed in this way, as *call*, invitation, then it is essentially self-diffusing or self-sharing. For us to

share *in* it therefore means that we are called to share it: our participation in God's liberty is necessarily a participation in the act of
making free. And as God is present in the basic event of our liberation
in Jesus, so he is present in the Church as it struggles to make men
and women free and to understand more deeply the shape and the
nature of the liberty it is there to generate. 'God reveals himself'
means that the meaning of the word 'God' establishes itself among
us as the loving and nurturing advent of *newness* in human life –
grace, forgiveness, empowerment to be the agents of forgiveness and
liberation. This advent has its centre, its normative focus, in the record
of Jesus; it occurs among us now as the re-presentation of Jesus
through the Spirit; and it rests upon and gives content to the fundamental regulative notion of initiative, creative or generative power,
potentiality, that is not circumscribed by the conditions of the empirical world – the *arché* of the Father, the ultimate source.

Notes

1. I am – manifestly – indebted to various treatments of some of these themes
by Donald MacKinnon. See, for example, his remarks on 'dialogue' (*Explorations
in Theology*, London: SCM, 1979, pp. 161–5): to attend to the process of
discovering truth in 'dialogue' is to attend to the inexorability of fact, to avoid
the facile theoretical resolutions of a total intellectual structure. It is an attention
built into the very claims of 'realism'.

2. On the question of 'theonomy' as the foundation of authentic *autonomy*
see *Church Dogmatics* II.2, pp. 177–81, 184.

3. 'Toward a Hermeneutic of the Idea of Revelation', *Essays on Biblical
Interpretation*, ed. with an introduction by L. S. Mudge (London, 1980), pp. 73–
118.

4. Ibid., p. 101.

5. Ibid., p. 102.

6. Cf., in the same collection. 'The Hermeneutics of Testimony', pp. 119–54:
'testimony' relates to the particularities of events, not to supposed common
essences, and so calls forth an act, an event, in the interpreter. Thus a 'hermeneutic
of testimony' is opposed to the aspiration to absolute knowledge – knowledge
which is nobody's in particular. The parallels with MacKinnon are clear.

7. Cf. R. Williams, 'Poetic and Religious Imagination', *Theology*, May 1977
(pp. 178–87), pp. 185–6.

8. Ricoeur, *op. cit.*, p. 109.

9. *The Tribes of Yahweh. A Sociology of the Religion of Liberated Israel
1250–1050 B.C.E.*, London: SCM, 1979.

10. E.g. 'Yahweh's uniqueness lay in the fact that "he" was the symbol of a
single-minded pursuit of an egalitarian tribal social system' (p. 693). This is, of
course, intended as a sociological and historical observation, not intended to

foreclose any further discussion of the ontological status of such a symbol, or to suggest that YHWH is a mere 'projection'.

11. *Unfinished Man and the Imagination. Toward an Ontology and a Rhetoric of Revelation* (New York, 1968), especially pp. 83–105.

12. Ibid., p. 99.

13. A good discussion in Karl Rahner, *Visions and Prophecies* (London, 1963). I am grateful to Mr Rex Tomlinson for directing my attention to this work.

14. *Church Dogmatics* 1.1 section 8; for a fuller discussion, see R. Williams, 'Barth on the Triune God', in *Karl Barth. Studies of his Theological Method*, ed. S. W. Sykes (Oxford, 1979).

15. Jn 16.15.

16. Ricoeur, *op. cit.*, p. 101.

Kathryn Tanner, 'How I Changed My Mind'

in Darren Marks (ed.), *Shaping a Theological Mind: Theological context and methodology*, Aldershot: Ashgate, 2002, pp. 115–21.

In addressing the question of theological method, *Kathryn Tanner highlights some important questions for those interested in learning more about theological reflection. She traces how scholarship within systematic theology has taken a decisively practical turn in the past generation, referring to this as a shift from 'methodological to substantive' considerations. Due largely to the influence of theologies of liberation, which highlight both the social location of the theologian and the practical, ethical or political implications of theological reflection, theologians have developed a greater preoccupation with the* relevance *as well as the philosophical coherence of their endeavours.*

There is much material here for the basis of further discussion: for example, on the role of theological scholarship in the academy, which is Tanner's own professional setting. How does academic theology claim legitimacy in a secular or non-confessional university? Similarly, can theology claim currency beyond the confines of the Christian community, assuming a role of cultural critic out of its own historical symbol systems? Finally, is the theologian one who provides a description of how people of faith use the sources and resources of religion in the conduct of their lives, or is the theologian required to develop a 'constructive' theology that offers normative guidance in a more prescriptive fashion (p. 33)? Tanner concludes that professional theologians must necessarily adopt the latter stance, 'in order to establish a consistent Christian outlook on life' (p. 35), and that professional theologians can serve as guardians of an approach to theological reflection that is comprehensive, historically minded, ecumenical and challenging.

When I was in graduate school at Yale in the early 1980s (working primarily with Hans Frei, George Lindbeck and Louis Dupré), the main worries of both theologians and philosophers of religion were methodological in nature: to justify religious thought, either by show-ing how it met the usual standards of meaning, intelligibility and truth endorsed by other disciplines, or (the preferred tactic of Frei and Lindbeck) by showing, with an ironic display of academic rigour, why no such effort of justification was necessary. Epistemological issues (such as how meaning and truth were conveyed linguistically through signs and symbols) and biblical hermeneutics were the bread and butter of our studies. Methodological preoccupations were what distinguished theological schools (Yale and the University of Chicago), and these fights were formulated as a continuation of controversies within neo-orthodoxy and Karl Barth (our hero), on the one hand, versus Rudolf Bultmann and Paul Tillich, on the other. The history of Christian thought, another main focus of our study, was taught with these same methodological emphases in mind.

My teachers, Frei and Lindbeck, often half-jokingly quipped that one day they would eventually *do* theology, rather than spend all their time talking about how to go about it; but neither of them, as it turns out, made it to that point in their own work. Nowadays, however, their hopes (at least in this regard) have come to fruition in the new generation of US theologians, who (whatever their method-ological backgrounds or proclivities) dare to say something as 'con-structive' theologians, reworking Christian themes to address the challenges of today's world. Pick up almost any work in theology today and you are liable to find a discussion of the Trinity and its implications for politics, or a reformulation of God's relation to cre-ation as an impetus to ecological responsibility, or a rethinking of the atonement in light of trauma theory. Frei, my old friend, at once so cautious and generous, would no doubt be astounded and grateful; and perhaps a little envious too, pleasantly surprised but concerned for the brazen boldness of it all.

This shift from methodological to substantive preoccupations is partly a response to, and incorporation of, the lessons of liberation theology, which effectively undercut the Enlightenment as the taken-for-granted starting point for theological work. The need is not so much to show the meaningfulness of Christianity in today's world but rather what Christianity can contribute to making the world a better place. The same sort of shift is also encouraged by post-modern trends in academic disciplines. With the onset of a post-modern humility about pretensions to such things as universality and disinterestedness, the particularism of specifically Christian sources of insight and the advocacy stance assumed by many theologians are far less suspect than they used to be. The theoretical deficiencies of which theology has been accused are now so spread around that they appear to be the defining fault of no one field in particular, and significant differences among fields in this regard seem mere matters of degree. The legitimacy of theology, to the extent it remains a question in American intellectual life, is no longer a matter of whether theology can meet some scholarly minimum in its procedures. Theology's warrant now centres on the question of whether theologians have anything important to say about the world and our place in it. What, if anything, can the Christian theologian positively contribute to the search for the true and the right on particular issues of importance in the twenty-first century? What resources does the Christian symbol system provide for resolving such issues? How might that symbol system be creatively recast in the process?

Answers to these questions require new methods. Theology's closest analogue is no longer a perennial philosophy, addressing the most general questions of human moment purportedly common to every time and place, but a political theory (broadly construed) of cultural meanings that is quite situation-specific in its focus. In other words, the theologian – like a Weberian social scientist or a Gramscian political theorist – now asks about the way Christian beliefs and symbols function in the particulars of people's lives so as to direct and justify the shape of social organization and the course of social action. As a historian of Christian thought and practice, the theologian needs a thorough knowledge of the way these intersections of culture and politics have panned out across differences of time and place: a thorough knowledge of the various permutations of the Christian symbol in all its complicated alignments with social forces for good or ill. With this knowledge in hand, the constructive theologian is better positioned to intervene in the current situation adroitly, effectively and responsibly, with suggestions for both rethinking Christian claims and refiguring human life for the sake of the greater good.

My own theological trajectory has followed this outline. I initially turned to theology from philosophy, which in my day at Yale as an undergraduate involved (unusually for the time) the broad study of both continental and analytic philosophy, and familiarity with

American pragmatism and process thought. The linguistic turn had been made, deconstruction was in the air, Thomas Kuhn had initiated a sociology of knowledge that chastened the objectivist ideal of science as a paradigm for all other disciplines; but the blurring of philosophy into anthropology and literary theory – now so common – had yet to take hold. Theology held for me the hope of addressing questions of meaning in a comprehensive fashion that philosophers themselves now seemed reluctant to pursue. Theology as a form of intellectual inquiry was clearly about something (not talk about talk about talk) and offered direction and significance to the pursuit of the true and the right through a community of inquiry outside itself – the Church. Theology, in short, seemed to matter to 'someone'. Under the impact of post-liberalism, which had just begun to solidify around the work of Frei and Lindbeck during my time in graduate school, my work has increasingly made that community of inquiry (religious people in their efforts to forge a way of life) its focus as both subject matter and object for intervention with a corresponding broadening of methods, away from philosophy as traditionally construed.

My first book, *God and Creation in Christian Theology* (1988), was a wide-ranging analysis of patterns of discourse about God and creation in Christian thought. It discussed the way such patterns of discourse modified habits of speech in the wider society in order to show (rather than explain) the coherence of various Christian claims about God and the world; and discussed how those patterns of discourse were distorted and coherence was lost, under modern strain. Because Christian language was never adequate to the God to which it referred, the theologian was concerned, not directly with that referent, but with the habits of speech and action that amounted to God's direction of Christian lives. Intellectual difficulties arising out of everyday Christian practice (for example, the inability to resolve how I am to be responsible for the character of my life while dependent, nevertheless, on God's grace) set off theological questions about the compatibility of asserting both human and divine responsibility for our actions; and those questions were resolved by altering the way we usually speak of action in common.

My next book, *The Politics of God* (1992), moved to a more overt discussion of the function of religious discourse in Christian lives by exploring how beliefs about God and creation shaped the political stances of Christians. Discourse in an analytic mode, the method of the first book, was insufficient here; the method was now something closer to that of sociology or anthropology. This book did not simply describe Christian practice (while commending it for its coherence, as the first book did). It argued a normative case, how beliefs about God and creation *should* shape Christian lives, in self-conscious opposition to the way those beliefs have commonly functioned to ill effect in the past and present. The next book, *Theories of Culture: A New Agenda for Theology* (1997), raised this new method up as the primary subject for discussion. The latest, *Jesus, Humanity and the Trinity: A Brief Systematic Theology* (2001), ventures a clear vision of the whole 'Christian thing' (as David Kelsey, another of my Yale teachers, would put it) – Trinity, creation, covenant, Christology and eschatology, all oriented towards the idea of God as gift giver – in order to establish a consistent Christian outlook on life and the corresponding character of human responsibilities.

Despite the idiosyncrasies of my own trajectory, this constructive focus on Christianity as a world-view and orienting point for social action, and the way it brings theologians into conversation with social scientists, is, I have said, not particularly unusual on the present scene: liberation, African-American and feminist theologies, historicist and pragmatist-influenced theologies, theologies originating in a Tillichian brand of correlation, are often found moving in these same directions. One thing that sets my own efforts apart is the place of historical study for a creative reworking of Christian ideas and symbols to meet present challenges.

Relevant in this connection is the fact that one of the things that originally attracted me to theology was its oddity in the secular university and on the contemporary scene (despite the characteristically modern rise of fundamentalism as a world historical force). Theology had the ability to propose the unexpected, to shock and startle. It offered an escape from the taken-for-granted certainties of life, by referring them to something that remained ever beyond them, resisting capture and encapsulation. The theologian respects that capacity, it seems to me, not by dressing up contemporary commonplaces in religious terms, but in seeking what lies beyond a contemporary outlook and beyond the immediate context of one's work. A theology that starts from, and uses as its toolbox for creative ends, materials gathered from the widest possible purview is, in my opinion, a theology with that imaginative expansiveness. Such a theology looks to the Christian past not for models for simple imitation but for a way to complicate one's sense of the possibilities for present Christian expression and action. It looks to the past not to restrict and cramp what might be said now but to break out of the narrowness of a contemporary sense of the realistic. It complements an understanding of the complex variety of pre-modern theologies in the West with an understanding of the complex forms of Christianity's global reach now and in the past. It reaches beyond the narrowness of denominational confines to the broadest ecumenical vision, and sees beyond elite forms of theological expression, primarily in written texts, to the popular theologies of everyday life.

All of that is what I mean by a 'constructive' theology that is historically funded: the pre-modern, the popular, the global and the ecumenical put to use to shake up, reorient and expand what one would have thought one could do with the Christian symbol system, in the constructive effort to figure out the proper Christian stance for today's world.

The breadth of this understanding of the historical, and the focus here on the historical complexity and variability of Christian forms of life, indicate ways that I have moved beyond my Yale training, where the talk was commonly of *the* biblical world and *the* Christian tradition. I have also done so in refusing to understand Christian ways of living in isolation from the wider culture. Christian ways of speaking and acting are not created out of whole cloth but are constituted by odd modifications to ways of speaking and acting that are current in the wider society. It is therefore impossible to understand their meaning and social point without understanding the culture of the wider society and what Christian habits of speech and action are saying about it through modifications made to it. For example, when Christians call Jesus 'Lord' that is a comment on the Lords of the wider society which is impossible to understand without knowing what is unusual about that attribution in the context of its use; for example, contrary to its usual application, 'Lord' in Christian uses refers to a person shamefully crucified like a criminal and enemy of the state. Similarly, the significance of eating in church is not clear until one understands the eating practices of the wider society, modifications to those practices in church becoming a kind of commentary on them (for example, a criticism of the exclusions of ordinary table fellowship).

Theological construction, figuring out what it is that Christians should 'say' and 'do' in one's present context, therefore requires a highly complicated and subtle reading of the whole cultural field into which Christianity figures. One is helped here again by historical analysis (in my broad sense) that incorporates such a holistic cultural perspective. Theology is always a matter of judgments regarding the practices of the wider society and about the degree and manner in which they should also figure in Christian lives. Knowledge of how

Christians have made such judgments at other times and places, and one's own sense, in hindsight or at a distance, about whether they did so correctly, in suitably Christian fashion, provide invaluable insights and practice in tackling the issues of one's own time and circumstance when the personal stakes are much higher.

Method, I have learned, is not a safeguard for such judgment. Karl Barth was shocked by his teachers' support for the First World War into a rejection of the method of Protestant liberalism. But I have been shocked by many of my American theological colleagues' responses to the political upsurge of the Christian right in the United States, and the present culture wars here, into the sense that method (as it has been traditionally conceived) is not sufficient. Too many of my teachers (and here I mean 'teachers' very broadly as those already established on the theologian scene and from whom I therefore expected wisdom and guidance) read, it seemed to me, the upsurge of the religious right simply as a salutary entrance of religion into the public square, promising an elevation in the seriousness with which theological exchange would have to be taken from now on by the wider society. *What* the religious right was promulgating was of less interest to them. Shame at the fact that Christianity stood so publicly for *this* was not, as far as I could see, at a premium. Given the at least superficial similarities between the post-liberalism of my immediate circle of teachers and that of the religious right (for example, preoccupation with the world of the Bible, repudiation of apologetics and a stance in opposition to liberal culture), the failure of post-liberal theologians to criticize the right could easily be taken for an endorsement. So that silence not be taken for praise, the situation required, it seemed to me, only the most forceful repudiation of the right's political judgments, something that I tried to do, in my own limited way, in *The Politics of God*. The post-liberal reluctance to be more than a witness to the wider society had to be overcome. It seemed to me, instead, that one's sense of that witness itself was to be formed in direct engagement with the political developments of the day.

What I carry away from this time (which unfortunately is not over) is the belief that it is misguided to search for proper theological method with the expectation that it will make clear, all by itself, the proper Christian stance on the contested sociocultural issues of one's day. Search for proper method with that expectation encourages blanket judgments about the wider culture as a whole – it is to be resisted, or welcomed as the ground floor for the contributions of grace, or transformed as a whole – when what is really necessary is an often more difficult and nuanced discernment about particulars.

Advocating either the Word as norm for Christian judgment with Barth or critical correlation with Tillich does not help very much when the question is how to read the situation in a Christian light. What, for example, does feminism or the movement for gay liberation represent in Christian terms? An instance of moral irresponsibility which Christians should resist or an intent to further full human flourishing to which Christians should be sympathetic? Such judgments have much more to do with the substantive character of one's understanding of what Christianity is all about than they do with the method used to come up with it. To make a simplistic parallel with Barth again, Christians supported the Nazis not because they neglected the Word in favour of cultural trends but because they had a misguided understanding of Christianity. Hitler's National Socialism was wrong on a Christian understanding of things because its policy towards Jews (and others) was un-Christian and not because it forced the neglect of the Word by making the nation-state all. Clearly, a nation-state could respect the Word and persecute Jews, depending on its understanding of what Christianity was all about, and that would merit as grave a theological condemnation as any the Barmen Declaration offered. Christians are always influenced, one way or another, by the cultural trends of the day and respect for the Word does not exempt them from its effects (as Barth himself recognized in *Church Dogmatics*, I/2).

It is what Christians do with those influences that matters, as they grow into an understanding of their Christian commitments by way of complex processes of revision, appropriation and resistance to those cultural trends, taken one by one. One never rejects everything, since one's Christianity always remains parasitic to some extent on the wider society's forms of life. Nor (one hopes) does one accept everything, because Christian justifications even for courses of action shared with the wider society alter their sense and point. One's judgments about different aspects of the wider society's practices need not, moreover, be the same. For example, my grave worries about economic inequalities that are the product of global capitalism need not spill over onto the greater economic opportunities for women that are also a feature of recent economic developments in the West. An equal resistance to both, simply because they are the 'world' that Christianity is to reject, leads to dishonesty about the way that the world inevitably figures in even the best Christian lives, and to a lazy reneging on Christian responsibilities to judge particulars with care.

As I have argued in *Theories of Culture*, I think that theologians have to be honest about the complexities of Christian lives and the way Christian beliefs and symbols figure there. Doing so means taking seriously what disciplines such as sociology and anthropology reveal: the often messy, ambiguous and porous character of the effort to live Christianly. Trained historians of Christianity – particularly historians who also avail themselves of the insights of these other disciplines – were not surprised by my methodological recommendation in that book. Theologians, commonly in my experience, have yet to make the leap.

Terry Veling, 'What is Practical Theology?'
in *Practical Theology: on earth as it is in heaven*, New York: Maryknoll, 2005, pp. 3–7; 13–18.

Veling's extract represents a progressive Roman Catholic position on the subject of practical theology. Influences reflect post-Vatican II trends and liberationist perspectives within theology: note the passing reference, unacknowledged, to the conciliar document 'Gaudium et Spes' (joy and hope) at the end of the section entitled 'On Earth'.

Veling's attempts to define the discipline of practical theology may speak to the frustration of many students on approaching the study of practical or pastoral theology for the first time, who are told that all theology is practical. Veling insists it cannot be compartmentalized, however, and this is what characterizes its particular approach. Yet he is also sensitive to the need for further rigour: are people 'reflecting theologically' just by thinking about something? Veling's response is that theology may emerge out of reflection on the practice of faith, but it is not reducible to casual reflection.

It is possibly the theme of incarnation that informs Veling's understanding of practical theology most strongly. Theological reflection is certainly about attentiveness to God, but that is a God who is disclosed in history and in the life of Jesus Christ. Nevertheless, Veling argues that humanity experiences itself as apprehended and called by God, from whom the initiative flows. Once again, therefore, we see how practical theologians attempt to maintain the tension between theological reflection as both mediated through human culture and experience, yet flowing out of a divine invocation. This Veling characterizes as the meeting of earth and heaven: theological reflection is charged with reading the conditions of human situations in the light of the vision of the kingdom of heaven (p. 48). It is an attempt to subject the conditions of experience to the unconditional demands of

God, who represents love and grace that is not bounded by the contingent questions of culture or history.

There is an inherent difficulty in describing practical theology. For a start, it is often dogged by what Edward Farley calls the 'fragmentation of theology', the division of theology into defined and specialized fields (as when we speak, for example, of systematic theology, or pastoral theology, or historical theology, etc.).[1] Into this scenario comes yet another branch called 'practical theology,' which leads many to ask, 'So what does practical theology specialize in?' However, there is an important sense in which practical theology is an attempt to heal this fragmentation of theology, such that it resists being slotted into yet another theological specialty.

In his book *The Love of Learning and the Desire for God*, Jean Leclercq paints a wonderful picture of monastic culture in which we get a feel for what theology was like before it became fragmented and specialized.[2] Leclercq evokes a time when study and the love of learning was part and parcel of the desire for God, and was never divorced from liturgy and prayer, human work and labor, contemplation of the scriptures, the search for wisdom (in philosophy and the arts), or pastoral concern and the 'love of neighbor'.

While this may sound like a serene and untroubled scenario, it nevertheless presents an image of what practical theology is perhaps seeking to reclaim – a certain reintegration of theology into the weave and fabric of human living, in which theology becomes a 'practice' or a way of life. This is what makes practical theology difficult to define, as though it were one 'type' of theology as opposed to another 'type'. It resists a certain branding or labeling, and makes its appeal to a more integrated theological sensibility that attempts to honor the great learnings of theological wisdom with the desire for God and the coming of God's kingdom 'on earth, as it is in heaven'.

There is another particular difficulty with defining practical theology. In asking, 'What is practical theology about?' we are asking about its 'theory'. In our highly specialized world, we have grown accustomed to first clarifying the 'theory' of something and then, as a second step, seeking its practical application. However, as might be expected from its very name, the 'theory' of practical theology, as Karl Rahner suggests, 'indwells the practice itself'.[3] Theory 'indwells' practice, not in the sense that we *put* theory *into* practice; rather, in the sense that it is only in the practice or doing of theology that we begin to realize and understand its meanings and its workings more deeply. As the Christian community, for example, engages in the practices of prayer, study, hospitality, forgiveness – as we do these things – we begin to deepen our understanding of what the kingdom of God is all about, and what it means to be a people of God.

Anyone who writes 'about' practical theology faces the peculiar quandary of falling into either one of the 'traps' named above, that is, turning it into a theological discipline that exists alongside other theological disciplines, or bringing it to theoretical clarity so that people can then know what to do with it. There is no assured way of avoiding this struggle, but we need to begin somewhere, and so in this introductory chapter I would like to present some 'snapshots' of practical theology that attempt to open the scene for the chapters ahead. Practical theology is a large subject matter. Indeed, Rahner goes so far as to say that *'everything* is its subject-matter'.[4] So there is little hope of really capturing it; rather, there is the hope of 'whetting our appetites' for the love of learning and the desire for God.

Practical Theology is not a 'Thing'

'To think and act practically in fresh and innovative ways', writes Don Browning, 'may be the most complex thing that humans ever attempt'.[5] Practical theology, as its name suggests, is less a thing to be defined than it is an activity to be done. In this sense, it resists our attempts to pin it down and define it. Practical theology is more 'verb-like' than 'noun-like'. In many ways, we would be better to speak of 'practicing theology' rather than 'practical theology'. So a better question to ask would be, 'What does it mean to practice theology?'

Theology is often seen as a speculative enterprise in which people think about important questions concerning God, faith, belief, and the religious meaning of life. And most people, if you were to ask them about 'practical theology', would probably say, 'Oh, that's about applying our faith and our beliefs to life in the real world'. There is the 'world of theology' – somewhat abstract and aloof – and then there is the 'real world' where theological knowledge is applied and put into practice.

This is a fairly common understanding of theology. Indeed, it is reflected in the long-standing division of theology into two primary areas, namely, 'systematic theology' and 'pastoral theology'. Systematic theology is where we do all our theoretical work, and pastoral theology is where we apply this learning to the life of the church and the needs of the world. According to Thomas Groome, this is the standard paradigm of theology. We begin with heavy doses of theology's theoretical disciplines (systematics, church history, scripture studies, etc.) and then tag on, almost as an afterthought, some training in pastoral skills in order to apply this theory to practice. Such a paradigm 'presumes a one-way relationship between theory and practice with theory always the point of departure; theory is something from "outside" to be applied and practice something to receive it'.[6] Practical theology is an attempt to heal this division, so that pastoral theology is never simply an afterthought or a derivative of systematic theology. So that theological reflection can regain its intrinsic connection to life. So that we can overcome the artificial distinction between thinking and acting and become more serious about both.

Life in the World

One of the greatest philosophers of the twentieth century, Martin Heidegger, delivered somewhat of a jolt to his contemporaries when he suggested that philosophy is concerned with our life in the world. Hardly a mind-blowing thought, you might say! However, Heidegger was suggesting that the Western philosophical tradition had spent so much time inquiring into life and its meaning that it had forgotten to attend to life itself. He spoke of this forgetfulness as a 'forgetfulness of Being'.[7] How is it possible, one may wonder, to inquire into life's 'being' and yet be forgetful of life at the same time?

Heidegger's response is that we have forgotten that 'Being' carries the resonance of a verb rather than the 'thingness' of a noun. We have tended to treat Being as though it were some*thing* that we can approach and gain knowledge of, as though it were some*thing* that we can know and apprehend, as though it were some*thing* 'out there' that we can probe and analyze. Rather than seeing Being as a thing 'out there' – aside and apart from us – Heidegger preferred to speak of our 'being-in-the-world'. He suggested that we do not stand over the world in order to know the world. We are not bare, thinking subjects who reach out to know a world of objects. Rather, we are absorbed and immersed in the world, never over against it as a subject to an object.

Life means living, and living is preeminently what we *do*. We do not simply exist; rather, we are alive and we *live* – and our living is vital and dynamic, whereas much of philosophy's talk about Being always seems so detached and lifeless. Heidegger sought to renew our appreciation of the verblike quality of Being – 'to be' – not what is, but the verb, the very 'act' of being. Knowledge of the world can never be detached from being-in-the-world, and if we want to know (if we want to understand), we need to engage our whole way of being – our memories, our feelings, our imagination, our thinking, our actions.[8]

In a similar fashion, practical theology suggests that we cannot separate knowing from being, thinking from acting, theological reflection from pastoral and practical involvement. Theology is always shaped by and embodied in the practices of historical, cultural, and linguistic communities. Our understandings always emerge from our practices, or from the 'forms of life' in which we participate.

Practical theology does not really have a head for great systems of thought, even though it may admire these systems as one admires a great cathedral. There is something wonderful about towering thoughts, but even so they still cast a shadow. Our serene theories with their grand visions of life too often deny to knowledge any origin in the practical difficulties of life, but rather seek to transcend these difficulties into a vision of Being that is pristine and unaffected by human affairs.

What is typically called 'systematic theology' is often tempted to gather everything into a 'grand narrative' as though it already knew the story's whole plot – the beginning, the middle, and the end. Systematic theology seems to soar on eagle's wings, flying high above life and offering us a spectacular, God-like view. What it then leaves for us is to take this grand vision and to apply it to our lives, a task typically associated with the role of 'pastoral theology' – taking what we have learned in the great system and applying it to the more lowly and everyday practices of Christian living.

Life, however, is not very 'systematic'. As Rowan Williams suggests:

> A religious discourse with some chance of being honest will not move too far from the particular, with all its irresolution and resistance to systematizing: it will be trying to give shape to that response to the particular that is least evasive of its solid historical otherness *and* that is also rooted in the conviction that God is to be sought and listened for in all occasions.[9]

According to the Brazilian educator and thinker Paulo Freire, the danger with intellectual systems is their tendency to confuse thought with existence. The speculative thinker forgets that knowledge involves passion, struggle, decision, and personal appropriation, that we must live and act out of our knowing. 'Knowledge emerges only through invention and re-invention,' writes Freire, 'through the restless, impatient, continuing, hopeful inquiry people pursue in the world, with the world, and with each other.'[10]

Practical theology wants to keep our relationship with the world open, so that we are never quite 'done' with things; rather, always undoing and redoing them, so that we can keep the 'doing' happening, passionate, keen, expectant – never satisfied, never quite finished. 'Be perfect as your Father in heaven is perfect' (Matthew). Perhaps practical theology – as a constant 'doing' – is a passion for perfection in an imperfect world. Impossible! Yet that is probably why all the 'perfect' systems are left feeling so uneasy and insecure when poets and prophets show up. Practical theology is suspicious of any theology that is too solid, too well-built, too built-up. Rather, it is a theology that is given over to a passion for what could yet be, what is still in-the-making, in process, not yet, still coming ('Thy kingdom come!').

. . .

Truth and Goodness

Living attentive, thoughtful lives is important to practical theology. To try to live reflectively is to try to live in truthful ways – with integrity and honesty. It is to try to live responsibly, rather than with numbed silence or cold indifference. However, the test of truth is not so much measured against our great theories of life. Rather, truth is measured by the fruit it bears. When I am in the presence of a good and holy person, I am amazed at the truth I see – more than I have gleaned from books alone.

Emmanuel Levinas says that Goodness should always preside over the work of truth. The question of meaning and existence carries no sense on its own, unless it is first underwritten by the question of the ethical and the Good. This is the crux of Levinas's insistence: Whether or not existence is ethical and carries the value of the 'Good' is a more urgent question and claims priority over whether or not existence is meaningful and carries the clarity of the 'True'. 'Morality', writes Levinas, 'presides over the work of truth.'[11] The Good must preside over the True, in the sense that the value of my life for you presides over the meaning of my life for me. The question of existence cannot be answered within the realms of my own self or from the resources of my own self-reflection. Rather, it is given to me by the other who *provokes* the question of my existence, even as I try to justify its meaning. It is given to me by the one who is suffering, even while I live. It is given to me by the stranger and the immigrant, even while I recline at home. What is always first, what is always prior, is not the meaning of my existence as 'being-there', but the responsibility of my existence as 'being-for'. All of Levinas's thinking hinges on this one crucial affirmation, that we are responsible for each other, that my existence is not an existence unto myself, but an existence 'to you' and 'for you'.[12]

In the Jewish tradition, when the rabbis come across a difficult biblical text, they always look for the *ethical* message of the text, even when it is not especially evident. If the ethical message is not immediately apparent to them, it must be that they are not reading or interpreting the text correctly. They will stay with the text, bending and twisting it until its ethical import rings free. God's word, the Torah, is always about the *way one should live*, and the meaning of a text is always determined according to its ethical truth.[13]

In a similar way, in the Christian tradition, Augustine proposed that a basic principle of a *good* interpretation of scripture is whether or not the interpretation leads to a greater love of God and neighbor. The *good* interpretation will never lead one astray even if it may fall short of being the 'true' or 'correct' interpretation. Augustine writes that if someone 'is deceived in an interpretation which builds up charity, which is the end of the commandments, he is deceived in the same way as a man who leaves a road by mistake but passes through a field to the same place toward which the road itself leads'.[14]

Knowing the truth means little, according to St. Paul, unless it is infused with love. 'If I have all the eloquence of men or angels, but speak without love, I am simply a gong booming or a cymbal clashing' (1 Cor. 13.1). Love and goodness must always lead the way, presiding over the work of theology, and not merely relegated into an 'after-thought' – as happens, for example, when we create a subset of theology and call it 'moral' or 'pastoral' theology. Questions of morality, ethics, justice, and mercy must accompany all our theological work, such that the 'theoretical' and the 'practical' are not originally distinguishable.

A Craft more than a Method

It is not uncommon to read books on practical theology that devote considerable time to the question of methodology, that is, how we can best proceed with the task of practical theology. Learning the various methods of practical theology is important, but we should be wary of turning these methods into a simple 'how to'. Our world is inundated with 'how to' books.

In his best-known work, the philosopher Hans-Georg Gadamer draws a distinction between 'truth and method' (his book's title). Gadamer felt that our approaches toward reading and interpreting life were too captivated by methodological concerns.[15] He felt that we had become too preoccupied with finding the best methods to analyze human life, be it ancient texts, historical periods, other cultures, religious symbols. Getting the method right seemed as important, if not more important, than the truth we were seeking to discover. Moreover, our attachment to method gave us a smug sense that we were in control of our search and that all discoveries were finally in our hands.

In contrast to method, Gadamer preferred to speak of 'truth' or 'understanding'. Whereas method tends to distance us from what we seek to know – as though we were mere observers of life – understanding seeks to invite our very selves into the interpretive process. Rather than standing apart, analyzing and probing with our refined methods, understanding seeks to draw us in. Inevitably we will lose something of the 'control' that our methods afforded us, but we will become more receptive and open to that which is seeking to speak to us, to show itself to us, to reveal its truth to us.

In an interesting passage, Martin Heidegger offers the analogy of a woodworker learning the craft of cabinetmaking. He writes:

> A cabinetmaker's apprentice, someone who is learning to build cabinets and the like, will serve as an example. His learning is not mere practice, to gain facility in the use of tools. Nor does he merely gather knowledge about the customary forms of the things he is to build. If he is to become a true cabinetmaker, he makes himself answer and respond above all to the different kinds of wood and to the shapes slumbering within the wood – to wood as it enters into man's dwelling with all the hidden riches of its nature. In fact, this relatedness to wood is what maintains the whole craft. Without that relatedness, the craft will never be anything but empty busy-

work. . . . Every handicraft, *all human dealings*, are constantly in that danger.[16]

Along with learning the 'tools' and methods of practical theology, we must also develop an essential 'relatedness' to theology, whereby theological practice becomes a way of life, where it enters our dwelling in the world and reveals 'all the hidden riches of its nature'. Practical theology is a craft in which we continually 'answer and respond' to the call and vocation of apprenticeship and discipleship in God's ways.

In philosophy this process is known as *phronesis* – a 'practical wisdom' that is shaped over years of practicing the wisdom of a craft, a teaching, or a discipline that becomes a 'way of life'. For practical theology, this process is known as a *habitus*, a disposition of the mind and heart from which our actions flow naturally, or, if you like, 'according to the Spirit' dwelling within us.[17]

On Earth

Practical theology necessarily attends to the *conditions* of human life. It is concerned with the unique, the particular, the concrete – this people, this community, this place, this moment, this neighbor, this question, this need, this concern. Vatican II's Pastoral Constitution (*Gaudium et spes*) reminds us that without attention to 'the joy and hope, the grief and anguish of the people of our time', practical theology would have little or no connection to the coming of God's kingdom 'on earth'. That same document tells us that '*at all times*, the Church carries the responsibility of reading the signs of the times and of interpreting them in the light of the Gospel' (nos. 1, 4).

'At all times' is another way of saying that the theological task must be performed *each* and *every* time – not *once* and *for all time*. In many ways, all good theology is practical theology – attentive, searching, responsive. Indeed, even the great classic works of theology (Augustine or Aquinas, for example) represent theological responses worked out in response to contemporary pastoral situations – bold and innovative attempts to listen to and understand present realities rather than simply regurgitating answers from the past.

There is nothing easy about practical theology. Trying to interpret present realities is an incredibly difficult and complex task. Often, it will require of theology a partnering with other disciplines, especially the social sciences, to help us get a better 'read' of what is actually going on in our situation. Another valuable resource for 'reading the signs of the times' can be found in our poets and songwriters, novelists and artists – those who are best able to unmask our cultural blinders to current realities.

It is easy to be lulled into our present, and to fail to notice how askew things really are. In Luke's Gospel, Jesus says to the crowds, 'When you see a cloud looming up in the west you say at once that rain is coming, and so it does. And when the wind is from the south you say it will be hot, and it is. Hypocrites! You know how to interpret the face of the earth and the sky. How is it you do not know how to interpret the present time?' (12.54–56). How indeed? There is a reproof in this question. We seem to be able to read and interpret that which is predictable and familiar to us, but when it comes to interpreting the present time, we 'hear and hear again, but do not understand; see and see again, but do not perceive' (Isa. 6.9; cf. Matt. 13.13–15).

To read the signs of the times is one of the most difficult theological tasks, yet it is a theological imperative. Too often we do not behold the announcement of God in our present reality. Rather, we cling to what we already know of God, to tired and weary theological frameworks that have lost their sense of timeliness, to religious truths that lull us to sleep rather than provoke us to wakefulness. Any sense of expectation, announcement, or the coming of the kingdom is lost to us. Knowing the ways and purposes of God becomes as customary and familiar as forecasting the weather, yet we are cautioned to 'stay awake' lest we hear but do not hear, see but do not see. This vigilance does not come easily because it challenges theology to be observant and mindful – to 'think again' – to be alert and attentive. We are called to think and act for these times, for this reality, in the face of 'the joy and hope, grief and anguish of the people of our time, especially of those who are poor or afflicted . . . in deep solidarity with the human race and its history'.

As it is in Heaven

'Is there a way', asks Emmanuel Levinas, 'for the wisdom of heaven to return to earth?'[18] While it is crucial that practical theology attend to the concrete *conditions* of human existence, it must seek to read or interpret those conditions in the light of 'the kingdom of heaven'. What is the kingdom of heaven like? In many ways, the whole of the biblical tradition is an attempt to answer this question – or rather, to *provoke* this question – like the unsettling, demanding cries of the Hebrew prophets, or the disruptive parables of Jesus that keep turning things around, or the irritating lives of crazy saints with their impossible visions and out-of-place utopias.

When we pray, 'Thy kingdom come', we are subjecting the *conditions* of human existence, 'on earth', to the *unconditional* claims of God's word, 'as it is in heaven'. There are, for example, no conditions that limit or circumscribe the biblical message of mercy and justice, as though we could ever put up our feet and say, 'No more is required of me'. Each new age and every new generation must wrestle again with the question of what it means to act with justice and yet to love tenderly and be merciful.

The biblical message is not timeless (or 'heavenly') in the sense that it has nothing to do with time or history. Rather, it is timeless in the sense that it proclaims a 'surplus of love' or an 'amazing grace' that knows no bounds, a love that refuses to be measured by the history of human events, but that continually bursts forth and breaks into human history as an immeasurable love that awakens, inspires, and agitates our lives.

Practical theology is an effort to always honor the appeal to human experience, drawing our attention to questions of history, culture, and society, urging us to respond to the real needs of our world, to the conditions of human existence, 'on earth'. This is perhaps what is meant by the word 'practical'. Yet it is practical *theology* – an effort to regain the transcendent appeal of God's word to humanity, an appeal that calls out to us and asks us to be people of God, people of faith, people of hope, people of justice and mercy – a people living and acting on earth, 'as it is in heaven'.

. . .

Notes

1. See Farley, *Theologia* and *The Fragility of Knowledge*.
2. See Leclercq, *The Love of Learning and the Desire for God*.
3. Rahner, 'Practical Theology within the Totality of Theological Disciplines', *Theological Investigations*, 9:104.
4. Ibid.
5. Browning, *A Fundamental Practical Theology*, 7.
6. Groome, 'Theology on Our Feet: A Revisionist Pedagogy for Healing the Gap between Academia and Ecclesia,' in Mudge and Poling, eds. *Formation and Reflection*, 57.
7. See Heidegger, 'Being and Time: Introduction', in *Basic Writings*, 41–89.

8. See Groome's major work, *Sharing Faith: A Comprehensive Approach to Religious Education and Pastoral Ministry*.

9. Williams, *On Christian Theology*, 6–7.

10. Freire, *Pedagogy of the Oppressed*, 46.

11. Levinas, *Totality and Infinity*, 304.

12. Levinas's work is explored further in chapter 7 of Veling's book, 'Can the Wisdom of Heaven Return to Earth?'

13. This is something I learned while studying Talmudic texts under the wise guidance of Professor Michael Rosenak at the Hebrew University of Jerusalem. Readers may like to consult his works, *Commandments and Concerns: Jewish Religious Education in Secular Society; Roads to the Palace: Jewish Texts and Teaching; Tree of Life, Tree of Knowledge: Conversations with the Torah*.

14. Augustine, *On Christian Doctrine*, bk. 1.36.41.

15. Gadamer, *Gadamer in Conversation*, 40–42.

16. Heidegger, 'What Calls for Thinking?' in *Basic Writings*, 355–56.

17. *Phronesis* is a term that Gadamer borrows from Aristotle (see *Nicomachean Ethics*, Bk. 6). For Gadamer's reflections, see *Truth and Method*, 312ff. In *Theologia*, Farley focuses on theology as a *habitus*, a practical knowing having the primary character of wisdom.

18. Levinas, *Basic Philosophical Writings*, 158.

Theological Reflection: References and Further Reading

Charry, E. T. (1997), *By the Renewing of your Minds: The Pastoral Function of Christian Doctrine*, New York: Oxford University Press.

Farley, E. (1983), *Theologia: The Fragmentation and Unity of Theological Education*, Philadelphia: Fortress.

Pattison, S. and Lynch, G. (2005), 'Pastoral and Practical Theology', in D. F. Ford and R. Muers (eds.), *The Modern Theologians*, Oxford: Blackwell, 3rd edition, 408–25.

Jenkins, D. E. (1971), 'Concerning Theological Reflection', *Study Encounter* Vol. VII, No. 3, Geneva: World Council of Churches.

Killen, P. O. and de Beer, J. (1994), *The Art of Theological Reflection*, New York: Orbis.

Kinast, R. (2000), *What Are They Saying About Theological Reflection?* New York: Paulist Press.

Maitland, S. (1995), *A Big-Enough God: Artful Theology*, London: Mowbray.

I

Theology by Heart

Introduction

This method of theological reflection looks to the self and the interior life as the primary space in which theological awareness is generated and nurtured. It is a method with a long history; it could even be said to date back to the Psalms, where in poetry and prayer addressed to God, a turn is made to the inward life. The ways in which the Psalms have been recited through the centuries in a variety of public and private contexts, bringing together perennial themes that resonate within the heart, offer a fascinating example of how this method of theological reflection operates.

The method comes to its explicit shape in Augustine's writing: his work was groundbreaking in the way he used personal autobiography to open up theological questions and debates. Since then spiritual writers, theologians and religious people have turned to the self and written of their heartfelt inner experience, as they have also engaged with the world around them and with the place of God in their lives. As they have done so, they have reflected theologically; showing a particular method, and also leaving behind a theological resource for future generations.

Understood broadly, the method employs journal-writing, personal letters, verbatim accounts of pastoral encounters, spiritual autobiography and other contemporary forms of creative writing as the means to 'turn-life-into-text'. The subject matter can range widely, from the struggle with self expressed in dialogue with self, or with God, with some other imaginary or real reader; to ruthless self-examination and honesty in the face of some life crisis or sense of conscience; to an intense encounter with a sense of God in the natural world and an exploration of mystical experience. The styles adopted can also be varied: from prose to poetry; from dialogue to prayer forms, and the liveliest place in which this method is currently employed is in the many web-logging sites that are emerging as theologians make use of the facilities of the Internet to reflect and communicate with others.

The texts that result from this method of theological reflection can be described as 'living human documents'. The text itself takes on a life of its own that speaks of a particular time and place, and yet enables others to identify with similar or different issues. These living texts enable conversations to come to life: they do not only contain the perspective of their authors but also witness to encounters with other people, other world-views and with God. As such this method of theology by heart provides a rich resource, based in personal writing, but made public and applicable in different contexts and times.

Augustine, *Confessions*

translated by R. S. Pine-Coffin, London: Penguin, 1961, Book X, Chapters 6, 8, pp. 211–13, 215–16.

St Augustine was 43 when he wrote the Confessions *in 397. He had been consecrated Bishop of Hippo the year before. As Christianity began to emerge as a dominant religion from the crumbling civilization of the Roman world, Augustine was a leading figure in its engagement with classical philosophy, other religions and different interpretations of the Christian faith itself.*

We see in this passage how Augustine addresses God in the Confessions, *an astute move that enables him to make the whole work a prayer of praise and confession, as he explores his own nature and the quality of his relationships – with God and with other people. In making God his main dialogue partner he effectively makes his reader identify with himself, drawing the reader into the text and inspiring others to engage in this theological reflection 'by heart'.*

His subject in this passage is God's love and how it can be discerned in and through the natural world, and yet is distinct from it. Augustine writes beautifully; the section that begins 'But what do I love when I love my God?' is pure poetry. In a piece of writing about beauty, and how God is revealed in beauty, the elegance of his own expression drives home his theological point.

He turns in the second extract from the vast beauty of God's creation to the immensity that is within; his memory is 'a vast immeasurable sanctuary'. Augustine speaks of his 'mind's eye' that remembers the world, and sees its vastness and yet knows that there is more than that which is contained in the mind. In other places in the Confessions *Augustine relates conversations with others; here he is in dialogue with himself as he tries to comprehend how fearfully*

and wonderfully he is made. The intensity of Augustine's introspec-
tions and theological exploration of God, self and the world make the
Confessions *a work of enduring brilliance, and a classic illustration of*
this way of reflecting theologically.

6

My love of you, O Lord, is not some vague feeling: it is positive and
certain. Your word struck into my heart and from that moment I
loved you. Besides this, all about me, heaven and earth and all that
they contain proclaim that I should love you, and their message never
ceases to sound in the ears of all mankind, so that there is no excuse
for any not to love you. But, more than all this, *you will show pity*
on those whom you pity; you will show mercy where you are merci-
ful;[1] for if it were not for your mercy, heaven and earth would cry
your praises to deaf ears.

But what do I love when I love my God? Not material beauty or
beauty of a temporal order; not the brilliance of earthly light, so
welcome to our eyes; not the sweet melody of harmony and song; not
the fragrance of flowers, perfumes, and spices; not manna or honey;
not limbs such as the body delights to embrace. It is not these that I
love when I love my God. And yet, when I love him, it is true that I
love a light of a certain kind, a voice, a perfume, a food, an embrace;
but they are of the kind that I love in my inner self, when my soul is
bathed in light that is not bound by space; when it listens to sound
that never dies away; when it breathes fragrance that is not borne
away on the wind; when it tastes food that is never consumed by the
eating; when it clings to an embrace from which it is not severed by
fulfilment of desire. This is what I love when I love my God.

But what is my God? I put my question to the earth. It answered,
'I am not God', and all things on earth declared the same. I asked the
sea and the chasms of the deep and the living things that creep in
them, but they answered, 'We are not your God. Seek what is above
us.' I spoke to the winds that blow, and the whole air and all that
lives in it replied, 'Anaximenes[2] is wrong. I am not God.' I asked the
sky, the sun, the moon, and the stars, but they told me, 'Neither are
we the God whom you seek.' I spoke to all the things that are about
me, all that can be admitted by the door of the senses, and I said,
'Since you are not my God, tell me about him. Tell me something of
my God.' Clear and loud they answered, 'God is he who made us.'
I asked these questions simply by gazing at these things, and their
beauty was all the answer they gave.

Then I turned to myself and asked, 'Who are you?' 'A man,' I replied. But it is clear that I have both body and soul, the one the outer, the other the inner part of me. Which of these two ought I to have asked to help me find my God? With my bodily powers I had already tried to find him in earth and sky, as far as the sight of my eyes could reach, like an envoy sent upon a search. But my inner self is the better of the two, for it was to the inner part of me that my bodily senses brought their messages. They delivered to their arbiter and judge the replies which they carried back from the sky and the earth and all that they contain, those replies which stated 'We are not God' and 'God is he who made us'. The inner part of man knows these things through the agency of the outer part. I, the inner man, know these things; I, the soul, know them through the senses of my body. I asked the whole mass of the universe about my God, and it replied, 'I am not God. God is he who made me.'

Surely everyone whose senses are not impaired is aware of the universe around him? Why, then, does it not give the same message to us all? The animals, both great and small, are aware of it, but they cannot inquire into its meaning because they are not guided by reason, which can sift the evidence relayed to them by their senses. Man, on the other hand, can question nature. He is able to *catch sight of God's invisible nature through his creatures*,[3] but his love of these material things is too great. He becomes their slave, and slaves cannot be judges. Nor will the world supply an answer to those who question it, unless they also have the faculty to judge it. It does not answer in different language – that is, it does not change its aspect – according to whether a man merely looks at it or subjects it to inquiry while he looks. If it did, its appearance would be different in each case. Its aspect is the same in both cases, but to the man who merely looks it says nothing, while to the other it gives an answer. It would be nearer the truth to say that it gives an answer to all, but it is only understood by those who compare the message it gives them through their senses with the truth that is in themselves. For truth says to me, 'Your God is not heaven or earth or any kind of bodily thing.' We can tell this from the very nature of such things, for those who have eyes to see know that their bulk is less in the part than in the whole. And I know that my soul is the better part of me, because it animates the whole of my body. It gives it life, and this is something that no body can give to another body. But God is even more. He is the Life of the life of my soul.

. . .

8

. . .

All this goes on inside me, in the vast cloisters of my memory. In it are the sky, the earth, and the sea, ready at my summons, together with everything that I have ever perceived in them by my senses, except the things which I have forgotten. In it I meet myself as well. I remember myself and what I have done, when and where I did it, and the state of my mind at the time. In my memory, too, are all the events that I remember, whether they are things that have happened to me or things that I have heard from others. From the same source I can picture to myself all kinds of different images based either upon my own experience or upon what I find credible because it tallies with my own experience. I can fit them into the general picture of the past; from them I can make a surmise of actions and events and hopes for the future; and I can contemplate them all over again as if they were actually present. If I say to myself in the vast cache of my mind, where all those images of great things are stored, 'I shall do this or that', the picture of this or that particular thing comes into my mind at once. Or I may say to myself 'If only this or that would happen!' or 'God forbid that this or that should be!' No sooner do I say this than the images of all the things of which I speak spring forward from the same great treasure-house of the memory. And, in fact, I could not even mention them at all if the images were lacking.

The power of the memory is prodigious, my God. It is a vast, immeasurable sanctuary. Who can plumb its depths? And yet it is a faculty of my soul. Although it is part of my nature, I cannot understand all that I am. This means, then, that the mind is too narrow to contain itself entirely. But where is that part of it which it does not itself contain? Is it somewhere outside itself and not within it? How, then, can it be part of it, if it is not contained in it?

I am lost in wonder when I consider this problem. It bewilders me. Yet men go out and gaze in astonishment at high mountains, the huge waves of the sea, the broad reaches of rivers, the ocean that encircles the world, or the stars in their courses. But they pay no attention to themselves. They do not marvel at the thought that while I have been mentioning all these things, I have not been looking at them with my eyes, and that I could not even speak of mountains or waves, rivers or stars, which are things that I have seen, or of the ocean, which I know only on the evidence of others, unless I could see them in my mind's eye, in my memory, and with the same vast spaces between them that would be there if I were looking at them in the world outside myself. When I saw them with the sight of my eyes, I did not draw them bodily into myself. They are not inside me themselves, but only their images. And I know which of my senses imprinted each image on my mind.

Notes

1. Rom. 9.15.
2. Anaximenes of Miletus, the philosopher, who lived in the sixth century B.C. His teaching was that air is the first cause of all things.
3. Rom. 1.20.

Thomas Merton, *The Seven Storey Mountain*
6th impression, London: Sheldon Press, 1988, pp. 410–13, 419–23.

Merton's book The Seven Storey Mountain *has proved to be a modern classic of the religious life. Merton's life, and the telling of it in this autobiography, expressed for many the search for meaning in the post-war years, and a renewed interest in what enclosed orders might offer to a world that had a new sense of itself as global. Insights from the religious practices of the Middle and Far East were permeating through to the Christian world-view of the West, and Merton came to travel extensively, studying and lecturing on the religious life. He met his death, accidentally, in Bangkok in 1953.*

These passages offer a valuable insight into the conflict he experienced when he made his profession (taking lifelong vows) at the Cistercian monastery at Gethsemani at this time of religious revival. Already a published poet, he found that he could not shake off the former identity of writer and entrepreneur; an identity that followed him into the cloister, leaving him with the sense that either one of them would need to die for the other to thrive. The way Merton explores the split identity he experienced and struggled with the two different directions in which he sensed a vocation, and how he described the guidance he received from his religious advisors, including the Abbot, offer here an exquisite example of this method of theological reflection. The writing is dialogical and in the second excerpt, which concludes the book, Merton, like Augustine, addresses God directly and writes out an imagined reply from God. This reveals the anguish and difficulties that Merton associated with the burning

*and refining that were necessary as he sought solitude and had
to relinquish the control of knowing where God was leading him.
The Latin postscript means 'Here ends the book, but it is not the
end of the searching'; a fine epithet to the spirit of this man and the
book.*

ii

By this time I should have been delivered of any problems about my
true identity. I had already made my simple profession. And my vows
should have divested me of the last shreds of any special identity.

But then there was this shadow, this double, this writer who had
followed me into the cloister.

He is still on my track. He rides my shoulders, sometimes, like the
old man of the sea. I cannot lose him. He still wears the name of
Thomas Merton. Is it the name of an enemy?

He is supposed to be dead.

But he stands and meets me in the doorway of all my prayers, and
follows me into church. He kneels with me behind the pillar, the
Judas, and talks to me all the time in my ear.

He is a business man. He is full of ideas. He breathes notions and
new schemes. He generates books in the silence that ought to be sweet
with the infinitely productive darkness of contemplation.

And the worst of it is, he has my superiors on his side. They won't
kick him out. I can't get rid of him.

Maybe in the end he will kill me, he will drink my blood.

Nobody seems to understand that one of us has got to die.

Sometimes I am mortally afraid. There are the days when there
seems to be nothing left of my vocation – my contemplative vocation
– but a few ashes. And everybody calmly tells me: 'Writing is your
vocation.'

And there he stands and bars my way to liberty. I am bound to the
earth, in his Egyptian bondage of contracts, reviews, page proofs, and
all the plans for books and articles that I am saddled with.

When I first began to get ideas about writing, I told them to Father
Master and Father Abbot with what I thought was 'simplicity'. I
thought I was just 'being open with my superiors'. In a way, I suppose
I was.

But it was not long before they got the idea that I ought to be put
to work translating things, writing things.

It is strange. The Trappists have sometimes been definite, even
exaggerated, in their opposition to intellectual work in the past. That

was one of the big battle cries of De Rancé. He had a kind of detestation for monkish dilettantes and he took up arms against the whole Benedictine Congregation of Saint Maur in a more or less quixotic battle that ended in a reconciliation scene between De Rancé and the great Dom Mabillon that reads like Oliver Goldsmith. In the eighteenth and nineteenth centuries, it was considered a kind of a monastic sin for a Trappist to read anything but Scripture and the lives of the saints: and I mean those lives that are a chain of fantastic miracles interspersed with pious platitudes. It was considered a matter worthy of suspicion if a monk developed too lively an interest in the Fathers of the Church.

But at Gethsemani I had walked into a far different kind of a situation.

In the first place, I entered a house that was seething with an energy and a growth that it had not known for ninety years. After nearly a century of struggle and obscurity, Gethsemani was suddenly turning into a very prominent and vital force in the Cistercian order and the Catholic Church in America. The house was crowded with postulants and novices. There was no longer any room to hold them all. In fact, on the Feast of St. Joseph, 1944, when I made my simple profession, Father Abbot read out the names of those who had been chosen for the first daughter house of Gethsemani. Two days later, on the Feast of St. Benedict, the colony left for Georgia and took up its abode in a barn thirty miles from Atlanta, chanting the psalms in a hayloft. By the time this is printed there will have been another Cistercian monastery in Utah and another in New Mexico, and still another planned for the deep South.

This material growth at Gethsemani is part of a vaster movement of spiritual vitality that is working throughout the whole Order, all over the world. And one of the things it has produced has been a certain amount of Cistercian literature.

That there should be six Cistercian monasteries in the United States and a convent of nuns soon to come: that there should also be new foundations in Ireland and Scotland, all this means a demand for books in English about the Cistercian life and the spirituality of the Order and its history.

But besides that, Gethsemani has grown into a sort of a furnace of apostolic fire. Every week-end, during the summer, the Guest House is crowded with retreatants who pray and fight the flies and wipe the sweat out of their eyes and listen to the monks chanting the office and hear sermons in the library and eat the cheese that Brother Kevin makes down in the moist shadows of the cellar that is propitious for that kind of thing. And along with this retreat movement, Gethsemani has been publishing a lot of pamphlets.

There is a whole rack of them in the lobby of the Guest House. Blue and yellow and pink and green and grey, with fancy printing on the covers or plain printing – some of them even with pictures – the pamphlets bear the legend: 'A Trappist says . . .' 'A Trappist declares . . .' 'A Trappist implores . . .' 'A Trappist asserts . . .' And what does a Trappist say, declare, implore, assert? He says things like this: It is time you changed your way of looking at things. Why don't you get busy and go to confession? After death: what? and things like that. These Trappists, they have something to tell laymen and laywomen, married men and single men, old men and young men, men in the army and men who have just come out of the army and men who are too crippled up to get into the army. They have a word of advice for nuns, and more than a word for priests. They have something to say about how to build a home, and about how to go through four years of college without getting too badly knocked about, spiritually, in the process.

And one of the pamphlets even has something to say about the Contemplative Life.

So it is not hard to see that this is a situation in which my double, my shadow, my enemy, Thomas Merton, the old man of the sea, has things in his favor. If he suggests books about the Order, his suggestions are heard. If he thinks up poems to be printed and published, his thoughts are listened to. There seems to be no reason why he should not write for magazines. . . .

At the beginning of 1944, when I was getting near the time for simple profession, I wrote a poem to Saint Agnes on her feast in January, and when I had finished it my feeling was that I did not care if I never wrote another poem as long as I lived.

At the end of the year, when *Thirty Poems* were printed, I still felt the same way, and more so.

So then Lax came down again for another Christmas, and told me I should be writing more poems. I did not argue about it. But in my own heart I did not think it was God's will. And Dom Vital, my confessor, did not think so either.

Then one day – the Feast of the Conversion of Saint Paul, 1945 – I went to Father Abbot for direction, and without my even thinking of the subject, or mentioning it, he suddenly said to me:

'I want you to go on writing poems.'

iii

. . .

Before we were born, God knew us. He knew that some of us would rebel against His love and His mercy, and that others would love Him from the moment that they could love anything, and never change that love. He knew that there would be joy in heaven among the angels of His house for the conversion of some of us, and He knew that He would bring us all here to Gethsemani together, one day, for His own purpose, for the praise of His love.

The life of each one in this abbey is part of a mystery. We all add up to something far beyond ourselves. We cannot yet realize what it is. But we know, in the language of our theology, that we are all members of the Mystical Christ, and that we all grow together in Him for Whom all things were created.

In one sense we are always travelling, and travelling as if we did not know where we were going.

In another sense we have already arrived.

We cannot arrive at the perfect possession of God in this life, and that is why we are travelling and in darkness. But we already possess Him by grace, and therefore in that sense we have arrived and are dwelling in the light.

But oh! How far have I to go to find You in Whom I have already arrived!

For now, oh my God, it is to You alone that I can talk, because nobody else will understand. I cannot bring any other man on this earth into the cloud where I dwell in Your light, that is, Your darkness, where I am lost and abashed. I cannot explain to any other man the anguish which is Your joy nor the loss which is the Possession of You, nor the distance from all things which is the arrival in You, nor the death which is the birth in You because I do not know anything about it myself and all I know is that I wish it were over – I wish it were begun.

You have contradicted everything. You have left me in no-man's land.

You have got me walking up and down all day under those trees, saying to me over and over again: 'Solitude, solitude'. And You have turned around and thrown the whole world in my lap. You have told me, 'Leave all things and follow me,' and then You have tied half of New York to my foot like a ball and chain. You have got me kneeling behind that pillar with my mind making a noise like a bank. Is that contemplation?

Before I went to make my solemn vows, last spring, on the Feast of St Joseph, in the thirty-third year of my age, being a cleric in minor orders – before I went to make my solemn vows, this is what it looked like to me. It seemed to me that You were almost asking me to give up all my aspirations for solitude and for a contemplative life. You were asking me for obedience to superiors who will, I am morally certain, either make me write or teach philosophy or take charge of a dozen material responsibilities around the monastery, and I may even end up as a retreat master preaching four sermons a day to the seculars who come to the house. And even if I have no special job at all, I will always be on the run from two in the morning to seven at night.

Didn't I spend a year writing the life of Mother Berchmans who was sent to a new Trappistine foundation in Japan, and who wanted to be a contemplative? And what happened to her? She had to be gate-keeper and guest-mistress and sacristan and cellaress and mistress of the lay sisters all at the same time. And when they relieved her of one or two of those jobs it was only in order to give her heavier ones, like that of Mistress of Novices.

Martha, Martha, sollicita eris, et turbaberis erga plurima . . .

When I was beginning my retreat, before solemn profession, I tried to ask myself for a moment if those vows had any condition attached to them. If I was called to be a contemplative and they did not help me to be a contemplative, but hindered me, then what?

But before I could even begin to pray, I had to drop that kind of thinking.

By the time I made my vows, I decided that I was no longer sure what a contemplative was, or what the contemplative vocation was, or what my vocation was, and what our Cistercian vocation was. In fact I could not be sure I knew or understood much of anything except that I believed that You wanted me to take those particular vows in this particular house on that particular day for reasons best known to Yourself, and that what I was expected to do after that was follow along with the rest and do what I was told and things would begin to become clear.

That morning when I was lying on my face on the floor in the middle of the church, with Father Abbot praying over me, I began to laugh, with my mouth in the dust, because without knowing how or why, I had actually done the right thing, and even an astounding thing. But what was astounding was not my work, but the work You worked in me.

The months have gone by, and You have not lessened any of those desires, but You have given me peace, and I am beginning to see what it is all about. I am beginning to understand.

Because You have called me here not to wear a label by which I can recognize myself and place myself in some kind of a category. You do not want me to be thinking about what I am, but about what You are. Or rather, You do not even want me to be thinking about anything much: for You would raise me above the level of thought. And if I am always trying to figure out what I am and where I am and why I am, how will that work be done?

I do not make a big drama of this business. I do not say: 'You have asked me for everything, and I have renounced all.' Because I no longer desire to see anything that implies a distance between You and me: and if I stand back and consider myself and You as if something had passed between us, from me to You, I will inevitably see the gap between us and remember the distance between us.

My God, it is that gap and that distance which kill me.

That is the only reason why I desire solitude – to be lost to all created things, to die to them and to the knowledge of them, for they remind me of my distance from You. They tell me something about You: that You are far from them, even though You are in them. You have made them and Your presence sustains their being, and they hide You from me. And I would live alone, and out of them. O *beata solitudo!*

For I knew that it was only by leaving them that I could come to You: and that is why I have been so unhappy when You seemed to be condemning me to remain in them. Now my sorrow is over, and my joy is about to begin: the joy that rejoices in the deepest sorrows. For I am beginning to understand. You have taught me, and have consoled me, and I have begun again to hope and learn.

I hear You saying to me:

'*I will give you what you desire. I will lead you into solitude. I will lead you by the way that you cannot possibly understand, because I want it to be the quickest way.*

'*Therefore all the things around you will be armed against you, to deny you, to hurt you, to give you pain, and therefore to reduce you to solitude.*

'*Because of their enmity, you will soon be left alone. They will cast you out and forsake you and reject you and you will be alone.*

'*Everything that touches you shall burn you, and you will draw your hand away in pain, until you have withdrawn yourself from all things. Then you will be all alone.*

'*Everything that can be desired will sear you, and brand you with a cautery, and you will fly from it in pain, to be alone. Every created joy will only come to you as pain, and you will die to all joy and be left alone. All the good things that other people love and desire and seek will come to you, but only as murderers to cut you off from the world and its occupations.*

'*You will be praised, and it will be like burning at the stake. You will be loved, and it will murder your heart and drive you into the desert.*

'*You will have gifts, and they will break you with their burden. You will have pleasures of prayer, and they will sicken you and you will fly from them.*

'*And when you have been praised a little and loved a little I will take away all your gifts and all your love and all your praise and you will be utterly forgotten and abandoned and you will be nothing, a dead thing, a rejection. And in that day you shall begin to possess the solitude you have so long desired. And your solitude will bear immense fruit in the souls of men you will never see on earth.*

'*Do not ask when it will be or where it will be or how it will be: On a mountain or in a prison, in a desert or in a concentration camp or in a hospital or at Gethsemani. It does not matter. So do not ask me, because I am not going to tell you. You will not know until you are in it.*

'*But you shall taste the true solitude of my anguish and my poverty and I shall lead you into the high places of my joy and you shall die in Me and find all things in My mercy which has created you for this end and brought you from Prades to Bermuda to St Antonin to Oakham to London to Cambridge to Rome to New York to Columbia to Corpus Christi to St. Bonaventure to the Cistercian Abbey of the poor men who labor in Gethsemani:*

'*That you may become the brother of God and learn to know the Christ of the burnt men.*'

SIT FINIS LIBRI, NON FINIS QUAERENDI

C. S. Lewis, *A Grief Observed*
London: Faber & Faber, 1989, pp. 16–18, 25–9.

In A Grief Observed C. S. Lewis departed so radically from his main corpus of work that he published this little book under the pseudonym of N. W. Clerk, and it was only revealed as his work in 1963 after his death. In it he is no longer the author of allegorical children's

*books, or an apologist for Christianity, but someone struggling in-
tensely and personally with the loss of Joy, the woman he married
rather late in life, and with whom he shared too short and passionate
a length of time. In these passages his rigorous honesty is apparent
as he worries about constructing her in his own image and according
to his own needs. He delights in the way she was so resistant, so
other to himself when she was alive; how she challenged him out of
his 'old bachelor pipe-dreams', showing how important, in this
method of theological reflection by heart, the other is to the self and
its growth.*

*In the second passage there is no sense of complacency about
Lewis's struggle with his faith in a good God: he rails against God
with a bitterness that is out of keeping with the self-confidence of his
other writing. He faces the utter meaninglessness of life without love,
where it seems he is 'just hanging about waiting for something to
happen', and yet, in the tradition of the anger and frustration of the
writers of the Psalms, he can find no peace of mind in these early
days of grief.*

For the first time I have looked back and read these notes. They appal
me. From the way I've been talking anyone would think that H's
death mattered chiefly for its effect on myself. Her point of view
seems to have dropped out of sight. Have I forgotten the moment of
bitterness when she cried out 'And there was so much to live for'?
Happiness had not come to her early in life. A thousand years of it
would not have made her *blasée*. Her palate for all the joys of sense
and intellect and spirit was fresh and unspoiled. Nothing would have
been wasted on her. She liked more things and liked them more than
anyone I have known. A noble hunger, long unsatisfied, met at last
its proper food, and almost instantly the food was snatched away.
Fate (or whatever it is) delights to produce a great capacity and then
frustrate it. Beethoven went deaf. By our standards a mean joke; the
monkey trick of a spiteful imbecile.

I must think more about H. and less about myself.

Yes, that sounds very well. But there's a snag. I am thinking about
her nearly always. Thinking of the H. facts – real words, looks,
laughs, and actions of hers. But it is my own mind that selects and
groups them. Already, less than a month after her death, I can feel
the slow, insidious beginning of a process that will make the H. I
think of into a more and more imaginary woman. Founded on fact,
no doubt, I shall put in nothing fictitious (or I hope I shan't). But

won't the composition inevitably become more and more my own? The reality is no longer there to check me, to pull me up short, as the real H. so often did, so unexpectedly, by being so thoroughly herself and not me.

The most precious gift that marriage gave me was this constant impact of something very close and intimate yet all the time unmistakably other, resistant – in a word, real. Is all that work to be undone? Is what I shall still call H. to sink back horribly into being not much more than one of my old bachelor pipe-dreams? Oh my dear, my dear, come back for one moment and drive that miserable phantom away. Oh God, God, why did you take such trouble to force this creature out of its shell if it is now doomed to crawl back – to be sucked back – into it?

. . .

Come, what do we gain by evasions? We are under the harrow and can't escape. Reality, looked at steadily, is unbearable. And how or why did such a reality blossom (or fester) here and there into the terrible phenomenon called consciousness? Why did it produce things like us who can see it and, seeing it, recoil in loathing? Who (stranger still) want to see it and take pains to find it out, even when no need compels them and even though the sight of it makes an incurable ulcer in their hearts? People like H. herself, who would have truth at any price.

If H. 'is not', then she never was. I mistook a cloud of atoms for a person. There aren't, and never were, any people. Death only reveals the vacuity that was always there. What we call the living are simply those who have not yet been unmasked. All equally bankrupt, but some not yet declared.

But this must be nonsense; vacuity revealed to whom? Bankruptcy declared to whom? To other boxes of fireworks or clouds of atoms. I will never believe – more strictly I can't believe – that one set of physical events could be, or make, a mistake about other sets.

No, my real fear is not of materialism. If it were true, we – or what we mistake for 'we' – could get out, get from under the harrow. An overdose of sleeping pills would do it. I am more afraid that we are really rats in a trap. Or, worse still, rats in a laboratory. Someone said, I believe, 'God always geometrizes'. Supposing the truth were 'God always vivisects?'

Sooner or later I must face the question in plain language. What reason have we, except our own desperate wishes, to believe that God is, by any standard we can conceive, 'good'? Doesn't all the *prima facie* evidence suggest exactly the opposite? What have we to set against it?

We set Christ against it. But how if He were mistaken? Almost His last words may have a perfectly clear meaning. He had found that the Being He called Father was horribly and infinitely different from what He had supposed. The trap, so long and carefully prepared and so subtly baited was at last sprung, on the cross. The vile practical joke had succeeded.

What chokes every prayer and every hope is the memory of all the prayers H. and I offered and all the false hopes we had. Not hopes raised merely by our own wishful thinking; hopes encouraged, even forced upon us, by false diagnoses, by X-ray photographs, by strange remissions, by one temporary recovery that might have ranked as a miracle. Step by step we were 'led up the garden path'. Time after time, when He seemed most gracious He was really preparing the next torture.

I wrote that last night. It was a yell rather than a thought. Let me try it over again. Is it rational to believe in a bad God? Anyway, in a God so bad as all that? The Cosmic Sadist, the spiteful imbecile?

I think it is, if nothing else, too anthropomorphic. When you come to think of it, it is far more anthropomorphic than picturing Him as a grave old king with a long beard. That image is a Jungian archetype. It links God with all the wise old kings in the fairy-tales, with prophets, sages, magicians. Though it is (formally) the picture of a man, it suggests something more than humanity. At the very least it gets in the idea of something older than yourself, something that knows more, something you can't fathom. It preserves mystery. Therefore room for hope. Therefore room for a dread or awe that needn't be mere fear of mischief from a spiteful potentate. But the picture I was building up last night is simply the picture of a man like S.C. – who used to sit next to me at dinner and tell what he'd been doing to the cats that afternoon. Now a being like S.C., however magnified, couldn't invent or create or govern anything. He would set traps and try to bait them. But he'd never have thought of baits like love, or laughter, or daffodils, or a frosty sunset. *He* make a universe? He couldn't make a joke, or a bow, or an apology, or a friend.

Or could one seriously introduce the idea of a bad God, as it were by the back door, through a sort of extreme Calvinism? You could say we are fallen and depraved. We are so depraved that our ideas of goodness count for nothing; or worse than nothing – the very fact that we think something good is presumptive evidence that it is really

bad. Now God has in fact – our worse fears are true – all the characteristics we regard at bad: unreasonableness, vanity, vindictiveness,
injustice, cruelty. But all these blacks (as they seem to us) are really
whites. It's only our depravity makes them look black to us.

And so what? This, for all practical (and speculative) purposes
sponges God off the slate. The word *good*, applied to Him, becomes
meaningless: like abracadabra. We have no motive for obeying Him.
Not even fear. It is true we have His threats and promises. But why
should we believe them? If cruelty is from His point of view 'good',
telling lies may be 'good' too. Even if they are true, what then? If His
ideas of good are so very different from ours, what He calls 'Heaven'
might well be what we should call Hell, and vice-versa. Finally, if
reality at its very root is so meaningless to us – or, putting it the other
way round, if we are such total imbeciles – what is the point of trying
to think either about God or about anything else? This knot comes
undone when you try to pull it tight.

Why do I make room in my mind for such filth and nonsense? Do
I hope that if feeling disguises itself as thought I shall feel less? Aren't
all these notes the senseless writhings of a man who won't accept the
fact that there is nothing we can do with suffering except to suffer it?
Who still thinks there is some device (if only he could find it) which
will make pain not to be pain. It doesn't really matter whether you
grip the arms of the dentist's chair or let your hands lie in your lap.
The drill drills on.

And grief still feels like fear. Perhaps, more strictly, like suspense.
Or like waiting; just hanging about waiting for something to happen.
It gives life a permanently provisional feeling. It doesn't seem worth
starting anything. I can't settle down. I yawn, I fidget, I smoke too
much. Up till this I always had too little time. Now there is nothing
but time. Almost pure time, empty successiveness.

One flesh. Or, if you prefer, one ship. The starboard engine has
gone. I, the port engine, must chug along somehow till we make
harbour. Or rather, till the journey ends. How can I assume a harbour? A lee shore, more likely, a black night, a deafening gale, break-
ers ahead – and any lights shown from the land probably being waved
by wreckers. Such was H's landfall. Such was my mother's. I say their
landfalls; not their arrivals.

Annie Dillard, *Pilgrim at Tinker Creek*

New York: HarperCollins, 1988, pp. 18–19, 23–5.

*Annie Dillard's work needs to be located within the American tran-
scendentalist tradition of nature writing;* Pilgrim at Tinker Creek *can
be seen as a critical tribute to Thoreau, to whom she refers throughout
the text. There are also resonances with William Blake in her search
for a sense of the presence of God in the world. This is not, however,
a benign, kind God, but a divinity who is there in the brutal beauty
of the particular.*

*The first passage illustrates her preoccupation with what it means
to see and to observe as acutely as possible. Seeing becomes a mystical
experience as she seeks the essence of what is observed, even the death
of a frog, sucked dry by a giant water bug. She writes of what she
sees, but in the writing she crafts not only the objectivity of what is
before her, but also her own sense of identity and engagement with
the world. She writes as much of the patience required, the frustrations she feels and dramatic impact upon her as she does of the
phenomena itself: 'I couldn't catch my breath', she writes.*

Pilgrim at Tinker Creek *has been recognized as a modern classic
of spiritual writing that does theology from the heart; a form of
autobiography that does not set out the chronology of a life so much
as attempt to capture the encounter of self with a power that is divine.
She is the explorer, the stalker, who is pummelled by power, by the
gale force of the spirit and who with consummate skill writes a text
that is a rich meal of different encounters and conversations with
other philosophers and with nature itself.*

A couple of summers ago I was walking along the edge of the
island to see what I could see in the water, and mainly to scare frogs.
Frogs have an inelegant way of taking off from invisible positions on
the bank just ahead of your feet, in dire panic, emitting a froggy
'Yike!' and splashing into the water. Incredibly, this amused me, and,
incredibly, it amuses me still. As I walked along the grassy edge of
the island, I got better and better at seeing frogs both in and out of
the water. I learned to recognize, slowing down, the difference in
texture of the light reflected from mudbank, water, grass, or frog.
Frogs were flying all around me. At the end of the island I noticed a
small green frog. He was exactly half in and half out of the water,
looking like a schematic diagram of an amphibian, and he didn't
jump.

He didn't jump; I crept closer. At last I knelt on the island's winter-killed grass, lost, dumbstruck, staring at the frog in the creek just four feet away. He was a very small frog with wide, dull eyes. And just as I looked at him, he slowly crumpled and began to sag. The spirit vanished from his eyes as if snuffed. His skin emptied and drooped; his very skull seemed to collapse and settle like a kicked tent. He was shrinking before my eyes like a deflating football. I watched the taut, glistening skin on his shoulders ruck, and rumple, and fall. Soon, part of his skin, formless as a pricked balloon, lay in floating folds like bright scum on top of the water: it was a monstrous and terrifying thing. I gaped bewildered, appalled. An oval shadow hung in the water behind the drained frog; then the shadow glided away. The frog skin bag started to sink.

I had read about the giant water bug, but never seen one. 'Giant water bug' is really the name of the creature, which is an enormous, heavy-bodied brown beetle. It eats insects, tadpoles, fish, and frogs. Its grasping forelegs are mighty and hooked inward. It seizes a victim with these legs, hugs it tight, and paralyzes it with enzymes injected during a vicious bite. That one bite is the only bite it ever takes. Through the puncture shoot the poisons that dissolve the victim's muscles and bones and organs – all but the skin – and through it the giant water bug sucks out the victim's body, reduced to a juice. This event is quite common in warm fresh water. The frog I saw was being sucked by a giant water bug. I had been kneeling on the island grass; when the unrecognizable flap of frog skin settled on the creek bottom, swaying, I stood up and brushed the knees of my pants. I couldn't catch my breath.

. . .

Like the bear who went over the mountain, I went out to see what I could see. And, I might as well warn you, like the bear, all that I could see was the other side of the mountain: more of same. On a good day I might catch a glimpse of another wooded ridge rolling under the sun like water, another bivouac. I propose to keep here what Thoreau called 'a meteorological journal of the mind', telling some tales and describing some of the sights of this rather tamed valley, and exploring, in fear and trembling, some of the unmapped dim reaches and unholy fastnesses to which those tales and sights so dizzyingly lead.

I am no scientist. I explore the neighborhood. An infant who has just learned to hold his head up has a frank and forthright way of gazing about him in bewilderment. He hasn't the faintest clue where he is, and he aims to learn. In a couple of years, what he will have learned instead is how to fake it: he'll have the cocksure air of a squatter who has come to feel he owns the place. Some unwonted, taught pride diverts us from our original intent, which is to explore the neighborhood, view the landscape, to discover at least *where* it is that we have been so startlingly set down, if we can't learn why.

So I think about the valley. It is my leisure as well as my work, a game. It is a fierce game I have joined because it is being played anyway, a game of both skill and chance, played against an unseen adversary – the conditions of time – in which the payoffs, which may suddenly arrive in a blast of light at any moment, might as well come to me as anyone else. I stake the time I'm grateful to have, the energies I'm glad to direct. I risk getting stuck on the board, so to speak, unable to move in any direction, which happens enough, God knows; and I risk the searing, exhausting nightmares that plunder rest and force me face down all night long in some muddy ditch seething with hatching insects and crustaceans.

But if I can bear the nights, the days are a pleasure. I walk out; I see something, some event that would otherwise have been utterly missed and lost; or something sees me, some enormous power brushes me with its clean wing, and I resound like a beaten bell.

I am an explorer, then, and I am also a stalker, or the instrument of the hunt itself. Certain Indians used to carve long grooves along the wooden shafts of their arrows. They called the grooves 'lightning marks', because they resembled the curved fissure lightning slices down the trunks of trees. The function of lightning marks is this: if the arrow fails to kill the game, blood from a deep wound will channel along the lightning mark, streak down the arrow shaft, and spatter to the ground, laying a trail dripped on broad-leaves, on stones, that the barefoot and trembling archer can follow into whatever deep or rare wildnerness it leads. I am the arrow shaft, carved along my length by unexpected lights and gashes from the very sky, and this book is the straying trail of blood.

Something pummels us, something barely sheathed. Power broods and lights. We're played on like a pipe; our breath is not our own. James Houston describes two young Eskimo girls sitting cross-legged on the ground, mouth on mouth, blowing by turns each other's throat cords, making a low, unearthly music. When I cross again the bridge that is really the steers' fence, the wind has thinned to the delicate air of twilight; it crumples the water's skin. I watch the running sheets of light raised on the creek's surface. The sight has the appeal of the purely passive, like the racing of light under clouds on a field, the beautiful dream at the moment of being dreamed. The breeze is the merest puff, but you yourself sail headlong and breathless under the gale force of the spirit.

Rubem A. Alves, 'Words and Flesh'
in *The Poet, The Warrior, The Prophet*, London: SCM Press, 1990, pp. 48–52.

The Poet, The Warrior, The Prophet results from the Edward Cadbury Lectures of 1990 delivered by Rubem Alves, the professor of philosophy at the State University of Campinas in São Paulo, Brazil. His style is poetic and theological as he explores a number of subjects, like 'silence', 'poetry and magic', 'prophecy', and throughout the text the recurring theme of food emerges. In this passage Alves reflects on how his father-in-law's sense of taste was constructed by the cultural and religious upbringing he had received to the extent that his body reacted automatically and differently when what he thought was (delicious) cauliflower was in fact (repulsive) brain. Alves' theology by heart becomes 'theology by body' here as he explores the power of words, the body and blood of Christ, the Word of God.

My father-in-law was born in Germany. He moved to Brazil after the first world war. He was the son of a Seventh-Day Adventist pastor. As you know, members of this religious group are very strict about their eating habits. They do not eat pork and blood, and don't drink liquor, tea or coffee. My father-in-law, even though he was no longer a believer, could not forget the prohibition words which had been written in his body. And he even had an extra prohibition, which was his alone: he could not eat brain. Even though he had never tried brain before, the fact was that he did not like it . . . One day he was invited to a dinner. He was the guest of honour. And he was very pleased as he saw that the main dish was breaded cauliflower. He must have thought that the hostess was an expert in the rules of etiquette: she must have known about his almost vegetarian habits. He ate and had more. Delicious . . . At the end of the dinner, the alchemy of assimilation having already begun, and body and soul satisfied with the food, he gave a compliment.

'The breaded cauliflower was divine . . .'

'Oh! No!' said the hostess. 'It is not breaded cauliflower; it is breaded brain . . .'

Poor lady! She could never have imagined the kind of storm which an innocent word in the mouth could produce in the body ... My father-in-law, forgetting all rules of propriety, jumped off his chair, rushed to the bath room, and vomited everything ...

How can we account for what happened?

The 'thing': was it not delicious? Had not the body tasted and approved it? What physical or chemical changes could have occurred after the word 'brain' was said? None. My father-in-law knew this in his head. And yet his body did not agree. What had been good to eat before the word, ceased to be after the word was heard. What strange entity is this, which has the power to bring to nothing the hard realities of physics and chemistry? One single word triggered the digestive storm. It was not the taste, it was not the smell, it was not the touch, it was not the sight: one single word. Which leads us to a strange conclusion: my father-in-law did not vomit a 'thing'; he vomited words. What gives pleasure – and displeasure – are not things, but words, the words which dwell in them. As Zarathustra suggested, what makes things refreshing are the names and sounds which are given to them (*PN* 329). Somehow, for reasons unknown, the word 'cauliflower' was, in my father-in-law's body, the beginning of a beautiful world, whereas the word 'brain' invoked repulsive images. One single word suffices to transform a prince into a frog. No witches are needed. The prince himself can perform the black magic ...

The body has a philosophy of its own. Reality, for it, is not what we usually call by this name. It is not something given. It is rather the *result* of an alchemic operation whereby a nameless 'stuff' is mixed with words. And its world is created. This, and only this, is what is given to the body to be eaten. Guimarães Rosa showed great familiarity with the wisdom of the body when he said that 'everything is real because everything is invented'. 'Dreams is what we are made of', says Norman O. Brown (*LB* 254). My father-in-law did not vomit the 'thing'. He vomited the bad dreams, nightmares, which were invoked by the bewitching word ...

My thoughts dance and jump from this disastrous dinner to mediaeval sacramental theology. In describing what took place in the eucharist they used the word transubstantiation. Protestant theologians could not understand this concept because, for them, words have no magical power; they are only raw material for thinking. I suspect that this is due to the fact that their fathers-in-law never experienced the embarrassment of an indigestion provoked by one single word. These two situations: are they not rigorously alike? Bread and wine: the basic 'stuff' for the meal. Then a word is pronounced.

Nothing changes. Under the scrutiny of objective criteria of know-ledge, bread remains bread and wine remains wine. As mediaeval theologians said, the 'accidents' remain the same. And yet they affirmed that by the power of the word an imperceptible change took place: a new 'substance' is there, in the place of the old: the body and the blood of Christ.

But which word is this, with such a magical power? Is it not the word which announces the absence? Is not the eucharist a meal before the Absent One? 'Eat and drink in remembrance of me' (I Cor. 11.25). If it is done in 'remembrance' it is because something or someone is absent. Bread and wine are physical entities. They serve to nourish the body. Even ants and bees know that. But when certain words are pronounced, a great void is opened inside our bodies, we feel 'saudades', and our bodies are transubstantiated by the power of the absence. The villagers were resurrected because of the power of the Void: they heard words which named their longings. They understood that they are lost, without the help of that which does not exist.

What a strange world – the reality of which is mystically sur-rounded by a transparent rainbow of absences . . . Its language we no longer know. 'Have you brought the key?', it asks. But we have not. Indeed we have many keys, many words. But we don't know where we have left the key, the word . . .

Our keys open the doors of a world which is familiarly known by all and about which we talk. It is solid, securely tied around hard things, and those who know it have no difficulty in repeating its gospel:

'In the beginning it was the thing . . .'

Words come after, as consequences.

First the original, then the copies.

First the trees, the clouds, the mountains; then their inverted reflec-tions on the surface of the lake.

But we all know that reflections have no reality. They are nothing more than light playing with our eyes. They do not have power. They have meaning, only. They are the finger which points to the moon, but woe to the one who takes the finger for the moon.

But the keys we don't have lead us through the looking glass . . . One dives through the shining surface of the lake, and there the words are no longer reflections but fishes which swim in dark waters: the magical, sacred universe which is hidden inside our flesh. These words are more real than things.

Now it is the things which are the reflections of the word.

In the beginning, before anything existed, and there was nothing

to appear reflected on the surface of the waters, there was the Void.
No true word could be said because there was nothing to be reflected.

And yet, a word was heard, 'ex nihilo', filling the primordial silence.

It had to be God's word, because it had the power to bring into
existence the world which did not exist.

In the beginning, the Word.

Then, the Universe.

God's mirror. The Word taking on a visible form.

Universe.

uni-Verse.

In Hegelian terminology: the objectification of the Spirit.

It is not the Universe which is the meaning of the Word.

It is the Word which is the meaning of the Universe.

It is not the finger which points to the moon.

It is the moon which points to the finger.

The meaning of the universe is

the verse

which lies hidden, unspoken,

inside its silence.

References

LB Brown, Norman O., *Love's Body*, New York: Vintage Books, 1966
PN Kaufman, Walter, *The Portable Nietzsche*, New York: The Viking Press, 1965

Gillian Rose, *Love's Work*
London: Chatto & Windus, pp. 31–6.

Gillian Rose's short autobiography Love's Work *provides a relatively
accessible way into a profound mind. As a philosopher writing at the
end of the twentieth century, she is preoccupied by questions of politics and religion, of power and identity, anticipating many of the
issues and conflicts that seem set to dominate as the twenty-first
century begins. The cross-cultural and hybrid nature of identity
emerges from this passage, as does the way in which different religious
traditions of protest and the law come together as individuals struggle
to find meaning. Rose's fascination with words is made more intense
by her dyslexia; and she describes how formative the struggle with it
became as she learned to read. For her 'reading was never just reading:
it became the repository of my inner self-relation: the discovery,
simultaneous with the suddenly sculpted and composed words, of*

distance from and deviousness towards myself as well as others'. Her sense of identity is shaped, in part, by the journey she makes, again and again, between the Judaism of her fathers and a sense of Protestantism that provides a creative antithesis in her thinking and sense of self.

The reflexive nature of her writing, coupled with the metaphorical and psychological insights she incorporates as she explores the nature of her identity, make this a fascinating example of 'theology by heart'.

I was never an innocent child. I was forever accompanied by four wicked and energetic Particles, secret and clever companions, who never allowed me any inhuman innocence of beginning, and who kept me prodigiously busy. These imps were called 'Im', 'A', 'Di' and 'Dys': 'Im-migration', 'A-theism', 'Di-vorce', 'Dys-lexia'. Dyslexia, the last of these genies, is really the first: for, by discovering from very early on that the desert of stony words could be made to bloom, that I could channel what I could not overcome, I acquired a puckish strategy for enchanting the agents of adversity. The fourth disability could be made to germinate the other three.

In Jerusalem, Paul Mendes-Flohr's son, Itamar, is so profoundly dyslexic that, at the age of twelve, he cannot read a single word in any of the three languages which he speaks fluently: Hebrew, American-English and Arabic. Rita, his mother, is a Sephardi Jew from Curaçao, hence the 'Mendes' in the family name. His father, Paul, is an American Jew. Itamar bears five names: his parents' amalgamated surname, and three given names, one Israeli, one Arabic, one English.

Itamar's parents, secular Zionists, are pro-Palestinian and active in the peace movement. Rita, his mother, architect and artist, stands daily in the roaring midday sun, dressed in heavy, black, long garments, with other women, mostly Ashkenazim, members of the protest movement, 'The Black Palestinian Women'. They expect the insults hurled from marauding bands of right-wing youths, who also congregate in the square. Itamar's father, Paul, hosts a group of Arab intellectuals and Israeli academics who assemble weekly at the American Colony Hotel, situated between the Damascus Gate and Herod's Gate, the one location in Arab East Jerusalem where you see vehicles parked next to each other, some with Israeli and some with Arab numberplates. Paul, who combines his political activities with being Professor of German-Jewish intellectual history at the Hebrew

University, has lost the sight in one of his eyes by neglecting to procure any treatment for a detached retina.

Dyslexia in a Jewish child is fraught with significance. For childhood is the preparation for the reading of the portion of the law at thirteen, the *bar mitzvah*, when the child becomes an adult, 'a son of the law'. In Itamar's case, I suspect, as in mine, the inability to read is a blind protestantism, an unconscious rebellion, against the law, the tradition of the fathers, and against the precipitous fortress of the family. The stuttering in the face of the Written Word enacts a mimesis of the embattled and shattered truth of father and family. The confusion of names marks the child with the stigmata of the fantasised identity which he cannot assume – and so he stumbles against its central asylum, the written names of the law.

My conviction that I harboured secret, malign and crafty powers was encouraged by the adult treatment of me as a well wound-up mechanical toy that perversely refused to work. The emotional and symbolic meaning of my dyslexia was overlaid and obscured by several physical disabilities, which received a lot of attention.

Quite recently I was propelled out of an optician's chair with the impetus of primitive and long forgotten despair, when the optician remarked to me casually that I have a 'lazy' eye. On recovering my equilibrium and equanimity, I had it explained to me that the epithet 'lazy' is employed to render the nature of a squint intelligible to children. I riposted that this vicious metaphor can only be heard by a child as a harsh, personal judgement on her very being, on her good intentions and on her willingness to collaborate. Since the defect in my vision and the defect in my comprehension of words on the page were not distinguished from each other, the pronouncement 'lazy' tore down through me and made me determined, once I learnt to read, never to rest in the work of deciphering dangerous and difficult scripts.

The uncoupling of my wandering eye and my wandering mind did not finally occur until I was seven years old. I woke up in a hospital bed to find myself in the unaccustomed presence of both my father and my mother, which made me immediately aware, before I'd fully regained consciousness, that something very important and serious was happening to me. A row ensued between the two of them as to whether I should be permitted to eat or not. I cannot remember whose view prevailed, but I do remember being fed mashed banana, which I promptly vomited up. Meanwhile, the operation to correct the squint was successful, and now I could concentrate on learning to read.

Reading, however, did not interest me. With a persistent, dreary ache, my habit of sounding out words backwards, of not seeing sense in the unit of conjoint letters, gave me the dull conviction that I was a closed creature where reading was concerned. The special teacher, to whose house I was taken unwillingly every day after school, her voluminous, unified breast bolstered on the table next to the tall glass of cold milk and the plate of dry, predictable biscuits, did not seem a likely anagoge into recalcitrant mysteries which possessed only a dubious claim on my soul.

The only paradises cannot be those that are lost, but those that are unlocked as a result of coercion, reluctance, cajolery and humiliation, their thresholds crossed without calm prescience, or any preliminary perspicacity. Reading was never just reading: it became the repository of my inner self-relation: the discovery, simultaneous with the suddenly sculpted and composed words, of distance from and deviousness towards myself as well as others. My disastrous judaism of fathers and family transmogrified into a personal, protestant inwardness and independence. Yet, as with the varieties of historical Protestantism, progenitor of modernity, the independence gained from the protest against illegitimate traditional authority comes at the cost of the incessant anxiety of autonomy. Chronically beset with inner turmoil, the individual may nevertheless become roguishly adept at directing and managing the world to her own ends. Little did I realise then how often I would make the return journey from protestantism to judaism.

Frances Ward, 'Learning to Write'

in *Lifelong Learning*, London: SCM Press, pp. 133–43.

In this book designed for those who seek to reflect theologically as they continue to learn through the practice of ministry, Ward turns to the notion of the 'living human document', an expression first coined by Anton Boisen, the founder of the Clinical Pastoral Education movement. A 'living human document' can be a journal, or a creative piece of writing, or a verbatim account of a situation that enables the reflective practitioner to examine life-turned-into-text and thereby grow in understanding of self in the context of life and ministry. This passage develops the dialogical nature of this practice of knowing oneself, drawing on literary theory to understand more clearly the nature of the conversations, both internal and external, that lie at the heart of a sense of self.

Such dialogue is never innocent of power relations, nor can it be divorced from the body, which locates the interchange between self and other in an encounter that is always marked by desire and challenge. 'From the dialogue of voice, to the otherness of face, to the crafting of body': Ward shows how 'theology by heart' is a necessary theological method for anyone who recognizes the need to be aware of themselves in the varied and various contexts of life and ministry.

The Dialogical Self

The living human document, the life-turned-into-text, which is reflective of practice and reflexive of self, is embedded in dialogue, with words and thoughts going between self and others in an ongoing conversation which is both internal and external. To understand identity in this way is to draw upon dialogical theory. Dialogical theory really began with the work of Mikhail Bakhtin. Bakhtin (1895–1975) was a literary theorist who lived and worked in Russia after the Revolution. Years of intense creativity in collaboration with his two friends Medvedev and Voloshinov become increasingly dangerous after Stalin began to consolidate his power in the 1920s. Bakhtin was arrested in 1929 and spent six years in exile in Soviet Central Asia. Voloshinov died of TB in 1936; Medvedev was shot in 1938. Bakhtin has been seen as a writer who kept a sense of freedom alive through Stalin's terror. His writing on carnival, seemingly innocent to the authorities, carried a subversive sub-text that challenged totalitarian power. His writing on the ways in which texts, and particularly novelistic texts, bear various different voices (heteroglossia), and his exploration of dialogical, as opposed to monological, literary forms has opened up many fruitful lines of thought through the twentieth and twenty-first centuries in his influence on many later philosophers and literary theorists.

In one of his essays in *The Dialogic Imagination* (1996), entitled 'Epic and Novel', he writes about the epic form and its main character, the hero:

As such he is a fully finished and completed being. This has been accomplished on a lofty heroic level, but what is complete is something hopelessly ready-made; he is all there, from beginning to end he coincides with himself, he is absolutely equal to himself . . . He has already become everything he could become, and he could become only that which he has already become. He is entirely externalized in the most elementary, almost literal sense: everything in him is exposed and loudly expressed. (p. 34)

In his description of such a figure – a literary type, to be sure – you can hear, I think, Bakhtin commenting on a totalitarian mindset: the Stalinist bureaucrat dehumanized by his functionality so that no longer was there any play between internal and external, no dynamic growth or sense of development. There is no nuance of appearance or action, no subtlety of voice or layer of meaning. It is a characterization. It is an extreme description. But I use it because I think it is possible to detect traces of this heroic type, sometimes, when the word 'formation' is used, and in particular understandings of ministry that rely upon a clericalized paradigm.

By way of contrast to the static and received form of the hero of the epic, Bakhtin opens up the novel as a text in which a variety of voices is to be heard:

> The novel orchestrates all its themes, the totality of the world of objects and ideas depicted and expressed in it, by means of the social diversity of speech types and by the differing individual voices that flourish under such conditions. Authorial speech, the speeches of narrators, inserted genres, the speech of characters are merely those fundamental compositional unities with whose help heteroglossia can enter the novel; each of them permits a multiplicity of social voices and a wide variety of their links and interrelationships (always more or less dialogized). These distinctive links and interrelationships between utterances and languages, this movement of the theme through different languages and speech types, its dispersion into the rivulets and droplets of social heteroglossia, its dialogization – this is the basic distinguishing feature of the stylistics of the novel. (p. 263)

Again, you can read into this text Bakhtin's subversion of the monoculture of Stalinism. Here he celebrates the diversity of voice and the complexity of interaction between different characters, including the author, which can be found within a novel. Life itself, you might say, is to be discovered in all its multiplicity of dialogue and speech, in its diversity, its social heteroglossia.

Incomplete, unfinished, a dialogical self is constructed as one amongst many voices, in constant negotiation. Lynne Pearce says that 'the Bakhtinian subject ... is formed and re-formed through a never-ending process of sociolinguistic interaction' (1994, p. 89).

Formation, when understood in these terms as a constant forming and re-forming, loses that connotation of static completeness, that sense of arrival. Instead it is possible to see the self as in a continuous process where the encounter with many others in ongoing conversations shapes us and reshapes us, transforming and changing the way we are, who we are. So instead of taking a stance and making pronouncements, as Bakhtin would see it, in a monological way, we need to be there, in the thick of the dialogue, contributing ourselves and what we think, but always open to what others are saying and thinking, always open to be changed. There is provisionality about this dialogic sense of self, which encourages the ability to be creative with possibilities rather than reliant upon certainties.

So where does dialogue take place within ministry? Most obviously in the encounters with work colleagues, members of the congregation, others in the local community, as the minister collaborates on a project, or negotiates a shared vision for the future. As Robert visited Peter's family, as Sarah talked with Bob. But the dialogue is also an internal one. Consider the significant others with whom you converse in your mind as you walk the children to school. As you wonder what your mother or father would say to a particular course of action you are thinking about. What comment a soul friend, or mentor, or spiritual director might make. And as we fall into the hands of the living God, we dialogue in prayer, in listening to biblical texts for the voice of God; we are engaged in dialogue which transforms us. Sarah, in her subsequent email to me, indicated something of the internal dialogues she had been having, including prayer. Internally she was playing with and considering different possibilities, different ways in which she might have responded in that situation. We form practical judgements; we use practical wisdom, phronesis, which is shaped in conversation, external and internal. When I first started exploring whether ordination was the right path for me, I spoke with my parish priest at the time, and over subsequent years built up a good friendship with him. He died over ten years ago now, but I still find myself in conversation with him, imagining what he would say, taking on board and being changed, even now, by his influence. And as John V. Taylor would say, the go-between God is present in such encounters, enabling that conversation, whether external, with real people, or internal – imagined, but nonetheless a powerful dialogue – that forms and transforms our sense of self.

Dialogue: Difference and Power

Such dialogues, especially the external ones, need to be understood as always belonging to specific times and places and permeated through with different registers of difference. Our conversations – how and what we say – are dependent upon the context and the people with whom we are speaking. We talk differently to a child, to our boss, to a friend, to someone of another faith and culture, and our conversations are always pervaded by explicit or implicit relations of power. Robert, as he shared his faith with Peter's family who were reluctant to let any mention of God be made at the funeral, was nervous because he felt he had to share his faith and feared they would reject something important to him. He took the risk that he might be interpreted as imposing his faith on others. The conversation was power-laden in complex ways. Robert Stam has written:

> To speak of dialogue, without speaking of power, in a Bakhtinian perspective is to speak meaninglessly, in a void. For Bakhtin, language is thus everywhere imbricated with asymmetries of power. Patriarchal domination and economic dependency make sincere interlocution impossible. There is no 'neutral' utterance; language is everywhere shot through with intentions and accents; it is material, multiaccentual, and historical, and is densely overlaid with the traces of its historical usages. (1989, p. 8)

Stam refers here to patriarchal power and economic dependency. He argues that to be in a dynamic where one is economically dependent or subordinated in a dominant patriarchal culture mars the conditions of free speech – can even destroy them. It is not that interlocution cannot happen at all; it just will not be 'sincere' if the imbalance of power between those conversing is too great.

Stam says that no utterance is ever 'neutral' – it will always carry with it some negotiation with or from a position of dominance and subordination. As we consider what enables effective reflective practice, it is important that we attend reflexively to our own position in terms of the power relations we have with those we dialogue with.

How do you understand power to be present in the funeral visit that Robert made with Peter's family?

Consider a situation when you have felt constrained or silenced by differentials of power. How did you feel? What did you do?

Those who have used Bakhtin's ideas have argued that all dialogue is permeated by power relations, and an important aspect of reflexivity in ministry is the appreciation of one's own positionality and power in any encounter: that we are part of a conversation that is a constant negotiation with others, with the self, and with God. Relations of power permeate all dialogue. Stam says here that dialogue is material. It is not as if voices float around in the ether, but that every dialogue, every conversation takes place in a real situation, in a real context between real bodies, between embodied self and embodied other. To be engaged in dialogue with sensitivity, one needs to be aware of the complex ways in which we communicate with others.

A Dialogical, Embodied Self

The way in which self negotiates with others has become an increasingly important aspect of twentieth- and twenty-first-century thought. Emmanuel Levinas wrote in the aftermath of the Holocaust about the necessity of encounter with 'the other'. He was born in 1906 into an orthodox Jewish family in Lithuania, and as Martin Buber enquires into the 'I and Thou', Levinas examined the relationship between the self and other, but brought a different emphasis to the encounter by focusing upon the face, the most obvious material point of contact. Levinas, after the experience of Nazism and the Holocaust, argued that the other could not be understood, as Buber had done, as 'friendly'; rather the face of the other questioned the self, challenged the self with its misery. There was no necessary communication between self and other, but rather dia / logue, marked by rupture. From his experiences he could envisage a gulf of non-communication. He attended to what was silenced in any encounter, to that which is 'not said'. Instead of the subject, the knowing I who relates as an autonomous self with its others, Levinas thought of the self as first and foremost a 'me', placed in the accusative, accused by its others, responsible to its others. In the relationship with the other, the self is challenged, 'wrench[ing] from ourselves the autonomy of our consciousness and intentions, by the demand of the other and the responsibility this lays (and has always laid) upon us' (Ward, 2000, p. 101). The other is found in the face, in the encounter that can be a terrible non-encounter. Behind that (non-) encounter is otherness that is radically different, wholly other, and which cannot be captured in words. Levinas distinguished between the said, which is done with, completed, and the infinite, the unsaid, the unthinkable which leaves its trace in what is said, and perhaps here Levinas could be seen to refer to God. As Ward writes:

> The infinite (and God) enters Levinas' work because the saying which arrives with the face of the other person bears witness to an elsewhere, a transcendence which is totally other . . . Here we move beyond being . . . towards that which is otherwise than being. This is the Good beyond being . . . [and] it is from this transcendental Good that the command, the saying, the call to and of responsibility issues. (2000, p. 102)

In this call is located desire: Levinas marks human being and existence with desire. It is the sense of being divided, incomplete, that draws us on in desire: 'we are both commanded by, and attracted to, the other which draws us ever beyond – beyond ourselves, beyond the given, beyond history, beyond Being itself. We submit as servants, as suffering servants, both to the command and the attraction' (2000, p. 104). So here, in contrast to the theology of the presence of the Holy Spirit as the go-between God, going between self and other, we have a sense of God who is beyond language, beyond dialogue, the object of desire, and the subject to whom we respond as object, a subject who calls us ever beyond, encountered as the Other in the others with whom we dialogue.

Levinas enables us to see how a sense of self can be formed and transformed in dialogue with others, and in response to the Other, who draws us on into the future by the very difference and strangeness which is hinted to us in the face of the people with whom we dialogue, provoking our desire for what we are not. As Heather Walton has commented, 'the self is constituted through a mysterious meeting with what lies beyond its bounds' (2000, p. 12).

So if self is seen as always dialogical, and pulled towards the future in desire for the ultimate Other, then 'formation' is never complete. We ourselves need to view ourselves as partial, incomplete, open to encounter, open to transformation by the difference of the other, with whom dialogue may, at times, be extremely difficult, marked by rupture.

Think about a time when you have been in dialogue with another and have been aware that the cultural assumptions that lie beneath your conversation are very different, even incommensurable. Describe or draw how it felt.

How might Taylor's writing of the go-between God taken you forward?

If Levinas wrote about how the face relays the encounter with others, then, by extension, bodies too can be seen to convey meaning. How they are used, dressed, presented are important elements in communication. Many of these same issues of dialogue and communication between self and other are inscribed in ethnography, the discipline of researching and writing about culture. Ethnographers seek cultures to study that are not necessarily to be found on far distant shores: many today will look at a local congregation, or a school and its subcultures, as 'fields' of research. The local, close to home, the familiar can provide as much interest as the very strange. Amanda Coffey carried out an ethnographic study on a firm of accountants, and noted how dress functioned to communicate certain values:

> The physical appearance of accountants is of course important. Certainly to an outsider the accountant is perceived as fulfilling certain expectations about dress and demeanour. In Western Ridge, the firm in which I conducted fieldwork, new recruits (in this case graduate accountants) were given implicit and explicit guidance on their personal appearance. This included not only dress but also advice on skin care, makeup, hair-style, body hair, and the use of props such as jewellery and briefcases. For these junior accountants the body was implicated in their daily work lives. By association it was also implicated in my personal and practical experiences of fieldwork. (1999, p. 66)

As she researched, Coffey found that she herself had changed her own appearance, unconsciously, in order to engage in the 'field' as effectively as possible:

> During my fieldwork I was not particularly self-conscious or reflexive about the production of my own body: certainly not beyond the realities of needing to look the part in order to achieve access and an acceptable fieldwork persona. In retrospect I have come to realize that I was engaged in negotiating and producing a fieldwork body. In doing so I was responding to norms and rules of the organization. I crafted my body as part of the crafting of the field, and this was not something that was confined to the actual fieldwork setting. The ways I 'chose' to dress, wear make-up, style my hair, even shave my legs were part of a bodily performance

which I subconsciously thought necessary for the successful accomplishment of the fieldwork. My body is part of the way in which I experienced fieldwork and an important aspect of my fieldwork memories. I will always remember the ways in which the graduate accountants sought to craft the image of accountant. As too I will remember the way in which my feet ached after a working day in high-heeled shoes! (p. 66)

A Dialogical, Embodied, Public Self

From the dialogue of voice, to the otherness of face, to the crafting of body. The (trans)formation of self calls for a constant negotiation with the otherness of the field or context, which includes the personal and emotional. Much of what Coffey writes for ethnographers applies equally well to ministers, who use, perhaps unknowingly, ethnographic methods of participant observation as they engage in local contexts and seek to understand the culture of a congregation or local organizations. As Coffey 'crafts' her body, so many ministers think carefully about what to wear for a funeral visit, or for a primary school assembly, or to lead both in one morning. What signals are given? Not always, today, a message of safety and reliability, but now often inviting the label of authoritarian, or patriarchal, or too traditional to understand the contemporary world, sometimes even incurring taunts and despising comment, or distrust. In different contexts of ministry, when working on a project, or with secular organizations, a self-reflexive minister will recognize the importance of developing such social and communication skills, attending to what is said and not said and how the body speaks.

How much consideration do you give to the way you present your body? What do you communicate, do you think, to others by the way you habitually dress?

To understand oneself as an embodied dialogical self will prompt consideration of the personal vulnerability, even risk, which can result from public ministry. The situations that call for caution will be different for men and for women, for able-bodied or ministers with physical difficulties. If you are black, or belong to an ethnic minority, then your awareness of threat in different situations will probably be enhanced. The negotiation of relations of power becomes an important aspect of the experience of ministry if you enter any given context knowing from past encounters that you may be on the receiving end of the prejudices of others. Levinas' ethical understanding of the self as subject to the other takes on a different depth of meaning when the self is someone who is used to working as a non-dominant person. Reflexivity and self-awareness will tend to be understood differently depending on the experience of the minister, and what the minister and any other person he or she encounters has internalized from the past in terms of the differentials of power around, for instance, age and generational issues, class, gender, ethnicity, faith, sexuality. A minister who is able to be reflexive will be aware to a greater or lesser extent of dominating in any situation.

Bibliography

Bakhtin, Mikhail M. (1996), *The Dialogic Imagination: Four Essays*, ed. Michael Holquist, trans. Caryl Emerson and Michael Holquist, Austin: University of Texas Press.

Coffey, Amanda (1999), *The Ethnographic Self: Fieldwork and the Representation of Identity*, London: Sage.

Pearce, Lynne (1994), *Reading Dialogics*, London: Edward Arnold.

Stam, Robert (1989), *Subversive Pleasures: Bakhtin, Cultural Criticism, and Film*, Baltimore and London: Johns Hopkins University Press.

Ward, Graham ([1996], 2000), *Theology and Contemporary Critical Theory*, London: Macmillan.

Ben Edson, 'What's in a Name?'

A blog entry available at http://benedson.blogs.com/benedson/2006/08/whatsinaname.html

'Blog' is an abbreviation of 'weblog', which is a personal journal on the web, and is an increasingly popular medium and activity. It lends itself to doing theology by heart as it enables personal reflection that can then be commented upon by others from around the world, carrying forward a conversation, or a number of conversations, over the Internet. Blogging is an obvious development of this way of doing theology: life without the Internet is inconceivable now. As with personal letters and journals, the Internet is being used as a medium that lends itself to self-expression and reflection in an interesting negotiation of the privacy of one's interior life and a public, even global, forum. People now blog as a way of turning-life-into-text. The blog becomes a living human document that can be read and analysed as others engage in conversation with what you have written.

It is dialogical in style, accessible, self-regulating and stylistically diverse.

Ben Edson is one of the leaders of Sanctus1, a fresh expression of church in the centre of Manchester, UK. Both he and the church have blogs, which can be found at http://benedson.blogs.com and http:// www.sanctus1.co.uk/blog/ respectively. In this 'post' from August 2006, Edson explores his sense of identity and the way in which he presents himself and what he does, prompting nine comments, which can be followed by visiting the blog itself.

When I was 16 my entire immediate family changed our surname . . . We went from being called 'Pratt' to 'Edson' – I can't believe I'm telling you this! I also decided to use my middle name rather than my first name so I went from John Pratt to Ben Edson; life has improved from then! The reason that we changed our name was quite simply about first impressions, it gave a bad first impressions and for a teenager this was not what was wanted. So when we moved to Devon the whole family changed to Edson.

On the blah tour I was chatting with Jonny and Karen about how we introduce ourselves to people outside the Church without alienating the person that we're talking to? (ie calling yourself a missionary can alienate a lot of people). Jonny said that at MBS London he called himself a 'spiritual creative', Karen refers to herself as an 'abbess'. My job title is city centre missioner, my title in the church is 'Captain' – both are hideous – but it would have been worse if we'd not changed our surname . . . Captain Pratt!

I think that often the titles that the Anglican church uses have overtones of power associated with them – Venerable, Reverend, Right Reverend etc. This is problematic as I think that ministry within the church should primarily be about serving the community that you are part of and none of these titles suggest a serving ministry.

So what should I call myself? A spiritual creative is ambiguous and this is one of the beauties of it! I usually say something like I'm a minister in Anglican church – but it's a bit non-descript and tends to close down a conversation rather than open one up . . . any thoughts?

Technorati Tags: *mission, spirituality*
in Misc. Religion. Spirituality Permalink Comments(9)

'Theology by Heart': References and Further Reading

Baker, Jonny, weblog: http://jonnybaker.blogs.com/jonnybaker
Bolton, G. (2001), *Reflective Practice: Writing and Professional Development*, London: Paul Chapman Publishing Ltd.
Brewin, Kester, weblog: http://thecomplexchrist.typepad.com
Jonze, Tim (2006), 'Death on MySpace', *Guardian*, 15 May 2006, available at: http://arts.guardian.co.uk/features/story/0,,1775112,00.html (accessed 4 July 2006).
Milner, M. ([1934] 1986), *A Life of one's Own*. London: Virago Press.
Radice, B. (trans.) (1974), *The Letters of Abelard and Heloise (Penguin Classics)*, Harmondsworth: Penguin.
Weil, Simone, (1950), *Waiting on God*, Glasgow: William Collins & Co.

2

'Speaking in Parables': Constructive Narrative Theology

Introduction

Constructive narrative theology is built upon two fundamental convictions. The first is that human beings create their world through the process of telling stories. We are born into story-formed societies and we find our own sense of self as we appropriate the tools of narrative construction and begin to tell the stories of our lives. These life stories are vivid tapestries of characters, events and consequences that reveal who we are. Because they are stories they are never closed or complete; there is always the potential for twists, turnings and surprises.

The second conviction is that Christians worship a 'storytelling' God. Revelation comes to us through images, symbols, narrative parables and proverbs. These enable us to encounter God at work in creatively shaping the story of creation, but they prevent us from ever believing that we can fully grasp or define who God is or what God is doing. The truth of God is far too rich, complex and subversive to be laid hold of in this way.

Within constructive narrative theology the work of theological reflection is understood as the task of bringing our own narratives into a relationship with the narrative of God. However, this is not seen as accommodating our human stories to a divine master narrative (as might be the case in some forms of canonical narrative theology) but rather the creative interweaving of many strands of human experience and sacred tradition into exciting new configurations. It is within these living narrative forms that ancient religious convictions maintain their vitality and authenticity. If they are not able to be reborn in the life narratives of believers then they have relinquished the power to transform lives and can no longer retain their sacred status.

Constructive narrative theology in the contemporary context has gained much from the insights of contemporary biblical studies into the parabolic nature of Jesus' preaching. Parables are no longer seen as straightforward aids to communication that enabled uneducated believers to understand what Jesus was saying. Rather they are seen as disturbing and provocative stories that encourage their hearers to leave the safety of their conventional understanding and encounter insights that are new, shocking and transformative. Parables possess the same qualities as metaphors in that they bring together diverse elements into new configurations that in turn enable reality to be perceived in new ways. The work of contemporary philosophers, like Paul Ricoeur, on the transformative power of metaphoric utterance has also contributed to the development of constructive narrative theology in recent times. Their work allows us to discern how stories not only create the world but also have the power to change it.

The Christian faith has always been communicated through narrative means but what the contemporary work of constructive narrative theologians points to is how much more stories accomplish than carrying a message. They can become sites of sacred meeting, a space for imagining, and those groups most marginalized within Christianity have found that stories have enabled them to explore themes that traditional theology has not found worthy of significant attention. Within practical theology narrative has recently become privileged as *the* most significant vehicle for pastoral care and important links are now being made between narrative, ritual practice and healing. In situations of extreme pain or suffering one of the most valuable aspects of constructive narrative theology is that it does not need to deny or reconcile the tragic elements of human life before approaching God. It does not require that wholeness, coherence and closure be achieved but rather that we 'encounter' those things that are strange, unaccountable and sacred. This was what the parabolic teaching of Jesus achieved and what constructive narrative theology struggles to perform today.

Stephen Crites, 'The Narrative Quality of Experience'

Journal of American Academy of Religion, Vol. 39, No. 3, 1971, pp. 291–311.

In this evocative essay by Stephen Crites we see articulated the fundamental insight of constructive narrative theology, which is that human beings are story-telling creatures and that we find our identity and place in the world through narrative means. In making this argument Crites distinguishes three forms of narrative. First there are sacred stories that lie 'deep in the consciousness of a people'; these he describes as dwelling places, they provide shelter and security and orient the life of a people through time. Second, there are mundane stories, which consist both of the literary resources of culture and the everyday narrative communications that facilitate daily living. Between sacred and mundane stories there is distinction without separation and mediating between them is a third type – that of experience as consciously grasped always in narrative form.

As well as generating identity, narrative sustains, nourishes and protects it. Narrative, as a means of structuring experience, preserves us from both immediacy and abstraction – present in our times in the political threat of totalitarianism (in either fascistic or global-capitalist forms). In times of danger, or rapid cultural change, the permeability of narrative forms enables people to perceive new configurations between their experience and the sacred stories of their culture. These together may generate new symbols, like comets blazing into our atmosphere, which enable human beings to reorientate their cultural identity to meet the challenge of new times.

> *La narration est toute l'épopée; elle est toute l'historie; elle enveloppe le drame et le sous-entend.*
>
> Balzac

The *forms* of cultural expression are not historical accidents. They are not products of culture, much less products of individual choice and contrivance, although actual cultural expressions are to some extent both. The *way* people speak, dance, build, dream, embellish, is to be sure always culturally particular: it bears the imprint of a time and a place. A people speaks a particular language, not the same as that spoken in another land nor quite the same as that spoken by their fathers, and each person adapts it with some originality to his own use. But the fact that people speak some language is no historical accident. It is a necessary mark of being human, i.e., being capable of having a history. That is also true of other persistent forms of cultural expression. They are the *conditions* of historical existence; their expressions are moulded in the historical process itself into definite *products* of particular cultures.

I do not know how to go about proving any such grandiose thesis. To me, I confess, it seems self-evident, in the sense that once the appropriate distinctions are made it becomes obvious. Be that as it may, I propose here to illustrate the point in relation to storytelling, which I take to be one of the most important cultural expressions. I want to argue that the formal quality of experience through time is inherently narrative.[1]

I introduce this thesis by briefly posing another, to which it is intimately related: the style of action through time is inherently musical. The relation of the two theses can be stated in an equation of positively luminous simplicity: narrative quality is to experience as musical style is to action. And action and experience interpenetrate. Let us see about that.

Style

We speak of the things we do as having a particular style. There is a style in the way a person writes and speaks. An artist paints in a certain style. A farmer exhibits a style in the way he plows his field; a dealer, in the way he keeps his store and arranges his wares. A man's style is formed by the way he is brought up, by the people among whom he has lived, by his training: by his experience. Westerners have, collectively, a different style from Easterners and Californians. Yet in its details a man's style is idiomorphic – as the ringmaster says, inimitable. What is style?

Suppose I walk with unbroken stride across a room. It is a single complex movement. If I were a dancer I could, perhaps, cross the room at a single leap. But even for a dancer the action involves not only a steady change of position in the space of the room, but a divisible duration. There are variations on a joke about a runner so fast that he can turn and see himself still at the starting line. The point of the joke is that however single and swift a movement is there is always before and after.[2] An action is altogether temporal. Yet it has a unity of form through time, a form revealed only in the action as a whole. That temporal form is what we mean by style. My gait has a particular style – an ungainly one, as it happens, of a sort developed in walking through cornfields. But you could not detect it in a still photograph, because the style is in the movement. The same is true of gestures, mannerisms, the putting together of words, the modulations of the voice in speaking the words. All of these are actions, conscious movements in time, and it is appropriate in each case to speak of their having a particular style.

Why conscious movements? Actions are the movements of bodies, but unlike other movements they are performed by bodies that are both the subjects of experience and purposive agents. It does not occur to us, in common speech, to attribute style to unconscious bodies.[3] Movements must be conscious to have a style. Yet that does not imply that one necessarily attends consciously to these movements or to their style. One may do so, and may even attempt to change or to perfect his style. But he has a style, regardless of whether he ever concerns himself with it. Typically, the style is formed quite unconsciously by an agent intent on the various projects to which he directs his action. I cross the room to look out the window or talk to a friend, not in order to perfect my style of walking. The formation of style is seldom the conscious intent or point of an action, except when someone is deliberately training himself, say, as an artist or an athlete. But it is in any case the inner concomitant of an action, whatever its aim: whatever the product of the action, its style is a by-product, or, as we may say in anticipating our comments on its musicality, it is its accompaniment.

It is no coincidence that musical performance exhibits the formal properties of style generally. The rhythms and melodic lines of music are inherently temporal. We do not hear them all at once, but in a succession of pulses and pitched vibrations; yet we experience them as a unity, a unity through time. The reality of a musical phrase, being inherently temporal, implies the evanescence of all its elements. So it is with style. Its elements, too, are evanescent, yet the style of an action exists in the rhythms and the varying pattern of intensities found in it as a whole. To say that my gait in crossing the room has a style is to say that it expresses certain antic rhythms, that it is a crude kind of dance. Similarly, there is something in the cadences and modulations of a voice in speech that is struggling to become a song. Even this essay, turbid as it is, does, after all, have a style, and if you would have to say that its style is flat compared to your favorite books of poems, I think that in the end you would be indulging in a kind of musical criticism of the two productions.

Style is, of course, musical only in a rudimentary sense. It is not yet music, is so to speak below the threshold of music. Yet there is a definite relation between music and style, and not merely a strained analogy. If style is the form of conscious movement, music is that form purified: to the extent that it becomes conscious art it is purged of any inherent relation to a moving body, except as its mere 'instrument'. The music itself is pure action, not the movement of any thing but simply movement itself: invisible, light as air, freed from the weight of a body and the confinements of space. It exists in time alone, and is, therefore, experienced in the only way we could experience an altogether temporal reality: as something heard, as sound. It must, to be sure, be produced by a body, by someone singing or someone beating, strumming, blowing an instrument. So it, too, will have a style. Yet in itself, as it sounds forth, it is the aesthetic idealization of style, it is, so to speak, the style of style. In music, style is no longer ancillary to an action with some other aim, but is itself the sole aim of the action.

But style generally, the form of all action, is the source of music, its basis in ordinary life. Because it has its source in an ineluctable feature of human existence, music is one of the universal cultural forms of which we spoke at the outset. It is not an arbitrary contrivance, but is a purified form of the incipient musicality of style itself. People take such satisfaction in music because it answers to a powerful if seldom noticed aspect of everything they do, of every gesture, every footstep, every utterance; answers to it and gives it a purified expression. Courtship, worship, even violent conflict, call forth musical expressions in order to give these activities a certain ideality, a specific ideality rooted in the activities themselves. That is why the music of a culture or subculture has such a vital connection, so revealing yet so hard to define, with its whole style of life. The music of a people, or even a cohesive group, is peculiarly its own. It is the particular musical style that permits a group's life style, its incipient musicality, to express itself in full dance and song. The connection is of course reciprocal: The musical style in turn moulds the life style. But it cannot be an altogether alien mold. There is a beautiful paradox in the peculiar intensity with which a person responds to music which is 'his own': even if he has not heard it before it is familiar, as though something is sounding in it that he has always felt in his bones; and yet it is really new. It is his own style, revealed to him at an otherwise unimaginable level of clarity and intensity.

Now I want to suggest that stories have a similar resonance for us. But the comments on the musical style of action are not merely for the sake of establishing an analogy with the narrative quality of experience. Narrative, after all, is the other cultural form capable of expressing coherence through time, though its temporality is not so pure as that of music. Particularly important for our purposes, furthermore, are the kinds of stories that have strong musical overtones, for which verse would be the most appropriate form. So let our comments on style sound quietly and perhaps even musically in the background of what follows.

Mundane Stories and Sacred Stories

There are powerful grounds for thinking that narrative form is arti-
fice; that it is simply one of the ways we organize a life of experience
that is in itself inchoate. We are being reminded nowadays that stories
are fictions after all.[4] Of course there have been many forms of narrative, epic, drama, history, the novel, and so on, and our knowledge
of the origins and development of such genres has given us a keen
impression of their cultural and historical relativity. Furthermore,
among some of the most important modern writers there has occurred
a determined reaction against all standard narrative forms, partly on
the grounds that such forms represent a subtle falsification of the
immediacies of experience, of the modern experience in particular.
Even writers who retain recognizably narrative forms have experi-
mented with them freely. The great storytellers of our time as well
as those who refuse to tell stories have made us aware of how much
art is involved in all story telling. It no longer appears natural and
innocent in our eyes.

The study of traditional folk cultures has also made us aware that
there is more to narrative form than meets the eye (or the ear), and
at least it raises the question whether that may also be true even for
a culture as fragmented, sophisticated, and anti-traditional as ours.
For within the traditional cultures there have been some stories that
were told, especially on festal occasions, that had special resonance.
Not only told but ritually re-enacted, these stories seem to be allusive
expressions of stories that cannot be fully and directly told, because
they live, so to speak, in the arms and legs and bellies of the celebrants.
These stories lie too deep in the consciousness of a people to be
directly told: they form consciousness rather than being among the
objects of which it is directly aware. As such they are intimately
related to what we have called 'style', and so it is not surprising that
these stories can hardly be expressed at all without an integral fusion
of music with narrative. Every serious attempt to express them creates
poetry. The expressions admit of great variation in detail, but no
variation fully grasps the story within these diverse stories.

We sometimes apply our ambiguous term *myth* to this 'story within
the story'. But it is not identical with the 'myths' or legends we are
able to read in ancient books, although these give us valuable access
to those stories which have so powerfully formed a civilization's sense
of itself and its world. We might also call these stories 'religious', except
that this designation implies modern distinctions between religious
forms and secular, artistic, political forms, and these distinctions are

misleading as applied to traditional cultures. Certainly these mytho-
poeic stories function quite differently in traditional cultures from the
way conscious art does in what we are pleased to call higher cultures.
They are anonymous and communal. None of our individualized
conceptions of authorship are appropriate to them, and while rich
powers of imagination may be expressed in them they are certainly
not perceived as conscious fictions. Such stories, and the symbolic
worlds they project, are not like monuments that men behold, but
like dwelling-places. People live in them. Yet even though they are
not directly told, even though a culture seems rather to be the telling
than the teller of these stories, their form seems to be narrative.
They are moving forms, at once musical and narrative, which inform
people's sense of the story of which their own lives are a part, of the
moving course of their own action and experience.

I propose, with some misgivings, to call these fundamental narrative
forms sacred stories, not so much because gods are commonly celebrated in them, but because men's sense of self and world is created
through them. For that matter, only the musical stories that form
men's living image of themselves and their world have been found fit
to celebrate the powers on which their existence depends. For these
are stories that orient the life of people through time, their life-time,
their individual and corporate experience and their sense of style, to
the great powers that establish the reality of their world. So I call
them sacred stories, which in their secondary, written expressions
may carry the authority of scripture for the people who understand
their own stories in relation to them.

The stories that are told, all stories directly seen or heard, I propose
to call mundane stories. I am uneasy about that term also, although
it is not meant to be in the least depreciatory. It simply implies a
theory about the objectified images that fully articulated stories must
employ, i.e., about words, scenes, roles, sequences of events within a
plot, and other narrative devices: that such images to be capable of
being plausible objects of consciousness, must be placed within that
world, that phenomenological *mundus*, which defines the objective
horizon of a particular form of consciousness. In order to be told, a
story must be set within a world. It may not be an everyday world,
i.e., it may be an imaginatively augmented world. But even the most
fanciful stories have their proprieties. We speak of a universe of discourse, and this too has its limiting firmament above and below,
beyond which nothing can be conceived to happen. Historically there
have been a variety of such worlds, correlative to the historical forms
of consciousness. The stories of an age or a culture take place within

its world. Only in that sense are they necessarily mundane. Here, in some world of consciousness, we find stories composed as works of art as well as the much more modest narrative communications that pass between people in explaining where they have been, why things are as they are, and so on. Set within a world of consciousness, the mundane stories are also among the most important means by which people articulate and clarify their sense of that world. In order to initiate their children in 'the ways of the world', parents tell them stories – although in recent times, particularly, the problem has arisen that the children find themselves having to make their way in quite a different world, for which they have to devise quite different kinds of stories than those their parents taught them.

Sacred stories, too, are subject to change, but not by conscious reflection. People do not sit down on a cool afternoon and think themselves up a sacred story. They awaken to a sacred story, and their most significant mundane stories are told in the effort, never fully successful, to articulate it. For the sacred story does not transpire within a conscious world. It forms the very consciousness that projects a total world horizon, and therefore informs the intentions by which actions are projected into that world. The style of these actions dances to its music. One may attempt to name a sacred story, as we shall try to do in our conclusion. But such naming misleads as much as it illuminates, since its meaning is contained – and concealed – in the unutterable cadences and revelations of the story itself. Yet every sacred story is creation story: not merely that one may name creation of world and self as its 'theme' but also that the story itself creates a world of consciousness and the self that is oriented to it.

Between sacred and mundane stories there is distinction without separation. From the sublime to the ridiculous, all a people's mundane stories are implicit in its sacred story, and every mundane story takes soundings in the sacred story. But some mundane stories sound out greater depths than others. Even the myths and epics, even the scriptures, are mundane stories. But in these, as well as in some works of literary art, and perhaps even in some merry little tales that seem quite content to play on the surface, the sacred stories resonate. People are able to feel this resonance, because the unutterable stories are those they know best of all.

It is possible for such resonances to sound in poetic productions that seem to defy all traditional forms of story telling. For the surface of conventional narrative forms may have become so smooth and hard that it is necessary to break it in order to let a sacred story sound at all. Such a necessity may signalize that the sacred story is altogether alive, transforming itself in the depths. Break the story to tell a truer story! But there are also darker possibilities in this situation, as we shall see.

The Inner Form of Experience: 1. The Chronicle of Memory

Between sacred story and the mundane stories there is a mediating form: the form of the experiencing consciousness itself. For consciousness is moulded by the sacred story to which it awakens, and in turn it finds expression in the mundane stories that articulate its sense of reality. But consciousness itself is not a blank. Consciousness has a form of its own, without which no coherent experience at all would be possible.[5] Aside from that formidable inconvenience, it is difficult to see how a consciousness, itself entirely formless, could be the fulcrum that I have suggested it is between sacred and mundane stories. I want further to propose that the form of active consciousness, i.e., the form of its experiencing, is in at least some rudimentary sense narrative. That is why consciousness is able to mediate between the sacred and mundane stories through which it orients itself in a world.[6] A square peg would not fit into a round hole. The stories give qualitative substance to the form of experience because it is itself an incipient story.

That is the central thesis of this essay. Of all the unlikely things that have been said thus far, it perhaps seems the least plausible. In attempting to explain and support it I want to do the usual thing in such straits, and appeal for the help of a favorite teacher. The teacher is Augustine of Hippo. Not that he would necessarily subscribe to my thesis. But being a good teacher, he has helped me find my way to my own notions, and even when I have pursued my own follies he has only given me help when I knew I needed it.

The help in this case is offered in his brooding reflections on memory and time in the tenth and eleventh books of the *Confessions*. Whether or not he succeeded in establishing the subjectivity of time in that famous discussion, whether indeed that is what he was trying to do, I want to invert the problem and suggest that he did succeed in establishing the temporality of the subject. Consciousness grasps its objects in an inherently temporal way, and that temporality is retained in the unity of its experience as a whole.

Augustine ponders the paradox that the future, which does not yet exist, should pass into the past which no longer exists, through a present that is difficult to *conceptualize* as more than a vanishing quasi-mathematical point. The paradox is resolved when past, present, and future are considered to be not necessarily independent metaphysical modalities, but unavoidable modalities of experience in the mind or experiencing consciousness (*anima*). For consciousness 'anticipates and attends and remembers, so that what it anticipates passes through what it attends into what it remembers' (XI:xxviii).[7] We will consider in the next section the highly developed temporality implicit in this threefold function of consciousness. But already in memory alone there is the simpler temporality of sequence, of before and after.

Without memory, in fact, experience would have no coherence at all. Consciousness would be locked in a bare, momentary present, i.e., in a disconnected succession of perceptions which it would have no power to relate to one another. It might be argued that that would already imply a temporality of the most elemental sort. It is already significant that experience has, in its present, this sheer momentary quality. But it is memory that bestows the sense of temporal succession as well as the power to abstract coherent unities from this succession of momentary percepts.

In Book X Augustine singles out this capacity of memory for analysis, and also for a kind of awe – Augustine is a thinker for whom awe and close analysis are intensified together:

> Great is this power of memory, excessively great, my God, a vast and infinite interior space: who has plumbed it to the depths? Yet this is a power of my mind and pertains to my nature, so that I myself do not grasp all that I am. (X:viii)

Yet, Augustine muses, people take this prodigy within themselves for granted. Ignoring this interior space, they are amazed by the great dimensions of mountains, oceans, rivers, the orbits of the stars. But greater than the wonder of these external, natural wonders is the simple fact that he himself can speak of these things even though he does not at the moment see them. That is possible because he sees 'inwardly in my memory' these things he had once seen outwardly with his eyes – yet it is not the very things themselves that appear in this inner vision: For

> still I did not absorb these things [into myself] in seeing them . . . not are they themselves attached to me, but their images only, and I know by what sense of the body each was impressed upon me. (X.viii)

Detached from things and lodged in memory, along with inner impressions of feeling and mood, these images are susceptible to the uses of thought and the play of imagination. Called up by the activities of the mind, they can be dismantled and reassembled or combined in original ways. When we do not attend to them they are 'submerged and they slide down, as it were, into the remote interior spaces' of memory. But from this 'dispersion' they can always be 'collected' again by our thought, i.e., literally, by our cogitations. Augustine likes to play on the etymological connection between *cogo* – collect – and *cogito*. (X:xi)

So there is an important distinction between memory and recollection that goes back at least to Augustine. All the sophisticated activities of consciousness literally re-collect the images lodged in memory into new configurations, reordering past experience. But that would be impossible were it not for the much more naïve functioning of memory itself, preserving the images drawn from experience. But I venture to suggest that memory does not contain its images quite so 'scatteredly and confusedly' as Augustine suggests in the passage cited above. The memory also has its order, not the recollected order formed by thought and imagination, but a simple order of succession. This succession is the order in which the images of actual experience through time have been impressed upon the memory. It constitutes a kind of lasting chronicle, fixed in my memory, of the temporal course of my experience. This chronicle does not need to be recollected strictly, but merely to be recalled: I need only call up again the succession of images which stand waiting in memory in the order in which I experienced them. Of course the recall is not total, the chronicle is not without lacunae. In fact, it is for great stretches quite fragmentary. But what we do succeed in calling up we find differentiated into fairly clear sequence. We are aware of what comes before and what comes after. When we are uncertain, or feel that a crucial scene is missing, we have the sense of 'consulting' our memory. The recall is not infallible, but we have the sense that this 'consultation' is possible, that the chronicle is 'there', in memory, to be consulted, that if we concentrate intensely on our remembering we will be able to recall a sequence of events accurately. I consult my memory in this way, for example, when I mentally retrace my steps in the effort to recall where I may have lost something.

Yet that odd consultation is not strictly an act of recollection. We must consult our memory in order to recollect its images, to reorganize them for the more sophisticated purposes of the mind. But remembering is not yet knowing. Its chronicle is too elemental, too fixed, to be illuminating. Experience is illuminated only by the more subtle processes of recollection. At least in this sense, all knowledge is recollection! So is all art, including the art of storytelling. It is an act. It has style. But mere remembering as such has no style, if we could isolate it from the process of recollection that in practice generally accompanies it.

Yet storytelling is not an arbitrary imposition upon remembered experience, altogether alien to its own much simpler form. Images do not exist in memory as atomic units, like photographs in an album, but as transient episodes in an image-stream, cinematic, which I must suspend and from which I must abstract in order to isolate a particular image. The most direct and obvious way of recollecting it is by telling a story, though the story is never simply the tedious and unilluminating recital of the chronicle of memory itself. And, of course, I can manipulate the image-stream in other ways. I can abstract general features and formal elements of it for purposes of theory, or suspend it in order to draw a picture, or splice episodes from it in a way that gives them new significance. I can contemplate a whole segment of the image-stream in a single glance of inner vision, then fragment it so that its elements are left twinkling in isolation like stars – yet even then memory is not shattered. Indeed, I can do such things because the original chronicle, the image stream, is always at hand, needing only to be recalled. I can even measure out its segments into long times and short times, recalling some episodes as having occurred a long time ago, others more recently (a phenomenon that Augustine ponders with great care in XI:xv–xxviii).[8]

I recall, for example, a sequence from my own memory. In telling it, of course, recollection already intervenes, but I recollect in a way as faithful as possible to the memory itself. I measure out 'a long time' and recall an episode from my childhood. I have not thought about it for many years, and yet I find its chronicle in good condition, extremely detailed and in clear sequence. In an impetuous fit of bravado I threw a rock through a garage window. I recall the exact spot on the ground from which I picked up the rock, I recall the wind-up, the pitch, the rock in mid-air, the explosive sound of the impact, the shining spray of glass, the tinkling hail of shards falling on the cement below, the rough, stony texture of the cement. I recall also my inner glee at that moment, and my triumph when a playmate, uncertain at first how to react, looked to me for his cue and then broke into a grin. Now I could cut and splice a bit, passing over hours not so clearly recalled anyway, except that my mood underwent drastic change. Then I recall that moment in the evening when I heard my father's returning footsteps on the porch and my guilty terror reached a visceral maximum the very memory of which wrenches a fat adult belly – for remembering is not simply a process in the head! The details of the scene that ensued are likewise very vivid in my memory.

Now it would be quite possible for me to tell this story very differently. My perspective on it has been changed, partly by the death of my father and the fact that I am now myself the father of children, partly, too, by my reading in the *Confessions* a story about a wanton theft of pears and by some reading in Freud on the rivalry of fathers and sons, and so forth. So I have many insights into this chronicle that I could not have had at the time its events occurred. Yet the sophisticated new story I might tell about it would be superimposed on the image-stream of the original chronicle. It could not replace the original without obliterating the very materials to be recollected in the new story. Embedded in every sophisticated retelling of such a story is this primitive chronicle preserved in memory. Even conscious fictions presuppose its successive form, even when they artfully reorder it.

The Inner Form of Experience: 2. A Dramatic Tension

In the chronicle of memory there is the simple temporality of succession, of duration, of before and after, but not yet the decisive distinction between past, present, and future, that provides the tension of experience and therefore demands the tenses of language. Memory, containing the past, is only one modality of experience, that never exists in isolation from those that are oriented to the present and the future. To understand the relation of the three we may again refer to Augustine.

He points out that past, present, and future cannot be three distinct realities or spheres of being that somehow coexist. Only the present exists.

> But perhaps it might properly be said: there are three times, a present of things past, a present of things present, a present of things future (XI:xx)

Only the present exists, but it exists only in these tensed modalities. They are inseparably joined in the present itself. Only from the standpoint of present experience could one speak of past and future. The three modalities are correlative to one another, in every moment of experience.

For these are in the mind as a certain triadic form, and elsewhere I do not see them: the present of things past is memory, the present of things present is direct attention, the present of things future is anticipation. (XI:xx)

I want to suggest that the inner form of any possible experience is determined by the union of these three distinct modalities in every moment of experience. I want further to suggest that the tensed unity of these modalities requires narrative forms both for its expression (mundane stories) and for its own sense of the meaning of its internal coherence (sacred stories). For this tensed unity has already an incipient narrative form.

The chronicle of memory, with its simple successiveness, its before and after, is in actual experience always already taken up into the more sophisticated temporality of tense. If we would attempt to isolate anticipation as we did memory we would again discover a very elemental narrative form. We might call it the scenario of anticipation.[9] I have in mind our guesses and predictions about what may happen, hunches generally formulated in the attempt to lay some plans about our own projected courses of action. Projected action often dominates this modality of experience, though one may simply worry about the future or indulge in euphoric dreams about it. But whether anticipation takes the passive form of dreams, worries, and wishes, or is instrumental in laying plans or making resolutions for projected actions, it seems intuitively clear that we anticipate by framing little stories about how things may fall out. As the term *scenario* implies, these anticipatory stories are very thin and vague as compared with the dense, sharp detail of the chronicle of memory. It is also clear that the course of events generally turns out quite differently from what we had anticipated. But the experience of thwarted expectations, or the comic situation when parties to an encounter come to it with very different scenarios in mind – e.g., she prepared for political discussion, he for romantic rendezvous – simply serve to show that we do orient ourselves to the future by means of such scenarios. Though they are generally vague they are not altogether formless. However freely our action may improvise upon the scenario, it is never simply random.

Now it is not as though the scenario of anticipation were set alongside the chronicle of memory, as two quite separate stories. Our sense of personal identity depends upon the continuity of experience through time, a continuity bridging even the cleft between remembered past and projected future. Even when it is largely implicit, not vividly self-conscious, our sense of ourselves is at every moment to some extent integrated into a single story. That on the one hand.

On the other hand, the distinction between memory and anticipation is absolute. The present is not merely an indifferent point moving along a single unbroken and undifferentiated line, nor is the temporality of experience such a line. Nor do past and future simply 'meet' in the present. Memory and anticipation, the present of things past and the present of things future, are tensed modalities of the present itself. They are the tension of every moment of experience, both united in that present and qualitatively differentiated by it. For precisely in this momentary present which embraces my whole experience, the past remembered is fixed, a chronicle that I can radically reinterpret but cannot reverse or displace: what is done cannot be undone! And within this same present the future is, on the contrary, still fluid, awaiting determination, subject to alternative scenarios.[10] Precisely as modalities of the present of experience, the past remembered is determinate, the future anticipated is indeterminate, and the distinction between them is intuitively clear and absolute.

But how can the present contain such tension, on the one hand unifying, on the other hand absolutely distinguishing its tensed modalities? It can do so because the whole experience, as it is concentrated in a conscious present, has a narrative form. Narrative alone can contain the full temporality of experience in a unity of form. But this incipient story, implicit in the very possibility of experience, must be such that it can absorb both the chronicle of memory and the scenario of anticipation, absorb them within a richer narrative form without effacing the difference between the determinacy of the one and the indeterminacy of the other.

We can define such a narrative form a little more fully by reminding ourselves that the conscious present has a third modality: the present of things present. This *praesens de praesentibus* Augustine designates as *contuitus* – direct attention. True enough, but there is something more. If discussion of the aetherial-seeming objects of memory and anticipation may have tempted us to speak of consciousness itself as if it were an invisibility suspended in a void, mention of its direct present must sharply remind us that consciousness is a function of an altogether bodily life. The conscious present is that of a body impacted in a world and moving, in process, in that world. In this present action and experience meet. Memory is its depth, the depth of its experience in particular; anticipation is its trajectory, the trajectory of its action in particular. The *praesens de praesentibus* is its full bodily reality.

It is, moreover, the moment of decision within the story as a whole. It is always the *decisive* episode in the story, its moment of crisis between the past remembered and the future anticipated but still undetermined. The *critical* position of this modality gives the story a dramatic character as a whole. And since action and experience join precisely at this decisive and critical juncture in the drama, the whole drama vibrates with the musicality of personal style.

Still, it is a drama of a rudimentary sort. Life is not, after all, a work of art. An artistic drama has a coherence and a fullness of articulation that are never reached by our rudimentary drama. But the drama of experience is the crude original of all high drama. High drama can only contrive the appearance of that crisis which the conscious present actually is. The difference between a fixed past and a future still to be resolved, which in experience is an absolute difference, must be artfully contrived on a stage by actors who know the outcome as well as they know the beginning. The art of drama imitates the life of experience, which is the true drama.

'Once Upon a Time ... Happily Ever After'

Life also imitates art. The stories people hear and tell, the dramas they see performed, not to speak of the sacred stories that are absorbed without being directly heard or seen, shape in the most profound way the inner story of experience. We imbibe a sense of the meaning of our own baffling dramas from these stories, and this sense of its meaning in turn affects the form of a man's experience and the style of his action. Such cultural forms, both sacred and mundane, are of course socially shared in varying degrees, and so help to link men's inner lives as well as orienting them to a common public world. Both the content and the form of experience are mediated by symbolic systems which we are able to employ simply by virtue of awakening within a particular culture in which those symbolic systems are the common currency. Prevailing narrative forms are among the most important of such symbolic systems. It is not as though a man begins as a purely individual consciousness with the incipient story and musicality of his private experience, and then casts about for a satisfying tale to lend it some higher significance. People awaken to consciousness in a society, with the inner story of experience and its enveloping musicality already infused with cultural forms. The vital-ities of experience itself may in turn make a man feel that some of the old stories have a hollow ring and may be the source of originality in the formation of new stories, or even new kinds of stories. But the *way* we remember, anticipate, and even directly perceive, is largely social. A sacred story in particular infuses experience at its root, linking a man's individual consciousness with ultimate powers and also with the inner lives of those with whom he shares a common soil.

There is an entrancing half-truth that has gained wide currency, particularly among American undergraduates. It is that time itself is a cultural product, e.g., the creation of certain grammatical forms.[11] Presumably we could be rid of it if we played our cards right, say, with a non-western deck. The kernel of truth in this idyllic vision is that particular conceptions of time are indeed imbibed from cultural forms, not only from the structures of a language but from the kinds of stories being told. For the temporality that I have argued is necessary for the very possibility of experience does not of itself imply any particular conception of time. The connections among its episodes or moments is not necessarily, for example, either magical, causal, logical, or teleological. Least of all does it imply any theory regarding the metaphysical status of time. The temporality of lived experience as such, with its inherent tensions and crises, can only, so to speak, raise questions about the reality and meaning of time. For the answers to these questions it must, as it were, turn to the sacred and mundane cultural forms lying at hand. In fact, the answers precede and sometimes preclude the questions! Stories, in particular, infuse the incipient drama of experience with a definite sense of the way its scenes are connected. They reveal to people the kind of drama in which they are engaged, and perhaps its larger meaning. So the fact that there are very different notions of time implicit in the cultural forms of different historical traditions does not contradict the inherent temporality of all possible experience. There is only one absolute limit to that diversity: it is impossible that a culture could offer no interpretation of this temporality at all.

In principle, we can distinguish between the inner drama of experience and the stories through which it achieves coherence. But in any actual case the two so interpenetrate that they form a virtual identity, which, if we may pun a little, is in fact a man's very sense of his own personal identity. The sacred story in particular, with its musical vitality, enables him to give the incipient drama of his experience full dramatic dimensions and allows the incipient musicality of his style to break forth into real dance and song. Hence the powerful inner need for expressive forms, the music played and sung and danced, the stories told and acted, projected within the world of which men are conscious.

So the narrative quality of experience has three dimensions, the sacred story, the mundane stories, and the temporal form of experience itself: three narrative tracks, each constantly reflecting and affecting the course of the others.

And sometimes the tracks cross, causing a burst of light like a comet entering our atmosphere. Such a luminous moment, in which sacred, mundane, and personal are inseparably conjoined, we call *symbolic* in a special sense. Of course, there is a more general sense in which every element in a story is a symbol, an imaginative representation conveying a meaning; but even in that sense the symbol is partly constituted by its position in the story. A story is not a mere assembly of independently defined symbols. Still less is a symbol in the more pregnant sense, e.g., a religious symbol, an atomic capsule of meaning that drops from the heavens or springs from the unconscious in isolated splendor.[12] The cross, or a holy mountain, receive their meaning from the stories in which they appear. Such a symbol imports into any icon or life situation or new story in which it appears, the significance given it in a cycle of mundane stories, and also the resonances of a sacred story. The shock of its appearance is like the recurrence in daylight of an episode recalled from dreams. For a religious symbol becomes fully alive to consciousness when sacred story dramatically intersects both an explicit narrative and the course of a man's personal experience. The symbol is precisely that double intersection.

Narrative form, and not the symbol as such, is primitive in experience. But narrative form is by no means innocent. It acknowledges and informs only what is contained in its own ordering of events. Even the most naïve tale begins 'once upon a time' – a time prior to which there is only darkness, no time so far as the temporality constituted by the story is concerned. That time begins with this 'once . . .' and when the tale has run its course there is nothing left. Its characters disappear into a timeless 'happily ever after'. It is meaningless to ask whether they really do. For they live only within the tensions and crises which constitute the significant time of the story, the narrative 'tick-tock',[13] between the tick of 'once upon a time' and the tock of happy resolution. Of course, the resolution may not be happy. We may leave our characters in a state of horror also outside all time and, therefore, pure and unambiguous. This happiness, this horror, are both beyond the possibilities of recognizable human experience. Only narrative form can contain the tensions, the surprises, the disappointments and reversals and achievements of actual, temporal experience. The vague yet unambiguous, uncanny happiness and horror are 'beyond'. The story itself may, to be sure, contain symbolic accents that refer to such a beyond, e.g., the resurrection, or images of eternal blessedness or torment, or descents into a nether region that is strangely familiar. Such symbolic accents are not necessarily intimations of immortality. Imagination is projected by them beyond any possible experience, and yet the projection itself takes place within the contingencies of experience. It belongs to the story. However deep into the bowels of hell Dante leads us, however high into heaven, it is remarkable how he and his sinners and saints keep our attention fixed on the little disk of earth, that stage on which the drama of men's moral struggles in time is enacted. Far from reducing the significance of this time-bound story in which we are embroiled, such visions of happiness and horror make it all the more portentous. Even in secularized projections beyond the ambiguity of history into social utopia or doomsday, a particular sense of the historical drama itself is implicit. For the meaning of both happiness and horror is derived, even in the uttermost leap of the imagination beyond our story, from our conception of the story itself.

If experience has the narrative quality attributed to it here, not only our self-identity but the empirical and moral cosmos in which we are conscious of living is implicit in our multidimensional story. It therefore becomes evident that a conversion or a social revolution that actually transforms consciousness requires a traumatic change in a man's story. The stories within which he has awakened to consciousness must be undermined, and in the identification of his personal story through a new story both the drama of his experience and his style of action must be reoriented. Conversion is reawakening, a second awakening of consciousness. His style must change steps, he must dance to a new rhythm. Not only his past and future, but the very cosmos in which he lives is strung in a new way.

The point is beautifully made in a passage from the *Protreptikos* of Clement of Alexandria, selections from which, in verse translation, are among the last things we have from the pen of Thomas Merton. Clement, himself a convert to Christianity, is writing at the time Christianity first emerged in a serious way into a classical culture already become decadent. In a passage entitled 'The New Song', he retells an old Greek legend but glosses it in a way that gives it a radical new turn. A bard named Eunomos was singing, to his own accompaniment on the lyre, a hymn to the death of the Pythian dragon. Meanwhile, unnoticed by the pagan assembly, another performance is under way.

Crickets were singing among the leaves all up the mountainside,
  burning in the sun.
They were singing, not indeed for the death of the dragon,
  the dead Pythian, but
They hymned the all-wise God, in their own mode, far superior
  to that of Eunomos.
A harp string breaks on the Locrian.
A cricket flies down on top of the lyre. She sings on the
  instrument as though on a branch. The singer, harmonizing
  with the cricket's tune, goes on without the lost string.
Not by the song of Eunomos is the cricket moved, as the myth
  supposes, or as is shown by the bronze statue the Delphians
  erected, showing
Eunomos with his harp and his companion in the contest!
The cricket flies on her own and sings on her own.

The subversive cricket sings the new song, to Clement old as creation
yet newly come to human lips, of the Christian logos.

See what power the new song has!
From stones, men,
From beasts it has made men.
Those otherwise dead, those without a share in life that is really
  life
At the mere sound of this song
Have come back to life. . . .
Moreover He has structured the whole universe musically
And the discord of elements He has brought together in an
  ordered symphony
So that the whole Cosmos is for Him in harmony.[14]

Modernity and Revolution: An Intemperate Conclusion

The form of consciousness to which we apply the name *modernity*
seems to represent a transformation as radical, though of a different
sort, as that celebrated by Clement. Some have even suggested the
emergence of a yet newer sensibility, so new and inchoate that it can
only be designated 'post-modern'. All this is too close to us to speak
of it with much assurance, but I yield to the temptation to offer some
suggestions that bear on our theme.
  I have argued that experience is moulded, root and branch, by

narrative forms, that its narrative quality is altogether primitive. At the same time, expression is obviously not limited to story telling. Mind and imagination are capable of recollecting the narrative materials of experience into essentially non-narrative forms. Indeed there seems to be a powerful inner drive of thought and imagination to overcome the relentless temporality of experience. One needs more clarity than stories can give us, and also a little rest. The kind of pure spatial articulation we find in painting and sculpture, with all movement suspended, gratifies this deep need. Also in meditation and in theoretical endeavors we are a little less completely at the mercy of our own temporality. Traditional myths, stories dominated by timeless archetypes, have functioned in this way: by taking personal and historical time up into the archetypal story, they give it a meaning which in the end is timeless, cosmic, absolute.

But an important feature of the modern situation is the employment of quite different strategies for breaking the sense of narrative time. At a very general level, these strategies fall into two opposite and indeed mutually antagonistic types: one is the strategy of abstraction, in which images and qualities are detached from experience to become data for the formation of generalized principles and techniques. Such abstraction enables us to give experience a new, non-narrative and atemporal coherence. It is an indispensable strategy for conducting many of the practical affairs of life in our society; we are all technicians, like it or not. In its more elaborated forms, the strategy of abstraction is the basis for all science. Its importance in the formation of modern institutions can hardly be exaggerated.

But strategies of the other type seem almost equally important in the formation of 'modern' consciousness. This other type we may call the strategy of contraction. Here narrative temporarily is again fragmented, not by abstraction to systems of generality, but by the constriction of attention to dissociated immediacies: to the particular image isolated from the image stream, to isolated sensation, feeling, the flash of the overpowering moment in which the temporal context of that moment is eclipsed and past and future are deliberately blocked out of consciousness. It is commonly assumed that this dissociated immediacy is what is concrete and irreducible in experience.

But the sweat and grit of the moment, which some so highly prize, is in fact a contraction of the narrative movement that is really concrete in experience, as generality is the abstraction from it. The point can perhaps best be made indirectly, by noticing that these two time-defying strategies have projected a distinctively modern version of a dualism in the idea of the self: the dualism of mind and body. We state the matter backwards if we say that something called *mind* abstracts from experience to produce generality, or if we say that 'the body' has feelings and sensations. It is the activity of abstracting from the narrative concreteness of experience that leads us to posit the idea of mind as a distinct faculty. And it is the concentration of consciousness into feeling and sensation that gives rise to the idea of body. Both mind and body are reifications of particular functions that have been wrenched from the concrete temporality of the conscious self. The self is not a composite of mind and body. The self in its concreteness is indivisible, temporal, and whole, as it is revealed to be in the narrative quality of its experience. Neither disembodied minds nor mindless bodies can appear in stories. There the self is given whole, as an activity in time.

Yet criticism alone cannot dissolve this mind-body dualism. The very fact of its stubborn persistence in our ordinary sense of ourselves, even though we know better (in theory!), testifies to the very great importance in the modern world of the two strategies on which it is based. The power to abstract makes explanation, manipulation, control possible. On the other hand we seek relief and release in the capacity to contract the flow of time, to dwell in feeling and sensation, in taste, in touch, in the delicious sexual viscosities. So 'the mind' dwells in the light, clear, dry, transparent, unmessy. 'The body' dwells in the damp privacy of a friendly darkness created by feeling and sensation. In principle, the powers of consciousness to abstract and to contract need no more be in conflict than day and night. But day and night form a rhythm within the continuum of time. If the abstraction and contraction of consciousness were merely temporary suspensions of the narrative quality of experience there would be no crisis.

But the modern world has seen these two strategies played off ever more violently against one another. One could show how the reification of mind and body has killed modern metaphysics by leading it into arid controversies among dualistic, materialistic, and idealistic theories. But this comparatively harmless wrangle among post-Cartesian metaphysicians is only a symptom of the modern bifurcation of experience. Its more sinister expression is practical: the entrapment of educated subcultures in their own abstract constructions, and the violent reaction against this entrapment, a reaction that takes the form of an equally encapsulating constriction of experience into those warm, dark, humid immediacies. One thinks of Faust in his study where everything is so dry that a spark would produce an explosion, and then Faust slavering and mucking about on the

Brocken. Against the inhumanly dry and abstract habitations of the spirit that have been erected by technological reason, the cry goes up, born of desperation, to drop out and sink into the warm stream of immediacy. Within the university the reaction and counterreaction have been especially violent in the humanities.

And that is ironical. For the material with which the humanities have traditionally dealt is predominantly narrative. There have been deep conflicts among different kinds of stories and divergent interpretations. Still, the humanities have kept the story alive in the university; and it is precisely the story, with its underlying musicality, that provides generality and immediacy their humanly fruitful functions. So long as the story retains its primary hold on the imagination, the play of immediacy and the illuminating power of abstraction remain in productive tension. But when immediacy and abstract generality are wrenched out of the story altogether, drained of all musicality, the result is something I can only call, with strict theological precision, demonic. Experience becomes demonically possessed by its own abstracting and contracting possibilities, turned alien and hostile to experience itself. When the humanities give up the story, they become alternately seized by desiccated abstractions and scatological immediacies, the light of the mind becoming a blinding and withering glare, the friendly darkness deepening into the chaotic night of nihilism. Ethical authority, which is always a function of a common narrative coherence of life, is overthrown by a naked show of force exercised either in the name of reason or in the name of glandular vitality. Contrary to the cynical theory that violent force is the secret basis of authority, it is in fact always the sign that authority has dissolved.

So much for modernity. Now one speaks, perhaps wistfully, of the emergence of a 'post-modern' sensibility. This new sensibility is sometimes called 'revolutionary', a term that sounds less empty than 'post-modern', but is still obscure enough. Certainly it is often discussed in terms of the same dualisms and wearisome strategies of abstraction and contraction that have plagued the 'modern' period. Some envision a 'revolution' that would consist in extending the control of abstract, technological reason to the whole life of society; maximum manipulation justified on the high moral ground that it would improve behavior – down to the least flicker of an eyelash. Others appear to hope for a society perpetually turned on and flowing with animal juices. The utopia schemed in the crystal palace, or that plotted in the cellar of the underground man: the lure of either of these utopias or any all-purpose combination of them can lead one to nothing more than a variation on an all too familiar refrain. Neither appears to catch the cadences of the new song that I think is struggling to be heard when people speak seriously of revolution.

I think that 'revolution' is the name that a post-modern consciousness gives to a new sacred story. I realize that if this essay has ever strayed into the sphere of sober theory, it has with this suggestion abandoned it altogether in favor of testimony. But if we really are talking about a sacred story, what can we do but testify? Certainly the sacred story to which we give this name cannot be directly told. But its resonances can be felt in many of the stories that are being told, in songs being sung, in a renewed resolution to act. The stories being told do not necessarily speak of gods in any traditional sense, yet there seem to be living continuities in this unutterable story with some of the sacred stories of the past. Certainly, too, revolution is more than the name for an idea or a program, though it is giving rise to many ideas and programs, some no doubt half-baked and quixotic – anything radically serious seems to gather a penumbra of lunacy – but also some that actively express the most intense needs of our times.[15] This revolutionary story has united the angry children of poverty and the alienated children of abundance in a common moral passion and a common sense of the meaning of their experience. Among those for whom the story is alive there is a revival of ethical authority otherwise almost effaced in our society. For it establishes on a new basis the coherency of social and personal time. It makes it possible to recover a living past, to believe again in the future, to perform acts that have significance for the person who acts. By so doing it restores a human form of experience.

Notes

1. That is to say that I conceive my undertaking to be phenomenological. It will not, however, be larded with citations from the great German and French phenomenologists. The phenomenology will be homemade.

2. Though not as if, like Zeno's arrow, one passed through a series of quasi-mathematical points in time. The temporality of which we speak is constituted by the movement itself, and not by the (essentially spatial) units of its measure.

3. However poetically we may express our appreciation for, say, the revolutions of the moon, we would not normally attribute style to it, nor even to the 'song' of a bird. And while we do speak of the style of a painting, I take it that that is an oblique way of referring to the style of the artist in his act of painting it: the 'painting' and not the artifact as such has style. Again, when people are asleep their style slumbers also; 'What style!' would be a nice comic caption for a cartoon picturing a woman pointing at her snoring husband.

4. The point is brilliantly argued and elaborated in Frank Kermode, *The Sense*

of an Ending (Oxford University Press, 1966). Professor Kermode warns that 'If we forget that fictions are fictive we regress to myth . . .' (p. 41). My argument may well illustrate what he is warning against. I do deny that all narratives are merely fictive, and I go on to deny that myth, or what I call sacred story, is a mere regression from a fiction. But it is ungrateful to single out my disagreements with a book from which I have derived uncommon profit in pondering my theme.

5. As Kant argued in *The Critique of Pure Reason*, though of course reaching quite different conclusions about the constitution of this necessary form. To make at the level of *strenge Wissenschaft* my case that the primary forms of possible experience are narrative, I should also have to follow Kant's lead by providing a transcendental deduction of these incipient narrative forms. But I content myself with the gestures in that direction contained in this and the following section.

6. There is an implicit circularity here that may as well be made explicit, since I am sure to be found out anyway. I appeal to the form of sacred and mundane story to suggest that the structure of experience informed by such stories must itself be in some sense narrative. But I have not really proven that what I have called sacred story is in any acceptable sense narrative itself, and among the reasons that make me think it is, the most important is that experience has at root a narrative form. Experience can derive a specific sense of its own temporal course in a coherent world only by being informed by a qualifying structure that gives definite contours to its own form. Very well. The points are mutually supportive, i.e., the argument is in the end circular, as any good philosophical argument is. And in the end it has only the explanatory power of this particular circle to commend it.

7. I take responsibility for the translation of extracts from *The Confessions* quoted here.

8. In recognizing the importance of this strange measurement of what no longer exists, Augustine does implicitly acknowledge the primitive order of succession within memory. Memory is not simply a vast interior space in which images tumble at random.

9. I have discussed such anticipatory scenarios in some detail in an essay to which the present one is in many ways a sequel: 'Myth, Story, History', published in a symposium entitled *Parable, Myth and Language* (Cambridge, Mass.: The Church Society for College Work, 1968), p. 68.

10. The fluidity of the future from the standpoint of consciousness has nothing to do with the truth or falsity of deterministic theories. The point is phenomenological, not metaphysical.

11. This view is usually linked with a loveable primitivism now in vogue. Students who make this link often seize upon the theories of Benjamin Lee Whorf, who had observed, for example, that characteristically western notions of time could not be expressed at all in the language of the Hopi Indians. See 'An American Indian Model of the Universe', in the collection of Whorf's writings entitled *Language, Thought, and Reality* (Cambridge, Mass.: M.I.T. Press, 1956). Cf. Richard M. Gale, *The Language of Time* (London: Routledge & Kegan Paul, 1968), pp. 45–48, for a critique of some of the general claims Whorf's observations led him to make. Those who cite Whorf are often less cautious than

he is claiming that time is the product of a particular culture, and therefore holding out the possibility that there are or might be peoples blessedly free of the conflicts and traumas of temporal existence. Among some of my favorite students it comes out like this:

O happy hippy Hopis
of pyote buds and herbs:
No tensions in their teepees,
no tenses in their verbs.

Far removed from this idyllic vision is the fine work of Georges Poulet, *Studies in Human Time* (trans. by Elliott Coleman, (Baltimore: Johns Hopkins Press, 1956). Poulet points up the radical developments and the subtle modulations in the sense of time within western culture itself, particularly in the works of a succession of important French and American writers.

12. It has been widely assumed that symbols are in some sense primitive in experience, and that myths and other narrative forms are secondary constructions that assemble the primal symbolic material into stories. That view, for example, in a highly sophisticated form, seems to be an important premise of Paul Ricoeur's fine studies in this field, e.g., *The Symbolism of Evil*, trans. by Emerson Buchanan (New York: Harper & Row, 1967). But such a view seems to presuppose an atomism of experience that I think is quite impossible.

13. Frank Kermode ingeniously treats 'tick-tock' as a model of plot, contrasting the organized duration between the 'humble genesis' of tick and the 'feeble apocalypse' of tock with the 'emptiness', the unorganized blank that exists between our perception of 'tock' and the next 'tick'. *The Sense of an Ending*, pp. 44–46.

14. Clement of Alexandria, Selections from *The Protreptikos*, an essay and translation by Thomas Merton (New York: New Directions, 1962), pp. 15–16, 17. It is significant that the early Christian preaching was largely a story-telling mission, offering people a new story, the Christian kerygma, to reorient their sense of the meaning both of historical time and of their own personal life-time.

15. There are also, of course, theories of revolution itself. For a dialectical theory is that most important theories of revolution are dialectical. For a dialectical theory is that form of generality that preserves in itself the vital pulse of temporal movement. A dialectical theory of revolution is not an alternative to a story of revolution, but is its exegesis.

Sallie McFague, 'Toward a Metaphorical Theology'
in *Metaphorical Theology: Models of God in Religious Language*
London: SCM Press, 1983, pp. 14–16, 17–19.

Sallie McFague has focused throughout her theological career upon the unsettling nature of religious language and how the human imagination encounters the presence of God. In her early work on the parables of Jesus, she shows that the stories of the kingdom are not homely illustrations but surprising, disturbing and challenging means of overturning assumptions and causing their hearers to realize their need to choose, change and act in response to them. In this extract from Metaphorical Theology *(1983), a transitional work, she argues that Jesus not only told parables but embodied a parable, a narrative unfamiliar and strange for us that nevertheless, in its surprising impact, draws us close to the heart of God. In this work, a direct link is made between parables and metaphors. Both bring familiar elements into surprising new conjunctions, causing us to question what we had once thought and see the world in new ways.*

McFague argues that genuine theological understanding is always metaphorical in that it draws all the conventions of daily life into question and results in a new naming of ourselves, our world and God. This is an insight which she has gone on to explore in later books such as Models of God *(1987) and* The Body of God *(1993). In these she actively creates new parables and metaphors that are intended to bring the resources of metaphorical theology to the pressing problems confronting the world today.*

Metaphorical Theology

If modernity were the only criterion, our task would be relatively easy. But such is never the case in theology. Christian theology is always an interpretation of the 'Gospel' in a particular time and place. So the other task of equal importance is to show that a *metaphorical theology* is indigenous to Christianity, not just in the sense that it is permitted, but is called for. And this I believe is the case. The heart of the Gospel in the New Testament is widely accepted to be the 'kingdom of God'; what the kingdom is or means is never expressed but indirectly suggested by the parables of the kingdom.[1] The parables are by no means the only form in the New Testament which deals with the kingdom and we must be cautious lest we make an idol of them. However, as the dominant genre of Jesus' teaching on the kingdom, they suggest some central, albeit indirect, clues to its reality. As a form of religious language, the parables of the New Testament are very different from symbolic, sacramental language. They do not assume a believing or religious perspective on the part of the listeners to whom they are addressed; they do not assume continuity between our world and a transcendent one; they do not see similarity, connection, and harmony between our ways and the ways of God. On the contrary, they are a secular form of language, telling stories of ordinary people involved in mundane family, business, and social matters; they assume a nonbelieving or secular attitude on the part of their audience; they stress the discontinuity between our ways and the ways of the kingdom; they focus on the dissimilarity, incongruity, and tension between the assumptions and expectations of their characters and another set of assumptions and expectations identified with the kingdom. In other words, they are a form peculiarly suited to what I have called the Protestant sensibility.

They are so suited because they are metaphors, not symbols. They are metaphorical statements about religious matters, about what both transcends and affects us at the deepest level of our existence. What is it about a religious metaphorical statement which makes it more powerful than a symbolical statement? The answer to this question centers on the nature of metaphor and especially of metaphorical statements. To many people 'metaphor' is merely a poetic ornament for illustrating an idea or adding rhetorical color to abstract or flat language. It appears to have little to do with ordinary language until one realizes that most ordinary language is composed of 'dead metaphors', some obvious, such as 'the arm of the chair' and others less obvious, such as 'tradition', meaning 'to hand over or hand down'. Most simply, a metaphor is seeing one thing *as* something else, pretending 'this' is 'that' because we do not know how to think or talk about 'this', so we use 'that' as a way of saying something about it. Thinking metaphorically means spotting a thread of similarity between two dissimilar objects, events, or whatever, one of which is better known than the other, and using the better-known one as a way of speaking about the lesser known.

Poets use metaphor all the time because they are constantly speaking about the great unknowns – mortality, love, fear, joy, guilt, hope, and so on. Religious language is deeply metaphorical for the same reason and it is therefore no surprise that Jesus' most characteristic form of teaching, the parables, should be extended metaphors. Less obvious, but of paramount importance, is the fact that metaphorical thinking constitutes the basis of human thought and language. From the time we are infants we construct our world through metaphor; that is, just as young children learn the meaning of the color red by finding the thread of similarity through many dissimilar objects (red ball, red apple, red cheeks), so we constantly ask when we do not know how to think about something, 'What is it like?' Far from being an esoteric or ornamental rhetorical device superimposed on ordinary language, metaphor *is* ordinary language. It is the *way* we think. We often make distinctions between ordinary and poetic language, assuming that the first is direct and the second indirect, but actually both are indirect, for we always think by indirection. The difference between the two kinds of language is only that we have grown accustomed to the indirections of ordinary language; they have become conventional. Likewise, conceptual or abstract language is metaphorical in the sense that the ability to generalize depends upon seeing similarity within dissimilarity; a concept is an abstraction of the similar from a sea of dissimilars. Thus, Darwin's theory of the survival of the fittest is a high-level metaphorical exercise of recognizing a similar pattern amid an otherwise incredibly diverse set of phenomena.

. . .

We have remarked that metaphor finds the vein of similarity in the midst of dissimilars, while symbol rests on similarity already present and assumed. But the difference is even more marked: metaphor not only lives in the region of dissimilarity, but also in the region of the unconventional and surprising. Both humor and the grotesque are distinctly metaphorical.[2] Humor is the recognition of a *very* unlikely similarity among dissimilars and we laugh because we are surprised to discover that such unlikes are indeed alike in at least one respect. A great many jokes take the form, 'How is a _____ like a _____?' Likewise, the grotesque forces us to look at radical incongruity, at what is outside, does not fit, is strange and disturbing. Both are extreme metaphorical forms which point up a crucial characteristic of metaphor: good metaphors shock, they bring unlikes together, they upset conventions, they involve tension, and they are implicitly revolutionary. The parables of Jesus are typically metaphorical in this regard, for they bring together dissimilars (lost coins, wayward children, buried treasure, and tardy laborers with the kingdom of God); they shock and disturb; they upset conventions and expectations and in so doing have revolutionary potential. In this regard, one could characterize symbolic, sacramental thinking as priestly and metaphorical thinking as prophetic. The first assumes an order and unity already present waiting to be realized; the second projects, tentatively, a possible transformed order and unity yet to be realized.[3]

Perhaps the most striking evidence of the revolutionary character of the New Testament parables is the redefinition they give to conventional understandings of the monarchical, hierarchical metaphors of 'kingdom' and 'rule'. God's 'kingdom', we discover from the parables, is not like any worldly reign; in fact, its essence is its opposition to the power of the mighty over the lowly, the rich over the poor, the righteous over the unrighteous. It is a *new* rule which is defined by the extraordinary reversal of expectations in the parables as well as in the life and death of Jesus.

The characteristics of metaphorical thinking we have suggested – ordinariness, incongruity, indirection, skepticism, judgment, unconventionality, surprise, and transformation or revolution – especially as they are realized in Jesus' parables, have persuaded many people to think of Jesus as a parable of God.[4] That is to say, the life and death of Jesus of Nazareth can be understood as itself a 'parable' of God; in order to understand the ways of God with us – something unfamiliar and unknown to us, about which we do not know how to think or talk – we look at that life as a metaphor of God. What we see through that 'grid' or 'screen' is at one level an ordinary, secular story of a human being, but also a story shot through with surprise, unconventionality, and incongruities which not only upset our conventional expectations (for instance, of what a 'savior' is and who gets 'saved'), but also involve a judgment on our part – 'Surely this man is the Christ'. In contrast to incarnational christology, however, parabolic christology does not involve an assumption of continuity or identity between the human and the divine; it is not a 'Jesusolatry', a form of idolatry. It is, I believe, a christology for the Protestant sensibility and the modern mentality.

All the foregoing comments on metaphor, parable, and Jesus as a parable require considerable elaboration. Perhaps, however, these brief introductory remarks are sufficient for us to attempt to advance a case for a metaphorical theology. If metaphor is the way by which we understand as well as enlarge our world and change it – that is, if the only way we have of dealing with the unfamiliar and new is in terms of the familiar and the old, thinking of 'this' as 'that' although we know the new thing is both like *and* unlike the old – if all this is the case, then it is no surprise that Jesus taught in parables or that many see him as a parable of God. For he introduced a new, strange way of being in the world, a way that could be grasped only through the indirection of stories of familiar life which both 'were and were not' the kingdom. And he himself was in the world in a new, strange way which was in many respects an ordinary life but one which also, as with the parables, called the mores and conventions of ordinary life into radical question.

A metaphorical theology, then, starts with the parables of Jesus and with Jesus as a parable of God. This starting place does not involve a belief in the Bible as authoritative in an absolute or closed sense; it does not involve acceptance of a canon or the Bible as 'the Word of God'. In fact, such a perspective reverses the direction of authority suitable both to Scripture and to the Protestant sensibility. For what we have in the New Testament are confessions of faith by people who, on the basis of their experience of the way their lives were changed by Jesus' Gospel and by Jesus, *gave* authority to him and to the writings about him. The New Testament writings are foundational; they are classics; they are a beginning. But if we take seriously the parables of Jesus and Jesus as a parable of God as our starting point and model, then we cannot say that the Bible is absolute or authoritative in any sense except the way that a 'classic' text is authoritative: it continues to speak to us. What must always be kept in mind is that the parables as metaphors and the life of Jesus as a metaphor of God provide characteristics for theology: a theology guided by them is open-ended, tentative, indirect, tensive, iconoclastic, transformative. Some of these characteristics appear 'negative', in the sense that they qualify any attempts at idolatry, whether this be the idolatry of the Bible, of tradition, of orthodoxy, or of the Church. In such a theology *no* finite thought, product, or creature can be identified with God and this includes Jesus of Nazareth, who as parable of God both 'is and is not' God. Against all forms of literalistic realism and idolatry, a metaphorical theology insists that it is not only in keeping with the Protestant sensibility to be open, tentative, and iconoclastic but that these are the characteristics of Jesus' parables and of Jesus' own way of being in the world.

Notes

1. Leander Keck voices the position of many New Testament exegetes in the following statement: 'The whole network of words, deeds, and death which we call "Jesus" was pulled into a pattern by the magnetic power of the kingdom and hence reflected the impingement of that kingdom on his life and work. This was not simply a matter of Jesus working out the implications of a root idea. Rather, it was a matter of being grasped by a perception in such a way that the whole career became a celebration of the kingdom's coming and thereby its vanguard as well' (*A Future for the Historical Jesus: The Place of Jesus in Preaching and Theology*, Philadelphia: Fortress Press, 1981, pp. 218–19).

2. See Kenneth Burke, *Permanence and Change: An Anatomy of Purpose*, New York: New Republic, 1935.

3. I am indebted to F. W. Dillistone for his distinction between analogical and metaphorical thinking. Of analogy he writes: 'In any organic system the single member is related to the whole according to some pattern of order and proportion; no figure of speech is more fitted to express this relation than analogy'

(*Christianity and Symbolism*, London: William Collins, 1955, p. 152). He notes that one can move from the known to the unknown because the part participates in the whole and is similar to it. Analogical thought is positive, comprehensive, and systematic. Analogy has links with the simile, metaphor with the contrast. Metaphor focuses attention on variety and the openness of reality, and on dissimilarity rather than similarity. Metaphor holds together similarity and dissimilarity in a resolution:

> The resolution is not final, for there are ever wider areas of conflict to embrace. But every metaphor which holds together two disparate aspects of reality in creative tension assumes the character of a prophecy of the final reconciliation of all things in the kingdom of God. It is the favorite tool of all the great poets ... Through it the imagination performs its task, the task which Coleridge describes as dissolving, diffusing, dissipating in order to recreate, as reconciling opposite or discordant qualities, as struggling to idealise and to unify. Through it the prophet leaps outside the circle of present experience, the realm of the factual and the commonsense, the typical and the regular. He parts company with those who are travelling the surer and steadier road of analogical comparison. By one act of daring he brings into creative relationship the apparently opposite and contrary and, if his metaphorical adventure proves successful, gains new treasure both for language and for life (Ibid., p. 161).

Finally, Dillistone notes that while analogy tends toward petrification, metaphor moves toward renovation and that Jesus was a metaphorical thinker, disrupting the old by seeing it in a new light.

4. Among the several New Testament critics who see Jesus as a parable of God are Leander Keck and John Donahue. Keck writes: 'Jesus concentrated on parabolic speech because he himself was a parabolic event of the kingdom of God' (*A Future for the Historical Jesus*, p. 244). Donahue writes: 'Responding to the parable of Jesus in Mark is engagement in the ultimate paradox of the Christian life' ('Jesus as the Parable of God in the Gospel of Mark', *Interpretation* 32 [1978], p. 386). Both exegetes substantiate their claim by a comparison of Jesus' life with the characteristics of parables: their metaphoricity, mundanity, realism, strangeness, indirection, shocking disclosive power, and existential engagement.

Alicia Ostriker, 'Entering the Tents'

in *The Nakedness of the Fathers: Biblical Visions and Revisions*, New Jersey: Rutgers University Press, 1997, pp. 5–8, 13–16.

In this extract, Alicia Ostriker vividly describes the problems women have in relating to the sacred narratives of religious traditions. Not only are women marginalized and casually despised within the pages of Scripture but, for thousands of years, they have been denied the privilege of studying and interpreting the holy books. Ostriker argues that despite the alienation this causes, women cannot turn their backs on what is precious and desirable in the traditions within which they

*have been formed. However, they must enter into a new relationship
with the texts that delight and deny them.*

*Ostriker is a poet and a literary critic as well as a feminist theo-
logian. Her creative work involves re-reading, re-writing and reconstructing the stories of her Jewish faith. This work serves to make
visible the exercise of power performed by sacred texts and gives
voice to the silent women who inhabit the ancient narratives. She
accomplishes this task in the spirit of Midrash, which insists that
other interpretations are always possible and that fresh meanings
can always emerge from generative texts. While this process is not
submissive it is deeply faithful. The texts provoke her attention, they
call out to her and, in a spirit 'of love and anger', she responds.*

Entering the Tents

*Would to God that all the Lord's
people were prophets!*
NUMBERS 11:29

*You don't want me to dance, too bad,
I'll dance anyhow.*
ELIE WIESEL, *THE GATES OF THE FOREST*

I am and am not a Jew. I am a Jew in the sense that every drop of
blood in my veins is Jewish, or so I figuratively presume although
Jews have been a mixed multitude since they left Egypt. I am a Jew
because my parents are. So, naturally, is every thought in my head,
my habits of thinking, my moral impulses and burden of chronic
guilt, my sense of humor if any, my confrontational and adversarial
inclinations. They say a Jew is somebody who loves to argue,
especially with God and other Jews. My laughter and tears are
Jewish laughter and tears. What else could they be? My ancestors
are Russian-Jewish ancestors. The shtetl mud is hardly shaken
from my roots. In the 1880's when the great pogroms swept
Russia and eastern Europe, it was me they hated and wanted to
kill. Me, an innocent girl in my babushka throwing grain to the
chickens. In 1944 it could have been me trembling, my long nose
no longer in a book, wetting myself in a railroad car a few kilomet-
ers out of Budapest, or among the soft stacked bodies like speech-
less tongues in the mouth of a ravine at Babi Yar. Here is my violin,
hidden in a closet of the Warsaw apartment, kicked to splinters

by a soldier's boot, going up in flames. And I have fantastically escaped and can breathe air, enjoy freedom, by merest chance. No way I can be anything else. Can't be a Buddhist like Allen Ginsberg (who anyway gets more and more rabbinical), or a Sufi like Doris Lessing. It would be a joke, silly to pretend. When I stand before a classroom to discuss a Shakespeare sonnet, who stands inside me? Isn't it a long row of rabbis waving their bony index fingers, cantankerous and didactic, analyzing a bit of Aramaic phrasing? When I march in a peace demonstration, the prophet Isaiah goes in front of me. Beat your swords into plough-shares, he shouts. Do not hurt or destroy. And I hurry to step and chant alongside him. Could I despise the drops of blood in my body? To deny my Judaism would be like denying the gift of life, the reality of sorrow, the pleasures of learning and teaching. To reject Judaism would be to surrender an idea of justice inseparable from compassion.

But I'm not a Jew, I can't be a Jew, because Judaism repels me as a woman.

To the rest of the world the Jew is marginal. But to Judaism I am marginal. Am woman, unclean. Am Eve. Or worse, am Lilith. Am illiterate. Not mine the arguments of Talmud, not mine the centuries of ecstatic study, the questions and answers twining minutely like vines around the living Word, not mine the Kaballah, the letters of the Hebrew alphabet dancing as if they were attributes of God. These texts, like the Law and the Prophets, are not-me. For a thousand years and longer I am not permitted to discuss sacred writings. I am not permitted to be a scholar. I am not given access to the texts, although my very bones command me to go and study. It is said: Woe to the father whose children are girls. It is said: Whoever teaches his daughter Torah, teaches her obscenity. It is said: The voice of woman leads to lewdness.[1] I am told to light candles in honor of the holy word, revere my husband and raise my children, cook and clean and manage a joyous household in the name of these texts. What right have I to comment? None, none, none. What calls me to do it? I have no answer but the drops of my blood, that say *try*.

Is there a right of love and anger?

I'm afraid: but it seems obvious, doesn't it. *Everyone is afraid. Do what you fear.* I don't know if it says that in some text, but women have to run on these hobbled legs, have to pray and sing with our throttled voices. We have to do it sometime. We have to enter the tents/texts, invade the sanctuary, uncover the father's nakedness. We have to do it, believe it or not, because we love him. It won't kill him. He won't kill us.

Touch me not, thou shalt not touch, command the texts. Thou shalt not uncover. But I shall. Thou shalt not eat it lest ye die. I shall not surely die.

The stories call me simultaneously from outside and from within myself. They are composed, we are told, by a male God dictating them to a male visionary, Moses, so they are composed by not-me. The heroes of the stories are not-me. Likewise the innumerable generations of commentators, who until now have been not-me, but wise and learned men who would consider it improper or perhaps sacrilegious for a woman to express opinions regarding Scripture. What then compels me to comment? What made me recognize when I first read these tales that I had known them always, as if they were dreams of my own that I had forgotten? The tales of the tribe. My tribe, therefore my stories. The shapes my soul has always unconsciously or half-consciously assumed. But to say this is to say nothing. What do the stories mean to me and what do I mean to them? I cannot tell until I write.

(To make each story open to me, as I climb into and into it. To make each story open, as I climb down into its throat.)

. . .

The stories are part of a book compiled over a span of perhaps a thousand years, equivalent to the time between Beowulf and T. S. Eliot, and edited for a period lasting from about four hundred years before the birth of Jesus to over a hundred years afterward. A thick quilt, patchwork, braiding, embroidery. No single author. Multiple authors. Some threads of language go back to Phoenician, Hittite, Ugaritic, Sumerian poems. The stories form a sequence which is itself a story, the tale of our, that is my, long relationship with God.

Reader, you are supposed to ask: does God exist. Is the Holy One in that book real or imagined. And then what about Abraham, Moses, and so on, what is their status vis-à-vis 'reality'. Is Abraham in other words a body, a material fact, or is he a spirit, an imagined fact. I confess these questions do not interest me. For who among us, solid flesh though we are, is not partially fictional. And who among us supposes herself the inventor of her own fiction. And who is not just such an aggregation of scraps, just such a patchwork as Abraham, a basket containing millennia. Is God a myth? A set of myths? Then so am I, so are you.

Let me suppose that Abraham is an imagined fact. Let me suppose that God is another. Let me suppose that I am a third. We are all equally real in the dimension of language, which is where we intersect. It is here that we meet, marry, wrestle, bargain, love and fear one another, find ecstasy and desolation, form some kind of tangled ganglia, push and pull one another forward in the story.

The story of history, the movement into and through time. In the beginning, in Genesis, there is much more woman. As in myths, as in dreams, or as in families. In one telling of the story it is said that woman and man are alike, at the very beginning, created simultaneously in the image of their creator. In another it is said that woman is more powerful, more intellectual, more ambitious and daring than her mate, he a first draft made of mud, she the improved version.[2] Then man gradually becomes more powerful, while woman continues to act, laugh, talk, and in part control the course of the narrative. Later there is less and less woman. As in most nation states. As in 'public' life. As in law, theology, and war. After the Exodus women start to become insignificant. Shepherds and their domestic stories become warriors and their military stories. The penis, that flexible flesh, hardens into the metal of the sword.

> The sword thins to the sceptre.
> The sceptre dictates and the pen is born.

Myth moves forward into legend, legend melts into history. Annals, records, myths, legends, rituals, laws converge: they become the accepted canon, the official texts. The women disappear, they cease to act, they become objects of the law, they become property, they become unclean, they become a snare, they become a metaphor. The disappearance of the women is the condition and consequence of the male covenant. Meanwhile at every step the men advance into individuality. No two alike. Forward march our patriarchs, our heroes, our judges, our kings. Abraham, Isaac, Jacob, Joseph. Moses and Joshua. Samuel, Saul, David, Solomon. They carry populations in their loins, in their orbits, in their mysterious magnetic fields. They embody and enact the will of the Holy One, enduring the lava of punishments and promises poured over their covenanted heads. Their circumcision the sign of the covenant.

My fathers, whom I intend to pursue. Their stories mine. My fathers, whose meanings I am laboring to understand, since to understand them is to understand myself. Needing to know whom

I love, whom I hate. Needing to remember that I am my fathers,
just as much as I am my mothers.

Yet the beginning is not the beginning. Inside the oldest stories are
older stories, not destroyed but hidden. Swallowed. Mouth songs.
Wafers of parchment, layer underneath layer. Nobody knows how
many. The texts retain traces, leakages, lacunae, curious figures of
speech, jagged irruptions. What if I say these traces too are mine? If
I pull at the texts like the yard worker who goes out with a rake in
early spring. She pulls at the compacted layers of leaves, heaving them
up from the ground. Wet and soggy, they resist, they cling to the
earth. She stands in the yard sniffing the fresh air. Under the compost
there is bare ground from which a few thin chartreuse sprouts have
begun to uncurl. A dog barks somewhere in the neighborhood.
Another beginning, I tell myself. Nor is the canonized text a final text,
nor can the writing be finished. For I remember slavery; I remember
liberation from slavery. This is what the Lord did for me when I came
out of Egypt. I remember a covenant in which I promised to serve
God's purposes. And what if I say the purposes have not yet been all
revealed?

> They say no, they say blasphemer, they say false,
> They say whore, they say bitch, they say witch,
> They say ignorant woman, they lock me up for crazy
>
> *Of course I'm crazy*
> *Digging and digging*
> *Smelling the ground*
> *I talk to myself and see things*
> *I remember things, and sometimes I remember*
> *My time when I was powerful, bringing birth*
> *My time when I was just, composing law*
> *My time playing before the throne*
> *When my name was woman of valor*
> *When my name was wisdom*
> *And what if I say the Torah is*
> *My well of living waters*
> *Mine*

Notes

1. In traditional Judaism women could not (and among the Orthodox still cannot) be counted in a minyan or lead religious services; could pray in synagogue only behind the mechitza, a curtain which separated them from the males; their testimony (like that of minors, deaf-mutes, and idiots) was inadmissable in a Jewish court. Whether or not women should study Torah was debated for centuries, but the dominant view in Talmudic and rabbinic tradition is that women are endowed with a simple spirituality which should be centered in the fulfillment of household tasks, the basic moral education of their children, and the support of their husbands; they should not be educated as scholars, although the ideal Jew spends his life studying sacred texts. The most famous exception to the rule that excludes women from learning is Beruriah, wife of the great rabbi Meir, who became a scholar in her own right and whose opinions are quoted in Talmud. Legend relates that Rabbi Meir in order to prove that women were immoral ordered one of his students to seduce her. After protracted resistance, Beruriah succumbed, and then killed herself. The rabbinical consensus is that Rabbi Meir's case was proved, and that learning endangers woman's virtue regardless of her intelligence.

2. The two creation narratives in Genesis provide the most familiar example of the redactors' attempts to join accounts from heterogeneous sources. In Genesis 1:1–3 the simultaneous creation of male and female earthlings climaxes the creation of nature and is followed by the sabbath; but in Genesis 1:4–3:19 God creates first man, then other animals, then woman, and the woman proceeds to show all the initiative in the story. These and similar textual inconsistencies ('fault lines' to Geoffrey Hartman, 'the abrasive frictions, the breaks, the discontinuities of readability' to Roland Barthes) make Scripture a garden of delight to the exegete, the theologian, the mystic, and the poet such as myself. I return again and again to these places of mystery.

Herbert Anderson and Edward Foley, 'The Power of Storytelling'

in *Mighty Stories, Dangerous Rituals: Weaving Together the Human and the Divine*, San Francisco: Jossey Bass, 1998, pp. 9–16, 18–19.

In Mighty Stories, Dangerous Rituals, *the North American pastoral theologians Herbert Anderson and Edward Foley discuss the different roles narrative plays in personal and social well-being. They use categories devised by John Dominic Crossan (1975) to distinguish between mythic and parabolic stories. Mythic stories help people to mediate and reconcile life experiences into a coherent whole and offer a sense of unity, solidity and structure and hope. Parabolic stories, in contrast, highlight irreconcilable opposites, the dangerous contradictions that unsettle us and the challenges that provoke difficult choice. Human beings require both types of stories in order to attain a mature and responsive outlook on life. Both also function as ways to encounter the divine. However, the natural tendency to seek ease and safety can result in us failing to attend to parabolic narratives until forced to do so by tragedy or personal loss.*

Their consideration of the significance of narrative leads Anderson and Foley to conclude that at the heart of pastoral care is the need to help people find ways of narrating the stories of their lives in a manner that helps them respond positively to 'new worlds of possibility'. For religious believers a crucial aspect of this process entails weaving personal narratives together with the sacred texts and ritual practices of their traditions. The stories of God we encounter in Scripture, and re-enact in sacraments and celebrations, have the power to become revelatory for us only as an integral part of the stories of our own lives.

When Stories Conceal

Stories, as such, are not fundamentally designed to provide essential facts or data about ourselves or our world, although that may some-times be a purpose. Even so, it is important that our stories fit the understanding and interpretation of our life by others. Sometimes our storytelling is used only as a tool to develop an identity and offer a respectable self-interpretation of ourselves for ourselves. Thus we shape the events and circumstances of our lives into a story that reinforces our self-identity and worldview without attention to the interpretation of others. When our narrative does not square with the stories that others tell of us, we isolate ourselves.

Consider the following narrative as an exercise in self-deception. Chris believes that life owes him much more than he has thus far received. At thirty-two, he is likeable and seemingly well-motivated but always in trouble financially or relationally. When confronted with one more loss of a job, end of a relationship, or arrest for public intoxication, Chris will explain his situation by reminiscing about his wonderful childhood.

The way he remembers it, Chris was raised in an idyllic family setting with indulgent parents, who gave him and his siblings what-ever they wanted. His childhood home in rural Ohio was spacious and well-appointed on the inside and crowned outside with a huge swimming pool. Because his parents entertained a lot, there was always a party on the horizon, with more than adequate amounts of food, recreational drugs, and liquor. Chris began drinking in his early teens, about the same time he began smoking marijuana. Things began to fall apart when Chris was in his early twenties. The family business failed, the homestead was sold, the money disappeared, and the good life came to an end. After a falling out with his parents, Chris moved to Texas and took a job waiting tables. Now he is stuck in a trade that he hates.

Chris reports that he despises his life. He cannot understand why the family business failed. He is very bitter that his parents sold the home he loved so much. 'It's not fair,' he often complains. 'I deserve better than this.' The tragic symbol of his unhappy life is the ever-present lottery ticket in his pocket. 'One day I am going to win a million bucks,' he announces. 'Then I'm going back to Ohio and buy back the old house. Everything will be as it should be.'

This story, which Chris repeats with unflagging consistency after a few beers, illustrates how the privilege of self-interpretation can be abused. His narrative does not include any episodes about his drinking, his various arrests for driving while intoxicated, or the many demolished relationships that have unraveled in the midst of his drinking sprees. The most dominant force in his life – his alcoholism – is never mentioned. Rather, his carefully constructed tale is of a congenial childhood and a promise of a great future gone awry. What appears to Chris to be a matter of survival actually fabricates an identity that disconnects him from the present and traps him in a past that never was. The private interpretation of his story has led Chris into a cul-de-sac of only private meanings. We are in danger of being isolated in our life narrative whenever our storytelling conceals more than it reveals.

When Stories Reveal

When we tell stories about ourselves, we are often amazed to discover unknown commonalties that bond us quickly with strangers or deepen the affections of friends or family. Not every exercise of our narrative function is self-evading. When our autobiographical tales are self-effacing, disarming, or amusing, they reveal the kind of openness that is necessary for building community. Storytelling not only makes us human; it creates vulnerability. Melissa Musick Nussbaum admits that her autobiographical stories, which originated as stories told to her own children, have such a purpose. A particular favorite of hers – and her children – is titled 'The Time I Wet My Pants at Sue Harris's Wedding':

> I was Sue Harris's flower girl. I was dressed in a stiff full slip undergirding an explosion of pastel taffeta. The slip crackled when I sat. It was an outfit almost too gorgeous to bear, and the feel of it against my skin sent me into tremors of hopping on one leg in delight. My mother interpreted this as a full bladder hop. She was partly right. A few minutes before the wedding was about to begin my mother suggested, then demanded, that I go to the bathroom. Of course, I needed to go, but I couldn't bear to miss the various domestic dramas being performed around me in the vestibule . . .
>
> I have tried to remember as I mopped puddles over the years how it felt to want so badly to stay for the action and so badly to relieve one's bladder that one did both. Which is what happened to me at Sue Harris's wedding. I did need to urinate, and I did need to stay. So I let loose all over the solemn stone floor of the First Methodist Church in Tulia, Texas. I stepped away from the grown-ups, over to the side in a dark corner to urinate. A janitor happened by and, seeing the yellow stream trickling down the steps, asked me suspiciously, . . . 'Where did that water come from?' I looked him sweetly in the eye and said, 'I don't know; it must be raining,' and marched soggily down the aisle, strewing rose petals and savoring the interesting sensation of my lace-socked feet squashing in my Sunday shoes [Nussbaum, 1995, p. 696].

Nussbaum admits that this kind of storytelling reveals something about herself that is important for her children. Having them imagine her shamefaced before others, when they are so often shamefaced before her, allows her children 'to imagine themselves as grown-ups' and to know that things will not always be as bewildering as they are in childhood. Nussbaum concedes, however, that such storytelling is not only important for her children; it is also important to her. In her words, 'To tell the story allows me to remember how it was to be a child: noisy, sticky, curious, bold, clumsy, eager, cruel' (p. 696).

Telling stories or fashioning a narrative are not, at their root, just speech patterns but life patterns – not simply a way of talking to explain the world or communicate ourselves but a way of being in the world that, in turn, becomes the basis of our explanations and interpretations. Our stories are not so much a part of experience as they are the premise of experience. An amazing dynamic exists between our lives and our stories: each one shapes the other. Our collective life experiences are interpreted through a personal narrative framework and shaped into a master story that, in turn, influences subsequent interpretations. Each of us carries a personally constructed narrative framework into each situation we encounter. This framework becomes a key for interpreting reality and determines to what extent the stories we compose reveal and conceal.

Each of us is a storyteller, actively composing the story of our life. Chris, for example, is not simply mouthing stories about his life that deny his alcoholism; he is living a narrative that does the same. Even so, we do not shape this narrative alone. There are many outside influences over which we may have very little control. Chris's parents did indulge him and his siblings. The family business did fail, and financial stability deteriorated. Chris's alcoholism is a disease, traceable to his mother's drinking problem and socially traceable to a family that perpetually partied. Like the rest of us, Chris is more a coauthor than a solitary narrator of his life.

A life narrative is a joint product of person and environment. The reality that we coauthor our narrative with others parallels the idea that becoming a person is an ongoing process shaped by and shaping a wide range of agents and institutions. Fashioning stories is an act of creating one's life in ways that include these coauthors, whose influences should not be minimized or ignored. Theologian Rebecca Chopp has described this process in a way that bypasses old battles about determinism. 'Our stories are related to but not determined by factors such as events beyond which we have no control, other actors to which we are in relation, and traditions that we appropriate or resist' (Chopp, 1995, p. 32). Although Chopp is using narrative agency to identify the new freedom women have to name their experience, women and men alike need to recognize that writing one's story is a complex process with more than one collaborator.

We will return later to the theme of coauthoring when we consider the connection between divine and human narratives. Understanding our story in relation to God's story is necessary for persons of faith. Nonetheless, even though others, including God, have a part in authoring our story, we are ultimately responsible for the narrative. For that reason, we need not be trapped in or by our story. Even Chris, while mired in a powerful tale of self-deception, has the capacity – although maybe not the will – to author a different life and craft a different narrative. The power of interpretation is always ours. It is therefore always possible to narrate our lives in another way.

Consequently, storytelling is an act of hope, and even defiance, because it carries within it the power to change.

Mythic and Parabolic Narratives

As previously noted, we use stories to construct meaning and communicate ourselves to one another. Thus our storytelling could be envisioned as having an internal purpose (making sense of the world) and an external purpose (communicating ourselves to others). As the stories of Chris and Melissa illustrate, however, there are many ways to narrate our lives. In some measure, this diversity exists because of the great differences in characters and events that distinguish one story from another. Each of us has different coauthors, different set designers, different choreographers, production managers, and supporting casts. Stories differ in content and complexity. The dissimilarities in our stories may also come from our different styles of developing them. Some storytelling has a didactic or apologetic character. Other stories amuse us, or they satirize or lampoon an event, a personality, or even ourselves. Apart from apology or satire, we also fashion stories as mysteries or romance, comedies or tragedies, adventures or character studies.

If understanding the ambiguity of life and communicating that understanding to others are basic reasons for the narratives we fashion, then we need to reflect upon which form of storytelling will most accurately convey our particular understanding. Of all the classifications possible for understanding how we fashion our stories, John Dominic Crossan's polar opposites of myth and parable are two of the most useful. In his classic study on parables, *The Dark Interval* (1975), Crossan argues that myth and parable define the limits of a story's possibilities. Crossan suggests that all narration can be understood as existing someplace along a continuum between these two binary opposite forms.

Myth for Crossan does not mean a pleasant story that is untrue, or what he calls sophisticated lying. Nor is it some type of legend populated with gods and goddesses. Rather, in the technical sense in which he employs it, *myth* refers mostly to mediation and reconciliation. Crossan draws upon the work of the French philosopher Claude Lévi-Strauss, whose basic thesis, Crossan explains, is that 'myth performs the specific task of mediating irreducible opposites' (Crossan, 1975, p. 51). Myth bridges the gap between apparently irreconcilable stances, individuals, or situations and demonstrates that mediation is possible.

The classic fairy tale *Beauty and the Beast* is a myth. In its simplest form, the story is about Beauty, the youngest and most beautiful daughter of a once-wealthy merchant. She is dedicated to her father, even though he has lost his fortune and has been abandoned by his other children. When the father becomes lost in a forest and accidentally wanders into the den of the fearsome Beast, he becomes the Beast's captive. Eventually the father is ransomed by his daughter Beauty, who exchanges places with him. In turn, the Beast falls in love with Beauty. When the Beast finally wins her over and she consents to marry him, the Beast is released from the spell that had possessed him and revealed to be a handsome and wealthy prince.

This fairy tale is a myth in Crossan's technical sense. It is a tale of many opposites: beauty/beast, poor/rich, commoner/royalty, woman/man, captive/free. In the conclusion of the story, however, all of these apparently opposing forces are reconciled. In the process, the core meaning of myth is revealed: mediation is possible. Crossan concludes, 'What myth does is not just to attempt the mediation in story of what is sensed as irreconcilable, but in, by, and through this attempt it establishes the possibility of reconciliation' (Crossan, 1975, p. 53). The double function of myth is this: to resolve particular contradictions and, more important, to create a belief in the permanent possibility of reconciliation.

Parable, on the other hand, is not about mediation but about contradiction. It creates irreconcilability where before there was reconciliation. According to Crossan, parable has a double function that opposes the double function of myth. Parable not only introduces contradiction into situations of complacent security, 'it challenges the fundamental principle of reconciliation by making us aware of the fact that we made up the reconciliation' (Crossan, 1975, p. 57). If the stories we create are to be authentic reflections of the lives we live, we need room for ambiguity and vulnerability. Parabolic narratives show the seams and edges of the myths we fashion. Parables show the fault lines beneath the comfortable surfaces of the worlds we build for ourselves. Myth may give stability to our story, but parables are agents of change and sometimes disruption. For that reason, parable is often an unsettling experience.

Flannery O'Connor was a novelist who excelled in parable. In her short story 'Revelation', an upstanding Christian woman, Ruby Turpin, and an acne-scarred college girl named Mary Grace meet in a doctor's office. Ruby Turpin chatters away about her great gratitude to God for giving her such a blessed life. While others ignored Ruby or listened politely, Mary Grace was enraged. Finally, no longer able to bear Mrs Turpin's public 'thank you Jesus', Mary Grace hurled a book at Ruby and then leapt on top of her. Mrs. Turpin was stunned not only by the physical attack but by the girl's chilling words, 'Go back to hell where you came from, you old wart hog.'

While Ruby was not physically hurt, she could not shake the memory of the girl's hateful words. Why had she, a hardworking, churchgoing Christian, been singled out for this message? There were real trash in that same waiting room who really deserved those words. In her final confrontation with God, Ruby thought that if God liked trash so much she might just join their ranks, quit work, and spend her days lounging around. Ruby could be shiftless like the other trash. The thought of Mary Grace's insult seemed as though it was an insult from God. Anger rose strong and quickly inside of Ruby until she shook her fist to the heavens and shouted out to God. 'Who do you think you are?'

It was at that point that Ruby Turpin had her 'revelation', for as she looked toward the heavens she seemed to see a whole company of white trash, now clean for the first time, moving toward heaven. There were

> battalions of freaks and lunatics shouting and clapping and leap-
> ing like frogs. And bringing up the end of the procession was a
> tribe of people whom she recognized at once as those who, like
> herself and [her husband] Claud, had always had a little of every-
> thing and the God-given wit to use it right. She leaned forward
> to observe them closer. They were marching behind the others
> with great dignity, accountable as they had always been for good
> order and common sense and respectable behavior. They alone
> were on key. Yet she could see by their shocked and altered faces
> that even their virtues were being burned away [O'Connor, 1965,
> pp. 217–218].

Ruby Turpin's encounter with Mary Grace had shattered her vision of God's well-ordered universe and pulled the rug out from under her own secure place in that world. The vision she saw contradicted all of her tidy expectations. She was a hardworking, decent, Christian woman who had the world and God figured out. Everything was in its place. After her encounter with Mary Grace, however, Ruby Turpin found herself in a very different world, confronted with an unexpected kind of God. As we leave her at the end of 'Revelation', stunned and vulnerable, it is unclear how well Ruby will navigate this new terrain. What is clear, however, is that her view of the world has been turned upside down by a parabolic vision of clean trash 'rumbling toward heaven'.

Living Between Myth and Parable

Mythic narrations comfort us and assure us that everything is going to be all right; parables challenge and dispute the reconciliation that our myths have created. Myths allow us to dream and to believe in a future better than the present; parables disallow us from living in a dream world, call us to confront the present, and deter us from trusting in any hope that does not face the hard reality of the present. The irony, of course, is that these are complementary narrative forms, and human beings need both of them.

If our narrative is out of touch with the parabolic, for example, there is the real danger that we will be trapped in a dishonest dream, as Chris's story demonstrates. Although his body is shutting down from years of alcoholic poisoning, and his personal life is crumbling, Chris continues to narrate the tale of his idyllic childhood. And with every purchase of a lottery ticket, he wagers that the dream can be recovered. The hope he lives, however, is more than simply false – it is destructive. His unwillingness and inability to demythologize his childhood and wager on something other than winning the lottery is figuratively and literally killing him. The problem is not that Chris has dreams; the problem is that in his mythic fashioning of life, he has nothing else.

A life devoid of mythic narration, on the other hand, is a life without the possibility of reconciliation and ultimate peace. It is true that parables challenge our myths and the reconciliations we have created. But parables can only subvert a world already created in and by myth. In doing so, parables give rise to a new reconciliation and therefore to a new myth. Melissa Musick Nussbaum's parabolic revelation of her childhood challenges the myth of the perfect parent who was once a perfect child. Her children love the myth-shattering pants-wetting story:

> Since their birth, I have been set up before them as the final arbiter in matters of morals and hygiene ... I'm the one who, to little children dribbling on the toilet and absentmindedly picking their noses, is Other, She-Who-Is-Always-Right. But to hear that story, and others like it, is to know that I, appearances and admonitions to the contrary notwithstanding, have walked a familiar road [Nussbaum, 1995, p. 696].

Nussbaum's parabolic narration debunks the myth of the perfect parent, the pure arbitrator and the unmoved mover. In doing so, it creates a new myth: that imperfect children can grow up to be lovable, imperfect adults. Thus parables are not about eliminating reconciliation; rather, they are about challenging the reconciliation with which we are comfortably living. The elimination of all myth, without the ultimate possibility for harmonizing all of those discordant strands in our lives, could leave us awash with meaninglessness or on the brink of despair.

While both mythic and parabolic stories are necessary for an authentic narrative, the parabolic story is more difficult to master. Human beings are much more inclined to revel in the world of the mythic. There are obvious reasons for this. The underlying message of mythic narration is that things are going to be all right. For example, in terms of the fairy tale *Beauty and the Beast*, one might imagine, 'If things could work out for Beauty – who was separated from her poor and ailing father, and was the captive of a Beast – then they could certainly work out for me.' Myth engages the natural optimism of the human spirit and the physiological instinct of the human organism. Our bodies struggle to live, and with every ounce of strength, they reject the ultimate parable of our own death. It is the death parable, however, which ultimately must be embraced in order to make the transition to the myth of eternal life.

. . .

We Are Our Stories

There are several implications for pastoral ministry from constructing meaning and communicating ourselves through story. The first is that people such as Chris need not be trapped in their stories. It is possible to find new stories for shaping meaning in our lives and by so doing bring forth new worlds of possibility. The task of pastoral care is to help people reframe their lives in the light of God's story for the sake of greater freedom and responsibility.

Second, it is more difficult to be absolute about any interpretation of reality from a narrative perspective. If all reality is socially constructed, constituted through narrative, and organized and maintained through stories, then we need to allow for the possibility of several meanings of the divine story as it has been mediated through the Bible and religious traditions.

Third, linking the human and the divine story becomes a creative but very complex activity that depends on respecting differences. Although we construct stories to organize the disparate elements of our lives and make sense of the world for ourselves, the stories we fashion will enhance or diminish the possibility of community. Stories that conceal more than they reveal are likely to foster isolation rather than intimacy. Therefore, since creating community is one aim of telling stories, honesty, authenticity, and a recognition of the parabolic in life should be part of every story. We will revisit this theme throughout this book.

Finally, it is important for the sake of Christian ministry to acknowledge that fashioning a narrative is a personal responsibility even though we are never the sole author of the story. Each life narrative is an individual creation achieved largely through improvising rather than pursuing a vision already defined or living out someone else's narrative. And yet each narrative is composed of many stories with many coauthors. For persons of faith, God is understood as one of those authors. One key way to increase our awareness of the enduring link between God's narrative and ours is to foster greater reciprocity between worship and pastoral care in the practice of ministry. Stories are mighty and dangerous, but so are rituals, especially those connected with religious expression. Ritual is one place in our regulated lives where we remember the stories of God that have the power to transform us and take us to a new place. As we will demonstrate throughout this book, worship and pastoral care are two complementary aspects of ministry that have a special capacity for respecting and merging the divine and human story.

What is most important about this theme is that we cannot and need not escape the narrative structure of human life. Telling stories is the way to be human. Even as we create our stories, we are at the same time being shaped by the stories we fashion. This narrative approach to life is risky, however. Authentic life as individuals and in community reveals more than it conceals. It keeps the tension between mythic and parabolic stories so that the stories we tell will reveal enough ambiguity and vulnerability to create and sustain human communities.

References

Chopp, R. *Saving Work: Feminist Practices of Theological Education*, Louisville, Ky.: Westminster, John Knox Press, 1995.

Crossan, J. D. *The Dark Interval: Towards a Theology of Story*, Niles, Ill.: Argus, 1975.

Nussbaum, M. M., 'Sleeping on the Wing.' *Assembly*, 1995, 21(5), 696–697, 702.
O'Connor, F., *Everything That Rises Must Converge*, New York: Noonday Press, 1965.

James Nelson, 'Doing Body Theology',

in *Body Theology*, Louisville, Kentucky: Westminster John Knox Press, 1992, pp. 42–46, 50–4.

Constructive narrative theology entails weaving together divine and human stories and sees this as possible because God has become flesh and human beings are also speakers of the transcendent word. In this extract from his important book Body Theology *(1992), James Nelson explores the significance of the body as a source for knowledge of God.*

For too long, he argues, Christians have viewed their bodies as an impediment to theological thinking rather than a site of revelation. A new awareness will entail telling the stories of our embodied experience in a way that makes clear the authority of bodily knowing. Our appreciation of the delicacy, interconnectedness and beauty of life will make for better understandings of what it means to be human. They will also contribute to profound reassessments of such fundamental doctrinal categories as incarnation and salvation as we begin to learn what it means to acknowledge, 'Good is the flesh that the Word has become'.

[O]ur religious tradition has too often forgotten the embodied self. Through the centuries, most theologizing, unfortunately, has not taken seriously the fact that when we reflect theologically we inevitably do so as embodied selves. Male theologians, in particular, have long assumed that the arena of theology is that of spirit and mind, far removed from the inferior, suspect body. Consequently, we have begun more deductively than inductively. We have begun with propositions and attempted to move from the abstract to the concrete. The feminist and the lesbian/gay liberation movements have now reminded us to take body experience as important theological data.

For centuries, however, it was not generally recognized that human bodies are active sources of meaning. Rather, it was believed that bodies were like cameras in a photographic process, simply recording external things mechanistically, things that were passed through the nervous system to form images in the brain according to physical laws. Now, however, there is reason to understand differently.[1] The body has its own ways of knowing. The body often speaks its mind.

Thus, our concern here is not primarily with the 'body-object', as studied by the anatomist or physiologist, but rather the 'body-subject', the embodiment of our consciousness, our bodily sense of how we are in the world. Our concern is the interaction of the 'givenness' of our fleshly realities and the ways in which we interpret them. It is our bodily sense of connections to the world, our bodily sense of the space and time we are in, our bodily knowing of the meanings of our relationships.[2]

Starting with Experience

Body theology begins with the concrete. It does not begin with certain doctrinal formulations, nor with certain portions of a creed, nor with a 'problem' in the tradition (though all of these sources may well contribute insight later). Rather, body theology starts with the fleshly experience of life – with our hungers and our passions, our bodily aliveness and deadness, with the smell of coffee, with the homeless and the hungry we see on our streets, with the warm touch of a friend, with bodies violated and torn apart in war, with the scent of a honeysuckle or the soft sting of autumn air on the cheek, with bodies tortured and raped, with the bodyself making love with the beloved and lovemaking with the earth.

The task of body theology is critical reflection on our bodily experience as a fundamental realm of the experience of God. It is not, in the first instance, a theological description of bodily life from a supra-bodily vantage point (as if that were possible, which in actuality it is not). Nor is it primarily concerned with articulating norms for the proper 'use' of the body. Body theology necessarily begins with the concreteness of our bodily experience, even while it recognizes that this very concreteness is filtered through the interpretive web of meanings that we have come to attach to our bodily life.

After all, we know the world and respond to it through our embodiedness. That is how as little children we learned to differentiate ourselves from other persons: we touched them, heard their voices, saw their movements as other than our own. As children we learned to make sense of language through body motions and images.

If as adults we have been taught to abstract much of our knowledge from the body, that only makes both our knowledge and our bodies less real. Moral knowledge, for example, is bodily: if we cannot somehow feel in the gut the meanings of justice and injustice, of hope and hopelessness, those terms remain abstract and unreal.

The way we feel about our embodiedness significantly conditions the way we feel about the world. Studies in body psychology, for example, disclose strong correlations between self-body connectedness and the capacity for ambiguity tolerance. The more connected and comfortable I am with my bodily reality, the more I am able to accept the confusing mix of things in the world I experience. Contrarily, there are also strong correlations between body alienation and the propensity toward dichotomous reality perceptions: the more I feel distant from my body, the greater my tendency to populate my perceived world with sharply etched 'either-ors' (either me or not-me, we or they, good or bad, right or wrong, black or white, sick or well, true or false, heterosexual or homosexual).[3] Our body realities do shape our moral perceptions in ways we have seldom realized.

'We do not just *have* bodies, we *are* bodies.' This sentence is both a hopeful statement of faith and a lived experience. It is part of our faith heritage. Hebraic anthropology was remarkably unitary about the bodyself, and when the Christian tradition is purged of its dualistic accretions it too incarnationally proclaims the unitary human being. But let us be clear about the difference between a *dualism* and a *duality*. A dualism (like a dichotomy) is the experience of two utterly different elements at war with each other. At times they may exist in uneasy truce, but always there is hostility. A duality (or polarity) is the perception of two elements which, while distinguishable from each other, truly belong together. Sometimes the two elements may be experienced in creative tension, but always they belong together. Thus, the alienation of body from spirit is dualism, or polarization. The sense that there are different dimensions of myself but that I am essentially one is the perception of duality, or polarity, within my essential unity.

While our self-experience is too frequently dualistic and divisive, we also know the reality of our bodyself unity. That, too, is our lived experience. We feel 'most ourselves' when we experience such bodyself integration. When, in illness, the body feels alien to us we say, 'I'm not myself today.' And we feel most fully ourselves when bodily connected with each other and the earth. The unitary bodyself, then, is not simply an abstract hope, a revelation 'from outside' imposed on a very different reality. We are able to articulate this faith claim and we are moved to do so precisely because this too is part of our body experience.

On the other hand, we do live between the times, knowing well the ravages of our body dualisms very personally, but also socially and planetarily. We have been taught that not only is the body different from the real core of selfhood, it is also lower and must be controlled by that which is higher. Our language itself is often strongly dualistic: to say, 'I *have* a body' seems much more 'natural' than 'I *am* a body.' Certain experiences – notably illness, aging, and death – seem to confirm the otherness of my body. In those situations, my body seems radically different from me. Though the body is 'me', the body is also 'it', a thing, a burden to be borne, to be put up with, to be tolerated, sometimes an enemy lived with in warfare or uneasy truce. Then, though the body is 'mine,' I am also 'its'.

Thus, for good and for ill, the body has theological and ethical relevance in a host of ways. And our bodily experience is always sexual. Such experience, obviously, is not always genital – actually, only infrequently so. Sexuality is far more than what we do with our genitals. It is our way of being in the world as bodyselves who are gendered biologically and socially, who have varying sexual orientations, who have the capacity for sensuousness, who have the need for intimacy, who have varied and often conflicting feelings about what it means to be bodied. It is all of this body experience that is foundational to our moral agency: our capacities for action and power, our abilities to tolerate ambiguity, our capacities for moral feeling. Our bodily experience significantly colors our interpretations of social relations, communities, and institutions which are the stuff of ethics.

Similarly, our body experience lends considerable shape to our basic theological perspectives. These days we have been frequently and rightly reminded that the images and metaphors we find most meaningful to our experience of God are inevitably connected to our lifelong body experience. In contrast to the anti-body images of experiencing God, listen to the positive body revelation in Brian Wren's hymn 'Good Is the Flesh' (based on Gen. 1:31, John 1:14, and John 14:23):

> Good is the flesh that the Word has become,
>   good is the birthing, the milk in the breast,
>   good is the feeding, caressing and rest,
>   good is the body for knowing the world,
> Good is the flesh that the Word has become.

Good is the body for knowing the world,
  sensing the sunlight, the tug of the ground,
  feeling, perceiving, within and around,
  good is the body, from cradle to grave,
Good is the flesh that the Word has become.

Good is the body, from cradle to grave,
  growing and ageing, arousing, impaired,
  happy in clothing, or lovingly bared,
  good is the pleasure of God in our flesh,
Good is the flesh that the Word has become.

Good is the pleasure of God in our flesh,
  longing in all, as in Jesus, to dwell,
  glad of embracing, and tasting, and smell,
  good is the body, for good and for God,
Good is the flesh that the Word has become.[4]

. . .

Defining an Incarnational Body Theology

What, then, is body theology? It is nothing more, nothing less than our attempts to reflect on body experience as revelatory of God. How can we understand both the givenness of our body realities and the meanings that we ascribe to them, and how can we interpret these in ways that nurture the greater wholeness of our lives in relation to God, each other, and the earth? Obviously, there is no single path. But one approach of crucial importance to Christians is in exploring the meanings of 'incarnation'.

Webster's primary definition for incarnation is simply *embodiment* – being made flesh. Theologically, it means *God's* embodiment. Christianly, it means *Christ*. In particular, it means Jesus as the Christ, the expected and anointed one. Through the lens of this paradigmatic embodiment of God, however, Christians can see other incarnations: the *christic* reality expressed in other human beings in their God-bearing relatedness. Indeed, the central purpose of Christology, I take it, is not affirmations about Jesus as the Christ. Rather, affirmations about Jesus are in the service of revealing God's christic presence and activity in the world now.

While this understanding of the main purpose of Christology may seem at odds with much in the tradition, I believe it faithful to tradition's intent. Christologies, our reflections about the meanings of Christ, serve best when they clarify the present activity and embodiment of God, not when they keep our vision fixed on a past epiphany. Indeed, traditional Christologies frequently have raised difficult problems. The formula of a hypostatic union of two natures was largely based on a dualistic metaphysic and has perpetuated it. Beginning with the assumption that divine nature and human nature were essentially foreign to each other, the question then became, how can these two utterly different natures be united in one being?

Confining the divine incarnation exclusively to Jesus has tended to make him a docetic exception to our humanity and has disconnected the christic reality from our experience. Docetism – the early heresy that believed God took on only the *appearance* of human flesh in Jesus, but did not really enter a fully human being – is, unfortunately, still alive and well. Further, focusing on who Jesus was (the divine and human natures) has relegated his actions and relationships to secondary importance. By suggesting to many Christians that belief in a certain Christological formula is necessary for their salvation, such theologies have encouraged Christian triumphalism and have been oppressive to many persons.[5]

I have spoken of essentialism in views of the body and of objectivism in value theory. While I find some truth in each of these, they become distorted, indeed, when taken as the whole truth. Now it is time to name the parallel danger in our views of Jesus Christ. The danger becomes manifest whenever Christology succumbs to one-sided essentialism and objectivism. This happens when claims are made that through God's unilateral decision and action the 'objective' divine essence became embodied in Jesus, quite independently of his own faith, decisions, actions, relationships, and interpretations. When such interpretation holds sway, not only is Jesus' humanity effectively undercut, but also all other human beings are effectively excluded from participation in the christic reality.

What is at stake for body theology is not the paradigmatic importance of God's revelation in Jesus. In our faith community's history, it is this figure and not another who has been and who is central for us. It is through him that we measure the ways we are grasped by the christic presence. But the marvelous paradox is that Jesus empties himself of claims to be the exclusive embodiment of God, and in that self-emptying opens the continuing possibility for all other persons.

The union of God and humanity in Jesus was a moral and personal union – a continuing possibility for all persons. Incarnation is always a miracle of grace, but the essence of miracle is not 'interference' in the 'natural' world by the 'supernatural'. It is the gracious (hence miraculous) discovery of who we really are, the communion of divine and human life in flesh. One essential criterion of Christological adequacy must be the moral test. Does this interpretation of Christ result in our bodying forth more of God's reality now? Does it create more justice and peace and joyous fulfillment of creaturely bodily life? Do we experience more of 'the resurrection of the body' now – the gracious gift of a fundamental trust in the present bodily reality of God, the Word made flesh?

All this suggests that the human body is language and a fundamental means of communication. We do not just use words. We *are* words. This conviction underlies Christian incarnationalism. In Jesus Christ, God was present in a human being not for the first and only time, but in a radical way that has created a new definition of who we are. In Christ we are redefined as body words of love, and such body life in us is the radical sign of God's love for the world and of the divine immediacy in the world.[6]

This incarnational perspective, only briefly sketched here, is one critical way of beginning to move into the deeper meanings of our body and sexual experience. There are other ways. Yet this path is an important part of the Christian tradition, even if it has often been muted.

It was present, for example, in the later period of the Byzantine Empire, a time in which Christ's transfiguration was seen to be at the very center of our understanding God, ourselves, and the world. It was a time that affirmed that while the final mystery of God will always remain beyond the reach of our faculties, nevertheless, in the energies of the divine action and presence, God is revealed to our bodily senses. This vision of a transfigured world, a vision at the heart of Eastern Orthodoxy, was also present in the Anglican vision of the seventeenth century. In Thomas Traherne's work, for example, it finds remarkable expression: 'By the very right of your senses, you enjoy the world ... You never enjoy the world aright, till the sea itself floweth in your veins, till you are clothed with the heavens and crowned with the stars, and perceive yourself to be the sole heir of the whole world, and more than so, because others are in it who are everyone sole heirs as well as you.'[7]

True, the developments in science and philosophy in the latter days of the seventeenth century muted that theme in the West, and ever since then it has been more difficult to see the bodily consequences of an incarnational faith. The time is upon us for recapturing the feeling for the bodily apprehension of God. When we do so, we will find ourselves not simply making religious pronouncements about the bodily life; we will enter theologically more deeply into this experience, letting it speak of God to us, and of us to God.

The significance of all this has not escaped Toni Morrison in her Pulitzer prize-winning novel, *Beloved*. A central character is Baby Suggs, grandmother and holy woman of the African American extended family who had escaped from slavery in the South only to find continued oppression by the Northern whites. Speaking to her people, Baby Suggs 'told them that the only grace they could have was the grace they could imagine. That if they could not see it, they would not have it. "Here," she said, "in this place, we flesh; flesh that weeps, laughs; flesh that dances on bare feet in grass. Love it. Love it hard. Yonder they do not love your flesh. They despise it . . . You got to love it. You." '[8] Note carefully Baby Suggs's counsel. The only grace we can have is the grace we can imagine. If we cannot see it, we will not have it.

Notes

1. See Don Johnson, *Body* (Boston: Beacon Press, 1983), esp. ch. 3.

2. See Kenneth J. Shapiro, *Bodily Reflective Modes: A Phenomenological Method for Psychology* (Durham, N. C.: Duke University Press, 1985).

3. See Seymour Fisher, *Body Experience in Fantasy and Behavior* (New York: Appleton-Century-Crofts, 1970); *Body Consciousness* (Englewood Cliffs, N.J.: Prentice-Hall, 1973); *Development and Structure of the Body Image*, vol. 2 (Hillsdale, N.J.: Lawrence Erlbaum Assocs., 1986). Fisher says, 'Although we are still in the early stages of understanding body image phenomena, we have discovered that body attitudes are woven into practically every aspect of behavior. The full range of their involvement cannot be overstated' (*Development and Structure*, 625). There is reason to assume that our bodyself experiences as females and as males are more similar than dissimilar. Here I am dealing in the basic human commonalities of body experience. Nevertheless, there are also certain important differences of world perception related to our different sexual biologies as well as to our sex-role conditioning. I have described some of these with their possible theological-ethical implications in *The Intimate Connection: Male Sexuality, Masculine Spirituality* (Philadelphia: Westminster Press, 1988).

4. Brian Wren, *Bring Many Names* (Carol Stream, Ill.: Hope Publishing Co., 1989). I wish to record my genuine gratitude to Brian Wren for dedicating this hymn to me.

5. For a helpful and extended discussion of these problems, see Tom F. Driver, *Christ in a Changing World* (New York: Crossroad, 1982).

6. Two writers who have grasped this insight well are Charles Davis, *Body as Spirit: The Nature of Religious Feeling* (New York: Seabury Press, 1976), and Arthur A. Vogel, *Body Theology* (New York: Harper & Row, 1973).

7. Thomas Traherne, *Poems, Centuries and Three Thanksgivings*, ed. Anne Ridler, 174, 177, quoted in A. M. Allchin, *The World Is a Wedding: Explorations in Christian Spirituality* (New York: Crossroad, 1982), 41.

8. Toni Morrison, *Beloved* (New York: New American Library, 1987), 88.

Heather Walton, 'This Common Road': Palm Sunday in a time of War'

in Elaine Graham and Anna Rowlands (eds), *Pathways to the Public Square*, Münster: Lit Verlag, International Practical Theology, 2005, pp. 315–18.

It is a characteristic feature of constructive narrative theology that it seeks to bring human stories into conjunction with sacred stories in order that both can be seen in a fresh way. In this sermon, delivered on Palm Sunday, Heather Walton tells the story of Jesus' entry into the city against the context of the imminent war in the Middle East in 2003. In so doing she links the modern urban environment, experienced as complex, alienating and dangerous, with the ancient Christian motif of the eschatological city of God, all set within the framework of another timeless religious practice, that of pilgrimage.

In much traditional Christian thinking, the point of a sermon is to offer an exegesis of a text and apply it to contemporary life. A narrative sermon cannot directly convey a message in this way. Rather, through the use of image, symbol and metaphor it evokes a response or, as the French philosopher Paul Ricoeur describes this, provokes an encounter. Walton uses these linguistic devices to encourage her audience to look with renewed vision at contemporary events in order to 'glimpse the mystery that surrounds us' and to interpret what they see as an epiphany of God.

In Matthew's gospel the road Jesus travels is from Jericho towards Jerusalem.

It is the final journey. Jesus stands in the ancient streets of Jericho and looks up at the solid city walls. Walls the old ones say once trembled and fell at the sound of a ram's horn. He says to his friends, those who will go with him, 'The rulers of the nations are tyrants. They lord it over their people. Don't let it be like that with you. Whoever wishes to be great amongst you must be the servant of all'. These are the words that Jesus spoke before he journeyed from the city of Jericho towards Jerusalem. He entered David's city gently, humbly, riding on a donkey.

I remember that in my children's picture book Bible Jesus was shown heading up a procession to the gates of Jerusalem. Before and after the road is clear. Someone must have stopped the road for this Palm Sunday parade. But those of us who have walked alongside Jesus from Jericho to Jerusalem know that this is a crowded route. Our small company tries to guide a couple of wayward donkeys – and perhaps one of us carries a ram's horn just for luck. We are jostled by the other travellers. Some of these believe the road belongs to them. The soldiers, the traders and the pilgrims would call this road their own.

The soldiers, of course, believe all the roads to all the cities are theirs to travel. Their ghost roads stretch across the deserts. In a skeleton tank a blackened warrior remains forever still and vigilant – guarding the military way.

In the darkened room the map of the city is flashed onto a bank of computer screens. Every road into the city can be traced. Each artery is visible. Every grid can be expanded. The city is x-rayed and revealed. It can be entered with surgical precision.

The soldiers are our friends. They carry in the big, flap, button-down pockets of their uniforms a folded document wrapped in plastic to protect it from sand or rain or snow. It is the road map for peace given to them by the rulers of the nations. It is not a map that we have been shown yet. But our small group cannot worry about this. We are trying to persuade these stubborn donkeys to tread the way we know we must follow.

Always with the soldiers travel the traders. They are enthusiastic about our journey. Glad that we are visiting their great city. 'The city is founded on trade' they tell us. 'Should the city fall we have, signed in our briefcases the contract for its reconstruction. The walls of Jericho stand again now stronger than before. For Jerusalem the tenders are in place.'

The traders are happy to talk for the essence of trade is communication. In the heart of the city is the market and 10,000 telephone lines link it to the world. Futures are bought and sold here. The traders have the ear of the government and a hot-line to the presidential palace. They travel along the electronic super-highway. They believe a fast road from the airport is essential. Along all this route are the billboards and the banners, the arches of triumph. Welcome, Welcome, Welcome. To the city of culture, the city of sport, heritage city, the city of the future. World city – sponsored by . . .

Travel quickly along this broad, bright road the traders tell us. But we cannot travel quickly. We are the wedding party and we are the funeral procession. We move slowly because of the tender love we have for the one who travels with us. We move slowly so that other wedding guests and mourners can join us. Coming out of the narrow streets and dark alleyways now: the daughter of Jerusalem and all her children.

The pilgrims believe that before the soldiers came and surveyed this straight smooth route, before the traders came with their wayside stalls and flags and banners, there was an ancient pathway to the Holy City. 'The route was not marked by the signs we now see', they tell us, 'but the true way was known to the faithful'. Beneath the paving still lies the pilgrim way – coming up from Jericho towards Jerusalem.

The soldiers listen and say nothing. They know how the rulers of the nations authorise travel, grant safe passage and send their garrisons to guard the sacred sites. The traders smile because the number of pilgrims has been predicted to rise year on year. They contribute significantly to the national economy. They have a graph to show that this is so and shares in 47 religious broadcasting companies.

We walk beside the pilgrims for a while. Sometimes it comforts us to sing the old songs and hear the deep strong harmonies. But the pilgrims tell us that the city towards which we are travelling is not real. Only the temple is real. 'City walls tumble', they say, 'but the temple walls stand firm'. The pilgrims seem to be walking the same road as us but we realise that they are in truth following their own invisible path. Jesus asked us to walk with him from Jericho to Jerusalem. This common road.

This common road. Marked by craters. Barred by checkpoints. Which is becoming crowded now. Our small band has been swollen by lines of prisoners walking in single file. The daughter of Jerusalem clutches her baby beneath her black veils and hurries to avoid the crossfire and the curfew. Those whose limbs are shattered limp beside us. There are those whose eyes are blank because they have seen too much and children who cry and cry and cry.

I can see this road. I can see this long road between Jericho and Jerusalem. The military way, the trade route, the pilgrim path and the road trod by all those others who chose, or who did not choose, to accompany Jesus on his journey.

It is the road that I have seen on my television screen for the past month now crowded with tanks and refugees. It is the road to hell and the long road to freedom. It is the road we all travel each holy week when we take in our hands the palms that will become ashes. It is the road of my life for I have been compelled to join the wedding party/funeral procession as it winds its way up the hillside to the city walls. It is probably me who is carrying the ram's horn (just for luck). I slap the side of the donkey when it stops dead in the road. I can see myself, I can see us, I can see all of us as we enter the city. We are there just on the threshold when the miracle takes place.

Jesus travelled from Jericho to Jerusalem. As he entered the city the huge walls trembled and the stones broke into song. The trees flung down their branches. The prisoners tore off their uniforms to lay them on his path – and their guards did also. The eyes that had been blind could see again and the lame could dance. The children cried. Hosanna, Hosanna. Behold daughter of Zion your lord is coming to you. Gentle, humble, riding on a donkey.

I can see that moment as we enter the city and everything and everyone rejoices. This is my vision – our common vision. It has been given to us as a sign.

It is a sign that not in some other place but right here in this city God comes to us in gentleness and humility but with a transforming power that makes the stones tremble and the trees clap their hands. Look around and catch the glimpses of a mystery that surrounds us. It can be seen. It can be felt.

It is a sign that not amongst some other people but right here amongst us the sweetness of God enters – not to overcome or subdue but to empower. It is the daughter of Zion who raises her head to see who enters. It is the little ones we have seen crying on the road who raise their palms and sing Hosanna. Our heads are raised and our mouths are full of praise. We have witnessed that this can happen.

It is a sign that not at some other time but right now we must join the procession. Affirm that in this manner of coming amongst us God is most welcome. In this way of peace, that reclaims the ghost roads, that turns the tables of the traders and topples the temple – God is welcome amongst us. In the carnival chaos our weakness is turned to strength and we are filled with joy.

It is a sign that you must keep before you as we continue on our way through this week. The helicopter gun ships are now patrolling the streets and the daughter of Jerusalem is calling for her children. It is a sign you will need when the soldiers come to make their arrest, when he is traded for twelve pieces of silver and the pilgrims call for their sacrifice. It is the sign you will need as you follow the procession on the road that leads outside the city.

Raise your head and look. It is the sign you have been given.

'Speaking in Parables': References and Further Reading

Buttita, P. (1995), 'Theological Reflection in Health Ministry' in J. D. and
E. E. Whitehead (eds), *Method in Ministry: Theological Reflection and Christian Ministry*, Kansas City, Mo.: Sheed & Ward, pp. 112–22.

Bons-Storm, R. (1996), *The Incredible Woman: Listening to Women's Silences
in Pastoral Care and Counselling*, Nashville, Tn.: Abingdon Press.

Crossan, J. D. (1975), *The Dark Interval: Towards a Theology of Story*, Niles,
Ill: Argus Communications.

The Institute for Contemporary Midrash (online), available at: http://www.
icmidrash.org/

Ricoeur, P. (1994), *Oneself As Another*, trans. Blamey, K., London & Chicago:
University of Chicago Press.

3

'Telling God's Story': Canonical Narrative Theology

Introduction

Canonical narrative theology, as the name suggests, is a form of theological reflection that is based upon the story of Jesus as recounted in Scripture. For canonical narrative theologians the Gospel stories, and in particular those recounting Jesus' passion and resurrection, hold the key to interpreting the whole of existence. They constitute the heart of reality and everything else finds its meaning and significance through them. The aim of theological reflection in this perspective is not to discover some new truth appropriate to our own age and context, but rather to enable believers to locate their diverse and particular stories within the framework of the story *God told* through Christ. Having made this act of committed identification they should then discover how their own lives become transformed into a dramatic re-presentation of the gospel in the contemporary situation. Telling the story of God, through membership of the story-formed community of the Church, is never a matter of words alone. In this method of theological reflection it is understood as a 'habitus', or way of life, in which the claims of the gospel are acknowledged in every aspect of personal and communal living.

Since earliest times the Church has encouraged believers to reflect upon and identify with the story of Jesus as told in Scripture. The rhythms of the Christian year began to emerge within the first Christian communities and, as they are formalized today, are intended to aid worshippers making their own annual journeys from Bethlehem to Jerusalem. Imitating the life of Christ has also been a resonant theme in Christian spirituality from the beginning. It received fresh focus in medieval times when the radical challenges of Franciscan piety effected their renewing influence upon the Church. On the cusp of the modern era Anabaptists offered a new witness to the gospel through taking the example of Christ as their pattern for living and refusing to bear arms, swear oaths or accommodate their worship to the requirements of the civil authorities. They were savagely persecuted as a result.

It is interesting to note that these reforming movements emerged in times of social disruption in which the question of Christian identity was clearly posed. The contemporary rediscovery of the power of canonical narrative theology also emerged out of a period of turmoil. The Swiss theologian Karl Barth is credited with inspiring the forms of canonical narrative theology we encounter today. His work emerged as a direct result of his response to the sufferings of World War One and the inadequacy of liberal theology in responding to this human tragedy. His work came to fruition in the dark days of Hitler's rise to power. The conviction he had developed that only within the 'strange world of the Bible' do we discover the truth told through Christ proved a powerful platform from which to resist fascist claims to dominance in every aspect of social and religious life.

Many canonical narrative theologians working today treasure the ancient spiritual tradition of the imitation of Christ, acknowledge the inheritance of the Anabaptists and continue to reflect upon Barth's theological legacy. However, they also acknowledge that our postmodern culture raises significant challenges. Interestingly, an emphasis upon Christian narrative identity fits happily with the turn to narrative that accompanies the collapse of foundationalist epistemologies. Canonical narrative theologians, like Frei, Lindbeck and Hauerwas, have encouraged us to regard postmodern pluralism as freeing Christians from the mistaken belief that they should seek to build a social consensus upon Christian values and beliefs. The responsibility of the Church, they argue, is not to provide a firm foundation for our cultural order but rather to generate a radical alternative to contemporary cultural values. This counter-cultural witness is courageously rooted in a faithful return to the particularity of our own story and its celebration in the words, worship and social witness of the Christian community.

A Reconstruction of the 'Primitive' Rule of Saint Francis (1209/1210) from the Regula non Bullata (1221)

This reconstruction is by John R. H. Moorman, whose rationale is set out in his book *The Sources for the Life of St Francis of Assisi*, Manchester University Press, 1940, pp. 38–54.

The text which follows represents a careful reconstruction of the primitive Rule of St Francis, there being no copies of the original Rule, submitted to the Pope around 1209, in existence today. Although scholars are in broad agreement as to the spirit and content of the early Rule, there is still some controversy between them surrounding its status. This is largely because of the differences between it and a later form of the Rule composed in 1223 and approved by Pope Honorius III.

The first Rule originates in the passionate early days of the community around St Francis. This reconstruction portrays it as a dramatic call to an evangelical life patterned on the example of the poor Christ. It assumes that this is a path that the brothers can follow, as having 'abandoned their bodies to the Lord', they make their dwelling among the poor, the powerless and the sick. The later Rule comes from a rather different period. The numbers of brothers seeking to join the order had grown, creating the need for domestic provision, organizational structures and effective means of regulation and administration. The later Rule still retains a deep commitment to poverty as a special charism of the order; but the radical beauty of this primitive Rule has been transformed into a more conventional statement of the principles of monastic life. The controversy surrounding the various Rules is whether the latter develops and sustains the intention of the former. Or was Francis prevailed upon to modify his vision in the face of practical concerns and ecclesiastical pressures? This in turn raises the question of how far it is possible for communities of people (as opposed to individual saints and mystics) to live genuinely as Christ in the world.

1 In the name of the Father and of the Son and of the Holy Spirit. Brother Francis – and whoever is head of this religion – promises obedience and reverence to the Lord Pope Innocent and his successors.[1]

2 The rule and life of these brothers is this, namely: 'to live in obedience, in chastity and without anything of their own' and to follow the teaching and the

footprints of our Lord Jesus Christ, who says: *If you*
wish to be perfect, go, sell your possessions, and give
the money to the poor, and you will have treasure
in heaven; then come, follow me. And: *If any want*
to become my followers, let them deny themselves
and take up their cross and follow me. Again: *Who-*
ever comes to me and does not hate father and
mother, wife and children, brothers and sisters, yes,
and even life itself, cannot be my disciple. And,
Everyone who has left houses or brothers or sisters
or father or mother or children or fields for my
name's sake will receive a hundredfold, and will
inherit eternal life.[2]

Mt 19.21

Mt 16.24

Lk 14.26

Mt 19.29

3 If anyone, wishing by divine inspiration to accept
this life, comes to our brothers, let him be received
by them with kindness.

Mt 19.21   Let him sell all his belongings and be conscientious
in giving everything to the poor.

Let all the brothers wear poor clothes and, with the
blessing of God, they can patch them with sackcloth
and other pieces, for our Lord says in the Gospel:
Those who put on fine clothing and live in luxury
Lk 7.25   *are in royal palaces.*[3]

In accordance with the Gospel, it may be lawful for
Lk 10.8   them to eat of all the food that is placed before
them.[4]

4 Let all the brothers not have power or control especi-
Mt 20.25   ally among themselves; for, as the Lord says in the
Gospel. *The rulers of the Gentiles lord it over them,*
and their great ones are tyrants over them. It will
not be so among the brothers. *Whoever wishes*
to be great among them *must be* their *minister* and
Mt 20.26   *servant.* Whoever wishes to be first *among* them
Mt 20.27   *must be* their *slave.*[5]

Mt 20.27   Let no one be called '*prior*', but let everyone in gen-
Mt 23.8   eral be called a lesser brother. Let one wash the feet
of the other.[6]

5 None of the brothers may be treasurers or overseers
in any of those places where they are staying to serve
or work among others. They may not be in charge
in the houses in which they serve nor accept any
office which would generate scandal or *forfeit their*

Mk 8.36
Lk 22.26

life; let them, instead, be the lesser ones and be subject to all in the same house.

Let the brothers who know how to work do so and exercise that trade they have learned, provided it is not contrary to the good of their souls and can be performed honestly.

And for their work they can receive whatever is necessary excepting money. And when it is necessary, they may seek alms like other poor people.[7]

6 Let all the brothers strive to follow the humility and poverty of our Lord Jesus Christ and let them remember that we should have nothing else in the whole world except, as the Apostle says:

1Tm 6.8

If we have food and clothing, we will be content with these.

They must rejoice when they live among people considered of little value and looked down upon, among the poor and the powerless, the sick and the lepers, and the beggars by the wayside.

When it is necessary, they may go for alms. Let them not be ashamed.[8]

7 Let all the brothers be careful not to slander or engage in disputes; let them strive, instead, to keep silence whenever God gives them the grace. Let them not quarrel among themselves or with others but strive to respond humbly, saying: *We are worthless slaves.*

Lk 17.10

Let them love one another, as the Lord says: *This is my commandment, that you love one another as I have loved you.*[9]

Jn 15.12

8 When the brothers go through the world, let them *take nothing for* the *journey, no staff, nor bag, nor*

Lk 9.3

bread, nor money. Whatever house they *enter*, let them *first say, 'Peace to this house!'* They may eat and drink whatever is provided for as long as they

Lk 10.5

remain in that house.

Mt 5.39

Let them *not resist an evildoer. But if anyone strikes*

Mt 5.40

them *on the right cheek*, let them *turn the other also. If anyone wants to take* their *coat*, let them *give* their

Lk 6.30

cloak as well. Let them *give to everyone who begs from* them; *and if anyone takes away* their *goods, let them not ask for them again.*[10]

9 Wherever they may be, let all my brothers remember that they have given themselves and abandoned their bodies to the Lord Jesus Christ. For love of him they must make themselves vulnerable to their enemies, both visible and invisible, because the Lord says: *Those who want to save their life will lose it, and* Lk 9.24 *those who lose their life for my sake will save it* in eternal life.[11]

10 Let all the brothers be, live and speak as Catholics. If someone has strayed in word or in deed from catholic faith and life and has not amended his ways, let him be expelled from our brotherhood.
Let us consider all clerics and religious as our masters in all that pertains to the salvation of our soul and does not deviate from our religion, and let us respect their order, office and administration in the Lord.[12]

11 Whenever they may be it pleases them, all my brothers can announce this or similar exhortation and praise among all peoples with the blessing of God:
Fear and honour,
praise and bless,

1 Thess 5.18 *give thanks* and adore
the Lord God Almighty in Trinity and in Unity,
Father, Son and Holy Spirit,
the Creator of all.

Mt 3.2   Do penance,
performing worthy fruits of penance
because we shall soon die.

Lk 6.38 *Give, and it will be given to you.*
Lk 6.37b *Forgive and you will be forgiven.*
If you do not forgive others,
Mt 6.15 *neither will* the Lord *forgive your trespasses.*
Jas 5.16 *Confess your sins.*
Blessèd are they who die in penance,
for they shall be in the kingdom of heaven.

1 Jn 3.10 Woe to those who do not die in penance,
for they shall be *children of the devil*
whose works they do
Mt 18.8; 25.41 and they shall go *into the eternal fire.*
Beware of and abstain from every evil and persevere in good till the end.[13]

Col 3.17   **12** *In the name of the Lord Jesus!*
I ask all my brothers to learn and frequently call to
mind the tenor and sense of what has been written
in this life for the salvation of our souls. I beg God,
who is All-powerful, Three and One, to bless all who
teach, learn, retain, remember and put into practice
these things, each time they repeat and do what has
been written there for the salvation of our soul, and,
kissing their feet, I implore everyone to love, keep
and treasure them greatly.
Glory be to the Father, and to the Son, and to the
Holy Spirit. As it was in the beginning, is now, and
will be forever. Amen.[14]

Notes

1. Regula non Bullata Prologue v.1,3
2. RnB Chapter 1 v.1–5
3. RnB Chapter 2 v.1,4,14
4. RnB Chapter 3 v.13
5. RnB Chapter 5 v.9–12
6. RnB Chapter 6 v.3–4
7. RnB Chapter 7 v.1–3,7–8
8. RnB Chapter 9 v.1–4
9. RnB Chapter 11 v.1–3,5
10. RnB Chapter 14 v.1–6
11. RnB Chapter 16 v.10–11
12. RnB Chapter 19 v.1–3
13. RnB Chapter 21 v.1–9
14. RnB Chapter 24 v.1–3,5

C. Arnold Snyder, 'Discipleship: Following After Christ'
in *Following in the Footsteps of Christ: The Anabaptist Tradition*,
London: Darton, Longman & Todd, 2004, pp. 150–6.

*This extract, from Arnold Snyder's book on the history and principles
of the Anabaptist movement, testifies to the impact the tradition of
imitating Christ had made upon medieval spirituality. Owing much
to the inspiration of Francis, it appealed not only to defenders of
the Catholic Church, such as Ignatius Loyola, but also to many
Reformers and particularly the Anabaptists. Using the testimony of
Anabaptist preachers, prisoners and martyrs, Snyder displays the*

courage their Christian faith gave these radical disciples to oppose violence and to choose death rather than placing the demands of the civil authorities above the commandments of Christ.

One of the marks that distinguishes the Anabaptists from the other Reformation groupings is their great devotion to the example of Christ's life and teaching. They were criticized for this by those who thought that this betrayed a faith in 'works of righteousness' rather than in salvation through the atoning grace of God alone. In fact, within Anabaptist circles a distinctive understanding of the community's incorporation into the sufferings of Christ was developing. This not only continues to provoke radical discipleship among contemporary Anabaptists but has also inspired canonical narrative theologians from many different Christian traditions in our own times.

Non-Violence

When we turn to the Anabaptist teaching on non-violence we find an analogous case in which a direct biblical command – in this case to turn the other cheek and to love enemies – is cited explicitly in many Anabaptist testimonies. In 1589, Joost de Tollenaer wrote to his daughter Betgen from prison:

> We are to wish evil to no one, though in the law of Moses the contrary is written: 'Thou shalt love thy neighbour, and hate thine enemy.' But Christ takes this away; for that was in the law of revenge, but now we are under grace. Hence we must also show grace, and not punish, as Christ says: 'Ye have heard that it hath been said, Thou shalt love thy neighbour, and hate thine enemy. But I say unto you, Love your enemies, bless them that curse you, do good to them that hate you, and pray for them which despitefully use you, and persecute you; that ye may be the children of your Father which is in heaven: for he maketh his sun rise on the evil and on the good.' Matt. 5:43–45. Hence, dear child, one may not wish evil to his enemy, much less do him any evil. And do not hate him, neither avenge yourself, but give place to wrath; and be slow to wrath, for the wrath of man worketh not the righteousness of God; but as you would that men should do unto you, so do to them, and you will fulfill the law of Christ. Rom. 12:19; James 1:19, 20; Matt. 7:12.[1]

The words of Jesus to his disciples, particularly Jesus' words in the Sermon on the Mount, and the example of his own life, seemed clear enough scriptural testimony for disciples concerning God's will in Christ. The Anabaptist brothers who were marched to Trieste, condemned to be galley slaves, wrote in their confession of faith:

> All defence and physical resistance, all warring, fighting, insurrection, and resisting evil, and all litigation in worldly courts and quarrelling over temporal goods are excluded. Christ clearly forbids killing or angry resentment (Matt. 5[:38–40]). To this we add Paul who says: Do not avenge yourselves, my beloved, but give place to God's wrath (Rom. 12[:19]).[2]

Christ's command to his disciples is clear; so also is the testimony of the apostle Paul, and, for that matter, all apostolic testimony contained in the New Testament agrees.

The words of the New Testament were strong enough to make the point, but it was the example of Jesus himself that so often was held up in Anabaptist reflections on loving enemies and dealing with evil in the world. *Ausbund* hymn 46 contains the following lines:

> Yield yourself to God with wife and child,
> fully from the heart, with soul and body;
> He will truly enrich you.
> Show everyone spiritual fruit,
> love, and a gentle spirit.
> Meekly feed
> the enemy that troubles you.
> O brother of mine, show mercy
> to everyone,
> as does your Father . . .
> Be compassionate.
> Mirror yourself in the Lord Christ.[3]

Yieldedness (*Gelassenheit*) to God will bear the spiritual fruit of gentle love, a mirror image of Christ himself.

Placing Christ at the centre of the Christian life as the example to be 'mirrored' and followed was not original to the Anabaptists, but rather had been one of the strongest and deepest spiritual emphases in the late medieval West. Thomas à Kempis' classic, the *Imitation of Christ*, begins in book one, chapter one by saying:

'He that follows Me shall not walk in darkness,' says the Lord. These are the words of Christ, by which we are urged to imitate His life and virtues, if we wish to be truly enlightened and freed from all blindness of heart. Therefore, let it be our chief business to meditate upon the life of Jesus Christ. The teaching of Christ excels all the teachings of the Saints, and if a man have His spirit, he shall find therein a hidden manna.[4]

Christ is not to be 'imitated' in the sense of mere acting or aping, but rather those who 'study Christ' seek Christ's spirit, so that they can truly be imitators of Christ. So also the Taulerian *Theologia Deutsch* said:

Where the true Light is, there is a true righteous life, pleasing and precious to God. Although it is not the perfect life of Christ, it is nonetheless formed and righted according to it: the Christ life is loved and what flows from it: rectitude, order, and the rest of the virtues.[5]

The Holy Spirit, the true Light, brings forth a righteous life that is formed according to the life of Christ.

The Anabaptists were deeply nourished by this Christocentric spiritual tradition. 'Obeying the command of Christ' was central, of course, especially in the polemical argumentation of the sixteenth century, but the literal biblical command still did not get to the spiritual heart of the matter. Weapons are rejected, and enemies shown love, insofar as Christ's Spirit has been born within. Pilgram Marpeck wrote:

Revenge is no longer permitted in the New Testament for, through patience, the Spirit can now more powerfully overcome enemies than it could in the Old Testament. Therefore, Christ forbade such vengeance and resistance (Luke 9, 21; Matt. 5), and commanded the children who possessed the Spirit of the New Testament to love, to bless their enemies, persecutors, and opponents, and to overcome them with patience (Matt. 5; Luke 6).[6]

It is the Holy Spirit that makes possible the blessing of enemies, the 'Spirit of the New Testament' granted by Jesus Christ to the reborn children of God.[7] Paul Glock wrote from prison:

[Jesus] prayed life for those who killed him. In his last extremity he was still concerned about his enemies. Observe how the Father and the Son are one, friendly and forbearing ... Oh, you dearly beloved brethren and sisters, how few people there are who have the mind and spirit of Christ. May the Lord have mercy on us that more and more we may be removed from the unrighteous and defiled Adam into the new and undefiled Adam who is from heaven, the innocent lamb without blemish and without spot.[8]

The Anabaptists knew that the mind and spirit of Christ are not granted in perfect measure to human beings, this side of eternity. Nevertheless they were convinced, as was the *Imitatio* tradition that preceded them, that a good measure of the Christ-like life was possible on this earth for the reborn children of God, and so also was forbearing enemies and not retaliating with violence. An Anabaptist witness in 1529 stated the case negatively: 'our neighbours, the sword users (*Schwärtler*), also think they are Christians, but their works and deeds prove something much different. Their life accords very little and not at all with the teaching and life of Christ.'[9] It is by the measure of Christ's life that one's true spiritual condition is made evident.

Because of the cruel persecution they experienced, the Anabaptists had ample opportunity to reflect upon unjust suffering and perseverance. Many Anabaptists in prison took comfort in the words of Scripture that promised God's justice on those who had perpetrated injustice.[10] But it was not unusual for them also to reflect on the positive actions to which they felt called, in imitation of Christ. Bartholomeus Panten, executed in 1592, wrote an instruction from prison 'to all lovers of the truth; together with a brief account of his examination', in which he admonished them:

Dear friends, if we want to be of His servants, we must serve the Lord according to His divine will and demands. That is, we must suffer and bear here, and not resist; else we should live to ourselves, and not to the Lord, and so doing we should not follow the footsteps of Christ, for we must bless, and not curse, them that persecute us. As Paul teaches us: 'Provide things honest in the sight of all men. If it be possible, as much as lieth in you, live peaceably with all men. Dearly beloved, avenge not yourselves, but rather give place unto wrath: for it is written, Vengeance is mine; I will repay, saith the Lord. Therefore, if thine enemy hunger, feed him; if he thirst, give him drink: for in so doing thou shalt heap coals of fire on his head. Be not overcome of evil, but overcome evil with good.' Rom. 12:17–21.[11]

Not seeking vengeance is a necessary first step; overcoming evil with good is a further step beyond. Followers of Jesus are called to both. So Pilgram Marpeck wrote:

> Be glad for I have overcome the world (that is, in patience, hope, and faith). You will be in need of patience (that is, patience in time of evil tribulation). 1 Pet. 3[:9–11], Rom. 12[:21] And do not resist evil with evil, but overcome evil with good. Thus and in no other way had Christ overcome the world that we may be joyful in hope and so to overcome and to await our Saviour, according to His promise, who will be our victory and our overcoming.[12]

Christ overcame the world by patient yielding, defeating evil with good; his disciples and children will overcome the world in the same way, through patience, hope and trust in Jesus' victory.

Of course, proponents of hard-headed political solutions in the sixteenth century posed the same questions as do their twenty-first-century counterparts: what do you non-violent Christians propose to do when enemies attack our territory? Hans Schmidt reported the following exchange in 1590:

> The overseer said, 'If a murderer came to you in the field and killed you while you could defend yourself and did not, you would be your own murderer. If the Turk were to come into the land, would you not defend yourselves either?' I said, 'No. We will defend ourselves with prayer and will refrain from fighting. God fights for us.'[13]

Reborn children of God do as Christ did: they do not take life, they give life. They do not kill or coerce others to make matters on earth turn out 'right', but rather they trust entirely in God and God's providential care for the world.

One of the earliest public expressions of this sentiment is found in the Schleitheim Articles of 1527, where Michael Sattler wrote concerning separation from the world: 'Thereby shall also fall away from us the diabolical weapons of violence – such as sword, armor, and the like, and all of their use to protect friends or against enemies – by virtue of the word of Christ: "you shall not resist evil."' As he explained at his trial a few months later: 'If the Turk comes, he should not be resisted, for it stands written: thou shalt not kill. We should not defend ourselves against the Turks or our other persecutors, but with fervent prayer should implore God that He might be our defense and our resistance.'[14] This was an answer that came perfectly from a spirituality of following after Christ in yielded submission to God's will, but it certainly was not a thought-out strategy for Christian participation in political affairs. The heirs of the Anabaptist tradition have had to struggle with the consequences of this spirituality down to the present day.

Notes

1. Thieleman van Braght, *Martyrs Mirror* (Scottdale, PA: Herald Press, 1972), p. 1079.

2. C. A. Snyder (ed.), *Sources of South German/Austrian Anabaptism* (Kitchener, ON: Pandora Press, 2001) p. 267.

3. Translation, slightly modified, taken from *Songs of the Ausbund*, vol. 1, p. 88.

4. Thomas à Kempis, *Of the Imitation of Christ*, trans. Abbot Justin McCann (New York: Mentor-Omega, 1962), p. 17.

5. *The Theologia Germanica of Martin Luther*, trans. Bengt Hoffman (New York: Paulist Press, 1980), ch. 38, p. 120.

6. William Klaassen and Walter Klaassen (eds), *Writings of Pilgram Marpeck* (Scottdale, PA: Herald Press, 1978), p. 63.

7. Stanza 9 of *Ausbund* hymn 110 reads: 'Blessed are the peaceable, they are the children of God. The Holy Spirit lives in their pure hearts; it directs and guides them in God's Word alone.' Translation, slightly modified, taken from *Songs of the Ausbund*, vol. 1, p. 255.

8. Snyder, *Sources*, pp. 304–5.

9. Cited in Walter Klaassen (trans. and ed.), *Anabaptism in Outline* (Scottdale, PA: Herald Press, 1981), pp. 273–4.

10. As just one example from literally hundreds, Joost Verkindert, martyred in 1570 in Antwerp, wrote to his wife: 'My chosen, comfort yourself in the Lord, and let us commit the matter to Him, and pray for those who afflict us with this; for, "Vengeance is mine, I will repay, saith the Lord." Rom. 12:19.', Van Braght, *Martyrs Mirror*, p. 853.

11. Van Braght, *Martyrs Mirror* p. 1084.

12. Klaassen & Klaassen, *Pilgram Marpeck*, p. 539.

13. Snyder, *Sources*, p. 371.

14. *Legacy*, pp. 38, 72.

G. Lindbeck, 'Scripture, Consensus and Community'

in *Church in a Postliberal Age*, edited by J. Buckley, London: SCM Press, 2002, pp. 204–06 and 217–22.

George Lindbeck is a leading exponent of canonical narrative theology, and in the extract below we find an articulation of its major themes. According to Lindbeck the life of the Church is inextricably bound with the Scriptures it reads. In the early days of Christianity, Lindbeck argues, believers made their faith in Christ the hermeneutical key to their reading of sacred texts. They believed the whole history of Israel pointed to the coming of Jesus. The Hebrew Scriptures were thus claimed as the narrative of their faith regardless of what part of the Roman Empire they called home. Lindbeck argues that the tradition of regarding the Bible as revealing the truth about history flourished as the Church grew. The true story it told was more real than everyday reality, which was 'absorbed' within it. In what Lindbeck describes as the tradition of 'classical interpretation' the Bible was read as presenting a 'followable' story that should be taken up within personal life and by the whole community of the Church.

The question that Lindbeck then addresses is whether this classical hermeneutical model can be revived today. The rise of biblical criticism resulted in a fragmentation of the biblical narrative and a loss of confidence in its authority. However, within the postmodern context we are looking again at the claims of Enlightenment rationalism. We are coming to recognize that narratives are a vital source of personal and social identity and are seeking texts capable of 'projecting imaginatively and practically habitable worlds'. This encourages Lindbeck to believe that the Bible can be read again, not uncritically but 'classically' and faithfully. This will enable believers once again to pattern their lives on the story they read.

The Classic Hermeneutic: Premodern Bible Reading

In the early days, to rehearse familiar facts, it was not a different canon but a distinctive method of reading which differentiated the church from the synagogue. Christians read the Bible they shared with the Jews in the light of their at first orally transmitted stories of the crucified and resurrected Messiah in whose name they prayed and into whom they were incorporated in baptism and Eucharist. Jesus was for them the climax and summation of Israel's history. When joined to him, even Gentiles became members of the enlarged people of God, citizens of the commonwealth of Israel (Eph. 2.12). Its history became their history, and its Bible their Bible. It was not simply a source of precepts and truths, but the interpretive framework for all reality. They used typological and, less fundamentally, allegorical techniques derived from their Jewish and Greek milieux to apply the canonically fixed words to their ever-changing situations.

As time went on, an explicit rule of faith and an enlarged canon came into existence. The two developments were synchronically inter-related. The rule of faith, in its various versions, articulated the liturgi-cally embedded Christological and Trinitarian reading of the Hebrew Scriptures; the selection of certain writings out of the many then circulating which claimed apostolic status depended on their useful-ness within the context of the *sensus fidelium* formed by this implicit or explicit rule of faith. (The use, and therefore meaning, of the text, be it noted, was the one it had in the canon-forming situation, not in some putative historically reconstructed original one.) Thus a certain way of reading Scripture (viz. as a Christ-centered narrationally and typologically unified whole in conformity to a Trinitarian rule of faith) was constitutive of the Christian canon and has, it would seem, an authority inseparable from that of the Bible itself. To read the Bible otherwise is not to read it as Scripture but as some other book, just as to read Homer's *Odyssey* for philological or historical pur-poses, for example, is to turn it into something other than an epic poem.

In the light of this interrelation of canon, hermeneutics and the *sensus fidelium*, the Catholic/Protestant arguments about whether Scripture or the Church are prior seem futile. Israel's Scriptures, read in the fashion we have noted, were constitutive of the communities which produced an enlarged canon in order to reinforce their identi-ties against Gnostic, Marcionite and other groups which called them-selves Christian. Looked at in terms of historical development, what we now call the Catholic Church of the first centuries was constituted by those Christian groups (in some times and places perhaps a small minority) for which the Hebrew Bible read Christologically was of special importance. (The 4th-century Donatists were perhaps the first major schismatic movement to retain the catholic reverence for the Old Testament.) Even though these Old Testament-oriented churches soon became overwhelmingly Gentile in membership, they developed a Christian analogue of the Jewish sense of being a single people. Their widely separated communities were bound together by ties of mutual helpfulness, responsibility and openness to each other's correction. Because of this, they were able to cooperate in developing, not only congruent versions of a single rule of faith and a common enlarged canon, but also unified, though not uniform, ministerial, liturgical and disciplinary patterns and structures. A far-flung, flexible and yet tenacious network of mutual aid societies came to span the Mediterranean world.

Not surprisingly, it was these communities which out-distanced all other claimants to the Catholic name (for Marcionites and others also claimed to be the one and only Catholic Church). It was their Scriptures, not some other canon, which became the basic Christian Bible; and in this sense the Church is prior to the Bible. Yet, on the other hand, it was Scripture – initially Hebrew Scripture read Christologically – which had the consensus, community and institution-building power to make of these communities the overwhelmingly dominant and therefore Catholic Church. It does not even seem far-fetched to say that it was the Bible which conquered the empire in defiance of the normal laws of sociological gravity: non-violently, despite persecution, and without special economic, social, cultural or ethnic support. Other texts in other contexts – the Koran and Buddhist scriptures, for example – have also formed and sustained major trans-ethnic communities, but never in comparable independence of external assistance. Thus the priority of the Bible seems at least as plausible as the priority of the Church. No choice is necessary, however: it is best to think of the co-inherence of Bible and Church, of their mutually constitutive reciprocity. It was, furthermore, the Church as *sensus fidelium*, not as separately institutionalized magisterial authority, which was decisive in this process. Those writings which proved profitable in actual use among the people were the ones which were included in the canon.

The canon is now closed for all those who believe in the finality, the eschatological decisiveness, of Jesus Christ. The balance, one might say, has shifted. The Church, whether as institutionalized magisterium or as the sense of the faithful, no longer forms scripture, but is rather formed by it. Yet the Bible's community-forming role, needless to say, is not independent of community. It helps constitute the *ecclesia* only when interpreted communally in accordance with a community-constituting hermeneutics. That hermeneutics remained for long centuries the classic one.

As the Middle Ages manifest, the Bible classically interpreted can shape communal and personal identities even when (in contrast to the early church) almost all lay folk are illiterate. The laity learned the fundamental outline and episodes of the scriptural drama through liturgy, catechesis and occasional preaching. That drama defined for them the truly real world, and within it they inscribed their own reality (as the products of the popular imagination from paintings, sculpture and mystery plays to oaths and proverbs make evident). Nor was this absorption of ordinary life by the Bible simply an imaginative matter. Charlemagne's typological identification of himself as a Christian King David set over God's people, for example, was not an empty metaphor but a history-transforming trope. The extraordinary unity of western culture in the Middle Ages – far greater than it is at present – would not have been possible without such institutional developments as the papacy and the Holy Roman Empire, but it was above all the result of the reality-defining power of a single pre-eminent text, the Bible, classically interpreted.

This is not to deny that the Bible was also grossly misinterpreted: classical hermeneutics is no guarantee of Christian faithfulness. Deviations of piety, theology and church structure can be treated as immemorial Christian tradition and retrojected into the Bible or the early church (e.g. The Donation of Constantine). Persecutions and inquisitions were biblically legitimated. Nor were those whose personal motives were selflessly Christian, even cruciform, exempt from these distortions: it was St Bernard who preached the Second Crusade which, to his horror, unleashed the second great antisemitic pogroms. (Nor, it must be hastily added, are such corruptions confined to the Middle Ages: it was Luther who wrote some of the most painfully anti-Jewish diatribes in history.) Yet the Bible within the classical framework resists definitive capture by even communally self-interested misreadings. The centrality of the stories of Jesus and the typological application to the present Church (in accordance with 1 Cor. 10) of the Old Testament tales of God's wrath, as well as mercy, against his ceaselessly unfaithful people confer self-correcting potential on communal interpretation. Those who denounce communally authorized misreadings, furthermore, are admonished by the example of the prophets, of Jesus and of the apostles to remain loyal to the community and, according to Paul as reported in Acts, respectful of its leaders even if they are unbelieving high priests (23.5). A more effective strategy for maintaining unity despite disagreement cannot easily be imagined.

The strategy failed at the time of the Reformation. As early Jewish Christians were cast out of synagogues despite their desire to stay, so Luther and his associates were excommunicated by Rome. The parallel has difficulties, not least the fact that Luther's language regarding the pope does not follow Paul's example as recorded in Acts 23.5;

but our purpose here is not to explore the shared responsibilities for the schism but to look at the unifying role of Scripture during the Reformation period. This role, needless to say, is chiefly evident on the Protestant side: the Catholic reform, great though it was, built more on purified tradition than directly on the sacred page.

It is the Reformed more than the Lutherans who in the 16th and early 17th centuries best exhibit the consensus-and-community-building power of a biblically informed *sensus fidelium*. They were led by the best-educated ministry in Christendom and appealed especially to the literate artisan and rising middle classes, and yet they also constituted an inclusive popular movement which was able in an impoverished rural country such as Scotland, for example, to sweep also the peasantry and the aristocracy into the fold. Their churches were scattered from Hungary to New England in highly diverse situations, and yet they constituted a self-consciously united communion held together by nothing except a common approach to Scripture. They had no overarching organizational structures, nor Book of Common Prayer, as did the Anglicans, nor unified body of confessional writings, as did the Lutherans. Yet they formed a single community of interpretation which was diverse yet tenaciously united.

Their reading of the Bible largely conformed to the classic pattern: they read it as the all-embracing story of the present as well as past dealings of the Triune God with God's people and God's world. While they carried further the medieval Aristotelian minimization of allegory, already well-advanced in Aquinas, they were not modern literalists, for typology and typological applications were crucial. Through endless sermons and continual reading, the laity in many congregations came to know the Bible from Genesis to Revelation with a thoroughness never equaled before or since. Under the guidance of their preachers – for their reading was communal, not individualistic – they searched the Bible with close attention both to its details and encompassing patterns in order to shape their lives and thoughts in obedience to God's Word. Calvin's commentaries and *Institutes* guided but did not control their interpretations: for several generations, their theology, church organization and practice developed within a broad consensus along similar lines.

. . .

Retrieval

In a contribution to a recent Festschrift for Professor Frei, Ronald Thiemann, Dean of Harvard Divinity School, speaks of the biblical stories as 'followable', as constituting a 'followable' world.[1] This is a convenient tag for what Scripture becomes when the classic hermeneutics is employed. The question in this section is the extent to which the Bible can again become followable, not only for individuals (it has never ceased to be that), but also for communities, and in ways which are unitive rather than divisive. I shall suggest, first, that the postmodern situation is favorable, and second, that there are some beginnings in biblical scholarship and theology. I shall then comment on the ways in which the *sensus fidelium* might be affected.

With the loss of Enlightenment confidence in reason and progress, the worlds within which human beings live are increasingly thought of as socially, linguistically and even textually constructed. Sociology, anthropology, history, philosophy and literary studies have all contributed to this development. We are aware as never before of the degree to which human beings and their perceptions of reality are socially and culturally determined. Nothing is exempt from this conditioning, not even the natural sciences. Within our own lifetime, historians of science such as T. S. Kuhn and philosophers such as Wittgenstein, Quine and Rorty (to mention examples only from the anglophone sphere) have undermined the 19th-century distinction between *Natur-u.-Geisteswissenschaften*. Physics and poetry are not differentiated ontologically or epistemologically: it is not that they refer to distinct types of reality or arise from distinct ways of knowing which makes them different. Rather they are seen as products of social practices which, though diverse in structure and purpose, have overlapping features. This explains the remark I made in the discussion that one hears rigorous scholars say, as if it were a commonplace, that the epistemological grounding of quarks and Homeric gods is basically the same. It is rhetorical force rooted in communal practice which gives them their cognitive status, and when rhetoric and practice change, so does that status. Homeric gods were real and quarks non-existent for ancient Greeks; their status is reversed for us, and there are no definitively formulatable context-free criteria for determining who is right and who is wrong (though there may be unformulated implicit ones).[2]

The recent literary emphasis on textuality becomes understandable against this background. Texts, understood as fixed communicative patterns embedded in rites, myths and other oral and representational traditions, are already basic in preliterate societies. They can be used in different contexts, for different purposes, and with different meanings, and thereby provide frameworks in which individual utterances ('speech acts') are socially significant and effective. This power is enhanced when they take written form, for they can then have a comprehensiveness, complexity and stability which is unattainable in other media (not even modern electronic and cinematographic ones). In short, texts project worlds in which entire cultures can and have lived.[3]

Furthermore, without such texts, it is difficult, perhaps impossible, for large-scale communities of discourse to develop. Sinic civilization as it spread from China into Korea, Japan and Vietnam depended on the Confucian corpus; the various types of Buddhism on interlocking Buddhist canons; and Judaism, Christianity and Islam, needless to say, on their respective sacred scriptures. Without a central core of privileged and familiar texts, social cohesion becomes more difficult to sustain and depends more on bureaucratic management, the manipulation of public opinion, and ultimately, perhaps, totalitarian force. Reason in the form of science or philosophy is too restricted in scope (it neglects imagination, for example), and too contradictory and changing in its pictures of the cosmic setting of human life to provide a satisfactory substitute. What is needed are texts projecting imaginatively and practically habitable worlds.

A habitable text need not have a primarily narrative structure (with the exception of the Bible, none of the canons earlier mentioned do), but it must in some fashion be construable as a guide to thought and action in the encounter with changing circumstances. It must supply followable directions for coherent patterns of life in new situations. If it does this, it can be considered rational to dwell within it: no other foundations are necessary or, in the contemporary climate of opinion, possible.

Much contemporary intellectual life can be understood as a search for such texts. Contemporary Marxists and Freudians, for example, now rarely seek to ground their favorite authors' writings scientifically or philosophically. They simply ask that they be followable, that they be construable in such a way as to provide guidance for society, in the one case, and for individual life, in the other. Thus it is that Enlightenment systems which once claimed rational foundations have now turned into foundationless hermeneutical enterprises.

Classic biblical hermeneutics was born in a similar foundationless era when followable texts were in short supply. The Jews had a great advantage: not only did the monotheistic character of their sacred book give it universal scope and unity, and not only did the long history and diversity of the writings it contained give it extraordinarily wide applicability in varying circumstances, but it had directive force and community-building power far superior to the philosophical systems which were its only real rivals. Once Scripture was made applicable to non-Jews by the Christian movement, it proved widely appealing. It was a pre-eminently habitable text in a world needing habitations, and the nations flocked into it.

Ours is again an age when old foundations and legitimating structures have crumbled. Even the defenders of reason think it unreasonable to ask anything more than that they be followable of philosophies and religions or of the texts which give them richness, comprehensiveness and stability. There are fewer and fewer intellectual objections to the legitimacy or possibility of treating a classic, whether religious or non-religious, as a perspicuous guide to life and thought. The only question is whether one is interested and can make it work.

There are, in the second place, some developments which suggest that it can be made to work. Biblical scholars are increasingly interested in the literary features, social and communal functioning and canonical unity of the scriptural text. It is, however, for others better qualified than I to comment on these beginnings. Instead, I shall simply mention the names of Karl Barth and Hans Urs von Balthasar. Here are 20th-century theologians whose use of the Bible is more nearly classical than anything in several centuries and who yet are distinctively modern (e.g. they do not reject historical criticism). Both are wary of translating the Bible into alien conceptualities; both seek, rather, to redescribe the world or worlds in which they live in biblical terms;[4] both treat Scripture as a narrationally (or, for von Balthasar, 'dramatically') and typologically unified whole; and in both the reader is referred back to the biblical text itself by exegetical work which is an integral part of the theological program. In short, these two theologians inhabit the same universe of theological discourse as the fathers, medievals and Reformers to a greater degree than do most modern theologians. Discussions between them are possible – perhaps even decidable – by reference to the text because they approach Scripture in basically similar ways; whereas in the case of most other theologians, major differences arise from the extrabiblical conceptualities (idealist, Marxist, etc.) by means of which they interpret Scripture and are therefore undecidable: sometimes there is not even a common language in which they can be discussed.

Yet their approaches to Scripture have not been widely adopted. Even Barth's followers (I do not know about von Balthasar's) are for the most part influenced by his theology, not his exegesis. This is understandable, for his exegesis is at times deeply flawed (even if corrigible).[5] What we have in these two authors is only a first, even if important, stage in the work of making the Bible followable in our day, of making it readable classically, and yet not anticritically. The analogous task in the Greco-Roman world took hundreds of years, and although it reached a kind of climax in Augustine and the Cappadocians, it could never, given the mutability of that and every world, be definitively completed. We are perhaps at the beginnings of retrieval in theology and biblical scholarship, but no more than that.

The third and most difficult question, however, is whether the Bible read classically but not anticritically can come to inform the *sensus fidelium*. The condition for this happening is that communities of interpretation come into existence in which pastors, biblical scholars, theologians and laity together seek God's guidance in the written word for their communal as well as individual lives. Their reading of Scripture will be within the context of a worship life which, in its basic eucharistic, baptismal and kerygmatic patterns, accords with that of the first centuries. They may differ in their views of the *de iure divino* status of the threefold pattern of ministry and of the papal institutionalization of the Petrine function, but not on the legitimacy of these forms of ministry as servants of word, sacrament and unity, nor on the fundamental character of the ministerial office as divinely instituted to feed and lead God's flock. There will be in these communities a renewed sense that Christians constitute a single people chosen to witness among the nations in all they are, say, and do to the salvation that was, that is, and that is to come, and guided by God in his mercy and judgment and in their faithfulness and unfaithfulness, toward the promised consummation. They will care for their own members and will also be deeply concerned about Christians everywhere. Openness to receive and responsibility to give help and correction from and to other churches will be embedded in their institutional and organizational fabrics.

This is a dream, a cloud no larger than a hand on the horizon, and yet if it began to be actualized, even if in only a few and scattered places, it would be living proof that Scripture is a unifying and followable text. The news would travel quickly (it always does in our day), and its influence would mushroom. Public opinion might be widely affected, perhaps even quickly, in all communions, and the transformation of the *sensus fidelium* (which takes longer) might follow in due course.

Not all the problems of how to reshape the Church in this age of transition would be solved by such a development. Christians will continue to differ, not only on political questions of peace and justice and of socialism and capitalism but also on matters of direct ecclesial import such as the ordination of women. Is the tradition against women's ordination basically cultural and thus similar to the Church's long accommodation to slavery? Retrieval of the classic hermeneutics even in combination with historical criticism does not decide this issue. Yet it changes the context of the debate. Attention focuses, not on entitlements, privileges and gender, but on the pastoral office itself as God's instrument for the nurturing of his people with word and sacrament. What builds up the Church is what counts. Sociologically and historically speaking, it is ultimately the *sensus fidelium* which decides in such matters in any case but to the degree the instinct of the faithful (their connatural knowledge, as Aquinas would say) is scripturally shaped, it not only does but *should* decide.

There is much in the more theologically oriented ecumenical discussions which points in the direction of these remarks. The life of worship and ministry which is the necessary (not sufficient) context for unifying communal Bible interpretation is basically that described in the Faith and Order Lima document, *Baptism, Eucharist and Ministry*. Similarly, to cite just one other item, the most recent report of the Lutheran/Roman Catholic International Study Commission, *Facing Unity*, marks the beginnings of cooperative thinking on how interconfessional communities of interpretation (though it does not call them that) might develop which would contribute to the reshaping and renewal rather than disruption of present church orders.

Yet it must be admitted that, even more than Church unity, the hope for the actualization of the consensus-and-community-building potential of the classic pattern of biblical interpretation in a post-modern setting seems impossibly visionary. It is not even being talked about, much less put into practice. Those circles in which serious Bible reading is most widespread – conservative Protestant, charismatic, Cursillo, base communities – are often fundamentalist and almost always precritical in their hermeneutics. They also need to recover the classic pattern.

On the other hand, there is no reason for discouragement. Scripture permits and perhaps urges us to dream dreams and see visions. Barriers have been erased, retrieval has begun, and we can begin to imagine far more than was possible a mere generation ago that Roman Catholics, Eastern Orthodox and heirs of the Reformation will learn to read the Bible together as the Christ-centered guide for themselves and their communities. God's guidance of world and church history has sown the seeds for the rebirth of the written word, and it is for believers to pray, work and hope against hope that God will bring these seeds to fruition through the power of the Holy Spirit.[6]

Notes

1. Ronald Thiemann, 'Radiance and Obscurity in Biblical Narrative', in *Scriptural Interpretation*, (ed.) G. Green, Philadelphia: Fortress, 1987, pp. 21–41.

2. In its Anglo-American forms, this recognition of radical historicity is not necessarily associated with scepticism, relativism or irrationalism. The truth available to human beings in this life is 'justified belief', and the fact that the canons of justification vary does not make the truth any less imperative. The kind of Aristotelianism and Thomism represented by such authors as Alasdair MacIntyre, Victor Preller, David Burrell and Fergus Kerr is compatible with this position, and its relation to Thomas Aquinas in particular is discussed by Bruce Marshall in *The Thomist*. The argument, much oversimplified, is that while Aquinas was wholly non-relativistic about truth (God knows things as they actually are), he is not so about knowledge (creaturely knowledge is in accord with ('the mode of the receiver'), and therefore has room for a recognition of historicity which is neither sceptical nor irrationalist. Needless to say, the present argument is also compatible with other philosophical positions.

3. It may be helpful to offer some clarifications in order to avoid confusion between this use of 'textuality' and Jacques Derrida's deconstructionism. Derrida, despite his exaggerations, is not wholly wrong in claiming that writing is prior to speaking and polysemy to univocity. It is not the text, but only the 'present' word, the word as used in a situationally specific speech act, which has a single, fixed meaning. Derrida's theological error is to suppose that Christians have historically understood the logos, the Word incarnate, in terms of the ontotheology against which he polemicizes. Jesus Christ has never been treated in practice (whatever may have been true of doctrine or theology) as similar to a speech act with a single unchanging meaning, but is now, as the ascended Lord, just as much a living person as in his days on earth. His present meaning – what he says to believers through Scripture, worship, etc. – continues to be 'new every morning'.

A further point is that the emphasis on textuality involves an endless and an undecidable play of signification only when one refuses (as do the deconstructionists) to give privileged status to a given text and given hermeneutic. This refusal, however, is arbitrary. It is as if one were to deny the legitimacy of taking as primary the geometric meaning of Euclid's *Elements* just because this book can also be viewed as intertextually related to the whole of literature, and can be read with an indefinite number of purposes and meanings, including self-subversive ones. Apart from such deconstructive narrowness, however, the emphasis on textuality vividly makes the point that a textbound faith, far from being rigidified, is open to hearing God speak in many ways through Scripture.

In summary, premodern Bible reading shares with deconstructionism the refusal to make primary such derivatives from the text as doctrines (understood, e.g., as universal propositional truths about reality), historical reconstructions or existential descriptions of the human condition (each of which, if thought to catch the deeper meaning of the text, involves a kind of 'ontotheology'). It also shares with deconstructionism the emphasis on close reading and multiple meanings. The difference is that there was, for premodern Jews and Christians, unlike modern deconstructionists, a privileged text and privileged mode of interpretation. Thus within the indicated limitations, modern literary approaches with their emphasis on textuality increase the possibility of a retrieval of the classic hermeneutics.

4. When whales and bats are redescribed as mammals they come to be understood as quite different from fish or birds, and yet they remain thoroughly distinct from each other and from other mammals. Similarly, the worlds of early, medieval, Reformation or contemporary Christians remain quite different from each other when biblically redescribed. 'Absorbing contemporary reality into the scriptural text', to repeat an earlier phrase, is logically the reverse of translating the scriptural message into contemporary thought forms, but it need not be an archaizing project.

Barth and von Balthasar, however, differ in their redescriptions in that the latter is more positive than Barth about the contributions to the faith of 'Christianized' worldviews or philosophies (e.g. Platonism). He seems to me, however, to be equally insistent (e.g. against Rahner), on the fundamental 'untranslatability' of the biblical message. The present argument is compatible on these points with both Barth and von Balthasar, though, where they differ, it perhaps tilts toward von Balthasar.

5. I have commented briefly on some of the strengths and weaknesses of Barth's exegesis in 'Barth and Textuality', *Theology Today* 43 (1986), pp. 361–76.

6. As I come to the end of this chapter I am finding myself acutely aware that it is a counter-instance of what it recommends: it does not refer the reader to the biblical text. It is too long as it is, and I have tried, not altogether successfully, to omit scriptural citations. Yet if the form were to fit the message, it should be rewritten, in premodern fashion as a commentary on such interglossing passages as Deut. 6.4–9; 2 Tim. 3.15–17 and Luke 2.45–7. Historical criticism would help in ascertaining the views to which these passages were opposed (both originally and canonically), and typology would provide the warrant for finding analogies (and therefore guidance) in later church history and the present. Augustine's precepts for applicative interpretation, especially the rule of charity, would have to be observed, as also the self-critical force of the *simul justus et peccator*. The resulting essay would be longer, but also more interesting. It would be genuinely theological, a first-order attempt to get guidance from Scripture, instead of a second-order account of the need and possibility of doing so. Yet everything in the present essay could also find a place in the rewritten one.

Stanley Hauerwas, 'Jesus: The Story of the Kingdom'
Theology Digest, Vol. 26, No. 4, Winter 1978, pp. 303–24.

Stanley Hauerwas is a Methodist theologian whose work has been deeply influenced by the Anabaptist witness for peace and against the values of contemporary capitalism. In this early essay, which carries the seeds of much of his later work, he draws upon the work of the Anabaptist theologian John Howard Yoder, who famously argued that Jesus did not teach a social ethic but embodied one; in other words Jesus is a social ethic. What Hauerwas means by this is that there are no abstract principles or ethical systems that are capable of guiding Christian living. We live as Christians when we live like Jesus. Being a Christian entails patterning our lives according to the story that the Church tells about the Christ whose presence continues to enliven the story-shaped community he has gathered around him.

Like many canonical narrative theologians, Hauerwas audaciously claims that the story of Jesus does not offer inspiration for exceptional people or circumstances, but rather that it is properly told and lived within the messy reality of the Church. Thankfully, Hauerwas reminds us, the diversity of the Gospels allows for diversity in interpretation as to what the story means. However, there is no escaping the claim this narrative lays upon us. We face exactly the same challenge as the first Christians to bear the burden of the story with joy and celebrate that through our obedience 'our stories become part of the story of the Kingdom'.

To anyone who wishes to argue with one about religion one can then only take the argument in cogent, logical terms as far back as his own first principles will allow. But because there comes a point at which such argument must cease, it does not follow that there is nothing more to say. It is no accident that the religious autobiography is a classic form of theological writing for this shows us how a man comes by the premises from which he argues. It goes behind the argument to the arguer. St. Augustine's *Confessions* are the classic document here. Thus it is not mere pious moralizing which connects the rise of unbelief with a lowering of the quality of Christian life. Where the Christian community is incapable of producing lives such as those of the saints, the premises from which it argues will appear rootless and arbitrary.

Alasdair MacIntyre[1]

For the searching and right understanding of the Scriptures there is need of a good life and a pure soul, and for Christian virtue to guide the mind to grasp, so far as human nature can, the truth concerning God the Word. One cannot possibly understand the teaching of the saints unless one has a pure mind and is trying to imitate their life. Anyone who wants to look at sunlight naturally wipes his eye clear first, in order to make at any rate some approximation to the purity of that on which he looks; and a person wishing to see a city or country goes to the place in order to do so. Similarly, anyone who wishes to understand the mind of the sacred writers must first cleanse his own life, and approach the saints by copying their deeds.

St Athanasius[2]

1. Christology and social ethics

Even though neither of these quotes seems immediately relevant to questions concerning christology or social ethics I hope to show that they raise central issues for both subjects. Though my topic is Christian social ethics I have a larger agenda in view. To be a Christian implies substantive and profound convictions about the person and work of Jesus of Nazareth. Christians have often disagreed about how to understand the significance of Jesus but the centrality of Jesus for Christian identity has never been questioned. Yet when Christians turn from avowals about 'being Christian' to social ethics the substantive claims they make about Jesus no longer seem operative. Or their appeals to Jesus to support various social strategies appear accidental as it is often apparent that the social strategy has been or can be better justified on grounds different from the appeal to Jesus.

The separation between Jesus and social ethics is exhibited by the very way we have learned to formulate the problem – i.e., 'What is the relation between christology and social ethics?' That we can ask such a question indicates that something is wrong. The question presupposes that the meaning and truth of commitment to Jesus can be determined separated from his social significance. In contrast I will argue that what it means for Jesus to be worthy of our worship is explicable only in terms of his social significance. In so arguing I am not only suggesting that a christology which does not properly treat Jesus' social significance is incomplete. I offer the more radical argument that a christology which is not a social ethic is deficient. From this perspective the most 'orthodox' christologies are inadequate when they fail to suggest how being a believer in Jesus provides and requires that we have the skills to describe and negotiate our social existence.

We often forget that social questions were at the heart of the controversies from which the great classical christological formulas emerged.[3] One reason we forget the social dimension of the earliest faith in Jesus is that we reduce that faith to formulas which are assumed to be self-explanatory. They then fail to direct our attention to how it is we are required to make Jesus' life our own. In order to try to recover the social meaning of discipleship I will suggest that the most significant christological formulation is still the most primitive – namely that the Gospel is the story of a man who had the authority to preach that the Kingdom of God is present. By recovering the narrative dimension of christology we will be able to see that Jesus did not have a social ethic, but that his story is a social ethic. For the social and political validity of a community results from its being formed by a truthful story, a story that gives us the means to live without fear of one another. Therefore there can be no separation of christology and ecclesiology, that is, Jesus from the church. The truthfulness of Jesus creates and is known by the kind of community his story should form.

1.1. *Jesus at the mercy of social ethics*

Before developing my constructive thesis I need to document some of the reasons for the separation of Jesus and social ethics and explain why it is a christological problem.[4] As John Howard Yoder has observed, mainstream Christianity has assumed that Jesus is not relevant to questions of social ethics.[5] For example, Ernst Troeltsch claims, '. . . it is a great mistake to treat all the ideas which underlie the preaching of Jesus as though they were primarily connected with the "Social" problem. The message of Jesus is obviously purely religious; it issues directly from a very definite idea of God, and of the Divine Will in relation to man. To Jesus the whole meaning of life is religious; His life and His teaching are wholly determined by His thought of God.'[6] Therefore according to Troeltsch the central problems of the New Testament are

> always purely religious, dealing with such questions as the salvation of the soul, monotheism, life after death, purity of worship, the

right kind of congregational organization, the application of Christian ideals to daily life, and the need for severe self-discipline in the interest of personal holiness; further, we must admit that from the beginning no class distinctions were recognized; rather they were lost sight of in the supreme question of eternal salvation and the appropriation of a spiritual inheritance. It is worthy of special note that Early Christian apologetic contains no arguments dealing either with hopes of improving the existing social situation, or with any attempt to heal social ills. Jesus began His public ministry, it is true, by proclaiming the Kingdom of God as the great hope of Redemption; this 'Kingdom', however, was . . . primarily the vision of an ideal ethical and religious situation, of a world entirely controlled by God, in which all the values of pure spirituality would be recognized and appreciated at their true worth.[7]

We have learned to state Troeltsch's position in more nuanced ways, but the structure of Troeltsch's position remains dominant. Thus Jesus' irrelevancy for the 'social questions' is said to be because: (1) he had an 'interim' ethic; or (2) he was a simple rural figure caring little about problems of complex organizations; or (3) he had no social ethic because he had no power or control over the political and social fortunes of his society; or (4) he did not deal with social change but offered new possibility for self-understanding; or (5) he was a radical monotheist who relativized all temporal values; or finally (6) Jesus came to provide forgiveness, not an ethic.[8] What is often overlooked is that such claims of Jesus' social irrelevancy presuppose an account of 'social ethics' that cannot be justified by Jesus' own life. The problem is not that Jesus had no social ethic, but that the one he had does not match up with the social ethic these positions want or require.

For the 'social ethic' required is one that provides the means to rule and control society. It is interesting that Troeltsch lists as 'purely religious' questions concerning 'the right kind of congregational organization, the application of Christian ideals to daily life, self-discipline in the interest of personal holiness, and appropriation of spiritual inheritance'. Such issues are not issues of a social ethic because he assumes that a social ethic must be relevant to the needs of an empire; he is not interested in parishes or families. Thus of Troeltsch's description of the three types of social strategies consistent with the gospel – church, sect, and mystical – only the first on his terms is a genuine social ethic as it alone realizes the possibility of developing a viable social ethic from the Gospels. Some 'natural law' account is thus assumed to be unavoidable. But what we must recognize is that Troeltsch's extremely useful account of the three types is done from the perspective of the 'church type'.[9]

And even allowing for the more sophisticated accounts of 'social ethics' developed since Troeltsch the main thrust of his view still dominates the perspective of Catholicism as well as mainline Protestantism. Richard McCormick suggests that the question of whether Christian faith adds material content to what is in principle knowledge by reason has tremendous implication for public policy. For 'if Christian faith adds new material content to morality, then public policy is even more complex than it seems. For example, if Christians precisely as Christians know something about abortion that others cannot know unless they believe it as Christians, then in a pluralistic society there will be problems with discussion in the public forum.'[10] But McCormick then concludes that Christians do not come to the public forum with any special insight because Jesus is regarded 'as normative because He is believed to have experienced what it is to be *human* in the fullest way and at the deepest level. Christian ethics does not and cannot add to human ethical self-understanding as such any material content that is, in principle, strange or foreign to man as he exists and experiences himself'.[11] McCormick's concern seems to be that Christians should articulate a social ethic sufficient to guide, and perhaps even produce, those who would rule society. And that has to be an ethic acceptable to non-Christians, an ethic, at least in matters of content, in which Jesus is irrelevant.

Philip Wogaman argues that 'we cannot concede that this is a "post-Constantinian age" or a "post-Christian era" if we mean by these terms that the church should now relinquish attempts to organize the world on the basis of Christian presumptions'.[12] For "the problem really is *not* whether or not Christian faith can tolerate attempts to direct the course of social history. Such attempts are inevitable. Nor is it whether or not Christian faith should countenance the use of extrinsic forms of motivation. This, too, is inevitable, even when we seek to avoid it within the life of the church itself. Rather, it is the faithfulness with which we do this planning.'[13]

Unlike McCormick, Wogaman appeals to the 'Gospel' in support of his position. If we wonder how he can find a charter for rulers in the Gospel, we discover that he looks not to the story of Jesus to determine what is 'Christian' about his ethic, but rather to a series of propositions: (1) the goodness of created existence, (2) the value of individual life, (3) the unity of the human family in God, and (4) the equality of persons in God.[14] Wogaman claims that these are drawn from the 'core' of the Christian faith, but it can be pointed out that these 'presumptions' require little reference to who Jesus was or what he did for their meaning or intelligibility.

It is not my purpose to try to document on a case-by-case basis how one's understanding of 'social ethics' determines whether or how Jesus is understood.[15] Rather I am content to make the conceptual point that our 'christologies' are determined by our social-ethical presuppositions. The answer to Jesus' question 'Who do men say that I am?' depends on how we understand our social position and responsibility.[16] It is possible to argue, as indeed I hope to do, that the dependence should be the other way around.

Yoder notes that recent christology has suggested that we must choose between the Jesus of history and the Christ of dogma,[17] between the Jesus who can be reconstructed by historical methods and the Christ who is the son of God.[18] Such a choice is usually assumed to result from historical research, yet if I am correct such a choice reflects a social ethic which has lost sight of the fact that Jesus is, in his person and in his work, a social ethic. In Yoder's words, 'The Jesus of history is the Christ of faith. It is in hearing the revolutionary rabbi that we understand the existential freedom which is asked of the church. As we look closer at the Jesus whom Albert Schweitzer discovered, in all his eschatological realism, we find an utterly precise and practicable ethical instruction, practicable because in him the kingdom has actually come within reach. In him the sovereignty of Yahweh has become human history.'[19]

1.2. *The story of Jesus is a social ethic*

It is not sufficient that the social context of the church and its social ethics determine its view of Jesus. The reverse is true, for if Jesus cannot be said to have a social ethic or have implications for a social ethic but his story is a social ethic, then the form of the church must exemplify that ethic. How one settles what is usually thought of as straightforward christological issues, which are usually treated separately from social ethical concerns, will determine whether it is possible to give an account of how Jesus functions as the social ethic of the church. As a way of developing this point I will try to show that even though my own position would generally be associated with so called 'high christologies', it also has many parallels with the christology of liberal Protestantism, especially as found in the social gospel. Even though I do not share the liberal rejection of the classical christological formulas, the liberal concern to recover the centrality of Jesus' life strikes me as right.

The liberal attempt to return to the 'Jesus of history' was motivated by an attempt to reformulate Christianity without being bound to the classic Christian dogmas associated with Chalcedon.[20] The tendency of Logos or 'high christologies' toward forms of subordinationism was not the liberals' concern, but they did see that in the classical christological formulation there was a 'precarious loosening of the connection of the Son's divinity with Jesus of Nazareth, God's historical revelation'.[21] Therefore, the search for the historical Jesus motivated by liberalism, in spite of its methodological shortcomings, at least helped to keep the church honest 'through the constant pressure of having to do with a real human, historic figure. The controversy over the historical Jesus in theology is simply the modern form of the old question of Docetism, that ancient (and perennial) theological tendency so to absorb Jesus into current theological understanding that he becomes its construct. The concrete historical reality of the whole fabric called "Jesus" cannot be inferred from the Christian conviction that the ever-living Lord is known in faith and is present in the heart of the believer, just as the character of that Jesus is not to be inferred from the believer's heart or theology.'[22]

Walter Kasper made much the same point when he observes that Chalcedon, in the language and in the context of the problem at that time, provided an extremely precise version of what the New Testament understands to be involved in Jesus' history: 'namely in Jesus Christ, God himself has entered into a human history, and meets us there in a fully and completely human way'. But compared with the witness of Scripture, 'the christological dogma of Chalcedon represents a contraction. The dogma is exclusively concerned with the inner constitution of the divine and human subject. It separates this question from the total context of Jesus' history and fate, from the relation in which Jesus stands not only to the *Logos* but to "his Father", and we miss the total eschatological perspective of biblical theology.'[23] I have no wish to suggest that the language of incarnation is inherently defective, but only that it has and can provide a warrant for the assumption that one can know who Jesus is or 'what' he was in terms of essences, substances, and natures without the necessity in some way of knowing Jesus himself, without, that is, being his disciple.[24]

To be sure any christology must deal with how this particular individual is also affirmed as the savior of all people. But the appropriate form of his universality is lost if metaphysical and anthropological theories are substituted for the necessity of Christian lives and communities to witness to the significance of his story. For witness presupposes and claims universality but in a manner that makes clear that the universal can be claimed only through learning the particular form of discipleship required by this particular man.

For example much has been made in modern theology that we know Jesus only from the perspective of the resurrection – that is, the only Jesus we know is already the Jesus of faith, the Jesus created by the church. Some think this is a decisive problem because it seems that the 'real' Jesus is forever lost. But there is no 'real Jesus' except as he is known through the kind of life he demanded of his disciples – that the Gospels display the grammar of such a life should not therefore surprise us. Rather it only makes clear that the demand for 'historical accuracy' is a-historical insofar as the Gospels exhibit why the story of this man is inseparable from how that story teaches us to follow him.[25] The Gospels make clear that only because the disciples had first followed Jesus to Jerusalem were they able to understand the significance of the resurrection.

I want to be especially careful, however, how this is understood. For to emphasize the inseparability of knowing Jesus from how we must follow him may suggest a too complete identification of christology with soteriology. For even though a separation of christology and soteriology is not possible or desirable, too often soteriological concerns have determined what Jesus should be. For when the soteriological issues become primary, one must ask with Pannenberg, whether we have dealt with Jesus at all: 'Does it not perhaps involve projections onto Jesus' figure of the human desire for salvation and deification, of human striving after similarity to God, of the human duty to bring satisfaction for sins committed, of the human experience of bondage in failure, in the knowledge of one's own guilt, and most clearly in neo-Protestantism, projections of the idea of perfect religiosity, of perfect morality, of pure personality, of radical trust?'[26]

Thus ironically the liberal concern to find the Jesus behind the dogmas foundered on its own awareness that the 'historical Jesus' too often turned out to look like our prior ideal of what a good man should be. The humanistic assumptions of liberalism turned out to be the functional equivalent of Logos christology as Jesus, now stripped of metaphysical pretentions, became simply the best example of the kind of moral life that could be known and achieved apart from Jesus.[27] Thus for Rauschenbusch the significance of Jesus is that through his personality he initiated the Kingdom by democratizing the concept of God and by teaching the infinite worth of each personality.[28]

As Gustafson points out, this is a danger for all christologies in which Jesus is primarily understood as the proponent of an ethic rather than how his ethic might be integral to his life. For whenever Jesus becomes a pattern for a universally valid moral way of life his meaning is distorted. 'Christ is a means of life which in turn has moral expression. Thus the Christian ethic is in its fullest sense a way and pattern of life for those whose faith in God has Jesus Christ as its center. It is not first of all a universally valid objective model of morality. This it may provide, but only as an expression of God's way to man in Jesus Christ.'[29]

Therefore the claim that the story of Jesus is a social ethic means that there is no moral point or message that is separable from the story of Jesus as we find it in the Gospels. There can be no Christ figure because Jesus is the Christ.[30] Jesus' identity is prior to the 'meaning' of the story. There is no meaning which is separable from the story itself. That is why there can be no easy parallels drawn between the story of Jesus and other redeemer-redemption accounts. The difference

> lies neither in the difference between the saving qualities and action nor in the difference between redemptive needs. It is simply the unsubstitutable person about whom the story is told – his unsubstitutable deeds, words, and sufferings – that makes the real difference. Such exclusive reference to the person of Jesus as is found in the Gospel story is characteristic of neither Gnostic nor mystery religions. The Gospel story's indissoluble connection with an unsubstitutable identity in effect divests the savior story of its mythical quality. The Gospel story is a demythologization of the savior myth because the savior figure in the Gospel story is fully identified with Jesus of Nazareth. The early Christians would substitute no other names.[31]

The Christian savior story and ethic is that of Jesus himself. Jesus determines the story as the crucial person in the story. Thus his identity is grasped not through other savior stories, but by learning to follow him as the necessary condition for citizenship in his kingdom.

Put in more traditional categories, I am contending that Jesus' person cannot be separated from his work, the incarnation from the atonement. The severance between incarnation and atonement 'is the result of a failure to grasp the link that connects them, viz., the historical life of the incarnate Christ which is attested in the Evangelical records, or, in other words, that if one party (Eastern) has sought to find the essence of the gospel at Bethlehem, and another (Western) at Calvary, and each of them thereby presented a distorted picture of the gospel, it is because neither of them took sufficient account of what lay between, in Galilee and Judea.'[32]

But to emphasize the particularity of Jesus' story makes another question unavoidable: How can this man also be God, and consequently lay claim to universal, absolute, and insurpassable significance?[33] As I indicated above the temptation is to anchor Jesus' universality in a metaphysical or anthropological account free from the vicissitudes of history.[34] But to do so separates Jesus from social ethics by freeing those who claim to be his disciples from facing the fact that his universality rests on their faithfulness to the demands of his Kingdom. For faith has no

> timeless platform that lifts it outside the vulnerabilities of the historical realm. It boasts no certainty other than what accrues to a contingent event from the past, with its promise of claiming the present in the name of a purposive future. The person-event of Christ precedes a purposive future. The person-event of Christ precedes particular responses of faith. Yet it is precisely by means of such responses – those of the original witnesses no less than their successors – that revelation has its ongoing content and power. So completely is the truth of faith tied in with what is transmitted historically. Christological language is meaningful in relation to the actual life and impact of the man Jesus. And this relationship is made accessible to the present generation through the contribution of those who have already responded to that alteration of social-personal existence which roots in this Jesus.[35]

It may be, as Pannenberg argues, that Jesus' universal relevance is determined by the fulfillment of the hopes and deep longings of humanity.[36] But such fulfillment comes only as it is manifested by a particular community who have been trained by a particular man to surface and articulate a particular set of needs and longings. For Jesus' universality is manifested only by a people who are willing to take his cross as their story, as the necessary condition for living truthfully in this life.[37] As his cross was a social ethic so they become the continuation of that ethic in the world, until all are brought within his kingdom.

2. *Jesus: the Autobasileia*

The claim that the story of Jesus is a social ethic can be made clearer if we attend to the obvious: The only way we learn of Jesus is through his story as we find it in the gospel and as we see it lived in the lives of others. This fact has often been overlooked or assumed to be accidental to the real meaning of the 'Incarnation', but I argue that the narrative character of the Gospels is integral to the affirmation of Jesus' redemptive significance. This does not mean that the Gospels are biographies in the usual sense. They are proclamation; but the proclamation takes the form of a story of a man's life.[38] When this is recognized we can understand how Jesus provided a story to determine the polity of the church.

It has become a commonplace that one of the great contributions of critical scholarship has been a renewed sense of the significance of the Kingdom of God in Jesus' preaching and ministry. Ethicists have found this useful because the notion of the kingdom sounds like it involves normative guidelines to inform a social ethic. The Scriptures can be scavenged for individual sayings that seem to determine the character of such a kingdom – love, justice, righteousness. But this strategy is doomed to failure because such norms fail to do justice to the eschatological character of the kingdom.

Though there is no agreement how the various passages on the Kingdom as present, future, or even as growing are to be reconciled, there is a general agreement that the Kingdom first and foremost is the claim of God's lordship, his rule over all creation and history. Thus the Kingdom is 'totally and exclusively God's doing. It cannot be earned by religious or moral effort, imposed by political struggle, or projected in calculations. We cannot plan for it, organize it, make it, or build it, we cannot invent it or imagine it. It is given (Mt 21: 43; Lk 12:32), "appointed" (Lk 22: 29). We can only inherit it (Mt 25: 34).'[39]

But the ambiguity surrounding the timing of the Kingdom or our inability to 'make' it happen are not the primary reasons why the Kingdom should not invite speculation about what constitutes a just or ideal society considered in itself. Rather the reason the Kingdom cannot be made an ethical ideal is that the Scripture refuses to separate the Kingdom from the one that is the proclaimer of the Kingdom. 'Jesus is Himself the established Kingdom of God.'[40] Or in Origen's classical phrase Jesus is the *autobasileia* – the Kingdom in person.[41]

For the New Testament the proclamation of the Kingdom of God and the acknowledgement of the Lordship of Jesus come together. The fact that Jesus pointed to and preached the Kingdom without calling attention to himself is but an indication of the kind of rule he brings. Who he is revealed through his relation to God and this gives him the authority to proclaim the Kingdom. 'His vocation comes from the depths of his being. In the New Testament representation of Jesus Christ his authority and identity are absolutely inseparable from each other. The Church cannot in good faith try to separate what the Holy Spirit has joined. Jesus Christ is its only valid warrant for preaching the Kingdom of God.'[42] Put differently, Jesus refuses to accept the role of Messiah as if it constituted a 'part' that he was playing. Rather, his whole self is an act of participation in God's purpose for man. 'He is the supreme agent of the Kingdom, agent both in the sense of one who acts, and in the sense of one who represents the interests of another. He holds nothing in reserve for some other role. His spirit does not recoil upon itself but leads him straightway into the most solid and massive relationship with the actual world. The religious term for this massive relationship is Lordship.'[43]

There is no way to know the Kingdom except by learning of the story of this man Jesus. For his story defines the nature of how God rules and how such a rule creates a corresponding 'world' and society.[44] There is no way to talk about the social ethics of Christianity except as they are determined by the form of Jesus' life as we find it told by the general narratives. 'The whole Jesus was permeated by the kingdom of God, and since that kingdom is the effectuation of God's reign, it is Jesus as a whole who points to the kingdom in a new way. Just as the parable does not illustrate ideas better stated non-parabolically, and so become dispensable, so Jesus is not merely an illustration for the kingdom which can be more adequately grasped apart from him – say in mystic encounters or in abstract formulation. His task was not to impart correct concepts about the kingdom but to make it possible for men to respond to it; as a parable of the kingly God, he invited men to look through him into the kingdom, with the result that his hearers could not respond to the kingdom without responding to him.'[45]

But what can it possibly mean to claim that Jesus determines the character of the Kingdom in terms of actual sociological and political alternatives? At the very least it means that we are required to rethink our everyday sense of the 'political'. For to know the kingdom through the story of Jesus requires us to believe that the polity into which we are called can only be based on that power which comes from trusting in the truth. No one has put this better than Rauschenbusch as he rightly sees that Jesus requires a polity that goes beyond the bounds of conventional social ethics. For as he points out Jesus wielded

> no sword but the truth. But mark well, that truth was a sword in his hands and not a yard-stick. It cut into the very marrow of his generation. It was mighty to the casting down of strongholds. So it has proved itself wherever it has been used in dead earnest. It reveals lies and their true nature, as when Satan was touched by the spear of Ithuriel. It makes injustice quail on its throne, chafe, sneer, abuse, hurl its spear, tenders its goal, and finally offer to serve as truth's vassal. But the truth that can do such things is not an old woman wrapped in the spangled robes of earthly authority, bedizened with golden ornaments, the marks of honor given by injustice in turn for services rendered, and muttering dead formulas of the past. The truth that can serve God as the mightiest of his archangels is robed only in love, her weighty limbs unfettered by needless weight, calm-browed, her eyes terrible with beholding God . . .
>
> Jesus deliberately rejected force and chose truth. Truth asks no odds. She will not ask that her antagonist's feet be put in shackles before she will cross swords with him. Christ's Kingdom needs not the spears of Roman legionaries to prop it, not even the clubs of Galilean peasants. Whenever Christianity shows an inclination to use constraint in its own defense or support, it thereby furnishes presumptive evidence that it has become a thing of this world, for it finds the means of this world adapted to its end.[46]

2.1. *Discipleship and Kingdom*

I cannot hope to provide the scriptural basis to defend the view that Jesus is best understood as the story that authorizes the preaching of the Kingdom. But I hope at least to suggest that this way of putting the matter is appropriate to the form and content of the gospels by calling attention to the pericope containing Peter's confession in Mark. Peter's failure to understand his confession is an indication that it is necessary to know Jesus' story and why the Gospels appear as a story. The brief encounter between Peter and Jesus makes clear that the story of Jesus, like most good stories, changes the hearer. A story that claims to be the truth of our existence requires that our lives, like the lives of the disciples, be changed by following him. The interrelationship between this demand and the character of Jesus' messiahship is made clear as Jesus here asks what no man should ask from another – his life.[47] The 'messianic secret' in Mark, whatever other purpose it was meant to serve, makes clear that to be a disciple of Jesus requires a training beyond what any of them had imagined. This is the lesson Peter had yet to learn.

> And Jesus went on with his disciples, to the villages of Caesarea Philippi; and on the way he asked his disciples, 'Who do men say that I am?' And they told him, 'John the Baptist; and others say, Elijah; and others one of the prophets.' And he asked them, 'But who do you say that I am?' Peter answered him, 'You are the Christ.' And he charged them to tell no one about him.
>
> And he began to teach them that the Son of man must suffer many things, and be rejected by the elders and the chief priests and the scribes, and be killed, and after three days rise again. And he said this plainly. And Peter took him, and began to rebuke him. But turning and seeing his disciples, he rebuked Peter, and said, 'Get behind me, Satan! For you are not on the side of God, but of men.'
>
> And he called to him the multitude with his disciples, and said to them, 'If any man would come after me let him deny himself and take up his cross and follow me. For whoever would save his life will lose it; and whoever loses his life *for my sake* and the gospel's will save it. For what does it profit a man, to gain the whole world and forfeit his life? For what can a man give in return for his life? For whoever is ashamed of me and of my words in this adulterous and sinful generation, of him will the Son of Man also be ashamed, when he comes in the glory of his Father with the holy angels.' And he said to them, 'Truly, I say to you, there are some standing here who will not taste death before they see the kingdom of God come with power' (Mk 8:27–9:1).

This is obviously not only an important passage for Mark but for the whole New Testament as it asks the central question, 'Who do

men say that I am?' Each answer represents different religious and
political options of the day. Peter at first seems to get it right, this is
the messiah whom we have long awaited. This is the one who will
restore us to power and glory, who will provide the power to return
Israel to her preeminence among the nations. Peter has indeed learned
the name.

But Jesus then begins to tell them that he is not going to be recognized as having such power, but indeed will be rejected and killed.
And Peter, still imbued with the old order, suggests this is no way for
a savior to talk; saviors are people with power to affect the world.
To save means to be 'in control', or to seek to be 'in control', and
Jesus seeks neither. His power is of a different order and the powers
of this world will necessarily put him to death because they recognize,
better than Peter, what a threat to power looks like. For here is one
who invites others to participate in a kingdom of God's love, a kingdom which releases the power of giving and service. The powers of
this world cannot comprehend such a kingdom. Here is a man who
insists it is possible, if God's rule is acknowledged and trusted, to
serve without power.

Jesus thus rebukes Peter who had learned the name but not the
story that determines the meaning of the name. For to say the name
rightly is to know how to narrate the history of Israel, to describe
Israel; 'to identify that people . . . with the identity of Jesus Christ is
to narrate the history of Jesus . . . in such a way that it is seen as the
individual and climactic summing up, incorporation, and identification of the whole people, by which the people receive their identification'.[48] But Peter had not learned what that kind of identification
entailed.

So Jesus tells him. But he first calls not only his disciples, but the
multitudes. This is not a word for the few. And the 'truth' turns out
to be that if we are to follow him we must learn to lose our lives not
as an end in itself, but for 'his sake'. We can understand, perhaps,
how we might need to lose our lives for family, homeland, or some
noble cause – but he says you must lose your life for him, Jesus. Nor
does he mean that self-sacrifice is a good in itself. Just as truth is not
freeing unless it is his truth, so sacrifice will not help us unless it is
the sacrifice that is done in the name and form of the Kingdom as we
find it in his life. There is no truth beyond him: His story is the truth
of the Kingdom. And that truth turns out to be the cross.

The cross was not something accidental in Jesus' life, but the necessary outcome of his life and of his mission. His death is of decisive
significance, not because it alone wrought salvation for us, but

because it was the end and fulfillment of his life. In his death he finished the work that it was his mission to perform. In this sense the cross is not a detour or a hurdle on the way to the kingdom, 'nor is it even the way to the kingdom; it is the kingdom come.'[49]

And it is such because the cross more than any other event reveals the social character of Jesus' mission. Jesus was the bearer of a new possibility of human and social relationships. That is why the incarnation is not the affirmation of God's approval of the human (as previously defined on other grounds), but God's breaking through the borders of man's definition of what is human to give a new and formative definition of the human in Jesus.[50] The cross of Christ 'was not an inexplicable or chance event, which happened to strike him, like illness or accident . . . The cross of Calvary was not a difficult family situation, not a frustration of visions of personal fulfillment, a crushing debt or a nagging in-law; it was the political, legally to be expected result of a moral clash with the powers ruling his society.'[51]

It is in this way that Christian discipleship creates a polity; it is in this way it *is* a polity: Being a Christian is an expression of our obedience to and in a community based on Jesus' messiahship. And it was this that Peter had not learned, he assumed that this Kingdom would look like the kingdoms of the world. But he was wrong: the kingdoms of the world derive their being from our fear of one another; the rule of God means that a community can exist where trust rules, trust made possible by the knowledge that our existence is bounded by the truth. Like Peter, few of us are ready for such 'knowledge', but insofar as we are able to make it part of our lives we in fact become citizens of his Kingdom.

2.2. *Discipleship and community*

To be a disciple is to be part of a new community, a new polity, which is formed on Jesus' obedience to the cross. The constitutions of this new polity are the Gospels. The Gospels are not just the depiction of a man, but they are manuals for the training necessary to be part of the new community. To be a disciple means to share Christ's story, to participate in the reality of God's rule.

I have tried to suggest that such a rule is more than the claim that God is Lord of this world. It is the creation of a 'world' through a story that teaches us how such a rule is constituted.[52] Through Jesus' life Christians learn the power of such a rule by loving as God has loved. That is, they love their 'enemies, and do good and lend without expecting return'; for, if they do their 'reward will be great, and you will be sons of the Most High; for he is kind to the ungrateful and the selfish. Be merciful, even as your Father is merciful' (Luke 6:35-36).[53]

It is through such love that Christians learn that they are to serve as he served. Such service is not an end in itself, but rather reflects the Kingdom into which Christians have been drawn. This means that Christians insist on service which may appear ineffective to the world.[54] For the service that Christians are called upon to provide does not have as its aim to make the world better, but to demonstrate that Jesus has made possible a new world, a new social order.

It is a new world because no longer does the threat of death force us into desperate measures to insure our safety or significance.[55] A people freed from the threat of death must form a polity because they can afford to face the truth of their existence without fear and defensiveness. They can even take the risk of having the story of a crucified Lord as their central reality. He is a strange Lord, appears powerless, but his powerlessness turns out to be the power of truth against the violence of falsehood.

The power that comes from trusting in truth is but a correlative of how we have learned through Jesus to accept our life as a gift. In Jesus we have met the one that has the authority and power to forgive our fevered search to gain security through deception, coercion, and violence. For to learn to follow Jesus means we must learn to accept such forgiveness, and it is no easy thing to accept, as acceptance requires recognition of our sin as well as our vulnerability. But by learning to be forgiving we are enabled to view other lives not as threats but as gifts. Thus in contrast to all societies built on shared resentments and fears, Christian community is formed by a story that enables them to trust the otherness of the other as the very sign of the forgiving character of God's kingdom.

By making the story of such a Lord central to their lives Christians are enabled to see the world accurately and without illusion. Because they have the confidence that Jesus' cross and resurrection are the final words concerning God's rule they have the courage to see the world for what it is: Our existence is ruled by powers and forces that we hardly know how to name, much less defend against.[56] These powers derive their strength from our fear of destruction, cloaking their falsehood with the appearance of convention, from their offering us security in exchange for truth. By being trained through Jesus' story we have the means to name and prevent these powers from claiming our lives as their own.[57]

From this perspective the church is the organized form of Jesus' story. The church provides the conditions we need to describe what is going on in our lives. That does not mean that all other descriptions are rendered irrelevant, but rather that we learn how to negotiate the limits and possibilities of those descriptions. We test them against the cross. It is in his cross that we learn we live in a world that is based on the presupposition that man, not God, rules.

Jesus is the story that forms the church. This means that the church first serves the world by helping the world to know what it means to be the world. For without a 'contrast model' the world has no way to know or feel the oddness of its dependence on power for survival. Because of the church the world can feel the strangeness of trying to build a politics that is inherently untruthful; the world lacks the basis to demand truth from its people. Because of a community formed by the story of Christ the world can know what it means to be a society committed to the growth of individual gifts and differences. In a community that has no fear of the truth the otherness of the other can be welcomed as a gift rather than a threat.

All politics should be judged by the character of the people it produces. The depth and variety of character which a polity sustains is correlative of the narrative that provides its identity and purpose. The contention and witness of the Church is that the story of Jesus provides a flourishing of gifts which other polities cannot know. It does so because Christians have been nourished on the story of a savior who insisted on being nothing else than what he was. By so being the son of God he provided us with the confidence that insofar as we become his disciples our particularity and our regard for the particularity of our brothers and sisters in Christ contributes to his Kingdom. Our stories become part of the story of the Kingdom.

The most striking social ethical fact about the church is that the story of Jesus provides the basis to break down the arbitrary and false boundaries between people. The church is an international society only because we have a story that teaches us to regard the other as a fellow member of God's kingdom. Such regard is not based on facile doctrines of tolerance or equality, but are forged from our common experience of being trained to be disciples of Jesus. The universality of the church is based on the particularity of Jesus' story and on the fact that his story trains us to see one another as God's people. Because we have been so trained we can see and condemn the narrow loyalties that create 'the world'.

3. Jesus: the story that forms the church

The account I have tried to provide, to illuminate how the story of Jesus is a social ethic, is often dismissed by those who are impressed by the fact that the Gospels do not give us the 'historical Jesus', but only the Jesus as the early Christians understood him.[58] We know that Peter could not have called Jesus the Christ because he did not speak Greek. Therefore it is alleged to be incorrect to speak of Jesus as a social ethic. The best we can do is speak of the gospels as a social ethic.

I have tried to show that, if we pay attention to the narrative and self-involving character of the Gospels, as the early disciples did, there is no way to speak of Jesus' story without it forming our own. The story it forms creates a community which corresponds to the form of his life. As Nils Dahl maintains,

> In all New Testament writings there is a close relationship between the church and Jesus, but within this relationship Jesus retains priority and sovereignty. Without doubt, it has always been possible to use the sovereignty of the Lord to conceal his servants' will to power and to enforce comformity upon lax and dissident members of the church. But at least in the major writings of the New Testament, the memory of Jesus transcends ecclesiastical expediency and collective needs. For this reason, both loyal Christians and outside critics have been able to use the Jesus tradition to rebuke the state and the practices of the church at any given time and place. Some of the New Testament authors themselves have done this. In doing so, they did not follow any uniform pattern but drew upon various aspects of the tradition, using it for their own purposes. Just this diversity within the New Testament canon makes it impossible for a conservative or critical orthodoxy to resolve the problem of the relations between the church and Jesus once and for all times. It rather calls for spiritual discernment, and the answer depends upon the ability to distinguish between the spirits.[59]

The social ethical task of the church, therefore, is to be the kind of community that tells and tells rightly the story of Jesus. But it can never forget that Jesus' story is a many-sided tale. We do not have just one story of Jesus, but four. To learn to tell and live the story truthfully does not mean that we must be able to reconstruct 'what really happened' from the four. Rather it means that we, like the early

Christians, must learn that to understand Jesus' life is inseparable from how we learn to live our own. And that there are various ways to do that is clear by the diversity of the Gospels.

To tell the story truthfully cannot be guaranteed through historical investigation, though it certainly can be in service to the truth, but by being the kind of people who can bear the burden of that story with joy. We, no less than the first Christians, are the continuation of the truth made possible by God's rule. We continue this truth when we see the struggle of each to be faithful to the gospel as essential to each of our lives. I understand my own story through seeing the different ways in which others are called to be his disciples. If we so help one another, perhaps, like the early Christians when challenged about the viability of their faith, we can say, 'But see how we love one another'.[60]

Notes

1. Alasdair MacIntyre, *Difficulties in Christian Belief* (New York: Philosophical Library, 1959), p. 118. I am not suggesting that the truthfulness of Christianity or any other faith depends only on exemplary lives, but rather whatever the rationale for religious truth claims they are inseparable from such lives. Individual challenges to the coherence of religious belief will need to be dealt with individually. It is often thought that the truthfulness of religious belief is dependent on one's being able to provide a foundational account of truth, but in contrast I am suggesting that the truthfulness of religious convictions needs no 'foundation' that is separable from the claims themselves. Even though this is an issue of religious epistemology it has christological implications since foundationalist accounts always tend to make Jesus' particularity accidental to the meaning of the 'Christ-event'. For positions similar to the one I am suggesting see Diogenes Allen, 'Motives, Rationales, and Religious Beliefs', *American Philosophical Quarterly*, 3:2 (April, 1966), 1–17; and James McClendon and James Smith, *Understanding Religious Convictions* (Notre Dame: U. of Notre Dame Press, 1975).

2. St. Athanasius, *The Incarnation of the Word of God* (New York: Macmillan, 1946), p. 96.

3. See for example George Huntson Williams, 'Christology and Church-State Relations in the Fourth Century', *Church History*, 20: 3 and 4 (September, 1951; December, 1951), 3–33; 3–26. He says, 'It is clear that the conception one has of Christ and his several offices will affect one's view of Caesar and the legitimacy of his claims. For what the Christian is willing to render unto Caesar depends in part on his understanding of Christ as God and of Jesus' commandments as divine. Perhaps no dominical injunction has been rendered by christological elaboration more difficult in Christian practice, personal and corporate, than Jesus' supposedly simple distinction between the proper claims of Caesar and

God ... [No. 3, pp. 3, 9]. Over against the Catholic insistence on the consubstantiality of the Son, eventually made also explicit for the Holy Spirit, and the full deity and full manhood of Christ, are the various forms of subordination of the Son and the Holy Spirit worked out among the different Arianizing parties of the fourth century. Roughly speaking these two christologies gave rise to, or are at least associated with, two main views of the Empire and the relationship of the Church thereto. According to one view the emperor is bishop of bishops. According to the other, the emperor is within the Church' (No. 3, p. 9). Part of the problem with the standard works that treat the early christological developments is they so seldom contextualize those debates for their social significance. See for example Aloys Grillmeier, *Christ in Christian Tradition* (New York: Sheed and Ward, 1965).

4. It is instructive, for example, that almost all christologies are written with almost no concern for the social form of Jesus' work or the sociological situation of the church. At best authors may include a last chapter on the 'social-ethical implications'. Without denying much valuable work is thereby done it is my contention that to so structure one's christology is to distort the kind of messiah Jesus was. I have in mind such significant and sophisticated presentations as Pannenberg, Rahner, Kasper, and Barth. A recent notable exception is Jon Sobrino's *Christology at the Crossroads* (New York: Orbis Books, 1978). I am in deep sympathy with Sobrino's intention especially as he locates discipleship as a central christological motive. Moreover, unlike much of 'liberation theology', he carefully controls the meaning of 'liberation' by insisting that its meaning be christologically controlled. (I continue to doubt, however, if 'liberation' should be the central metaphor to describe Christian life and existence especially in the light of Sobrino's sensitive discussion of the place of suffering in the Christian life.) I am also sympathetic with his emphasis on the 'historical Jesus' though I am doubtful whether his thesis that Jesus' understanding of the kingdom changed at the middle of his career can be historically established. Sobrino rightly emphasizes, however, that classical christological formulations, including claims about 'incarnation', must come at the end not at the beginning of our christological reflection.

5. John Howard Yoder, *The Politics of Jesus* (Grand Rapids: Eerdmans Publishing Co., 1972), pp. 15–19. My indebtedness to Yoder's position throughout should be evident.

6. Ernst Troeltsch, *The Social Teaching of the Christian Churches* (New York: Macmillan Co., 1931), p. 50.

7. Troeltsch, pp. 39–40.

8. Yoder, pp. 16–19.

9. For example Duane Friesen documents that Troeltsch's own understanding of the church-world problem was Lutheran and his typology was thus biased as it made the social ethic of the church type appear to be the only viable alternative. 'Normative Factors in Troeltsch's Typology of Religious Association', *Journal of Religious Ethics*, 3:2 (Fall, 1975), 271–283. H. R. Niebuhr's famous typology developed in *Christ and Culture* is more adequate, but in spite of Niebuhr's attempt not to choose one type against the other his general preference for the 'Christ Transforming Culture' type seems evident. Moreover Niebuhr's rather

indiscriminating use of 'culture' tends to distort the 'Christ against culture' type, as often it is part of the force of representatives of that type to discriminate between the various aspects of 'culture' in which the Christian can participate.

10. Richard McCormick, 'Christianity and Morality'. *Catholic Mind*, 75:1316 (October, 1977), p. 18.

11. McCormick, p. 28. What one would like to have is a fuller discussion from McCormick about what the christological implications are for the claim that Jesus is normative only because he experienced what it means to be *human* in the fullest manner. Where, for example, did McCormick find out what it means to be human? If that is determined on grounds prior to Jesus then is Jesus simply the best example we have of such an experience? If so then why prefer Jesus to Moses or Buddha? To be fair McCormick is not alone in his failure as an ethicist to develop the christological implications of his position as that is generally the case.

12. Philip Wogaman, *A Christian Method of Moral Judgment* (Philadelphia: The Westminster Press, 1976), p. 185.

13. Wogaman, p. 193.

14. Wogaman, p. 104.

15. The work of Reinhold Niebuhr and of Paul Ramsey are particularly interesting from this perspective. Niebuhr was of course explicit about the irrelevancy of Jesus for social ethics except as he provided an indiscriminate norm that stands in judgment over all social activity. In spite of his criticism of the social gospel much of Niebuhr's christology continued in the vein of treating Jesus not as the redeemer but as the perfect example or teacher of love. Ramsey seems to be trying to develop a more 'orthodox' christology though his emphasis on love as the essence of Jesus' teaching may continue to separate the teacher from the teaching. Thus, at least early in his career, Ramsey was willing to justify picking and choosing among Jesus' 'teaching'. In *Basic Christian Ethics* (New York: Charles Scribner's Sons, 1950) he argues that 'the radical content of Jesus' strenuous sayings depends, it seems, on his apocalyptic expectation. As a consequence they cannot be translated from their mother tongue without danger of serious loss of meaning. We cannot, for example, recommend non-resistance or returning good for evil as obvious to the degree in which anger or impure thoughts or even anxiety may be discouraged among men and sabbath observances set aside. Therefore, non-resistance has frequently first been turned into non-violent resistance, and this then generalized to fit perhaps any age or circumstance. Jesus' original teaching about non-resistance seems in contrast to suit only an apocalyptic perspective' (p. 35). In the absence of such a perspective Ramsey concludes that to take such a teaching seriously cannot be literally justified.

16. I am sympathetic with Segundo's claim that every theology is political and that is especially true of 'academic theology's' pretentious assumption that it is not 'political'. I am less sure than Segundo that it is easy to characterize 'academic theology', but he is certainly correct that much of the theology done in our universities ignores its tie with the political status-quo. Such theology is surely in 'bad-faith' when it tries to defeat 'liberation theology' by accusing it of politicizing theology. Given that, however, I find Segundo's general position misleading if not perverse. By turning everything into ideology, even if by the latter you only

mean a system that serves as a necessary backdrop of any human action, Segundo makes the question of truth irrelevant. And by denying the question of truth we also make Jesus irrelevant. He fails to see that it is not sufficient to claim that every theology is political, but more important is the question of the kind of politics required by the Gospel. For exactly the political power of the Gospel is its ability to provide the critical skills necessary to free us from those ideologies that would claim our lives. Juan Luis Segundo, *Liberation of Theology* (New York: Orbis Books, 1976).

17. Yoder, p. 106.

18. Nils Dahl argues that we cannot draw a sharp distinction between the Gospel message and the recollection of the apostles as that is a distinction that early Christianity did not know. 'On the contrary, for the evangelists – and we dare add, for the apostles themselves – it was precisely the encounter of the apostles with the resurrected Christ that revived their recollection of his earthy life.' *Jesus in the Memory of the Early Church* (Minneapolis: Augsburg Publishing House, 1976), p. 27. Leander Keck has developed a powerful argument that there is a stronger continuity between the 'historical Jesus' and the 'faith of the disciples' than the Bultmann school assumed. See his *A Future for the Historical Jesus* (Nashville: Abingdon Press, 1971).

19. Yoder, p. 107. Julian Hartt contends, 'The distinction between faith in Jesus Christ and the faith Jesus Christ himself held, is theologically unreal and Christianly unimportant. Even if historical scholarship were able to uncover the "faith" Jesus Christ held in the same sense in which the historian might be able to tell us what faith Abraham Lincoln held, we would have in that alone an insufficient reason, if a reason at all, for making the distinction here rejected.' *A Christian Critique of American Culture* (New York: Harper and Row, 1967), p. 181.

20. Keck, p. 19.

21. Wolfhart Pannenberg, *Jesus – God and Man* (Philadelphia: Westminster Press, 1968), pp. 164–165.

22. Keck, p. 127.

23. Walter Kasper, *Jesus the Christ* (New York: Paulist Press, 1977), p. 238.

24. In his account of Clarence Jordan, James McClendon gives an account of a conversation between Jordan and his brother, Bob, that makes this point well. Jordan has asked Bob, a lawyer, to help defend his interracial community farm. Bob responded:

'Clarence, I can't do that. You know my political aspirations. Why if I represented you, I might lose my job, my house, everything I've got.'
'*We* might lose everything too, Bob.'
'It's different for you.'
'Why is it different? I remember, it seems to me, that you and I joined the church the same Sunday, as boys. I expect when we came forward the preacher asked me about the same questions as he did you. He asked me, "Do you accept Jesus as your Lord and Savior." And I said, "Yes." What did you say?'
'I follow Jesus, Clarence, up to a point.'
'Could that point by any chance be – the cross?'

'That's right. I follow him to the cross, but not on the cross. I'm not getting myself crucified.'

'Then I don't believe you're a disciple. You're an admirer of Jesus, but not a disciple of his. I think you ought to go back to the church you belong to, and tell them you're an admirer not a disciple.'

'Well now, if everyone who felt like I do did that, we wouldn't *have* a church, would we?'

'The question,' Clarence said, 'is, "Do you have a church?"''

Biography as Theology (Nashville: Abingdon Press, 1974), pp. 127–128. The problem with the doctrine of the 'incarnation' is that it too often becomes an object in itself rather than direct us to the kind of life necessary to appreciate what it means to say that Jesus' life is the final revelation of God. We thus become admirers rather than followers.

25. Though my general christological approach is closer to those that want to do christology from 'below', I generally find the contrast between christology from 'above' or 'below' less than helpful. See for example Peter Hodgson's criticism of that way of conceiving the issue in *Jesus – Word and Presence* (Philadelphia: Fortress Press, 1971), pp. 60–71. He says, 'What is needed is a way of avoiding the supernaturalism and docetism of the Logos-flesh christology, of overcoming the subjectivistic bias of a self-transcending anthropology, and of moving beyond the impasse of the doctrine of the two natures entirely, while at the same time holding radically to the historical man Jesus as the criterion of christology' (p. 71).

26. Pannenberg, p. 47.

27. Those that are usually identified with a 'low christology' often appear more tolerant and open to other options. For by placing Jesus' significance in his moral teaching or his personality it seems what is important is whether someone exemplifies the morality rather than learn to follow Jesus. However what many fail to notice is when Jesus is primarily treated as the perfect example or teacher of morality he turns out to be remarkably anti-semitic. For then it must be shown that the Jews were somehow morally deficient if not degenerate to reject the obvious moral superiority of Jesus. Nowhere can this be more clearly seen than in Kant's portrayal of the Jews. He thus claims that in contrast to the Christian commitment to universal morality, 'Judaism is really not a religion at all but merely a union of a number of people who, since they belonged to a particular stock, formed themselves into a commonwealth under purely political laws, and not into a church; nay, it was intended to be merely an earthly state so that, were it possibly to be dismembered through adverse circumstances, there would still remain to it the political faith in its eventual reestablishment.' *Religion Within the Limits of Reason Alone* (New York: Harper Torchbooks, 1960), p. 116. The 'liberal' condemnation of the Jews is often attributed to their ignorance of Judaism, but I am suggesting that it is structurally built into their position. Their failure to appreciate the particularity of Jesus is a correlative of their assumption of the backwardness of the Jews. Ironically enough, and given proper qualifications, Kant's characterization of the Jews above is very close to my view of what the Church, and its corresponding christology, should entail. Central to my

position is the assumption that Jesus' significance can only be appreciated by recognizing he was the messiah to the Jews.

28. Walter Rauschenbusch, *Theology of the Social Gospel* (Nashville: Abingdon Press, 1917), pp. 146–187. I think there are other aspects of Rauschenbusch's position, however, that qualify his more explicit christological claims in a manner not too unlike the position I am trying to develop.

29. James Gustafson, *Christ and the Moral Life* (New York: Harper and Row, 1968), p. 183.

30. Hans Frei, *The Identity of Jesus Christ* (Philadelphia: Fortress Press, 1975), p. 65.

31. Frei, p. 59.

32. George Hendry, *The Gospel of the Incarnation* (London: SCM Press, 1959), p. 31.

33. Kasper, p. 17.

34. From this perspective I am sympathetic with Kasper's criticism of Rahner's christology. He rightly observes that Rahner takes too little notice of the fact that the true reality of 'history implies a determination of the transcendental conditions affecting the possibility of understanding. It is a determination which is not derivable from and not wholly conceivable in terms of those conditions' (pp. 48–52).

35. Warren Groff, *Christ the Hope of the Future* (Grand Rapids: Eerdmans, 1971), p. 47.

36. Pannenberg, p. 205.

37. In some ways the position I am defending has close affinities with Abelard's 'subjective' theory of the atonement, but I hope to avoid some of the legitimate criticisms of that theory by emphasizing the moral context and meaning of the way Jesus affects us.

38. Frei rightly argues that 'if the Gospel story is to function religiously in a way that is at once historical and christological, the central focus will have to be on the history-like narration of the final sequence, rather than on Jesus' sayings in the preaching pericopes ... Jesus' individual identity comes to focus directly in the passion-resurrection narrative rather than in the account and teaching in his earlier ministry. It is in this final and climactic sequence that the storied Jesus is most of all himself, and there – unlike those earlier points at which we can get to his individual identity only ambiguously – we are confronted with him directly as an unsubstitutable individual who is what he does and undergoes and is manifested directly as who he is' (pp. 141–143).

39. Kasper, p. 81.

40. Karl Barth, *Church Dogmatics* II/2 (Edinburgh: T. and T. Clark, 1957), p. 177.

41. Origen, 'Commentary on Matthew', in *Ante-Nicene Fathers* (New York: Scribner's Sons, 1926), p. 498.

42. Hartt, pp. 166–167.

43. Hartt, p. 198. Jesus is the son of God, therefore, to the extent he is the agent of the Kingdom. The quandary of how to account for the unity of his person in the traditional very God–very man formulas is less a problem from this perspective. Jesus' Sonship rests on his perfect obedience to the cross and his divinity is thus the form of his humanity.

44. The influence of some of the work in sociology of religion and knowledge is beginning to have a fruitful effect on the kind of work that is done in New Testament ethics. For example even though Gager's *Kingdom and Community* (Englewood Cliffs, New Jersey: Prentice Hall, 1975) implicitly seems to have a destructive intent his methodology makes clear that 'despite protests to the contrary, the churches from the very beginning presented Rome with a serious political problem. Christians were constantly amazed to find themselves cast as enemies of the Roman order, but in retrospect we must admit that it was the Romans who had the more realistic insight' (pp. 27–28). Or as Leander Keck observes, pursuing the 'concern for the ethos of early Christians, and the relation of the NT to it, would recast the study of early Christian ethics and theology. NT ethics would no longer be confined to an analysis of the ways in which the dialectic of indicative and imperative becomes concrete, nor would it be presented as a series of attempts to apply principles to situations or to spell out the Christian ideal. Once the ethos of Christians came into view, it would become clear that NT ethics was sweated out of the interaction between the ethos and the gospel, an interaction which in turn helped to produce an ongoing ethos.' 'On the Ethos of Early Christians' *Journal of American Academy of Religion*, 42:3 (September, 1974), 451.

45. Keck, *A Future for the Historical Jesus*, p. 245.

46. Walter Rauschenbusch, *The Righteousness of the Kingdom* (Nashville: Abingdon Press, 1968), pp. 92–93.

47. Kasper, p. 102. Kasper makes some very interesting suggestions how various aspects of Jesus' life implicitly rest on assumption of his authority as the messiah. His kind of approach has much to commend it as it avoids the concern with Jesus' consciousness and instead concentrates on his life. The historical and philosophical difficulties connected with the question of the messianic consciousness make that way of asking the question fruitless. Rather it is better to ask, Did this man teach and act with authority?

48. Frei, p. 159. Put differently, Peter had not learned, indeed, could not have yet learned at this point, that 'Christ' cannot be separated from Jesus. For the kind of 'Lord' Jesus is is revealed finally only in the cross, thus making it impossible to separate the meaning of being 'the anointed one' from his life. Too often the attempt to substantiate who Jesus was by trying to find the meaning of the various titles in the Gospel fails to acknowledge that the meaning of the titles is given new meaning from the narrative. As Sobrino suggests, 'The theological importance of the name "Jesus Christ," then, is that the two words are brought together. The abstract term cannot be separated from the concrete name. Isolated from the proper name, the term "Christ" is an abstract honorific into which people can project all sorts of ideas and yearnings. It could become the basis for some new religion, in the pejorative sense of that term. But the term loses its abstract air if it is linked with the proper name "Jesus"' (p. 285).

49. Yoder, p. 61.

50. Yoder, p. 101.

51. Yoder, p. 132.

52. The way the early Christians put this was simply that with Jesus a new 'aeon' had begun. Such an 'aeon' is not simply a 'worldview' but requires that a

social world be created in accordance with the new social relations envisaged. Elsewhere I have tried to suggest the Christian story teaches us to see the world differently, but such seeing requires a community if such a vision is to be sustained. See my *Vision and Virtue* (Notre Dame: Fides, 1974).

53. Anthony Burgess has recently put this well as he points out 'the technique of loving others has to be learned, like any other technique. The practice of love is, we may say, ludic; it has to be approached like a game. It is necessary first to learn to love oneself, which is difficult; love of others will follow more easily then, however. The serious practitioners of the game, or *ludus amoris*, will find it useful to form themselves into small groups, or "churches," and meet at set intervals for mutual encouragement and inspiration.' 'Love and Sin in 1985' *New York Times Book Review* (August 13, 1978), p. 3.

54. For a further development of this point see my 'Politics of Charity', in *Truthfulness and Tragedy* (Notre Dame: University of Notre Dame Press, 1977), pp. 132–143.

55. I have not explicitly tried to suggest how the resurrection is an integral aspect of Jesus' story though it certainly is. As Frei suggests the gospels seem to be saying something like this: 'Our argument is that to grasp what this identity, Jesus of Nazareth (which has been made directly accessible to us), is is to believe that he has been, in fact, raised from the dead. Someone may reply that in that case the most perfectly depicted character and most nearly lifelike fictional identity ought always in fact to have lived a factual historical life. We answer that the argument holds good only in this one and absolutely unique case, where the described entity (who or what he is, i.e., Jesus Christ, the presence of God) is totally identical with his factual existence. He *is* the resurrection and the life. How can he be conceived as not resurrected?' (pp. 145–146). It is, of course, true that the only Jesus the gospel writers know is the resurrected Christ but that does not mean that their depiction of his life is thereby distorted. For example see Nils Dahl's *Jesus in the Memory of the Early Church*, pp. 11–29.

56. For an account of the powers see Yoder, pp. 135–162. Richard Mouw also bases his account of a Christian Social Ethic on this theme. See his *Politics and the Biblical Drama* (Grand Rapids: Eerdmans, 1976), pp. 85–116. Mouw's criticisms of Yoder are interesting, but I think fail to challenge the primary point that the powers can only be brought back to their true nature by refusing to acknowledge their false claims of authority.

57. I still find Rauschenbusch's account of the forces that put Jesus to death – religious bigotry, graft and political power, corruption of justice, mob spirit and action, militarism, racial sin in class contempt – one of the most compelling accounts of the kind of powers Jesus exposed and redeemed. According to Rauschenbusch, theology 'has made a fundamental mistake in treating the atonement as something distinct, and making the life of Jesus a mere staging for his death, a matter almost negligible in the work of salvation.' *Theology for the Social Gospel*, p. 260. It is necessary to keep the two connected as otherwise we fail to see how Jesus' life provided the grounds for solidarity necessary to overcome those powers that conspired to put him to death.

58. For example see Schubert Ogden's review of Jon Sobrino, '*Christology at the Cross-roads: A Latin American Approach*', *Perkins Journal*, 31:4 (Summer,

1978), 47–49. Ogden criticises Sobrino for trying to start with the 'man Jesus' and his claim of the Kingdom of God, as such an approach is 'unhistorical' after half a century of form criticism. But Ogden's assumption that there is a scholarly consensus about the limits of making claims about Jesus is unfounded. Not only does Keck's work stand against this, but the methodological assumptions of those that emphasized the discontinuity between the faith of Jesus and the Jesus of faith are increasingly being called into question. Thus Nils Dahl argues, 'The social setting of the Jesus tradition has usually been sought and found in the mission and/or the communal life of the church which proclaimed Jesus as the crucified and risen Christ. Only a minority of scholars have taken serious account of the possibility that the disciples quoted sayings of Jesus and told stories about him while he was still alive. As a consequence, the interest in the social function of the tradition has tended to result in a social isolation of Jesus himself. This tendency is further strengthened by the widely accepted principle that among the sayings attributed to Jesus, those are most likely to be authentic which can not have originated either in contemporary Judaism or in the church after Easter ('the criterion of dissimilarity'). The irony of the matter is that the application of rigid critical principles opens the doors to new versions of a modernized Jesus who is separated both from the church and from his Jewish environment but relevant for our time.' *Jesus in the Memory of the Early Church*, p. 168. Moreover as Geza Vermes contends, 'the positive and constant testimony of the earliest Gospel tradition, considered against its natural background of the first-century Galilean charismatic religion, leads not to a Jesus unrecognizable within the framework of Judaism as by the standard of his own verifiable words and intentions, but to another figure: Jesus the just man, the *zaddik*, Jesus the helper and healer, Jesus the teacher and leader, venerated by his intimates and less committed admirers alike as prophet, lord, and *son of God*.' *Jesus the Jew* (New York: Macmillan, 1973), p. 225.

59. Dahl, *Jesus in the Memory of the Early Church*, p. 171. Keck maintains 'that probing the ethos of religious communities with respect to the functions of traditions and texts could help us see that the NT is not simply a compilation of the literary justifications for the (diverse) Christian ethos, but a series of trenchant critiques of that ethos as well. I also suspect that no small part of the ethos was the habit of being willing to submit to judgment by its own prophets and traditions, and those of sister churches and their leaders (e.g. Ignatius).' 'On the Ethos of Early Christians', p. 450.

60. I owe much to David Burrell, James Burtchaell, Bob Krieg, John Howard Yoder, Bill O'Brien, Robert Wilken, Michael Duffey and Tom Shaffer for reading and criticizing early drafts of this paper. The usual disclaimer of course applies.

Denise Ackermann, 'A voice was heard in Ramah'

in D. Ackermann and R. Bons-Storm (eds), *Liberating Faith Practices: Feminist Practical Theologies in Context*, Leuven: Peeters, 1998, pp. 75, 93–101.

Denise Ackermann's essay is rather different from the others included in this section to this point. It returns us to the place where Christians first began to understand themselves as being incorporated into the story of Jesus. It reflects upon the significance of the Eucharist, an enacted corporate narrative that is the Church's oldest and most important means of representing the faith by which it shares in the suffering and resurrection of Christ.

Making this affirmation is particularly important in the context of suffering and persecution. Ackermann's work reminds us of the need to lament the violence of war and oppression by bringing the experience of these into the life of worship. The Eucharist in particular is a space in which these can be acknowledged, respected and mourned. It is also a place of healing in which joy stands alongside the deepest sorrow. Theological reflection in this context is a process of recalling shared stories, personal and corporate repentance and the transubstantiation of remembrance into hope.

Five fragments

'Thembinkosi's cries are still hurting me today. I want to know from the police where they took my children. Where did they kill my children?' Nohle Anna Nika-Jonas whose three sons, at the time all in high school, were taken from their shanty by police on the night of July 1, 1976.

'Just in pieces . . . pieces of him, brains, splattered all over the room'. Catherine Mlangeni describing how she found her son Bheki's body after he had been blown up by a police booby trap.

Joyce Mtimkulu, mother of Siphiwo killed by police, said she blamed former president F. W. de Klerk: 'He must have known about it. He must have known what was going on. I have always said it was the system. I still feel very sad. I have suffered for a long time and I want to see the men who killed Siphiwo.'

Cynthia Ngewu, mother of Christopher 'Rasta' Piet killed by police, said her notion of reconciliation was to 'restore the humanity of the perpetrators . . . I don't want to replace one evil with another'.

Johan, a young, white, Afrikaner student of theology: 'My parents lied to me, my school lied to me, our leaders lied to me and the church lied to me. I don't even know the truth about God.'

. . .

Communities of faith: healing praxis in lament and the eucharist

My faith has largely been nurtured in small communities outside the church. The church has too often been an uncomfortable, ambiguous place where my search for affirmation and belonging has encountered many of the barriers familiar to feminist women. This experience has led me to differentiate between the institutional church and communities of faith. Communities of faith include those people, many of whom are women, who profess faith but who, for a number of reasons, find themselves outside the church. Such communities also include small groups of people who, although they are members of the church, cannot ignore the tug of their hearts to share and explore faith together in environments which favour closeness.

Despite the obstacles of male-dominance, exclusive language and discriminating practices, I still belong to my church and I continue to write hoping to be heard in the church.[1] Why? Chiefly for two reasons. First, in the communal sharing of the bread and the wine I have found grace and food for life. I am at heart a eucharistic being. Second, the church, despite its ambivalent role in combating racism, afforded me a place to join other critical voices in opposing apartheid. Now, my feelings of disquiet about the ethical and moral basis of our emerging society have made one thing clear: I want to continue the pursuit of justice, healing and freedom for my society as a member of my church. This ongoing struggle needs the nurturing of the bread and the wine, shared in community.

This ambiguous experience of finding sustenance both in small groups and in the rites of the eucharist merge in a feminist theological search for healing praxis. I have little faith in the ability of the institutional church to transform itself, certainly not speedily enough to be able to deal with the present pain of people. I do believe in the efficacy of small groups within the church. In the present climate of truth-telling, small groups have much to offer people who are willing to share their stories. A commitment to hear 'the other' and to respect the validity of her or his story in a common search for healing, is the ground rule for such groups. As stories unfold, awareness increases. We do not only hear the stories of others. We have our own stories to tell. As these stories intersect, they change and we too are changed. Not all stories are liberating or comforting; stories can reinforce oppressions. But when these stories and the truths of our faith enter into conversation with one another, our longings for healing and wholeness and our faith in God's promises of a mended world, touch our consciousness in new ways. Momentarily we glimpse our restored humanity.

Engaging with stories alone, is not enough. The most important aspect of this shared search for healing lies in embracing communal lament. We have so much to lament about.[2] Traditionally, lament has been the prerogative of the suffering victims. The psalms of communal lament,[3] the stories of Rachel, Hagar, Hannah, David and Job, express the cries of suffering people, seeking deliverance from God. Nohle Anna Nika-Jonas, Catherine Mlangeni, Cynthia Ngewu and Joyce Mtimkulu together with thousands of others who share their grief, have decades of suffering and loss to lament. It is their prerogative.

The question arises: is lament appropriate for whites in South Africa? Can we like David, lament, from 'the other side'? Can we afford not to lament? We need to cry out to God for deliverance from our shameful past and for healing from the wounds that perpetrators inflict on themselves as well as on others. The particular suffering born out of the growing awareness of our role in the history of our country, should be lamented. We can lament the misuse of power and privilege, and our lack of courage in not standing up to evil and injustice. Mothers can lament for their sons drafted into the defence force and emerging after two years, scarred and depressed, cynical or ready to leave for far shores while at the same time remembering other mothers whose sons were tortured, imprisoned, killed and exiled in cause of the same ideology of white power.

Lament is never utilitarian. It is an existential wail which comes from the human soul. The hope is that communal lament of people in small groups in which the lamentation of the afflicted is heard and responded to, will make for healing and the restoration of well-being. Although lament is expressed communally, it comes from individual hearts which are weeping and raging, seeking a response from God. The very nature of lament is profoundly spiritual and profoundly political. Remorse, anger, the need for accountability and justice, combine as we contend with God.

Sadly, Western Christianity has lost its ability to lament. Acts of lamentation have disappeared from our liturgies in our churches. Keening bodies addressing God directly, calling God to account for the intractability of suffering, are deemed to be liturgically inappropriate in mainline Christianity in my country. Yet, at the same time, at African funerals in townships and rural areas, women lead the communal lament which often lasts for days. These cultural and religious rituals of lament are, however, abandoned at the church door. Is their repudiation attributable to the fact that women lead the lament? Is the very bodiliness of lament too menacing to those who want to maintain authority through tight control of liturgical actions? Does the fact that the people take initiative and address God without intermediaries threaten the role of the clergy? The loss of lament is costly, not least of all because it is crucial in the search for healing.[4]

Facing the irresoluble enigma of human suffering and then learning to live in that vacillating zone between acceptance and rebellion, is strangely healing. The psalms have much to teach us here. Lament of victims dares to rail against God and the inexplicability of suffering. Then, virtually in the same breath, it turns to praise. Divine silence is assaulted with tears, petitions and then with praise. In the midst of all the questioning, we find a God in whom we can truly trust. In Walter Brueggemann's words, we find a God 'whose impotence is reshaped by pathos'.[5] Lament of perpetrators emerges from anguished guilt, heartfelt repentance and the desperate search for the grace of forgiveness and acceptance. The outcome of this search is affirmed by the fact that such lament also ends on a note of praise and hope. Lament is to move from 'candor about suffering [to] gratitude about hope'.[6]

Lamenting alone is not enough. Having keened and raged, wept and repented, we then recognise two further needs: the first is to wait in faith; the second is to place the tears and the acts of love in the communion cup. God, we are told, is good to those who seek and wait; 'It is good that one should wait patiently for the salvation of the Lord' (Lam 3:26). Waiting is an act of faith which requires risk and holds on to hope. Perhaps, in the waiting, the institutional church will see and hear the lament of these small groups of people. And then, who knows, lament may be recovered for the worshipping community.

In the waiting, we seek food for new life in the bread and the wine. These are testing moments, filled with doubts and stumbling blocks. Can we in the face of so much human suffering, remember God's justice, mercy and love at the table? Do we trust that God's work of making all things new, as revealed in the life and work of Jesus Christ, is ongoing and affirmed by our remembrance of what happened in the upper room? A further stumbling block is the continuing dominance of the eucharist by the largely male clergy. This has not only protected male power in the church but it has also separated the clergy from the laity, rendering the laity largely passive.[7] If the eucharist is a powerful symbol of sexism and separation, can it be a potentially healing rite?

When racist laws kept people apart in my country, the eucharistic rite of sharing one cup took on revolutionary significance. At some altar rails there was no apartheid. Further exploration of the radical implications of the eucharist calls for imaginative praxis. By combining memory and imagination, a feminist theology of praxis seeks to expand the meaning of the eucharist so that its potential for remembering, healing and transforming is realised more fully. 'The eucharist should be the symbol of our nurture, growth, and participation in the authentic human life of mutual empowerment', writes Rosemary Ruether.[8] For the small groups who, in trust, have lamented and praised together, the need to take these initial healing processes into the ritual of breaking bread and sharing the cup, is further affirmation that the life, ministry and death of Jesus offers us new life. This affirmation we express in ritual.

All human beings have a longing for ritual. All 'human life is shot through and through with ritual', writes Susanne Langer. She continues 'It is an intricate fabric of reason and rite, of knowledge and religion, prose and poetry, fact and dream'.[9] Human creativity, longing, need and faith come together when groups seek ways of expressing new found relationships. The eucharist holds this promise.

'Rituals are about relationships; religious rituals are about ultimate relationships – about a people's origins and destiny and their true identity and purpose even in ordinary life', writes Mary Collins. Healed relationships are our compelling need. She continues: 'People learn who they are and who they are becoming before God in their very physical positions and their assigned roles in sacred assemblies, by what they themselves do and say, by what is said and done to them and for them, by the transaction in which their participation is either prescribed or proscribed'.[10] When ritual learning is taken away from the people by clerical dominance of the sacraments, healing is delayed or impeded. Shared lament needs to be cemented promptly in the cup as a further affirmation that the healing is happening.

I imagine small, vital groups of people who, after lamenting together, give thanks for memories of God's loving power in the past and thereby affirm this power in the present. And, most importantly, faith in God's present desire to love, equips us to resist future evil. In particular God's dealings with women, children, the poor and the vulnerable, are remembered through recalling shared stories. This combination of memory and thanksgiving forges a new solidarity which is focused on Jesus, the one who was anointed to bring good news to the poor, to proclaim release to the captives, recovery of sight to the blind and freedom for the [oppressed].

Images of the very earliest celebrations of the eucharist feed my imagination: small groups of people meeting to break bread and drink wine, singing, praying and remembering the gospel events.[11] I imagine a eucharist which is celebrated in small groups seeking reconciliation across historical chasms caused by apartheid and across the divides of patriarchal ideologies. Eucharist, in essence thanksgiving, expresses our gratitude, our reasons for blessing God. How fitting to move from lament, to praise and then to be able to give thanks.[12] Those who have benefitted from being on the side of the oppressors need to examine what sacrifices they are called on to make which will advance healing of fractured relationships. Men are called to re-examine their places of power and participation in sexist systems. Victims are faced with grappling with the ideas of forgiveness and reconciliation as members of the community of faith.

These are complicated processes. For white women, for instance, the need to sacrifice unjust privileges which the apartheid years showered on us, is clear. Equally clear is the fact that we have experienced sexism and its demands for sacrifice. Oppressing and being oppressed are not neatly separated in our lives. The very idea of sacrifice requires in Marjorie Procter-Smith's words 'a high degree of discernment and the knowledge of intersecting oppressions . . .

Therefore an emancipatory use of the eucharistic motif of sacrifice must be informed by critical consciousness about both the demand for sacrifice of unjust power and the complexity of interlocking oppressions'.[13]

The community of faith, gathered to eat the bread and drink the wine, image the body of Christ in the suffering world. We recollect the suffering and the death of women, children and the victims of apartheid, as we recollect Christ's suffering and death. 'A voice is heard in Ramah, lamentation and bitter weeping . . .'. In the cup, suffering and memory fuse into the transforming power of God's love. We move from despair and brokenness into hope and healing. 'The Eucharist as eschatological feast offers imaginative hope, the visionary experience of the goal toward which we work in our daily struggle'.[14] As we celebrate we pray

> God bless Africa.
> Guard her children.
> Guide her rulers,
> And give her peace for Jesus Christ's sake, Amen.[15]

A final fragment

In May 1993, I visited Mozambique at the invitation of Bishop Dinis Sengulane, the Anglican Bishop of Lebombo. Together with Francis Cull, the seventy-eight year old director of the Institute for Christian Spirituality, we held workshops for the church in small communities who were trying to come together again after being uprooted during the long years of civil war. On our last evening in Maputo I was resting after a long and tiring drive from the north when the Bishop insisted that we accompany him to his chapel.

I shall never forget what followed. Fourteen year old Candida stood before the baptismal font. Her parents watched her anxiously. Two years previously, during preparation for confirmation and baptism, she had been abducted by Renamo forces when on a visit to her relatives outside Maputo. She had reappeared out of the bush that morning, her adolescent body criss-crossed by strips of rags 'to ward off evil'. Her father contacted the Bishop and said: 'She was ready two years ago. I am bringing her to church tonight. You must baptise and confirm her right away.' Watching Candida in her broken plastic sandals and old pink spotted dress, I saw trauma, disorientation and fear. I could hardly bear to think of what she had been through. My mind raced through a list of remedies – medication for trauma, long term therapy, tests for HIV. But in May 1993, Mozambique had no psychiatrists, psychotherapists or pathologists. Her parents did what they could. They brought her for initiation into the community of faith, to be covered with the prayers of the church and fed with the bread and the wine – the sole means of grace and healing available to the people of Maputo.

Notes

1. See Denise M. Ackermann, Jonathan Draper and Emma Mashinini (eds.), *Women Hold Up Half the Sky: Women in the Church in Southern Africa* (Pietermaritzburg: Cluster Publications, 1991).

2. Denise M. Ackermann, 'On hearing and lamenting: faith and truth-telling' in Botman and Petersen (eds.), *To Remember and to Heal*, pp. 47–56.

3. For examples, see Ps. 44, 60, 74, 79, 80, 83 and 89.

4. See Walter Brueggemann, 'The costly loss of lament', in his work *The Psalms and the Life of Faith* (Minneapolis: Fortress Press, 1994), pp. 98–111.

5. Brueggemann, *The Psalms*, p. 108.

6. Brueggemann, *The Psalms*, p. 196.

7. See Rosemary Radford Ruether, *Women-Church: Theology and Practice of Feminist Liturgical Communities* (San Francisco: Harper and Row, 1985), pp. 75–95 for the implications of clericalism.

8. Ruether, *Women-Church*, p. 77.

9. Susanne K. Langer, *Philosophy in a New Key: A Study in the Symbolism of Reason. Rite, and Art.* 3rd edn (Cambridge, Mass.: Harvard University Press. 1979), p. 36.

10. Mary Collins, *Worship: Renewal to Practice* (Washington: The Pastoral Press, 1987), p. 259.

11. See Gregory Dix, *The Shape of the Liturgy*, 2nd edn (London: Adam and Charles Black, 1978), pp. 16–21 and Robert Cabié, *The Church at Prayer: An Introduction to the Liturgy* (ed. A. G. Martimort), vol. 2: *The Eucharist* (London: Cassell Ltd., 1986), pp. 36–38, 239–240.

12. Cabié, *The Church at Prayer*, pp. 21, 26–29, 93–94.

13. Procter-Smith, *In Her Own Rite*, p. 162.

14. Procter-Smith, *In Her Own Rite*, p. 163.

15. This prayer the Anglican church in South Africa owes to Trevor Huddleston, a monk of the Community of the Resurrection, who allied himself to black resistance to apartheid in the 1950s.

Samuel Wells, 'How Common Worship Forms Local Character'

Studies in Christian Ethics, Vol. 15, No. 1, 2002, pp. 66–74.

This essay by Samuel Wells brings the thinking of Stanley Hauerwas on the character-forming nature of the Christian story into sharp focus. Wells reflects upon the training of the moral imagination that takes place as a result of regular participation in Christian worship. Although worship has as its chief end the glorification of God, it also inculcates values, habits and predispositions in those who take part. As the worshippers are drawn into the stories they hear read, and participate in these through corporate rituals, they are transformed into a living parable of God's presence. This not only deepens their fellowship but enables them to stand apart from the world in order to witness for the very different values that worship has taught them.

The strength of Wells's essay is the way he roots his understanding of the transforming story of God in the everyday and often unregarded rhythms of the Christian life. Going to Church rarely feels like a 'dramatic' act – and yet this is precisely what Wells claims it to be. Christians have active roles to play in the story that the Church performs. While worship can appear 'ordinary and mundane' it is through 'habit and repetition and learning through time' that believers come to share the form of Christ and embody God's love to others.

This paper attempts to show how the Eucharistic liturgy trains Christians in the moral imagination, in the habits, practices, notions and virtues of discipleship.[1] This is not what worship is for: worship isn't for anything – it is one of the few human activities conducted for its own sake. Our chief end, as the Westminster Confession reminds us, is 'to glorify God and enjoy him forever'.[2] Yet though worship has its own inner logic and intrinsic worth, it also prepares the disciple for witness and service. Each aspect of worship represents a vital dimension of moral formation. *Lex orandi, lex vivendi.*

What follows is a sequence of significant practices of Christian worship. The list is illustrative rather than exhaustive. Under each part of the liturgy I shall name skills that are taught, practices that are developed, habits that are formed, virtues that are acquired and notions that are shaped. I shall then describe how this aspect of the liturgy has been performed in a local church and the character that has emerged from its repeated embodiment over time. The examples are not intended to be remarkable: on the contrary, their very ordinariness points to the way worship helps Christians take the right things for granted.[3]

1. Gathering

When Christians gather together to worship, whether two or three or two or three thousand, they are quickly reminded or become aware of three things. The first is that they are in the presence of God. The ability to name the presence of God is a skill. It is a skill that the Scriptures train the Church to perform. The presence of God may be commanding, as for Abram in Haran; it may be troublesome or mysterious, as it was for Jacob at Bethel and Peniel; it can be echoingly silent, as for Elijah on Carmel, or awesome, as it was for Isaiah in the Temple. It can be perceived amid injustice, as for the centurion at the cross, or in human companionship, as for the disciples on the Emmaus Road.

By naming the presence of God the community develop the faculty of wonder. They have their imaginations stretched to perceive the greatness of God, the mystery of his deciding to make himself known, and the grace of his means of doing so. They are formed in the virtue of humility. They discover that this God has a purpose for his creation and that they themselves have a valued part to play – and they perceive that this story is not about them but about God. They learn to rest upon the notion of God's inextinguishable glory and unshakeable faithfulness. They enter a tradition of providence, encompassing Noah's rainbow, Isaac's ram, Moses' pillar of cloud, Hannah's prayer, Daniel's lions, Elizabeth's child, the stilled storm, the Great Commission, the new Jerusalem. In the presence of God the congregation learn the skill of alertness, readiness, anticipation, expectation: that the God who has acted, and keeps his promises, will reveal himself today.

At much the same time as the congregation become aware of the presence of God, they become aware of the presence of one another. They discover that the body of Christ has many members, and they learn about the diversity of the gifts that the Holy Spirit has given the body. They are reminded that those gifts are for the building up of the Church, and that the neglect of any of the gifts is to the detriment of the body. They realise the discipline of forming an identity separate from the world, a light, before once again returning to serve the world, as salt. By committing themselves to meet regularly together Christians practise the skills of politics, the non-violent resolution of conflicting goods in corporate life. They practise the habits of welcoming the stranger, and valuing the child. By faithfully meeting week by week the congregation are formed in the virtue of constancy. By making Sunday the focal day the congregation learn the skill of telling the time, of distinguishing the important from the urgent, of realising that God has given us enough time to do what he calls us to do. By taking time to worship they are formed in the virtue of patience.

More gradually, the congregation become aware of those who are not gathering together – those who are absent. Some are worshipping elsewhere; some have died; some are sick or unable to be present; some are estranged or hiding from God and/or the Church; some have never been invited; some have never heard; some have hardened or bruised or bewildered hearts. This is how the community develops the skill of memory for those who are no longer here, and awareness of the breadth of the body and the extent of the kingdom. This awareness shapes the practices of pastoral care and evangelism. It fosters the virtue of love for the lost. It gives substance to the notion of the communion of saints, whose constant worship of God the congregation join from time to time.

One local congregation chose to embody this last notion, the communion of saints, through a photography project. They sought to surround the area used for worship with photographs of notable characters, all of whom lived in the area around the church, but none of whom came to worship on a Sunday. A group of single mothers, who used the church for a weekly art class, identified the people concerned, shot, developed and mounted the photographs, and displayed them around the church. Thus the worshipping congregation were surrounded on a Sunday with those for whom they prayed. When a bid went from the neighbourhood to the government for large sums of urban regeneration funding, there was a sudden search for photographs that expressed what was good about the community. The photographs on the church walls were ideal for the purpose, and were duly used. Thus had the local church's faithful notion of gathering to worship helped a neighbourhood realise its human worth.

2. Confessing

When Christians come kneeling and humble before God in confession, they learn what it means to come naked and humble before God in baptism. They thus prepare themselves to come naked and humble before God in death. They develop the skill of naming their own sin. They learn the savage blinding power of self-deception. They see themselves in the brothers' speechlessness before Joseph, David's incomprehension before Nathan, and Peter's horror as the cock crowed. By confessing their sin corporately they recognise their participation in wider ignorance, selfishness and pride, in human and global fear and finitude. In resolving to sin no more the congregation register the weight of making promises that they may not be able to keep, and practise the habit of dependence on the grace of God. By bringing their confession to an end and handing their sin over in penitence, they are formed in the virtue of humility, for they must realise that the worst that they have done cannot alter God's love for them or his working out of his eternal purpose, and that they cannot wrest their destiny, or that of those they have hurt, out of his hands. The congregation practise the virtue of courage, in anticipating their own death, and faith, in committing themselves to the one who judges justly. In receiving absolution they inhabit the clothes of their baptism. They learn the notions of adoption by the Father, justification through the Son, new birth in the Spirit, liberation from slavery, the resurrection of the body and vocation to a life of prayer and service. They realise that salvation is a gift to be received, not a reward to be earned.

In one local congregation there was an elderly woman who had lived all her life in the neighbourhood. She had attended the church longer than anyone could remember – perhaps fifty years. Everyone in the church, from the wildest child to the oldest salt, loved and revered her. One day, during worship, she was asked why she attended church so faithfully. She was a person of action rather than words, and her life had been devoted to care rather than cleverness. Without pause, she simply responded, 'For my sins'. There was silence. If she, who was holy, came for her sins, where did that place everyone else? Clearly her joy came from knowing God's forgiveness, and her faithfulness came from knowing that that grace could be found nowhere else When she died, the congregation realised that she had symbolised everything they believed in. In her gentle way she expressed that she had been formed by the worship in which she had shared.

3. Listening

When Christians listen for God's word in scripture, they learn to listen for God's word in every conversation. They develop the skill of storytelling, of finding their place and role in the story. They grow in the ability to recognise beginnings and endings, to perceive how God sows his seed and reaps his harvest. They learn to see the author at work, noting the house style of exalted meek and dejected mighty. The congregation learn also the skill of listening, of taking in the whole of God, action, interpretation, intention. They realise how much there is to discover, and they practise fitting their own small story into the larger story of God. They are formed in the virtue of prophetic hope, the conviction that God has acted before to save his people and the trust that he will act again to set them free. They learn the notion of revelation, the belief that truth and meaning are communicated from God's side of the conversation. They grow in an understanding of truth, that accounts can be accurate, trustworthy and worthy of commitment. They practise communal discernment, as together they use their gifts to hear the word speak in their contemporary context. They learn the discipline of authority and obedience. They come to see history as theology teaching by examples. And they realise what it means to inhabit a tradition.

In one local congregation a custom has developed at the evening service. After the second reading the priest asks a question of the congregation that links with the scripture passages. The question does not seek a right or wrong answer but invites members to share their experience. It might be, 'I wonder if you have known someone with a disability'; or, 'I wonder who you think really runs the country'. The sermon that follows usually weaves some of these answers into a presentation of the word and an insight into the character of God and the practice of the Church. Sometimes members of the congregation add observations at the end. On one occasion the priest was particularly pleased with what he had in mind to say and forgot to ask the wondering question. The following morning an outraged member of the congregation sought him out. 'Last night', she said, 'you simply talked at us for fully fifteen minutes, and then just stopped. There was no opportunity for discussion whatsoever.' The priest, somewhat defensively and ironically, pointed out that this would have been her experience of worship every Sunday if she attended almost any other church both in that city and quite possibly throughout the world. Yet here was a woman, living in a deprived community, who had through the repeated practice of listening and discerning, come to take for granted that her experience was an important part of the proclamation of God's word, that she had a place in God's story. This was an assumption, a form of her faith, that liturgical habit had taught her. It helped her to see the unique opportunity her church was offering to its community – to find their story in God's story.

4. Interceding

When a congregation intercede together, they put themselves in place of others before God. They develop the skill of distinguishing pain from sin, as they come to separate what needs intercession from what needs confession. They learn the skill of distinguishing suffering from evil, as they perceive the difference between a call for God's mercy and a call for God's justice. They learn to distinguish need from want, as, like Israel before them, they discern what it is to be God's beloved, and how that differs from being like other nations. They practise the virtue of patience, as they come to understand that all bad things come to an end in God's time, and that God has prepared for those who love him such things as pass their understanding. They learn the virtue of persistence, as they look back over years of knocking on heaven's door, and see that change did come in South Africa, peace, of a kind, did come in Ireland, and so it must in God's mercy somehow come in Palestine. They are also shaped in the virtue of prudence, for they learn only to request what they can cope with receiving. Prudence helps the congregation see the difference between what God can do and what they believe it is in the character of God to do. They learn the notion of providence as they look back and see how God's hand has guided his flock from age to age. They deepen their understanding of the kingdom of God, as they look for God's ways with the world that go way beyond the breadth of the Church. They learn what it means to have an advocate before the Father.

In one local congregation a woman who often attended the Sunday evening service began attending an adult literacy class held in the church on a weekday. It became clear that she had never learned to read well. To help her grow in confidence, she was asked to read a lesson every third Sunday. She was encouraged simply to miss out the longer or unfamiliar words or names, and concentrate on the ones she could read confidently. Gradually her range of words increased. Eventually she was asked to lead prayers. She felt she could not do this spontaneously, as some others did, so she would spend the week asking people to jot down prayers for her to use, which she would then carefully type into her word processor, which she was learning to use on another adult education class. For her, leading intercessions was the summit of her years of attending church. She realised that this was the moment when she was like Jesus, standing before the Father bringing the people with her. It was also like the anticipated moment of her death, when she would stand face to face with God, and he would ask her, 'Where are all the others?' – and she could reply, 'Here, in my prayers'.

5. Sharing Peace

By having to share the peace before sharing the bread, Christians learn that reconciliation is as necessary to their lives as their daily bread. They develop the skill of admonition. When the desire to love is at least as great as the desire to tell the truth, admonition is an important practice. It affirms that Christians have nothing to fear from the truth, and that protecting others from the truth is seldom a statement of faith. Sharing the peace also develops in the congregation the habit of not letting the sun go down on their anger, of seeing the naming of resentment as the first step in the forming of a new relationship based on healing and forgiveness rather than tolerance and turning a blind eye. They practise the virtues of mercy and forbearance, virtues that depend on the knowledge that they too have sinned and been forgiven, that they too have grown through constructive criticism, that they too have moods and quirks and prejudices. They grow in the virtues of humility and honesty, virtues that rest on the realisation that the Christian life is not about arriving at perfection, but about making interesting mistakes on the way. They are formed in the virtues of patience and courage, which help them to try once more with challenging relationships and risk rejection by trying to reconcile. They learn the notion of forgiveness, the astonishing story of how the prodigal was not just received home but treated like a king. They learn again what it means for the baptised to be a body and for its members all to function. They learn the ultimate unity of grace and truth.

In one local congregation the intimate connection between reconciliation with God and with one another is brought out by the use of a human statue. Two members of the congregation are invited to kneel opposite one another in the centre of the church and rest their respective heads on one another's left shoulder. (Those who participate, often one adult and one child, must be self-nominated – efforts to nominate one's neighbour are rejected.) The statue affirms that one cannot be reconciled with God until one is reconciled with one's neighbour.

The statue also affirms the physical nature of the healing of the body. One local congregation had a parish away day during which a litany of complaints, anxious frustrations and a sense of helplessness about one aspect of the church's ministry rained down upon those responsible. That day, when the time came for the Holy Communion, the peace was shared without words – the simple handshake and holding of eye contact was a statement of trust and commitment and reconciliation after perhaps too many words had been said. In being able to share the peace after such a traumatic day, the congregation discovered that it was possible to name the truth without fear.

6. Sharing Communion

By sharing bread with one another around the Lord's table, Christians learn to live in peace with those with whom they share other tables – breakfast, shopfloor, office, checkout. They develop the skills of distribution, of the poor sharing their bread with the rich, and the rich with the poor. They develop the skills of inclusion, of perceiving that diversity only enriches integrity. Everyone is called to a place around the table, whatever their gender, their race, their class, whatever their orientation, their physical health or ability, their mental health or ability, whatever their social or criminal history. They develop the practices of offering and receiving. They hand over the first fruits of labour and receive back the first fruits of the resurrection. They learn what is meant by a gift, by offering their food and drink and money to God and allowing him to do whatever he wants with them. They develop the skills of participating in the life of heaven, in realising their simple actions anticipate God's eternal destiny. They learn to look around them as they eat, and speculate on whether these are the people with whom God predicts they will spend eternity, or whether he has other people in mind, and if so, why those people are not present now. The congregation practise the virtue of justice, as they ensure that all are treated with equal respect, and all have their role and place around the throne of God. They learn the virtue of generosity, as they realise that they have freely received more than enough from God, and can therefore freely give. They are shaped in the virtue of hope, as they are given a picture of what the heavenly banquet will be like. They learn the notion of regular dependence on God's abiding providence, as they realise they live not on bread alone, but on every word that comes from the mouth of God. They perceive that at the heart of fellowship is sacrifice. They discover that holiness is formation as a kingdom of priests, a community through whom God makes his name known in the world, a people who are what they eat, the body of Christ.

One local congregation found it difficult to decide whether they should sit, stand or kneel to receive communion. Kneeling seemed appropriate to some, because it embodied humility. But some said that, without an altar rail, it asked too much of people with disabilities. It seemed that sitting was the posture that stressed equality, because everybody looked and felt much the same. But it was felt that, besides being too comfortable, remaining in one's seat suggested that God made the whole journey, with almost no response from his people. Standing in a circle became the norm. It stressed the differences of height, age and physical ability, and it made it necessary for some to rest on the strength of others. Though some said they felt unworthy to stand, others pointed out the Christ had enabled, even commanded them to stand, and that standing was a symbol of resurrection. By standing in a circle, the congregation realised they did not just eat of one body – they were one body.

7. Being Sent Out

Finally when Christians are sent back out into the world they learn what it means to be salt and light, to be distinct yet among. They develop the practice of service, remembering that even the Son of Man came not to be served but to serve. They learn the habit of partnership, remembering that those who are not against Christ are with him. They practise seeking out the ways of God in the most benighted corners of the world. They learn the disciplines and techniques of co-operating with people of very different principles and stories, of resolving conflict without violence and standing beside the weak and afflicted. They work out the virtue of justice, in seeking the equality they experienced at the Lord's table. They develop the habit of peacemaking, seeking the reconciliation they experienced before they came to the Lord's table. They practise the virtue of temperance, learning to expect compromise and to be changed by those they seek to influence. They experience the cost of the virtue of love. They inhabit the notion of mission, as like the seventy they go out in order to bring back stories of what the Spirit has done. They learn the practice of witness, as they realise how the Church differs from the world and how to speak despite this difference. They explore the meaning of incarnation, as they translate their experience of the body of Christ into their context of home, work and leisure. And they discover again the notion of kingdom, that for all their mistakes, God will work his purpose out in ways beyond their imaginations.

In one local church the notices used to come just before the sending out. On one occasion the priest shared with the congregation that a group of young girls had been trying for several days to persuade him to use the church to dance in on a Saturday. He asked the congregation for suggestions. After a pause, one woman aged eighty-six put up her hand and said, 'I'll sit with them if you like'. After a few weeks, one of the girls' mothers took over and set up a dance club that flourished for three years. Challenged by the call to go and do likewise, the elderly woman proved to be a stirring example to the rest of the congregation. If an eighty-six-year-old could be a youth worker, everyone could.

Concluding Words

Worshipping together does not always feel like moral formation. It is about the ordinary and mundane, about habit and repetition and learning over time to take the right things for granted. In many churches, people feel that the practice of worship has departed considerably from any conscious embodiment of the virtues described here. But in almost all cases, when habit and memory are still alive, the potential for renewal is still high. And a strange thing happens when, at a public, secular gathering, people begin to articulate the need for their institution to divert from its daily business, name divisions and mistakes, tell stories and affirm mission statements, name needs, be reconciled and share food in order to be re-empowered for service of the community. Members of the Church may choose whether or not to claim a copyright, but at the very least they will raise an eyebrow. They may well wonder at this rediscovery of the Church's heritage, and be consoled that imitation is the sincerest form of flattery.[4]

Notes

1. I owe this way of understanding the ethical dimensions of the liturgy to Stanley Hauerwas. See his 'The Liturgical Shape of the Christian Life: Teaching Christian Ethics as Worship', *In Good Company: The Church as Polis* (Notre Dame, Ind.: University of Notre Dame Press, 1995), pp. 153–68.

2. 'The Westminster Shorter Catechism', in The Presbyterian Church (USA) *Book of Confessions* (Louisville, Ky.: Office of the General Assembly, 1983), Q.1.

3. The ordinariness of the examples is genuine, but I cannot hide that it is partly designed to engage with criticisms of Stanley Hauerwas's ecclesiology. Both David Fergusson and Robin Gill suggest Hauerwas's Church is in large measure a fantasy, or is inevitably or implicitly a rare Mennonite phenomenon. It is my experience and contention that this is not the case. See David Fergusson, *Community, Liberalism and Christian Ethics* (Cambridge: Cambridge University, Press, 1999); and Robin Gill, *Churchgoing and Christian Ethics* (Cambridge: Cambridge University Press, 2001).

4. I am grateful to John Sweet and the Readers Summer Course 2001, to Stephen Barton and the Society for the Study of Christian Ethics Conference 2001, and in particular to Jolyon Mitchell, Luke Bretherton and John Inge for

their reflections on earlier versions of this essay. A number of people have suggested that 'Doxology' in the form of music and hymns should form part of this pattern. This essay sets out to address the sequential aspects of the liturgy and I confess I have not yet found a way to integrate the pervasive aspects of worship without losing the simplicity of the essay's shape. I would welcome suggestions on this.

'Telling God's Story': References and Further Reading

Ford, D. F. (1981), *Barth and God's Story: Biblical narrative and the theological method of Karl Barth in the Church*, New York: Peter Lang.

Frei, H. (1993), *Theology and Narrative: Selected Essays*, eds. G. Hunsinger and W. C. Placher, New York: Oxford University Press.

Hauerwas, S. and West, S. (2004), 'The Gift of the Church and the Gifts God Gives It' in *The Blackwell Companion to Christian Ethics*, Oxford: Blackwell, pp. 13–27.

Winterson, J. (1985), *Oranges Are not the Only Fruit*, London: Unwin Hyman.

4

'Writing the Body of Christ': Corporate Theological Reflection

Introduction

This method of theological reflection is first and foremost a corporate activity, with a shift of emphasis from the individual to the congregation, church or faith community. It is the community, made up of individuals committed to each other and having a sense of belonging, that uses various resources, like biblical and traditional texts, to create and sustain their ongoing existence. Theological reflection upon the body (the incarnation and the bodily encounter of believers in Christ) is as old as Paul's reflections in his letters to the incipient churches in cities like Corinth, where he recommended and sought to develop communal living. His central image of 'the body of Christ' is a very good example of how a sense of community can be created by an image or symbol, and can shape a particular way of life together.

How a faith community engages with its seminal texts, or with other archetypal literature, falls under the umbrella of this method of theological reflection. Just as it has been shown that a sense of narrative can contribute to a sense of individual identity, so a faith community can tell its own story and thereby develop a coherent sense of itself, and some scholars of the congregation have done interesting research in drawing together literary theory and anthropology in their studies of faith communities.

To think about corporate theological reflection is to raise many questions about the shape of faith communities: what enables them to cohere; the relationship between present experience and past traditions; questions of power and internal conflicts and resolutions. The method recognizes how 'community' can be constructed or imagined in different ways, depending on its context and reason for existence, and in that recognition this method often turns to the insights of the discipline of congregational studies, where the complexities of researching the congregation are fully explored.

The ways in which different communities can be 'imagined' into being in particular eras and around particular symbols or practices is central, and so a sense of history and understanding of traditions can often prove invaluable. For example, the way in which a religious sensibility can contribute to the shaping of national identity and notions such as Christendom can be instructive; as can the ways in which such sensibilities change in different cultures and times. The media – whether in more traditional form such as icons, or the development of print and image, or the use of the Internet – also needs to be recognized for the part it plays in the construction of corporate identity.

Faith communities find themselves in contemporary times with the need to relate in complex networks as they engage with different localities, issues and faiths. This method of theological reflection offers the tools to interpret communal life in ways that strengthen that engagement. Whether it is local faith communities working to find a place within the world of globalized capitalism, or by developing online community by using the Internet, this method enables exploration of questions about the construction of community and corporate identity, not least the question of whether the need for physical connection is crucial to corporate religious life.

As a method of theological reflection upon the nature of corporate life, and on the way in which communities themselves reflect and, as they do so, create and sustain themselves, this method makes an invaluable contribution to contemporary practical theology.

Dietrich Bonhoeffer, 'Community'
in *Life Together* London: SCM Press, 1970, pp. 7–10.

'Communal life is again being recognized by Christians today as the grace that it is, as the extraordinary, the "roses and lilies" of the Christian life' (p. 226). So writes Bonhoeffer in this passage from Life Together, *a short book written halfway through the twentieth century. Bonhoeffer sets out to recommend the communal life and to offer the means by which it can cohere. A central theological theme emerges in this passage, that of the bodily life of Jesus Christ and how fellowship based upon bodily encounter is at the heart of Christian community: 'Visitor and visited in loneliness recognize in each other the Christ who is present in body . . .' (p. 225). The passage illustrates clearly how Bonhoeffer seeks to construct community, drawing on biblical material and theological reflection.*

'Behold, how good and how pleasant it is for brethren to dwell together in unity!' (Ps. 133.1). In the following we shall consider a number of directions and precepts that the Scriptures provide us for our life together under the Word.

It is not simply to be taken for granted that the Christian has the privilege of living among other Christians. Jesus Christ lived in the midst of his enemies. At the end all his disciples deserted him. On the Cross he was utterly alone, surrounded by evildoers and mockers. For this cause he had come, to bring peace to the enemies of God. So the Christian, too, belongs not in the seclusion of a cloistered life but in the thick of foes. There is his commission, his work. 'The Kingdom is to be in the midst of your enemies. And he who will not suffer this does not want to be of the Kingdom of Christ; he wants to be among friends, to sit among roses and lilies, not with the bad people but the devout people. O you blasphemers and betrayers of Christ! If Christ had done what you are doing who would ever have been spared?' (Luther).

'I will sow them among the people: and they shall remember me in far countries' (Zech. 10.9). According to God's will Christendom is a scattered people, scattered like seed 'into all the kingdoms of the earth' (Deut. 28.25). That is its curse and its promise. God's people must dwell in far countries among the unbelievers, but it will be the seed of the Kingdom of God in all the world.

'I will ... gather them; for I have redeemed them: ... and they shall return' (Zech. 10.8, 9). When will that happen? It has happened in Jesus Christ, who died 'that he should gather together in one the children of God that were scattered abroad' (John 11.52), and it will finally occur visibly at the end of time when the angels of God 'shall gather together his elect from the four winds, from one end of heaven to the other' (Matt. 24.31). Until then, God's people remain scattered, held together solely in Jesus Christ, having become one in the fact that, dispersed among unbelievers, they remember *him* in the far countries.

So between the death of Christ and the Last Day it is only by a gracious anticipation of the last things that Christians are privileged to live in visible fellowship with other Christians. It is by the grace of God that a congregation is permitted to gather visibly in this world to share God's Word and sacrament. Not all Christians receive this blessing. The imprisoned, the sick, the scattered lonely, the proclaimers of the Gospel in heathen lands stand alone. They know that visible fellowship is a blessing. They remember, as the Psalmist did, how they went 'with the multitude ... to the house of God, with the

voice of joy and praise, with a multitude that kept holyday' (Ps. 42.4).
But they remain alone in far countries, a scattered seed according to
God's will. Yet what is denied them as an actual experience they seize
upon more fervently in faith. Thus the exiled disciple of the Lord, John
the Apocalyptist, celebrates in the loneliness of Patmos the heavenly
worship with his congregations 'in the Spirit on the Lord's day'
(Rev. 1.10). He sees the seven candlesticks, his congregations, the
seven stars, the angels of the congregations, and in the midst and
above it all the Son of Man, Jesus Christ, in all the splendour of the
resurrection. He strengthens and fortifies him by his Word. This is
the heavenly fellowship, shared by the exile on the day of his Lord's
resurrection.

The physical presence of other Christians is a source of incompar-
able joy and strength to the believer. Longingly the imprisoned apostle
Paul calls 'his dearly beloved son in the faith', Timothy to come to
him in prison in the last days of his life; he would see him again and
have him near. Paul has not forgotten the tears Timothy shed when
last they parted (II Tim. 1.4). Remembering the congregation in Thes-
salonica, Paul prays 'night and day . . . exceedingly that we might see
your face' (I Thess. 3.10). The aged John knows that his joy will not
be full until he can come to his own people and speak face to face
instead of writing with ink (II John 12).

The believer feels no shame, as though he were still living too
much in the flesh, when he yearns for the physical presence of other
Christians. Man was created a body, the Son of God appeared on
earth in the body, he was raised in the body, in the sacrament the
believer receives the Lord Christ in the body, and the resurrection of
the dead will bring about the perfected fellowship of God's spiritual-
physical creatures. The believer therefore lauds the Creator, the
Redeemer, God, Father, Son and Holy Spirit, for the bodily presence
of a brother. The prisoner, the sick person, the Christian in exile sees
in the companionship of a fellow Christian a physical sign of the
gracious presence of the triune God. Visitor and visited in loneliness
recognize in each other the Christ who is present in the body; they receive and meet each other as one meets the Lord, in reverence, humility,
and joy. They receive each other's benedictions as the benediction of
the Lord Jesus Christ. But if there is so much blessing and joy even
in a single encounter of brother with brother, how inexhaustible are
the riches that open up for those who by God's will are privileged to
live in the daily fellowship of life with other Christians!

It is true, of course, that what is an unspeakable gift of God for the
lonely individual is easily disregarded and trodden under foot by

those who have the gift every day. It is easily forgotten that the fellowship of Christian brethren is a gift of grace, a gift of the Kingdom of God that any day may be taken from us, that the time that still separates us from utter loneliness may be brief indeed. Therefore, let him who until now has had the privilege of living a common Christian life with other Christians praise God's grace from the bottom of his heart. Let him thank God on his knees and declare: It is grace, nothing but grace, that we are allowed to live in community with Christian brethren.

The measure with which God bestows the gift of visible community is varied. The Christian in exile is comforted by a brief visit of a Christian brother, a prayer together and a brother's blessing; indeed, he is strengthened by a letter written by the hand of a Christian. The greetings in the letters written with Paul's own hand were doubtless tokens of such community. Others are given the gift of common worship on Sundays. Still others have the privilege of living a Christian life in the fellowship of their families. Seminarians before their ordination receive the gift of common life with their brethren for a definite period. Among earnest Christians in the Church today there is a growing desire to meet together with other Christians in the rest periods of their work for common life under the Word. Communal life is again being recognized by Christians today as the grace that it is, as the extraordinary, the 'roses and lilies' of the Christian life.

Benedict Anderson, 'Cultural Roots'
in *Imagined Communities*, London: Verso, 1983, pp. 12–19.

Benedict Anderson's book on the origin and spread of nationalism explores the way in which a sense of community or nationhood results from historical forces that come together and distil over time. As this happens, a sense of 'nation-ness' emerges that can then be understood as a cultural artefact, a constructed entity, to be 'imagined' in different ways. His notion of 'imagined communities' has had widespread influence. It can be understood as the way in which a collective sense of belonging is created by members who have an idea of the other members, the majority of whom they will never meet. Anderson draws an analogy with how a reader imagines the lives of characters in a novel, so the citizens of a nation can imagine the lives of others who belong to the same nationality. This imagination is sustained and continually created through popular press, newspapers and other media in which, as Anderson says, 'each communicant is well aware that the ceremony he performs is being replicated simultaneously by thousands (or millions) of others of whose existence he is confident, yet of whose identity he has not the slightest notion' (1983, p. 35).

Anderson stresses the importance of means of communication in creating a sense of nationality, arguing that it was as the modern era developed 'print capitalism' that different languages came into their own, with sufficient fixity to enable them to generate national cohesion, as the vernacular replaced the universal language of Latin. Print capitalism, always seeking new markets, enabled the dissemination of information and opinion at a popular level, laying the basis of national consciousness.

In this passage Anderson highlights the ways in which sacred language and written script drew down superterrestrial power and gave an inviolable truth to the texts that were central to the religious community, which saw itself as central to the world. Texts, for Anderson, were at the heart of the construction of religious community in the Middle Ages. Christendom, as an imagined community, relied upon a common language, Latin, that although it was not understood by the majority, was interpreted for them by the literate, trans-European Latin-writing clerisy (p. 230). The encounter with other cultures and traditions led to the development of a relativist and territorial understanding of culture; and as sacred language began to dissolve before the face of print capitalism, the nation state began to emerge in Europe.

This passage pinpoints a sense of a tension that, it could be argued, still persists today. To what extent do religious communities imagine themselves? As individual congregations? As national churches? As global communions? And how is the relationship with political secular forms of governance understood? Anderson's thesis of 'imagined communities' can be discerned in Samuel Huntington's thesis of a 'clash of civilizations', where '[c]ivilizations are the biggest "we" within which we feel culturally at home as distinguished from all the other "thems" out there' (Huntington 1996, p. 43). Huntington argues that one, though by no means the only, 'us' and 'them' in today's world is the 'West' and 'Islam', and tracing back the clash of civilizations to its roots in the Roman Empire in the fourth century and to the creation of the Holy Roman Empire in the tenth century, Huntington explores the fault lines between Western Christianity and Islam in today's world. His book itself is a good example of Anderson's thesis of how a community (or civilization) can imagine and thereby construct itself; indeed, many commentators argue that Huntington's very writing has 'imagined' community in a particular

*way, exacerbating the polarization between 'Islam' and 'the West' in
conflictual terms.*

The Religious Community

Few things are more impressive than the vast territorial stretch of the
Ummah Islam from Morocco to the Sulu Archipelago, of Christendom from Paraguay to Japan, and of the Buddhist world from Sri
Lanka to the Korean peninsula. The great sacral cultures (and for
our purposes here it may be permissible to include 'Confucianism')
incorporated conceptions of immense communities. But Christendom,
the Islamic Ummah, and even the Middle Kingdom – which, though
we think of it today as Chinese, imagined itself not as Chinese, but
as central – were imaginable largely through the medium of a sacred
language and written script. Take only the example of Islam: if
Maguindanao met Berbers in Mecca, knowing nothing of each other's
languages, incapable of communicating orally, they nonetheless
understood each other's ideographs, *because* the sacred texts they
shared existed only in classical Arabic. In this sense, written Arabic
functioned like Chinese characters to create a community out of signs,
not sounds. (So today mathematical language continues an old tradition. Of what the Thai call + Rumanians have no idea, and vice
versa, but both comprehend the symbol.) All the great classical communities conceived of themselves as cosmically central, through the
medium of a sacred language linked to a superterrestrial order of
power. Accordingly, the stretch of written Latin, Pali, Arabic, or
Chinese was, in theory, unlimited. (In fact, the deader the written
language – the father it was from speech – the better: in principle
everyone has access to a pure world of signs.)

Yet such classical communities linked by sacred languages had a
character distinct from the imagined communities of modern nations.
One crucial difference was the older communities' confidence in the
unique sacredness of their languages, and thus their ideas about
admission to membership. Chinese mandarins looked with approval
on barbarians who painfully learned to paint Middle Kingdom ideograms. These barbarians were already halfway to full absorption.[1]
Half-civilized was vastly better than barbarian. Such an attitude was
certainly not peculiar to the Chinese, nor confined to antiquity. Consider, for example, the following 'policy on barbarians' formulated
by the early-nineteenth-century Colombian liberal Pedro Fermín de
Vargas:

To expand our agriculture it would be necessary to hispanicize our Indians. Their idleness, stupidity, and indifference towards normal endeavours causes one to think that they come from a degenerate race which deteriorates in proportion to the distance from its origin ... *it would be very desirable that the Indians be extinguished, by miscegenation with the whites, declaring them free of tribute and other charges, and giving them private property in land.*[2]

How striking it is that this liberal still proposes to 'extinguish' his Indians in part by 'declaring them free of tribute' and 'giving them private property in land', rather than exterminating them by gun and microbe as his heirs in Brazil, Argentina, and the United States began to do soon afterwards. Note also, alongside the condescending cruelty, a cosmic optimism: the Indian is ultimately redeemable – by impregnation with white, 'civilized' semen, and the acquisition of private property, *like everyone else.* (How different Fermin's attitude is from the later European imperialist's preference for 'genuine' Malays, Gurkhas, and Hausas over 'half-breeds,' 'semi-educated natives,' 'wogs', and the like.)

Yet if the sacred silent languages were the media through which the great global communities of the past were imagined, the reality of such apparitions depended on an idea largely foreign to the contemporary Western mind: the non-arbitrariness of the sign. The ideograms of Chinese, Latin, or Arabic were emanations of reality, not randomly fabricated representations of it. We are familiar with the long dispute over the appropriate language (Latin or vernacular) for the mass. In the Islamic tradition, until quite recently, the Qur'an was literally untranslatable (and therefore untranslated), because Allah's truth was accessible only through the unsubstitutable true signs of written Arabic. There is no idea here of a world so separated from language that all languages are equidistant (and thus interchangeable) signs for it. In effect, ontological reality is apprehensible only through a single, privileged system of re-presentation: the truth-language of Church Latin, Qur'anic Arabic, or Examination Chinese.[3] And, as truth-languages, imbued with an impulse largely foreign to nationalism, the impulse towards conversion. By conversion, I mean not so much the acceptance of particular religious tenets, but alchemic absorption. The barbarian becomes 'Middle Kingdom', the Rif Muslim, the Ilongo Christian. The whole nature of man's being is sacrally malleable. (Contrast thus the prestige of these old world-languages, towering high over all vernaculars, with Esperanto or Volapük, which lie ignored between them.) It was, after all, this possibility of conversion through the sacred language that made it possible for an 'Englishman' to become Pope[4] and a 'Manchu' Son of Heaven.

But even though the sacred languages made such communities as Christendom imaginable, the actual scope and plausibility of these communities *can not* be explained by sacred script alone: their readers were, after all, tiny literate reefs on top of vast illiterate oceans.[5] A fuller explanation requires a glance at the relationship between the literati and their societies. It would be a mistake to view the former as a kind of theological technocracy. The languages they sustained, if abstruse, had none of the self-arranged abstruseness of lawyers' or economists' jargons, on the margin of society's idea of reality. Rather, the literati were adepts, strategic strata in a cosmological hierarchy of which the apex was divine.[6] The fundamental conceptions about 'social groups' were centripetal and hierarchical rather than boundary-oriented and horizontal. The astonishing power of the papacy in its noonday is only comprehensible in terms of a trans-European Latin-writing clerisy, *and* a conception of the world, shared by virtually everyone, that the bilingual intelligentsia, by mediating between vernacular and Latin, mediated between earth and heaven. (The awesomeness of excommunication reflects this cosmology.)

Yet for all the grandeur and power of the great religiously imagined communities, their *unselfconscious coherence* waned steadily after the late Middle Ages. Among the reasons for this decline, I wish here to emphasize only the two which are directly related to these communities' unique sacredness.

First was the effect of the explorations of the non-European world, which mainly but by no means exclusively in Europe 'abruptly widened the cultural and geographic horizon and hence also men's conception of possible forms of human life.'[7] The process is already apparent in the greatest of all European travel-books. Consider the following awed description of Kublai Khan by the good Venetian Christian Marco Polo at the end of the thirteenth century:[8]

> The grand khan, having obtained this signal victory, returned with great pomp and triumph to the capital city of Kanbalu. This took place in the month of November, and he continued to reside there during the months of February and March, in which latter was *our* festival of Easter. Being aware that this was one of *our* principal solemnities, he commanded all the Christians to attend him, and to bring with them *their* Book, which contains the four Gospels of the Evangelists. After causing it to be repeatedly perfumed with

incense, in a ceremonious manner, he devoutly kissed it, and directed that the same should be done by all his nobles who were present. This was his usual practice upon each of the principal Christian festivals, such as Easter and Christmas; and he observed the same at the festivals of the Saracens, Jews, and idolaters. Upon being asked his motive for this conduct, he said: 'There are four great Prophets who are reverenced and worshipped by the different classes of mankind. The Christians regard Jesus Christ as their divinity; the Saracens, Mahomet; the Jews, Moses; and the idolaters, Sogomombar-kan, the most eminent among their idols. I do honour and show respect to all the four, and invoke to my aid *whichever amongst them is in truth supreme in heaven.*' But from the manner in which his majesty acted towards them, it is evident that he regarded the faith of the Christians as the truest and the best . . .

What is so remarkable about this passage is not so much the great Mongol dynast's calm religious relativism (it is still a *religious* relativism), as Marco Polo's attitude and language. It never occurs to him, even though he is writing for fellow-European Christians, to term Kublai a hypocrite or an idolater. (No doubt in part because 'in respect to number of subjects, extent of territory, and amount of revenue, he surpasses every sovereign that has herefore been or that now is in the world.')[9] And in the unselfconscious use of 'our' (which becomes 'their'), and the description of the faith of the Christians as 'truest', rather than 'true', we can detect the seeds of a territorialization of faiths which foreshadows the language of many nationalists ('our' nation is 'the best' – in a competitive, *comparative field*).

What a revealing contrast is provided by the opening of the letter written by the Persian traveller 'Rica' to his friend 'Ibben' from Paris in '1712'.[10]

The Pope is the chief of the Christians; he is an ancient idol, worshipped now from habit. Once he was formidable even to princes, for he would depose them as easily as our magnificent sultans depose the kings of Iremetia or Georgia. But nobody fears him any longer. He claims to be the successor of one of the earliest Christians, called Saint Peter, and it is certainly a rich succession, for his treasure is immense and he has a great country under his control.

The deliberate, sophisticated fabrications of the eighteenth century Catholic mirror the naive realism of his thirteenth-century predecessor, but by now the 'relativization' and 'territorialization' are utterly selfconscious, and political in intent. Is it unreasonable to see a paradoxical elaboration of this evolving tradition in the Ayatollah Ruhollah Khomeini's identification of The Great Satan, not as a heresy, nor even as a demonic personage (dim little Carter scarcely fitted the bill), but as a *nation*?

Second was a gradual demotion of the sacred language itself. Writing of mediaeval Western Europe, Bloch noted that 'Latin was not only the language in which teaching was done, it was the *only language taught*.'[11] (This second 'only' shows quite clearly the sacredness of Latin – no other language was thought worth the teaching.) But by the sixteenth century all this was changing fast. The reasons for the change need not detain us here: the central importance of print-capitalism will be discussed below. It is sufficient to remind ourselves of its scale and pace. Febvre and Martin estimate that 77% of the books printed before 1500 were still in Latin (meaning nonetheless that 23% were already in vernaculars).[12] If of the 88 editions printed in Paris in 1501 all but 8 were in Latin, after 1575 a majority were always in French.[13] Despite a temporary come-back during the Counter-Reformation, Latin's hegemony was doomed. Nor are we speaking simply of a general popularity. Somewhat later, but at no less dizzying speed, Latin ceased to be the language of a pan-European high intelligentsia. In the seventeenth century Hobbes (1588–1678) was a figure of continental renown because he wrote in the truth-language. Shakespeare (1564–1616), on the other hand, composing in the vernacular, was virtually unknown across the Channel.[14] And had English not become, two hundred years later, the pre-eminent world-imperial language, might he not largely have retained his original insular obscurity? Meanwhile, these men's cross-Channel near-contemporaries, Descartes (1596–1650) and Pascal (1623–1662) conducted most of their correspondence in Latin; but virtually all of Voltaire's (1694–1778) was in the vernacular.[15] 'After 1640, with fewer and fewer books coming out in Latin, and more and more in the vernacular languages, publishing was ceasing to be an international [sic] enterprise.'[16] In a word, the fall of Latin exemplified a larger process in which the sacred communities integrated by old sacred languages were gradually fragmented, pluralized, and territorialized.

Bibliography

Auerbach, Erich, *Mimesis: The Representation of Reality in Western Literature*, trans. Willard Trask, Garden City, N.Y.: Doubleday Anchor, 1957.

Bloch, Marc, *Feudal Society*, trans. I. A. Manyon, Chicago: University of Chicago Press, 1961, 2 vols.

Febvre, Lucien, and Henri-Jean Martin, *The Coming of the Book: The Impact of Printing, 1450–1800*, London: New Left Books, 1976. [Translation of *L'Apparition du Livre*, Paris: Albin Michel, 1958]

Lynch, John, *The Spanish-American Revolutions, 1808–1826*, New York: Norton, 1973.

Montesquieu, Henri de, *Persian Letters*, trans. C. J. Betts, Harmondsworth: Penguin, 1973.

Polo, Marco, *The Travels of Marco Polo*, trans. and ed. William Marsden, London and New York: Everyman's Library, 1946.

Notes

1. Hence the equanimity with which Sinicized Mongols and Manchus were accepted as Sons of Heaven.

2. John Lynch, *The Spanish-American Revolutions, 1808–1826*, p. 260. Emphasis added.

3. Church Greek seems not to have achieved the status of a truth-language. The reasons for this 'failure' are various, but one key factor was certainly the fact that Greek remained a *living* demotic speech (unlike Latin) in much of the Eastern Empire. This insight I owe to Judith Herrin.

4. Nicholas Brakespear held the office of pontiff between 1154 and 1159 under the name Adrian IV.

5. Marc Bloch reminds us that 'the majority of lords and many great barons [in mediaeval times] were administrators incapable of studying personally a report or an account.' *Feudal Society*, I, p. 81.

6. This is not to say that the illiterate did not read. What they read, however, was not words but the visible world. 'In the eyes of all who were capable of reflection the material world was scarcely more than a sort of mask, behind which took place all the really important things; it seemed to them also a language, intended to express by signs a more profound reality.' Ibid. p. 83.

7. Erich Auerbach, *Mimesis*, p. 282.

8. Marco Polo, *The Travels of Marco Polo*, pp. 158–59. Emphases added. Notice that, though kissed, the Evangel is not read.

9. *The Travels of Marco Polo*, p. 152.

10. Henri de Montesquieu, *Persian Letters*, p. 81. The *Lettres Persanes* first appeared in 1721.

11. Bloch, *Feudal Society*, I, p. 77. Emphasis added.

12. Lucien Febvre and Henri-Jean Martin, *The Coming of the Book*, pp. 248–49.

13. Ibid., p. 321.

14. Ibid., p. 330.

15. Ibid., pp. 331–32.

16. Ibid., pp. 232–33. The original French is more modest and historically exact: 'Tandis que l'on édite de moins en moins d'ouvrages en latin, et une proportion toujours plus grande de textes en langue nationale, le commerce du livre se morcelle en Europe.' *L'Apparition du Livre*, p. 356.

James Hopewell, 'The Thick Gathering'

in *Congregation: Stories and Structures*, Philadelphia: Fortress Press, 1987, pp. 5–9.

Hopewell's book Congregation: Stories and Structures *(1988) marks an important point in the contemporary development of this method of corporate theological reflection. Hopewell had an abiding love and interest in congregational life. For him congregations had their own distinct identities: each one different, it constructed its identity through the stories and narratives it told about itself. Through spending time as a participant observer with a congregation he sought to uncover its symbolic life, expressed in its everyday activities and the values that emerged from understanding the stories that were told. Such an approach was new, and to develop his understanding of narrative he turned to literary theory and so opened up exciting hermeneutical possibilities in the whole field of congregational studies. He developed the idea that the identity of the congregation can be seen as a construction that was always narrative in form, with its own plot, characterization and world-view. It was the researcher's job to uncover the story that was always implicit as part of the congregation's identity.*

The way Hopewell worked with congregations to enable them to understand more fully their own corporate identity and life as story has contributed a great deal to the way this method of theological reflection has developed in contemporary times.

In this passage, Hopewell gives a flavour of the absorbing potential of congregations: how each is distinct, and the rich harvest for the sympathetic researcher. He makes the interesting move to see the idiom (using a literary term) of the congregation as the unfolding construction of the human imagination: the congregation in its rich particularity represents the unconscious symbolic life of its members, corporately and over time. Hopewell stresses the importance of learning this language; that different groups and individuals (like the pastor) need to do so, seeking to read the symbols that reveal the underlying values, for example, concerning the furniture, money or children.

To highlight the symbolic value of such phenomena, and to understand them theologically as part of a long tradition of reflection, and contextually as embedded within a particular culture and society, is to recognize that the congregation itself belongs to a theological tradition and to its contemporary culture. If the congregation is to be taken seriously, and especially if any changes are to be made, the language, symbolic life and idiom are important.

Idiom

What struck me first and most forcefully in these three churches – the one I led and the two others I studied – was the surprisingly rich idiom unique to each. As slight and predictable as the language of a congregation might seem on casual inspection, it actually reflects a complex process of human imagination. Each is a negotiation of metaphors, a field of tales and histories and meanings that identify its life, its world, and God. Word, gesture, and artifact form a local language – a system of construable signs that Clifford Geertz, following Weber, calls a 'web of significance'[1] – that distinguishes a congregation from others around it or like it. Even a plain church on a pale day catches one in a deep current of narrative interpretation and representation by which people give sense and order to their lives. Most of this creative stream is unconscious and involuntary, drawing in part upon images lodged long ago in the human struggle for meaning. Thus a congregation is held together by much more than creeds,[2] governing structures, and programs. At a deeper level, it is implicated in the symbols and signals of the world, gathering and grounding them in the congregation's own idiom.

Most of us can recall several quite distinct manifestations of parish idiom. A pastor moving from one charge to another encounters strikingly different expressions of value and style in the new church. To communicate effectively within the new congregation the pastor must master its particular language. Moreover, potential church members, like househunters, do not find a wide range of acceptable habitations in a new town. They may search diligently before discovering a congregation that catches the intonations of their own language. Some give up the search and stay home. It is not that the churches they rejected were not reasonably pleasant and worshipful, and it is not, as hyperactive help books on the market assert, that better or different programs would necessarily lure them in. In hunting for a church, Christians are not only buying a product that must be attractively presented, they are also testing their own symbolic expression against that of the prospective church. Silently they ask of the congregation: What does this place say about us? What does it signify about our values and the way we see the world?

For both pastor and laity, entry into a new church is only the beginning of the encounter with its idiom. Parish communication constitutes virtually every parish event. Conflicts of any duration usually arise from different interpretations of parish idiom. Parents and education committees perennially worry about how the young are to learn the church's language. Each week teachers struggle to relate standard curriculum materials to the information that the congregation's members already convey to each other. Members of boards and committees map out campaigns and policies along lines of discourse that function to gather the congregation. The youth group strives to entertain the church's sense of the absurd in its skit at the next parish supper. A recovered invalid chooses to express thanks to a helpful congregation in a manner authentic to its nature. The pastor spends much of the week weighing words – phrases in prayers, terms in appeals, points in sermons – so that they sink into the communicated stuff of parish idiom.

Later chapters will explore ways of analyzing the expressive nature of the congregation: how it views itself and the world, how it behaves symbolically, and how it communicates its character. To start, however, I want to call attention to examples of signals and symbols in parish idiom, the first feature of congregational expression to attract my own attention. So accustomed are all of us to conceive the church as an assortment of either consciously planned programs or irrational religious feelings that illustrations of symbolic interaction are necessary to warm us to the notion that congregations have cultures as well as activities, policies, and emotions.

Consider the church in which it has been the practice of the members to leave abruptly after the worship service. Appeals to conscience ('We are depending on *you* to help create a time of fellowship after church') or a planned program to attract after-church participation are unlikely to change the habits of most members. But suppose changes are made in the symbolic code by which worshipers may remain comfortably in each other's presence after service, perhaps by giving each a doughnut. Neither provided nor consumed for the sake of nutrition, the after-worship doughnut (and the manner of its provision and eating) is, rather, intended as new bit of idiom that

influences the tone, timing, and identity of life together. A doughnut
might seem a strange example of congregational language, but it is a
signal that conveys a message significant to the corporate life of the
congregation. A congregation knows its specific meaning, which is
an invitation to linger good-naturedly. Substances that express such
messages, many only locally understood, are part of a congregation's
idiom.

Most available substances do not have idiomatic implications. To
offer glasses of water in the church foyer after worship would cause
bewilderment, as would the distribution of gum or grits. 'What's this
for?' worshipers would ask, uncertain of the intended meaning. Some
substances, nevertheless, as well as some sounds, gestures, and marks
– and even some smells such as sanctuary musk and kitchen spices –
do serve as signals within a congregation, which by the convention
of its idiom understands each to stand *for* something else. Both universal and home-grown signals, their combinations, and the rules regarding their significance form the idiom of the local church. As many
testify, idiom differs from congregation to congregation, subtly but
insistently presenting in each its own character.[3] Each idiom is a
wondrously complex language, largely built of written and spoken
words and phrases, but also including matter as tangible as doughnuts
and mute as handshakes and pouts. Together the signals make up the
idiomatic code by which a congregation communicates itself, enabling
it to identify and integrate itself, to express its faith and love, to
govern and sometimes to change its corporate behavior.

Within congregational idiom are special signs called symbols. We
shall use 'symbol' to refer to a signal that commands markedly higher
recognition and respect from members as an element essential to
parish life. As an East Coast pastor recently discovered, symbols are
not tampered with:

> It was the damndest thing. I preach unorthodox, even heretical
> sermons fairly often, and, three years ago, the board took the results
> of the sale of some property, over a million dollars, and set the
> proceeds aside ... for the meeting of human need in this city.
> There's never a peep about the preaching, nor a single complaint
> about that dramatic action on the part of the board. But when we
> said that we wanted to move the pulpit a couple of meters to the
> left and the lectern just a couple to the right, there was a ... storm,
> and that is not too strong a term.

An arrangement of sanctuary furniture for this congregation proved to be more inviolable than either its budget or its sermons.

Symbols differ from signals like doughnuts in another way: the meaning of the symbol is markedly less specific. Even young children know what afterworship doughnuts mean, but probably no member in the East Coast church, no matter how irate, could explain what the sanctuary arrangement precisely meant. That 'multivocality', in Victor Turner's phrase, is in the nature of the symbol.[4] Members fight for its significance but cannot agree upon a single particular referent. Thus the meaning of a symbol is not easy to grasp because it abounds in meanings that touch many parts of a parish identity.[5] The transformative power of symbols resides in the abundance of meanings stored in them,[6] so members are quick to champion, but slow to explain, the symbols of their identity.

What an observer of parish symbols soon discovers is that a large portion of them are not specifically Christian in nature. Both signals and symbols in congregational idiom can arise from any source in the experience of the congregation's members. Money is such a powerful, not specifically Christian, symbol. Though the disposal of a million dollars did not seem very significant to the East Coast church, money is frequently an emotion-laden metaphor that both expresses and provokes the identity of a particular congregation. Different local churches use the symbol in different ways. One parish develops an elaborate system for hiding its display, issuing awkward campaign letters that barely mention the subject, publishing no budget, and treating the Sunday offering as an embarrassing moment to be quickly concluded. But in another church, just down the road, the subject of money comes up in most conversations. There it functions as a potent expression of superabundance and fertility. Yet another church close by treats money as a principal adversary, waging a symbolic and sometimes ingenious guerrilla war against its power to dominate. And a fourth congregation in the vicinity uses the topic of its financial difficulties primarily to voice its disappointment with a world that, through changing population patterns in the neighborhood, seems to have drained that church of its membership and power.

Jesus' insouciance toward money, taking it from the mouth of a fish, typifies the idiom of none of these congregations. Their seriousness about money comes from other sources. Such parentage does not mean that the ways they treat money are therefore sub-Christian, but rather that a household of God draws its idiom from its complex heritage of Christian and non-Christian sources.

Another world symbol in congregational idiom is children, also an emotion-laden metaphor. Different churches treat their children in different symbolic ways. One secretes them in soundproof rooms and becomes uncomfortable if too many appear in the sanctuary. A neighboring congregation, expressing its fecundity, arranges the public display of its children at worship. Another church close by devises creative campaign strategies to attract more young people and families with children, while yet another acknowledges the absence of children as it grieves its own aging.

As described here, there are similarities between the symbolic operations related to money and children. It is not the case, however, that a given congregation's idiom would express a similar action or attitude in each matter. A congregation may flaunt its money and hide its children. The distinctive idiom of a church rests on such permutations of many symbols and signs. Its language is constructed from key verbal phrases, furnishings, rituals of conflict and conciliation, displays of technical competence, ways of showing care and worth, and much more. Given the variety of options available within any of the categories, it is easy to see that the idiom of any single church is necessarily distinct.

The local church suffers when it does not take its idiom seriously. If the congregation views itself as merely the repository of meanings better expressed elsewhere, it fails to appreciate its genius, its microcosmic capacity to reflect in uniquely lived form the sociality of humankind. When a congregation considers its own language neither interesting nor important it devalues its identity and thus its names for and before God.

Notes

1. Clifford Geertz, *The Interpretation of Cultures*, chap. 1.

2. Wade Clark Roof, *Community and Commitment*, 178–79, takes issue with research that construes belief primarily from the credal statements of a church: 'Theological doctrines are always filtered through people's social and cultural experiences. What emerges in a given situation as "operant religion" will differ considerably from the "formal religion" of the historic creeds, and more concern with the former is essential to understanding how belief systems function in people's daily lives.'

3. 'Individual congregations within one judicatory have very different ideological systems . . . The difference between the extremes of the systematic value structure of congregations has grown tremendously' (James D. Anderson, *To Come Alive!* 32). 'Congregations are unique. No two congregations are alike' (Loren Mead, *New Hope for Congregations*, 96). Sociological confirmation of the heterogeneity of congregations within a single denomination is found in the

various articles of James D. Davidson; in Donald L. Metz, *New Congregations: Security and Mission in Conflict* (Philadelphia: Westminster Press, 1967), 25; and in William H. Anderson, 'The Local Congregation as a Subculture,' *Social Compass* 18 (1971): 287–91.

4. Victor W. Turner, *Dramas, Fields and Metaphors*, 29.

5. Referring to what he terms their 'multivocality', Victor Turner proposes that symbols condense within a single formulation a number of meanings and values significant to a people (*The Forest of Symbols: Aspects of Ndembu Ritual* [Ithaca, N.Y.: Cornell Univ. Press, 1967], 19–41). Cf. Turner's introduction to Edward R. Spence, ed., *Forms of Symbolic Action* (Seattle: Univ. of Washington Press, 1970). Turner finds in each symbol a polarization of physiological referents and those which disclose a 'depth world of prophetic, half-glimpsed images . . . Symbols resonate with meanings'.

6. Symbols perform, for Geertz, a synthesizing action that relates their stored meanings and depicts a social behavior they also evoke (*Interpretation of Cultures*, 87–141).

Chris Baker, 'Hybridity and Practical Theology: In Praise of Blurred Encounters'

Contact, No. 149 2006, Miscellany One, pp. 5–11.

Corporate theological reflection in the twenty-first century will inevitably be shaped by the dynamics of a globalized world as faith communities work out appropriate meaning and mission strategies in their local contexts. Baker's research in Manchester, UK, locates the faith communities he studied within a late capitalist city where increased migratory patterns of people and ever more sophisticated means of communication result in understandings of culture that are inherently unstable.

Hopewell, as we have seen in this section, drew on literary theory to enable his thinking about the congregation, and Baker draws on the work of Homi Bhabha, another literary theorist, and his central concept of hybridity, to draw together his thinking about the place of the faith community in contemporary times. Hybridity, Baker says, increasingly becomes the hallmark of communities that are moving from traditional monochrome and homogeneous identities to a diverse and mixed internal life which has blurred boundaries as it engages with the world around. Hybrid communities undermine 'us and them' polarized differences by emphasizing the creative mixture of subjectivity, whether individual or corporate. Baker draws upon the writing of Kwok Pui-lan and her book The Postcolonial Imagination and Feminist Theology *(2005) to show how Christological thinking can shape a corporate theological reflection for today's congregation. Pui-Lan speaks of the space between Jesus and Christ as a hybrid, unsettling idea that resonates with the way in which congregations increasingly construct themselves in local and practical ways as the body of Christ.*

Summary

The article explores the growing significance of hybridity as a concept for describing the pastoral mission and practical identity of the church in the 21st century. The idea of hybridity emerges from the post-colonial and globalized urban societies in which we now live. The article synthesizes the literary theory of the leading exponent of this idea, Homi Bhabha, and his concept of the Third Space, with a post-liberal theology of the blurred encounter. The article ends with a reflection on the significance of a hybrid Christology in the construction of local and performative theologies.

Hybridity is a concept which has 'come of age'. It is a major theory that increasingly shapes the way we understand our cultural and political world and our sense of identity. Hybridity is emerging from the disciplines of cultural studies and anthropology and is beginning to cross over into theological discourses. It is by nature a complex and ambiguous concept, but one which practical theology ignores at its peril if it wants to connect with the major problematic emerging in the 21st century: our relationship with the Other in our midst and how we engage with diversity and plurality.

In this article I shall explore some of the 'prejudices' against hybridity that a practical theology will have to overcome. I then outline its emergence as an indispensable category for interpreting post-modern and post-colonial society. I look briefly at some case studies of churches working with hybrid identities and methodologies within their local communities. I then reflect on how hybridity could become a major tool in the working out of practical theology.

Hybridity: a Dirty Word

Hybridity appears to be objectionable on at least two fronts. One is a cluster of objections emerging from the colonial period which regarded the physical mixing of races as a eugenic as well as moral and cultural threat to the fixed 'purity' of white Western culture. For example, debates around hybridity emerged during the late eighteenth century concerning sexual relationships between the indigenous black population – the men and women deployed as slave labour on the plantations – and the white plantation owners, their wives and managers. Edward Long in his *History of Jamaica* (1774) notes with grave concern that many White men of the colony are so infatuated with the Black women that they refuse to marry White women. 'In consequence of this practice, we have not only more spinsters in this small community than in most other parts of his majesty's dominions, but also a vast addition of spurious offsprings of different complexions' (quoted in Young, 1995: 151).

This aversion to the 'mixing' of races in the colonial period had at least three causes. One was fear of a genetic weakening of pure stock. Long opines that, 'In the course of a few generations more, the English blood will become so contaminated with this mixture – even to reach to the middle and upper orders of people, till the whole nation resembles the Portuguese or Moriscos in the complexion of skin and baseness of mind' (quoted Young, 1995: 150). Second, these fears of skin-colour change were related to issues of fertility; despite evidence to the contrary, it was held that half-breed populations would slowly die out because they challenged the racial givens of the White vs Black dichotomy and thus produced defective offspring. This fear was based on the idea that human beings derived from different species – the so-called *polygenesist* position which claimed that Black humans and White humans, and so-called Brown, Red and Yellow humans, were actually different species, with White clearly at the top of the hierarchical species tree. This theory, expounded openly until the 1930s, defined the difference between mongrel and hybrid. Mongrels survived because they crossed distinct races, whereas hybrids were much more prone to infertility because they crossed different *species*. (See, for example, the writings of T. H. Huxley in the 1860s, especially his 'helpfully' entitled *Lectures to Working Men*).

The final anxiety associated with what came to be called *miscegenation* (Latin *miscere*, to mix, and *genus*, race) was the decline in purity of morals and intellect, as identified in a table devised by the French anthropologist Count Gobineau in the 1850s. For example, under the category of 'intellect' he listed 'Black races' as 'feeble', 'Yellow races' as 'mediocre' and 'White races' as 'vigorous'.

Unfortunately, these offensive attitudes are still aimed at those of mixed heritage living in British society today. Disturbing research has recently emerged into how young people who define themselves as

Mixed (in the 2001 census) are treated by wider society. Because they have one Black parent, society apparently expects them to think of themselves as Black, which some are willing to do, but others are not. However, all mixed-race young people are subject to deep-seated racial discrimination, epitomized in such phrases as 'peanut', 'yellow-belly', 'half-breed' and 'redskin', which are not used for Black children. It is also apparent that they experience racist discrimination at the hands of Black as well as White communities, despite efforts at identifying with Black culture and ways of life (Brah and Coombes, 2002: 89).

The other cluster of objections is related to the theological charge that hybridity (allowing new patterns of worship and spiritual identity to emerge from the plural and diverse experiences within globalized localities) is synonymous with syncretism (the 'watering down' of the purity of the Christian gospel). This argument rehearses a recurring theme – the negotiation of identity and the transmission of the Christian message within a post-modernity characterized by competing truth claims and fluid cultural foundations.

Robert Schreiter (1997), as part of his strategy for creative church engagement with hybridity, argues for a more positive assessment of syncretism. He traces the fluidity of Christianity from its earliest historical roots, as a reform movement within the Judaism of its day, which looked both backwards to pristinate Jewish life and forward to see the Lord coming again. As a reform movement, Christianity has always had 'a certain asymmetry, a certain restlessness' (1997: 65). The *ecclesia semper reformanda* is both a positive and negative phenomenon with regard to syncretism. As Schreiter points out, the 'restlessness' inherent within Christianity can cause anxiety for those for whom 'an addition or amendment is potentially encumbering to pure faith' (1997: 65). On the other hand, as Chinese theologian Kwok Pui-Lan points out (2005: 129), syncretism (the ability of Christianity to adapt to its cultural context as needed) has ensured the viability of Christianity as a faith tradition. She cites the way early Christianity interacted with the Hellenistic culture and philosophy in which it was embedded, including dualistic notions of darkness and light and the influences of Plato and Aristotle on the doctrines of the early church fathers.

Hybridity: A Ubiquitous Fact of Globalized Life

One major driver of hybridity in our contemporary experience is the *diasporization* of the world's populations within the expanding global cities which now function as the hubs for late capitalism and the creation of a 24/7 financial and knowledge-based market. This phenomenon is nothing new, but the intensity, speed and hypermobility of global populations from the 1980s onwards is. According to the diasporization theory of globalization, sharply increased migratory patterns of human behaviour are having an unsettling and polarizing effect on social space, as migration and telecommunications bring differences much closer together. This increases the opportunities for interaction (a so-called *open* identity), but also for living out more sharply defined or *fixed* identities. Diasporic communities are often marginalized or ghettoized by the prevailing urban elite. Migrants who are *culturally disembedded* may seek to *re-embed* themselves within host societies in ways that don't smooth out difference, but accentuate it. Either way, traditional understandings of culture based on colonial ideas of the *centre* controlling the *periphery* no longer work. The periphery has come into the centre, thus destabilizing long-cherished ideals of the single nation-state. Late capitalist cities and societies are now contested spaces where old binary assumptions about the stability of culture as 'complex wholes' (different elements held within a bounded, territorial and coherent symbol system which everyone understands and signs up to) have given way to understandings of culture as inherently unstable (Papastergiadis, 2000).

Homi Bhabha, a leading exponent of hybridity, develops these ideas further, with the idea of the Third Space – an unpredictable and 'live' space that exists within the binary labelling by the Colonial of the Other. The way that colonial discourses always labelled the Other was a static process, robbing the Other of their vitality and autonomy. The Other used to be the *énoncé*, or object of enunciation. Now, due to the radical instability in culture and urban society, the *énoncé* – the migrant or the trafficked person, those voices from the 'borderlands' (Sandercock, 1998) – becomes the subject of their own discourse. They speak their own reality. Their cultural position is fluid and always lies outside the statement made about them. Their essential, particular being is not fixed anyway, and can never be fully covered by what is assumed by the proposer. In Bhabha's terminology, the *binary* descriptions of colonial discourse are replaced by the instability of the *Third* Space, where neither *generalized labelling* nor the *specific implications* of an utterance holds sway. Rather, meaning is negotiated between the two to create a new *hybrid* identity that rejects a colonial present and future, but also a mythologized past based on nostalgic reclamation of a pure, pre-existing cultural or ethnic identity.

One criticism of Bhabha's thinking is that it relies overmuch on literary theory and is thus detached from everyday life. However, most agree that his ideas of Third Space hybridity are important and creative. His hybridity is not based on ideas of *accretion* (the essence of one identity is added to another), nor is it a *synthetic* model (different elements of identity fuse together). If hybridity became either of these two things it would cease being hybrid, and become a closed system – as essentialist as the categories of either Black or White. Bhabha's hybridity acknowledges the *untranslatability* of some parts of culture, and the need to live with that discomfort which paradoxically drives some migrants ever forward to gain understanding of their new identities. His is not a redemptive understanding of how hybridity can rescue post-colonial society, riven as it often is by fear and distrust of the Other (Sandercock, 2003: 4). Rather, Third Space hybridity is more 'interrogatory' than strategic.

Hybrid Church: Constructing Local Theologies

I now focus on some emerging ecclesiological and theological implications of engagement with hybridity. I believe we need to find a *methodological* hybridity as well as a *doctrinal* one. The following case study comes from research undertaken by the William Temple Foundation over three years, observing and reflecting on the experience of different church projects engaging in rapid urban and social change in Manchester (Baker and Skinner, 2005).

The Eden Project is a collective name for a cluster of independent charismatic churches established in Manchester during the late 1980s under the auspices of the World Wide Message Tribe to attract young people to the Christian gospel. Its methodology involves establishing partnerships with sympathetic church bases, who provide physical infrastructure for youth-focused evangelism in return for free specialist youth workers. The distinctive feature of this project is the requirement that its staff commit themselves to living in the community, buying a house and using local services such as surgeries, schools and shops. They thus function as a locally embedded community within a community. The Eden Project is based in East Manchester, the seventeenth most deprived ward out of 8,400 in England and Wales. The project has now been running for five years. Two aspects of its engagement have been 'blurred encounters' and being 'active local residents'.

Blurred Encounters

References by this church to 'our evangelical heritage' are supported by explicit commitments to church growth, increased baptisms and a commitment to alternative lifestyles, especially in relation to issues of sexual morality. However, interwoven with this belief structure is a willingness to have the boundaries of identity blurred. As they live longer in the area, so church members learn more about the complexity of drug and alcohol abuse issues, child abuse, poor education, long-term unemployment and chronic poverty. The issues of 'friendship' with the wider community, and becoming 'increasingly part of the community', are superseding traditionally understood roles and labels.

'We used to do a lot of detached youth work, well . . . that kind of gets merged when you walk down the shop and bump into a bunch of kids that you know on the street corner and they ask you something . . . before you know it you spend half an hour talking and you've walked down the shop to buy a bottle of milk when you think, "What was that? Was that life? Was that shopping? Was that detached youth work?" . . .'

This 'blurring of identities' is now part of Eden members' daily experience in East Manchester. (I am also indebted to John Reader (2005) for his sustained and creative thinking in this area.)

Being Active Local Citizens

One Eden member reflected,

'Those are the kind of things that we need to be chivvying along an we need to keep saying, "But we need to make sure that my next door neighbour can actually have a house in the new estate."'

Chivvying along is a deceptively deprecating phrase for a vital role this church finds itself playing with regard to the proposed demolition of six hundred houses in East Manchester to make way for mainly private housing. An original principle agreed between the local

residents, developers and local authority was that 'the current community must be facilitated in all possible ways to stay together, to be
the community that lives on the new estate.' The current value of
residents' housing has risen to £40,000–50,000 (Dec. 2004), which
is approximately what they will receive under compulsory purchase
order payments. However, it has emerged that the cheapest family
housing provided by the developers will be £150,000, leaving a potential mortgage shortfall of £100,000, a mortgage normally available
only to those with jobs paying salaries of £25,000–30,000 per annum.
These jobs are not available in the local community. Meanwhile those
who have already paid off the mortgage on their old houses face the
prospect of having to take out another one, typically in the later stages
of their lives or working careers. As residents, the Eden members
understand some of the implications of this process and consequently
believe they will fall short in their collective responsibility to the
neighbourhood if 'in five to ten years' time it becomes just a suburban
estate with a lot of sort of business people living on it' (quoted in
Baker and Skinner, 2005: 56).

Hence the important role of 'chivvying' – reminding others of
important core values and negotiating as subtly but powerfully as
possible to ensure that these are respected.

This case study describes a hybrid methodology, constructing a
local theology by a local church community. The hybridity emerges
from a number of different elements that include

- openness to working with partners from different perspectives;
- combining a number of different methodologies and approaches
  simultaneously;
- risk and experimentation;
- expanding core identities, but to identities that are continuous
  rather than discontinuous with existing identities and values (in
  other words evolution, not revolution);
- being highly reflexive but also strategic;
- meeting the challenge of learning new skills (Baker and Skinner,
  2005: 63).

Hybridity is also expressed in the growing ethnic and social diversity of many of the congregations the Foundation worked with. For
example, some of the Black Majority Churches (BMCs) are making
a transition from entirely monochrome communities to more hybrid
congregations as second- and third-generation Black British Christians
not only create families with other ethnic groups, but also attract new

members from other diasporic communities from Africa and Eastern Europe. Some of these churches have also evolved a more hybrid theology to match: that is with more emphasis on tolerance, acceptance and practical problem-solving for life issues, rather than overt moralizing, judgement and separation from the prevailing culture.

The Hybrid Christ: An Open-Ended Christology

Charges of syncretism that have emerged in previous eras of Christian history may surface again as awareness of hybridity begins to emerge within mainstream theological debate. One such reply to these charges is the creative Christology of Kwok Pui-Lan, currently reaching a wide audience in her book *Postcolonial Imagination and Feminist Theology* (2005).

Pul-Lan begins her exploration of the hybrid Christ with the question Jesus himself asks of his own disciples – 'Who do you say I am?' – and finds this question 'an invitation for every Christian and every local faith community to infuse that contact zone with new meanings, insights and possibilities' (2005: 171). From her feminist and post-colonial perspective, the local is the context from which hybridity should be allowed to emerge: 'The richness and vibrancy of the Christian community is diminished whenever the space between Jesus and Christ is fixed, whether . . . as a result of the need for doctrinal purity, the suppression of syncretism, or the fear of contamination of native cultures, or . . . on account of historical positivism and its claims of objectivity and scientific truths about Jesus' (Pui-Lan 2005: 171).

That reference to 'historical positivism' is an allusion to the quest for the historical Jesus epitomized by Albert Schweitzer's book of the same name (1906). For Pui-Lan this 'scientific' account was symptomatic of colonialism's need to locate Jesus away from his Jewish and Middle Eastern origins into a more European model of humanity (2005: 62–64). This static, Eurocentric understanding of Jesus' role and identity, with its power of representation over and against other cultural perspectives, is now being replaced, in Pui-Lan's opinion, by the Quest for the Hybridized Jesus (2005: 170). This quest is not simply a post-colonial phenomenon. Rather, the hybridized Christ emerges from the pages of the New Testament itself, which describes situations that are highly pluralistic, arising out of the cultural 'inter-mingling' of Palestine, the Hellenistic Jewish diaspora, and the wider Hellenistic world.

Pui-Lan's Christology suggests that hybridity is located at the very centre of the Christian faith. It reminds us that the Incarnation of the Christ (the divine and eternal Logos or Word of God) was not confined to a point in time and a culture two thousand years ago, but is a continuous event whereby the love of God for creation takes the risk of being born into human cultures in a way that not only *translates* and *negotiates* with those cultures from the underside of human experience, but also is itself *translated* by that experience. It is a risky, kenotic theology which will often lead to messy or blurred encounters and will potentially subvert the *status quo*, but will always point towards the *telos* of justice, inclusivity and reconciliation.

Pui-Lan finds the transforming mystery of the Incarnation not in 'Jesus' or 'Christ' (binary symbols at either end of the human-divine spectrum), but in the tiny hyphen or stroke sign that one could insert in between these terms (Jesus-Christ, Jesus/Christ). In a memorable passage she says,

> The space between Jesus and Christ is unsettling and fluid, resisting easy categorisation and closure. It is the 'contact zone' or 'borderland' between the human and the divine, the one and the many, the historical and the cosmological, the Jewish and the Hellenistic, the prophetic and the sacramental, the God of the conquerors and the God of the meek and the lowly. (2005: 17)

To link Pui-Lan's Christology to the terminology of Homi Bhabha, we could describe Jesus as 'a truly insurgent act of cultural translation' (Bhabha, 1994: 6), a Third Space ministerial paradigm. I believe that is an interesting idea that resonates powerfully with the overriding pastoral agenda to discern and valorize diversity and plurality, in local and practical ways – in other words, to welcome the Other in our midst.

References

Baker, C. and Skinner, H. (2005) *Telling the Stories: How Churches are Contributing to Social Capital*, Manchester: William Temple Foundation.
Bhabha, H. (1994) *The Location of Culture*, London and New York: Routledge.
Brah, A. and Coombes, A. (eds.) (2002) *Hybridity and Its Discontents: Politics, Science, Culture*, London and New York: Routledge.
Papastergiadis, N. (2000) *The Turbulence of Migration*, Oxford: Polity.
Pui-Lan, K. (2005) *Post-colonial Imagination and Feminist Theology*, Louisville: Westminster John Knox Press.
Reader, J. (2005) *Blurred Encounters*, Vale of Glamorgan: Aureus.

Sandercock, L. (1998), *Towards Cosmopolis*, Chichester: John Wiley and Sons.

Sandercock, L. (2003), *Cosmopolis II – Mongrel Cities of the 21st Century*, London: Continuum.

Shreiter, R. (1997) *The New Catholicity*, Maryknoll: Orbis.

Young, R. (1995) *Colonial Desire: Hybridity, Culture and Race*, London & New York: Routledge.

Will Storrar, 'Perspectives on the Local Church'

in Helen Cameron, Douglas Davies, Philip Richter and Frances Ward (eds), *Studying Local Churches: A Handbook*; London: SCM Press, pp. 177–81.

Storrar's contribution to the collection of essays Studying Local Churches *brings together rigorous ethnographic research and theological reflection that draws on anthropological perspectives, particularly the writing of Michel de Certeau. He draws out a central image from comments made by the two women who led the congregation he studied over a period of time, that of 'the temple', and in this selected passage he shows how he develops theological reflection upon the theme. For him the temple is not so much to be thought of as an intrinsically holy space but more as a socially constructed space made meaningful by the use to which it is put. He writes, 'this is a post-modern temple where the boundaries between church and neighbour-hood, member and neighbour, church or community resources and funding, are permeable and at times blurred' (p. 252). Spaces – and congregations – are created by the human actions that happen there, where space, time and bodily action come together. Whereas Hope-well encouraged the researcher to understand the language, idiom and narratives of the congregation, Storrar directs attention to the way in which bodies move and construct spaces, and therefore congregations, in non-verbal ways.*

Temple: A Biblical Correlation

God's people inhabit many spatial sites in the Bible: wilderness and holy mountain, tabernacle, temple, synagogue and household, promised land and foreign land. Each image suggests ways of thinking spatially about the local church. Why the temple-image in this particular case study? In the temple in Jerusalem that features prominently in the history of Israel and the ministry of Jesus, there were outer and inner courtyards, leading to the inner sanctuary. The primary purpose is the worship of God, although many ancillary activities are pursued within its walls (as the gospel story of Jesus driving out the money-changers reminds us). Over three years, Lynn and Jean never used temple imagery; this was my own selected image as a researcher. However, they did speak of what they were doing in ways that later prompted such an interpretation. Jean described their plan to site the counselling centre within the church sanctuary itself like this:

> We designed it so because we feel that everything that goes on should really be part of the church as opposed to something that the church is doing away from the church because it is the place where we want to be.

Lynn echoed that remark. It was the building that declared the Christian identity of the congregation:

> There is a theory about doing things off the premises and starting up say a shop or something in the community, particularly in communities like this. People have gone into the idea of house churches and moving away from buildings. I think if you scrape the surface of most of the people in the church, they still feel that it should be around the church . . . and I feel it should be in the church. Not because I want the gathering in here but because I think it is important to make that connection, to be honest about it and say, 'This is who we are', and that the project will be run by people who, it doesn't matter if they have faith or not, we need them to do this job for the children, but there is something about linking it in to the memorial chapel and the tree and the services of remembrance we have had there for children as well as adults.

For both Lynn and Jean the church building was important as a place to connect the Christian faith and the needs of the community. The church café, memorial chapel and counselling centre functioned like the outer and inner courtyards of a temple, leading local people through different zones into the ritual place of worship at the heart. Nor was the worship escapist in the life and suffering of this community. As Lynn put it:

> . . . it seems to me that the importance of worship is where life is and so that's when you come back to the café, and you come back

to the suffering and you come back to, how do you bring this back into the life and worship of the church?

It is not immediately obvious that the use of temple imagery is compatible with New Testament views of the temple. Jesus is seen as the new temple in his own person (John 1.14; 2.21), replacing the Jerusalem temple as the place where God dwells. There are, therefore, no longer any buildings or places that are holy or sacred for Christians (John 4.19–24). It is the bodies of Christians, rather than their places of worship, that are described by Paul in 1 Corinthians as the 'temple of the Holy Spirit' (I Corinthians 3.17; 6.19). This has led many today to stress the church is a community of faith, the body of Christ with many members (I Corinthians 12.12–27), and not a church building.

However, feminist theology and biblical studies also bring to our attention the embodied nature of the biblical narratives. The new temple may not be a building but it is a body in space and place: Christ's body and the body of Christ. As the Jesus of John's Gospel moves in and through space with the women disciples, for example, they create new places for the gospel: a room filled with the perfume of a woman's costly ointment, preparing Jesus' body for his death. The households of the first Christians, which included women, gentiles and slaves, embodied a gospel of reconciliation. Movement and action in space, which create theologically significant place, are integral to the life of this new temple. At the very least, Christians cannot spiritualize away the embodied life of the church. It is their bodies in space that are the temples of the indwelling Spirit and it is their embodied lives that create places of true discipleship (I Corinthians 6.15–20).

By calling Millhill Church a temple-like place I am not thinking of it as intrinsically holy or sacred space, but rather as a socially constructed space where local people find healing and hope by their bodily movement in and through its building, reconfigured as a welcoming and worshipful set of places. Unlike the temple in Jerusalem, which excluded women, gentiles and sinners from its innermost courtyard and sanctuary, all people in this temple are encouraged to move through the different courtyards and the sanctuary itself. I am therefore calling the Millhill congregation a temple in a *double* sense: it is an *embodied spiritual temple* inhabiting a *temple-like building*, where people move, mingle and express faith in social, pastoral and liturgical practices. This is a postmodern temple where the boundaries between church and neighbourhood, member and neighbour, church or community resources and funding, are permeable and at times blurred. If we are to understand the people and resources here, then we must watch how they inhabit place and move through space, rather than simply measure formal membership and official activities over time. To explore further, we now correlate this biblical interpretation of spiritual and spatial embodiment with anthropological perspectives.

Walking: An Anthropological Correlation

In an essay on spatial taboos in the Australian Aboriginal landscape, Nancy M. Dunn argues that anthropology needs to work against 'abstracting the problem of space from that of the body and action' by co-ordinating space, time and bodily action in one paradigm of changing relations (Dunn, 2003, pp. 92–109). The need for such a paradigm also applies to congregational studies. Too often we study the congregation as an organization over time without reference to embodied action within its delineated space. For example, we could describe the Millhill counselling centre as an organized pastoral response to the number of bereaved children in the community. However, for Lynn, it is a pattern of movement within the building:

> It's hard without seeing the building but it's almost as though we've physically kind of walked up there anyway because . . . we had the memorial chapel and the things that are in it . . . We started a music room for bereaved children . . . and through that partly came [the centre]. Through working with the children and through visiting the parents we seemed to be walking toward the area at the back of the church anyway.

How are we to understand these references to walking? They echo a study of sheep farmers in the Scottish Borders by another anthropologist, John Gray. He draws on Michel de Certeau's famous interpretation of walking as a practice that creates 'places'. Pedestrians make cities their own place not by following the cartographer's map but in the improvised act of window-shopping or strolling. Gray interprets the life of a hill-farming community through observing this non-verbal practice of walking: 'My aim is . . . to analyze how, in going around the hill, shepherds make a variety of places to which they become attached as a matter of their identity as hill sheep people and Borderers' (Gray, 2003, pp. 226–8). Through walking around the hills, this human action in space creates places of 'human significance and emotional attachment' for the shepherds.

Similarly, by paying attention to the non-verbal practices of movement around the church building we can see how a congregation and its neighbours create similar 'places' to which they also become attached in terms of their spiritual identity. Through such anthropological insights into space and place, we realize that these are not only metaphors for congregational life but also a constitutive part of it, without which the local church cannot exist or be understood. Like the anthropologists, we also need a paradigm that integrates space, time and bodily action in congregational studies. Has the Christian tradition itself ever understood the local church in such spatial and bodily terms?

Bibliography

Dunn, N. M. (2003) 'Excluded Spaces: The Figure in the Australian Aboriginal Landscape', in S. M. Low and D. Lawrence-Zuniga (eds) *the Anthropology of Space and Place: Locating Culture*, Oxford: Blackwell, pp. 92–102.

Gray, J. (2003) 'Open Spaces and Dwelling Places: Being at Home on Hill Farms in the Scottish Borders', in S. M. Low and D. Lawrence-Zuniga (eds.) *The Anthropology of Space and Place: Locating Culture*, Oxford: Blackwell, pp. 224–44.

Frances Ward, 'Studying Congregation using Ethnographic Methods'

in Mathew Guest, Karin Tusting and Linda Woodhead (eds) (2004), *Congregational Studies in the UK: Christianity in a post-Christian Context*, Aldershot: Ashgate, pp. 126–9.

Congregational studies as a discipline draws upon a wide range of different research methods and approaches to understand the congregation, faith community or church. This passage looks at the ways in which the ethnographic researcher produces 'a coherent text from the scraps and fragments of life' (Guest et al, 2004, p. 126), often dealing with difficult and conflicting relationships on the ground, and a plethora of data, both of which develop in their own, often unforeseen ways. As a research project is carried forward, the initial focus can change and reshape as different data emerge and the researcher refines their thinking in the light of that data. Throughout the process of research, questions of accountability and negotiation continue to be central, and are sometimes in conflict with the direction in which the research is travelling. Determining what analytical approach to adopt, and sorting data as the written text is shaped, itself results in an imaginative construction that can be seen to parallel the way in which the congregation or faith community comes to cohere through practices and communal reflection. Both the activity of writing about, and the congregation that is the subject of the research, reveal a network of power relations and conflicts that call out for theological reflection.

Stage One: Making a Start

My initial research proposal was to do an ethnographic study of three congregations of different Christian denominations, investigating 'corporate identity', a concept that so intrigued Hopewell, among others (Dudley, 1983; Dudley *et al.*, 1991; Hopewell, 1987; Browning, 1991), and which continues to hold the attention of researchers (Becker, 1999). I was interested to discover how each understood itself and formed such identity in dialogue with its own tradition and with the traditions of the others. I was particularly intrigued to find out how the informal structures of communication, particularly gossip, consolidated – and fragmented – corporate identity (Heilman, 1976; Spacks, 1986; Hopewell, 1987). I decided to start with the Anglican congregation, basically because the access was easiest: I knew both the then rector and the curate reasonably well. The congregation had been 'researched' before, and being an Anglican myself, I would be on home ground, as it were. So I talked informally with that rector, and with the curate, outlining my project.

Perhaps the most obvious and immediately noticeable feature about this church at the time was its rector. For twelve or thirteen years his strength of personality and flamboyance had left its mark upon the church's liturgical style and engagement in local political issues and community concerns in a social context that had undergone much change and upheaval. In many ways his type of leadership gave this church a particular ethos and corporate nature. Then, just as I was about to start the project, it was announced that he had been appointed to another post.

With this unforeseen movement, my initial plans of doing a comparative study of the different denominations within the area became more difficult. His imminent departure would create too many variables between the congregations. So instead I decided to focus solely upon this Anglican church, and to study its internal dynamics during the period of the interregnum. The vacuum left after the departure of a strong leader would make more interesting the notion of 'corporate identity'. I talked informally with the curate and when it was clear that he would be happy for the research to continue, I wrote to the Bishop to clear the proposal with him and also negotiated with my employer for the time to initiate and carry forward the project. I talked with the Parochial Church Council (the P.C.C.) and, before the rector left, introduced the research project to the congregation as an exploration of the notion of 'corporate identity'. I explained that I would be with them over the next few months, observing worship and P.C.C. meetings and social gatherings to investigate what held them together as a group. The rector was to be leaving within a fortnight or so, so essentially I was beginning my research as an interregnum began. It was to extend into the beginning of the incumbency of the next rector.

I attended most Sundays, sitting up in the balcony, making copious notes of where people sat, their interactions, and the roles that individuals played within the practices of worship. Coffee followed the main service, and again I mapped where people sat, whom they regularly talked with. A few then adjourned to the pub and I would accompany them, making mental observations that I would write up later on. I also collected other forms of data during that period – material from interviews (I interviewed two-thirds of the congregation), observations, and local primary documentary sources.

The notion of 'corporate identity' started to unravel. I was taken further towards a consideration of the power dynamics within the congregation than Hopewell seemed to contemplate, though Becker's use of 'new institutionalism' (1999, p. 11) in her study of *Congregations in Conflict* offers a fascinating approach to the subject. Unlike her, though, I turned more towards Foucault and his analysis of power as the negotiation with dominance. I found myself asking: Who constructs the 'corporate identity' of this particular congregation? Who is dominant here? Who subordinated? Whose interests are served by the status quo? What or who gave the congregation cohesion? How did members, especially black members, of whom there was a majority, and women, again of whom there was a majority, negotiate their places within the body of the congregation? In the face of such dominant white leadership as I suspected the rector gave, how did members register any discontent? What did members *really* feel about the liturgy at the church? Did all feel equally at home with what it offered? This plethora of questions raised concerns about power relations between different cultures and races, and the part played by gender.

The North American literature within the discipline of congregational studies at the time I was writing was largely produced within a white Protestant milieu, and although latterly there has been growing attention to questions of racism and gender (Wind and Lewis, 1998; Bennison *et al.*, 1999), it seemed to have very little to offer to enable an adequate analysis of the institutional forms that might emerge within a church congregation. The more I read within the field, the more it appeared benign and blind to such uncomfortable issues (Becker's book being the exception).

To provide the analysis I felt necessary, I turned to the work of Michel Foucault. Foucault, particularly in his *Discipline and Punish*, suggested that the construction of an institution makes material the interests of the status quo, which in turn serve the dominant subject. By 'dominant subject' here I had in mind Foucault's portrayal of modern man in his essay 'Man and his Doubles', where 'man' only makes his appearance 'in an unavoidable duality' with its others ([1966] 1994, p. 326). Such a subject sustains itself in power by cloaking its own presence and by projecting 'otherness' onto those who are different: black, women, gay and lesbian people, people of different class. If that 'subject', within the Church of England, is taken to be the dominant white Anglo-Saxon culture, then how might 'others' negotiate their presence?

There was a wide diversity of people who worshipped regularly in this congregation, from eleven different countries of origin, from many different denominational backgrounds and from Anglican churches with a different ethos. They continued to come to this church, often having sampled other Anglican or Catholic churches, because it was welcoming, and gave them enough spiritual sustenance. They felt at home, yes, but to varying degrees. I began to be interested in how 'at home' members felt in this congregation. As I interviewed members, the different ways in which they negotiated with the dominant practices and ethos started to emerge. There was plenty of evidence suggesting that there was not the same sense of ownership of the liturgy among black members that I heard from the Anglo-Saxon interviewees.

The congregation, under the leadership of rector and curate, took awareness of racism extremely seriously and worked hard to counter and challenge racist attitudes both within its own culture and in wider society. This was the time of the Stephen Lawrence Inquiry and the MacPherson report into 'institutional racism' within the police forces of the UK, and such language came easily to one of the leading white men, when I interviewed him. Talking of the black members of the congregation, he made the comment:

And that's because we, the white race, have kicked them in the balls too many times. That's the institutionalized racism bit, if you like. And I accuse the Church of England of being institutionally racist.

In this first stage of the research I had already begun to refocus the central question. The initial notion of 'corporate identity' had now developed into an investigation into institutional racism and gender. When this happens in a project that does not involve fieldwork, it is a straightforward process of reassessing documentary data thus far accumulated. When your research involves people, how beholden to them are you to keep them informed of changes of direction you are taking? I had moved from the initial 'contract' I had established with the congregation and the rector (who was long gone anyway). Should I go back and re-negotiate? With whom, though? And risk in the process disrupting the delicate business of gaining trust? With that rector gone, I did talk at length with the curate about where my thinking was going. At no time, however, during the period of my field research did it seem appropriate to talk with members of the congregation as a whole to bring them up to date. It would have been disruptive, and also it would have made a difference between those I had already interviewed and what they said, and the people I was yet to interview. And, anyway, who would I have selected? Was my thinking in a sufficiently coherent state to be discussed? For various reasons the ground shifted, and a widening gap emerged between where I was going with the research and the understanding that most members of the congregation had of what I was doing. But with hindsight, perhaps I should have talked more. Perhaps I should have set up from the beginning a group of congregational members with whom to consult about such matters, or used the P.C.C. more readily to air the progress of my research. As it was I continued, with a vague sense of disquiet.

References

Becker, P. E. (1999), *Congregations in Conflict: Cultural Models of Local Religious Life*, Cambridge, UK, New York and Melbourne, Australia: Cambridge University Press.

Bennison, C. *et al.* (1999), *In Praise of Congregations: Leadership in the Local Church Today*, Boston, MA: Cowley Publications.

Browning, D. (1991), *A Fundamental Practical Theology*, Minneapolis, MN: Fortress Press.

Dudley, C. (ed.) (1983), *Building Effective Ministry: Theory and Practice in the Local Church*, San Francisco: Harper and Row.

Dudley, C. *et al.* (eds) (1991), *Carriers of Faith: Lessons from Congregational Studies*, a Festschrift in honor of Robert W. Lynn, Louisville, KY: Westminster/ John Knox Press.

Foucault, M. ([1966] 1994), 'Man and his Doubles', in *The Order of Things: An Archaeology of the Human Sciences*, trans. A. Sheridan-Smith, New York and London: Routledge, pp. 303–343.

Foucault, M. ([1975] 1991), *Discipline and Punish: The Birth of the Prison*, trans. A. Sheridan-Smith, London: Penguin.

Heilman, S. (1976), *Synagogue Life: A Study in Symbolic Interaction*, Chicago: University of Chicago Press.

Hopewell, J. ([1987] 1988), *Congregation: Stories and Structures*, ed. B. Wheeler, London: SCM.

Spacks, P. (1986), *Gossip*, Chicago: University of Chicago Press.

Wind, J. P. and Lewis, J. W. (eds) (1998), *American Congregations*, 2 vols, Chicago: The University of Chicago Press.

Heidi Campbell, 'On Being the Church Online'

in *Exploring Religious Communities Online*, New York: Peter Lang, 2005, pp. 162–7.

A significant development in the first years of the twenty-first century is the emergence of online church communities. The ease of communication offered by the Internet and the opportunities to form community around networks of interest rather than based in location enable imagined communities to develop in ways unforeseen by Anderson. Heidi Campbell's research on this development illustrates the way in which many use the Internet to connect with other like-minded people to find fellowship. These passages, drawing on the responses to questionnaires conducted online and face to face with people from various parts of the world, highlight some of the benefits and disadvantages of online fellowship and the relationship with offline church belonging, which can be strengthened and complemented by online participation. For many, the more intense encounters were those online, and often these encounters enabled them to remain with their church communities where relationships were often shallow by comparison. The opportunities for people with disabilities are evident in these passages, with people finding greater access online to worshipping communities than in their experience of the local church. What people seemed to miss about the local church were the physical support and the involvement with activities such as singing and group learning.

Following the success of the 2005 series called Monastery *on BBC television, in which five men joined the community for 40 days on journeys of personal exploration, the Benedictine monastery at Worth in Sussex, which hosted the exercise, has developed its website further (see www.worthabbey.org). The use of the Internet offers religious communities and churches the opportunity to engage with the world at large, and to develop their own reflection upon corporate life.*

The opportunities that online religious communities offer are in the process of being explored and developed; as is the reflection upon belonging and the nature of religious community itself.

'Community of Prophecy' (CP) as Altar of Remembrance

While some critics argue online involvement encourages people to leave the local church for fellowship through their computers, most CP members stressed that online Christian community supports the local church rather than becoming its replacement. Observations and comments made in the CP suggested online community could even encourage involvement in the local church. By providing a ministry outlet and forum for learning that was unavailable offline, the CP helped ease members' feelings of restlessness and resentment toward the local church. 'I have been more content with my local church, for one thing, because my need in the area of being discipled and having prophetic fellowship is being met through the CP' (CP Email Questionnaire Response, 28 Mar 1998).

One clear example of this was Louise, a single lawyer from a rural area of Michigan. She referred to the internet as an 'altar of remembrance', a place she continually returns to in order to remember 'God is in control and at work in the world' and relive the times when she has personally experienced this (Personal Interview in Michigan, June 1998). Louise became part of the CP as a result of a visit to the Toronto Airport Christian Fellowship, the church linked to the 'Toronto Blessing' Charismatic Renewal movement. Her pilgrimage to Toronto made a profound spiritual impact on her. She described it as an experience of inner healing of her childhood pain and encountering 'the love of the Father [God]' for the first time. When she returned home and shared this experience with her church friends she felt she was speaking a foreign language to them. She wanted a place where she could talk about these experiences with others who could relate and be supportive. A friend in Colorado introduced her to a Christian email list. For her, 'getting on the mail list was a continuation of what I saw in Toronto'. A few weeks later she heard about the CP online and joined the prophetic training class.

Interacting with the CP allows Louise to stay 'plugged in', reminding her 'there is a "move of God" happening' and she is part of it.

> We build our little altars of remembrance . . . when you are plugging into that on the internet, and you are seeing that God is saying the same thing to other people and he is working in the same way you are going, you know this is a real thing. It's really happening and God is really moving . . . It really is a lifeline in a lot of ways, 'cause it keeps you plugged in. (Personal Interview in Michigan, June 1998)

When Louise returns to this altar of remembrance, her experiences with God and the worldwide church are made alive again. However, this online involvement did eventually breed discontent within her toward her church. It is a small, rural, independent, Charismatic fellowship of about thirty people, which she described as having a narrow 'us and no more' mentality. The church's activity revolves around the Sunday morning meeting, with no organized opportunities for fellowship, prayer, or Bible study beyond that.

She finds being single in a small church composed mostly of families difficult. After church on a Sunday morning, 'I am always standing there like . . . let's talk . . . what is God doing in your life this week. But everybody is kind of wandering to their cars and leaving and so I kind of feel like I am left standing there.' The year preceding the interview was a 'time of crushing' for the fellowship, as the group experienced several significant relational problems. Tensions mounted until she felt she could no longer remain part of the fellowship. The internet, instead of drawing Louise away from her local fellowship, became a tool to encourage her to remain committed. It was a word shared on the CP that challenged her not to leave.

> I was getting ready to leave [my church] and then one day on the CP a word came forth that talked about not forsaking your local fellowship. It actually used the word fellowship . . . not church . . . so I felt that it was directly for me, just encouraging me to hang in there and not be so discouraged. (CP Email Questionnaire Response, 30 March 1998)

She printed off the post and placed it on her refrigerator for several months to remind her of the importance of commitment to a local church. This online exhortation motivated her to remain an active member and worship leader at her fellowship, and not to give up trying to build deeper relationships with others. In the meantime the CP helped meet her need for greater connection and support. She said, 'It really can plug you in when you are in a place where really that is all the fellowship that you have'.

Louise admitted that online community does not completely satisfy her desire for demonstrations of 'loving one another'. As an example she recounted a story of a family she knew who lost their home and a child in a fire. At that moment emailing words of encouragement was not enough. 'They needed people who could physically put their arms around them and cry with them.' While grateful people around the world were praying for them, 'When you've just lost a child, it's hard to be comforted online'. So while the CP can provide fellowship she feels is lacking in her local church, she also needs 'real life community'. As an altar of remembrance, the internet can be a place to reconnect with experiences of God by communicating to others with similar experiences and convictions. More importantly, it can encourage people to maintain offline connections by highlighting what the internet does well, connecting people, and what it lacks, physical support.

'Online Church' (OLC) Replaces Offline Church?

A majority of the OLC questionnaire respondents (10 of 12) viewed participation in their list as a supplement to local church involvement. However, the actions and behaviors of many of its members challenged this claim. Relational support was the main thing online community added for list members. As has already been discussed, the ability to develop Christian friendships and receive support were valued characteristics within the OLC. A majority described these relationships as more dynamic than those they had offline. As one OLC member active in a church commented, 'OLC members know how I feel, because they feel much the same. I do not have a chance to share at this level in my local church' (OLC Email Questionnaire Response, 12 Feb 1999).

Viewing the OLC as supplement meant members charged online community and offline church with different roles or tasks. Local church was portrayed as the place where members received teaching, and the OLC where they found Christian friendships and spiritual or emotional ties. Members distinguished the roles of online and offline church in terms of the types and quality of experiences they encountered in those contexts. Members saw these as interconnected yet distinct spheres of interaction. Few (4 of 12) indicated the OLC influenced their local church involvement. Those who did stressed that the OLC supplied them with information they could bring to their churches or provided another venue for prayer. These qualifications about the supplemental nature of the OLC seemed linked to members' level of dependency on the OLC for fellowship and support. This was directly tied to members' current or past church experiences.

For Arthur, online friendships tend to be more 'informal, because I can switch them off at any time'. He doesn't feel 'the same heavy obligations' for OLC members as compared to people in his local church. His involvement in the local community happens throughout the week, while he devotes much less of his time to the OLC. Yet because he believes Christians should be in daily contact with other Christians, he feels that the OLC can be an important place for fellowship. 'Jesus is still alive here at OLC', Arthur says, but this does not replace his involvement in the local Baptist church and his 'special ministry', focusing on one-to-one encouragement and support to marginalized people. It is not a formal church ministry, but one of his church leaders confirmed Arthur's 'ministry of encouragement', by giving examples of his 'coming alongside people who need a listening ear or encouragement, Arthur has a special gift for that'. Arthur also attends a weekly prayer meeting and helps out with regular Alpha courses.[1]

While committed to his local church, Arthur understands this kind of involvement is not possible for some OLC members. Physical limitations and the failure of some churches to accommodate or support those with special needs means many of Arthur's OLC friends feel distanced from or antagonistic toward church. Many OLC members indicated that offline church had not been an easy place to find acceptance, and offered examples of their struggles to find a church community they felt comfortable in. Three questionnaire respondents indicated they were currently not involved in a church. Two others indicated they were not satisfied with their churches due to a lack of support.

Rick described his experiences visiting churches as disappointing, as people he met did not live up to the Christian standards he has read about in the Bible. Church members, he said, had often been awkward toward him due to his blindness and hearing problems, either ignoring him or speaking to his wife instead of directly to him.

By contrast, the OLC functions in the way he believes the church should behave, and he uses it to evaluate his face-to-face church experiences.

> Anytime I am involved with the church I hardly hear anybody speak like a Christian person would do, like you see on the OLC. People still have the nature to complain or the nature to gossip and I hear that and I see that at church, my wife's church ... When people get together at church, it's pretty much business. Where OLC is more social, but it goes deeper than social, it's just like family. It's really like family. (Personal Interview in St Louis, Missouri, September 1999)

Because his online friends seem 'more real' and his face-to-face contact at church has been so disappointing, he prefers to stay at home while his wife and children attend a local Catholic church.

Disappointment is also the story of Katie, who told of several failed attempts to become involved in local churches where she lives in London. Due to their blindness she and her husband have found it difficult to physically locate churches, having to rely on public transporation or rides from others. Also, having two guide dogs has caused problems, as some church members have reacted negatively toward them.

> You've not just got the barrier of introducing yourself to Christians who can see and being on a different playing field to them ... having guide dogs ... All these other barriers put together have made it very difficult to get into a local church and make friends. (Personal Interview in London, April 1999)

Six years of feeling unaccepted and unable to integrate into a church have left Katie and her husband frustrated. At the time of the interview they had taken a hiatus from church searching, opting instead for listening to tapes, radio, or visiting websites to receive Christian teaching. Katie joined the OLC to be part of a Christian community with other visually impaired Christians who can relate to 'the same sort of difficulties that I have known in becoming integrated in a main stream church situation' (OLC Email Questionnaire Response, 13 Feb 1999).

In Katie's experience, local churches often lack the ability to provide the acceptance and assistance that blind people require. The OLC meets the need to be understood and to be able to talk about these issues. Her infrequent attendance is not because of a lack of desire to be involved in a local church; rather it has been a 'long saga' of finding it hard to fit in. This was illustrated by an incident when she and her husband had just started to attend a local church. One Sunday they got lost and were unable to find the church building, when they tried to make their own way to church after their ride did not show up. Katie later learned that several church members passed them on their way to the service and saw them going the wrong way, but no one stopped to ask if they needed help.

A contrasting incident occurred just before the interview, when she decided to take a break from the OLC due to an illness and a need to be offline and spend 'more time directly with God'. This break lasted only two weeks, because she received numerous personal emails from OLC members asking her to come back. Several members continually forwarded her the list messages, and one OLC friend emailed her every day.

> It indicated clearly to me the love and support of my OLC friends . . . So I think if anything I saw that they weren't going to let me go easy and they still wanted to communicate with me. I kept getting the 'come back' messages. (Personal Interview in London, April 1999)

While Katie emphasized that the OLC has become a significant part of her Christian support structure, it could not be a complete substitute for church. 'The fact that I do not have a regular church at present is of great sadness to me, but the OLC does not take the place of a local church for me and never will.' The OLC meets her need for the caring aspect of church, but not her desire for teaching. 'You can't live a total church life within OLC . . . You don't run Sunday school classes. You don't involve yourself singing, in leading music.' Katie values the role the OLC plays in her life, but still wishes she could find a church home.

Stuart, the list owner, agrees that ideally OLC members would be part of a local body of believers, but recognizes it is very hard for some to be involved in a church. 'I would hate to . . . use an electronic church as my only source of contact with other Christians, but if that's all a person has, then it can be a ministry to them as well' (Personal Interview in Colorado, September 1999). For him the OLC and the local church should work together, the electronic church serving as an extension of the church by connecting believers from all over the world and providing encouragement for those isolated from Christian contact. The difference is that a local church is community-minded, while an online community offers a global perspective. 'On OLC there's an atmosphere of fellowship that is generated just by the nature of the list itself and that's true in a local New Testament church.'

The OLC may be described as supplement to local church involvement, but in reality, for some members it becomes a substitute. Overall what the OLC supplements is a listening ear, understanding based on similar experience, Christian counsel, and an opportunity to serve and support one another. What the OLC lacks is significant Bible teaching, opportunities for proclamation or evangelism, and the opportunity for local involvement in other members' lives. These are aspects of church that members see as important.

Note

1. Alpha courses are evangelistic outreach courses featuring fellowship meals, videos, and small group discussions.

'Writing the Body of Christ': References and Further Reading

Anderson, Benedict (1983), *Imagined Communities*, London: Verso.

Browning, D. S. (1991), *A Fundamental Practical Theology: Descriptive and Strategic Proposals*, Minneapolis: Fortress Press.

Bhabha, H. (1994), *The Location of Culture*, London: Routledge.

de Certeau, M. (1984), *The Practice of Everyday Life*, Berkeley, CA: University of California Press, Part 3, 'Spatial Practices' and Chapter 7, 'Walking in the City'.

Guest, Matthew, Karin Tusting and Linda Woodhead (eds) (2004), *Congregational Studies in the UK: Christianity in a post-Christian context*, Aldershot: Ashgate.

Huntington, Samuel (1996), *The Clash of Civilizations and the Remaking of World Order*, New York: Simon & Schuster.

Kwok, Pui-lan (2005), *Postcolonial Imagination and Feminist Theology*, London: SCM Press.

5

'Speaking of God in Public': Correlation

Introduction

The correlative method conceives of theological reflection as occurring via a process of conversation (or 'correlation') between Christian revelation and surrounding culture. It understands the emergence of Christian practical wisdom as a synthesis between tradition and secular culture, such as philosophy, the arts, politics or natural sciences. The realms of 'grace' and revelation, and those of 'nature' or human reason, are partners in the process of theological reflection. Theologians such as Aquinas and Rahner stressed the possibility for human consciousness to apprehend the reality of God, however incompletely; and Tillich characterized the process of correlation as one of 'question and response' between the existential questions posed anew by every generation and the enduring power of the Christian tradition. Such exemplary figures share an essential conviction that there is a convergence between secular wisdom and the language of faith.

Some see such a synthesis or dialogue between 'Christ' and 'culture' taking place as an act of *apologetics*, of utilizing dialogue and public debate in order to commend the gospel to a particular non-Christian philosophical system or world-view. It is important that the Word of God is rendered accessible to its recipients on their own terms; but 'Christ' is always to be regarded as the completion and apotheosis of whatever 'culture' has already apprehended, however dimly. The realms of human reason and enquiry are therefore capable of manifesting God's truth, even if that remains to be brought to completion by a more complete revelation in Christ.

There is a second, more *revisionist* or *dialectical* strand of correlation, however, which finds contemporary expression in movements such as feminist theology and dialogues between science and religion. This argues that all theological tradition is still evolving, and that the 'usable tradition' from which theological reflection can draw is constantly being augmented or renewed. Thus, the correlational model shares with other models of theological reflection the assumption that revelation within human history is always awaiting completion. If no human institution is free from the limitations of sin, it is therefore inevitable that the tradition awaits further fulfilment. However, the revisionist tendency within the correlational model is distinctive in its assumption that truth and revelation may also speak to human hearts and minds through sources *beyond* the confines of tradition or the Church. Hence, correlation regards extra-theological understandings as exercising an important corrective influence in the face of the shortcomings and distortions of inherited tradition. Insights from secular sources can sometimes speak more powerfully of the nature of God and human destiny, and theological reflection that is open to such voices can call the tradition to a renewed sense of its own core values.

Given its emphasis on the validity of extra-theological wisdom, this model of theological reflection regards the articulation of theology and the practice of theological reflection as something necessarily undertaken *in public*. That is, a crucial test of the coherence and authenticity of the Christian tradition should be its readiness to be exposed to the scrutiny of non-Christian world-views.

Thomas Aquinas, *Summa Contra Gentiles*, Book 1

translated by A. C. Pegis, Notre Dame, IN: University of Notre Dame Press, 1975; Chapters 3, 4, 7, 8.

This extract expresses the core principle of critical correlation, namely that theological reflection needs to attend to voices and authorities from the 'secular' sphere as well as from religious tradition. Although divine self-revelation proceeds solely from the person of God, and is ultimately a gift of God's grace, knowledge of God is not some form of secret or esoteric wisdom, the preserve of an educated few (p. 273). Some aspects of God may surpass human understanding (p. 269), such that observation of the natural world will not of itself lead the human mind to God; yet basic properties of human reason are capable of providing prefigurations of divine presence. Creation and reason contain nothing that contradicts reason; grace does not undermine faith but brings it to fruition.

On one level, this is an essay about the incapacity of human reason alone to grasp the divine nature. Rather than preaching the inadequacy of human understanding, however, this essay says more about the ultimate mystery of the divine. It is a salutary reminder that no human can lay possession to the entire or final truth of God (pp. 270,

275). Yet at the same time it affirms the integrity of human efforts to
know and understand the world, subject to the promptings of divine
grace. There is a sense in which Aquinas views the process of theologi-
cal reflection as one necessarily rooted in a kind of divine pedagogy
(p. 273).

Chapter 3.
On the Way in which Divine Truth is to be Made Known

[1] The way of making truth known is not always the same, and, as
the Philosopher has very well said, 'it belongs to an educated man to
seek such certitude in each thing as the nature of that thing allows.'[1]
The remark is also introduced by Boethius.[2] But, since such is the
case, we must first show what way is open to us in order that we may
make known the truth which is our object.

[2] There is a twofold mode of truth in what we profess about
God. Some truths about God exceed all the ability of the human
reason. Such is the truth that God is triune. But there are some truths
which the natural reason also is able to reach. Such are that God
exists, that He is one, and the like. In fact, such truths about God
have been proved demonstratively by the philosophers, guided by the
light of the natural reason.

[3] That there are certain truths about God that totally surpass
man's ability appears with the greatest evidence. Since, indeed, the
principle of all knowledge that the reason perceives about some thing
is the understanding of the very substance of that being (for according
to Aristotle 'what a thing is' is the principle of demonstration),[3] it is
necessary that the way in which we understand the substance of a
thing determines the way in which we know what belongs to it.
Hence, if the human intellect comprehends the substance of some
thing, for example, that of a stone or of a triangle, no intelligible
characteristic belonging to that thing surpasses the grasp of the human
reason. But this does not happen to us in the case of God. For the
human intellect is not able to reach a comprehension of the divine
substance through its natural power. For, according to its manner of
knowing in the present life, the intellect depends on the sense for the
origin of knowledge; and so those things that do not fall under the
senses cannot be grasped by the human intellect except in so far as
the knowledge of them is gathered from sensible things. Now, sensible
things cannot lead the human intellect to the point of seeing in them
the nature of the divine substance; for sensible things are effects that

fall short of the power of their cause. Yet, beginning with sensible things, our intellect is led to the point of knowing about God that He exists, and other such characteristics that must be attributed to the First Principle. There are, consequently, some intelligible truths about God that are open to the human reason; but there are others that absolutely surpass its power.

[4] We may easily see the same point from the gradation of intellects. Consider the case of two persons of whom one has a more penetrating grasp of a thing by his intellect than does the other. He who has the superior intellect understands many things that the other cannot grasp at all. Such is the case with a very simple person who cannot at all grasp the subtle speculations of philosophy. But the intellect of an angel surpasses the human intellect much more than the intellect of the greatest philosopher surpasses the intellect of the most uncultivated simple person; for the distance between the best philosopher and a simple person is contained within the limits of the human species, which the angelic intellect surpasses. For the angel knows God on the basis of a more noble effect than does man; and this by as much as the substance of an angel, through which the angel in his natural knowledge is led to the knowledge of God, is nobler than sensible things and even than the soul itself, through which the human intellect mounts to the knowledge of God. The divine intellect surpasses the angelic intellect much more than the angelic surpasses the human. For the divine intellect is in its capacity equal to its substance, and therefore it understands fully what it is, including all its intelligible attributes. But by his natural knowledge the angel does not know what God is, since the substance itself of the angel, through which he is led to the knowledge of God, is an effect that is not equal to the power of its cause. Hence, the angel is not able, by means of his natural knowledge, to grasp all the things that God understands in Himself; nor is the human reason sufficient to grasp all the things that the angel understands through his own natural power. Just as, therefore, it would be the height of folly for a simple person to assert that what a philosopher proposes is false on the ground that he himself cannot understand it, so (and even more so) it is the acme of stupidity for a man to suspect as false what is divinely revealed through the ministry of the angels simply because it cannot be investigated by reason.

[5] The same thing, moreover, appears quite clearly from the defect that we experience every day in our knowledge of things. We do not know a great many of the properties of sensible things, and in most cases we are not able to discover fully the natures of those properties

that we apprehend by the sense. Much more is it the case, therefore, that the human reason is not equal to the task of investigating all the intelligible characteristics of that most excellent substance.

[6] The remark of Aristotle likewise agrees with this conclusion. He says that 'our intellect is related to the prime beings, which are most evident in their nature, as the eye of an owl is related to the sun.'[4]

[7] Sacred Scripture also gives testimony to this truth. We read in Job: 'Peradventure thou wilt comprehend the steps of God, and wilt find out the Almighty perfectly?' (11:7). And again: 'Behold, God is great, exceeding our knowledge' (Job 36:26). And St Paul: 'We know in part' (I Cor. 13:9).

[8] We should not, therefore, immediately reject as false, following the opinion of the Manicheans and many unbelievers, everything that is said about God even though it cannot be investigated by reason.

Chapter 4.
That the Truth about God to which the Natural Reason Reaches is Fittingly Proposed to Men for Belief

[1] Since, therefore, there exists a twofold truth concerning the divine being, one to which the inquiry of the reason can reach, the other which surpasses the whole ability of the human reason, it is fitting that both of these truths be proposed to man divinely for belief. This point must first be shown concerning the truth that is open to the inquiry of the reason; otherwise, it might perhaps seem to someone that, since such a truth can be known by the reason, it was uselessly given to men through a supernatural inspiration as an object of belief.

[2] Yet, if this truth were left solely as a matter of inquiry for the human reason, three awkward consequences would follow.

[3] The first is that few men would possess the knowledge of God. For there are three reasons why most men are cut off from the fruit of diligent inquiry which is the discovery of truth. Some do not have the physical disposition for such work. As a result, there are many who are naturally not fitted to pursue knowledge; and so, however much they tried, they would be unable to reach the highest level of human knowledge which consists in knowing God. Others are cut off from pursuing this truth by the necessities imposed upon them by their daily lives. For some men must devote themselves to taking care of temporal matters. Such men would not be able to give so much

time to the leisure of contemplative inquiry as to reach the highest peak at which human investigation can arrive, namely, the knowledge of God. Finally, there are some who are cut off by indolence. In order to know the things that the reason can investigate concerning God, a knowledge of many things must already be possessed. For almost all of philosophy is directed towards the knowledge of God, and that is why metaphysics, which deals with divine things, is the last part of philosophy to be learned. This means that we are able to arrive at the inquiry concerning the aforementioned truth only on the basis of a great deal of labor spent in study. Now, those who wish to undergo such a labor for the mere love of knowledge are few, even though God has inserted into the minds of men a natural appetite for knowledge.

[4] The second awkward effect is that those who would come to discover the abovementioned truth would barely reach it after a great deal of time. The reasons are several. There is the profundity of this truth, which the human intellect is made capable of grasping by natural inquiry only after a long training. Then, there are many things that must be presupposed, as we have said. There is also the fact that, in youth, when the soul is swayed by the various movements of the passions, it is not in a suitable state for the knowledge of such lofty truth. On the contrary, 'one becomes wise and knowing in repose,' as it is said in the *Physics*.[5] The result is this. If the only way open to us for the knowledge of God were solely that of the reason, the human race would remain in the blackest shadows of ignorance. For then the knowledge of God, which especially renders men perfect and good, would come to be possessed only by a few, and these few would require a great deal of time in order to reach it.

[5] The third awkward effect is this. The investigation of the human reason for the most part has falsity present within it, and this is due partly to the weakness of our intellect in judgment, and partly to the admixture of images. The result is that many, remaining ignorant of the power of demonstration, would hold in doubt those things that have been most truly demonstrated. This would be particularly the case since they see that, among those who are reputed to be wise men, each one teaches his own brand of doctrine. Furthermore, with the many truths that are demonstrated, there sometimes is mingled something that is false, which is not demonstrated but rather asserted on the basis of some probable or sophistical argument, which yet has the credit of being a demonstration. That is why it was necessary that the unshakeable certitude and pure truth concerning divine things should be presented to men by way of faith.[6]

[6] Beneficially, therefore, did the divine Mercy provide that it

should instruct us to hold by faith even those truths that the human reason is able to investigate. In this way, all men would easily be able to have a share in the knowledge of God, and this without uncertainty and error.

[7] Hence it is written: 'Henceforward you walk not as also the Gentiles walk in the vanity of their mind, having their understanding darkened' (Eph. 4:17–18). And again: 'All thy children shall be taught of the Lord' (Isa. 54:13).

. . .

Chapter 7.
That the Truth of Reason is Not Opposed to the Truth of the Christian Faith

[1] Now, although the truth of the Christian faith which we have discussed surpasses the capacity of the reason, nevertheless that truth that the human reason is naturally endowed to know cannot be opposed to the truth of the Christian faith. For that with which the human reason is naturally endowed is clearly most true; so much so, that it is impossible for us to think of such truths as false. Nor is it permissible to believe as false that which we hold by faith, since this is confirmed in a way that is so clearly divine. Since, therefore, only the false is opposed to the true, as is clearly evident from an examination of their definitions, it is impossible that the truth of faith should be opposed to those principles that the human reason knows naturally.

[2] Furthermore, that which is introduced into the soul of the student by the teacher is contained in the knowledge of the teacher – unless his teaching is fictitious, which it is improper to say of God. Now, the knowledge of the principles that are known to us naturally has been implanted in us by God; for God is the Author of our nature. These principles, therefore, are also contained by the divine Wisdom. Hence, whatever is opposed to them is opposed to the divine Wisdom, and, therefore, cannot come from God. That which we hold by faith as divinely revealed, therefore, cannot be contrary to our natural knowledge.

[3] Again. In the presence of contrary arguments our intellect is chained, so that it cannot proceed to the knowledge of the truth. If, therefore, contrary knowledges were implanted in us by God, our intellect would be hindered from knowing truth by this very fact. Now, such an effect cannot come from God.

[4] And again. What is natural cannot change as long as nature does not. Now, it is impossible that contrary opinions should exist in the same knowing subject at the same time. No opinion or belief, therefore, is implanted in man by God which is contrary to man's natural knowledge.

[5] Therefore, the Apostle says: 'The word is nigh thee, even in thy mouth and in thy heart. This is the word of faith, which we preach' (Rom. 10:8). But because it overcomes reason, there are some who think that it is opposed to it: which is impossible.

[6] The authority of St Augustine also agrees with this. He writes as follows: 'That which truth will reveal cannot in any way be opposed to the sacred books of the Old and the New Testament.'[7]

[7] From this we evidently gather the following conclusion: whatever arguments are brought forward against the doctrines of faith are conclusions incorrectly derived from the first and self-evident principles imbedded in nature. Such conclusions do not have the force of demonstration; they are arguments that are either probable or sophistical. And so, there exists the possibility to answer them.

Chapter 8.
How the Human Reason is Related to the Truth of Faith

[1] There is also a further consideration. Sensible things, from which the human reason takes the origin of its knowledge, retain within themselves some sort of trace of a likeness to God. This is so imperfect, however, that it is absolutely inadequate to manifest the substance of God. For effects bear within themselves, in their own way, the likeness of their causes, since an agent produces its like; yet an effect does not always reach to the full likeness of its cause. Now, the human reason is related to the knowledge of the truth of faith (a truth which can be most evident only to those who see the divine substance) in such a way that it can gather certain likenesses of it, which are yet not sufficient so that the truth of faith may be comprehended as being understood demonstratively or through itself. Yet it is useful for the human reason to exercise itself in such arguments, however weak they may be, provided only that there be present no presumption to comprehend or to demonstrate. For to be able to see something of the loftiest realities, however thin and weak the sight may be, is, as our previous remarks indicate, a cause of the greatest joy.

[2] The testimony of Hilary agrees with this. Speaking of this same truth, he writes as follows in his *De Trinitate*: 'Enter these truths by

believing, press forward, persevere. And though I may know that you will not arrive at an end, yet I will congratulate you in your progress. For, though he who pursues the infinite with reverence will never finally reach the end, yet he will always progress by pressing onward. But do not intrude yourself into the divine secret, do not, presuming to comprehend the sum total of intelligence, plunge yourself into the mystery of the unending nativity; rather, understand that these things are incomprehensible.'[8]

Notes

1. Aristotle, *Nicomachean Ethics*, I, 3 (1094b 24).
2. Boethius, *De Trinitate*, II (*PL*, 64, col. 1250).
3. Aristotle, *Posterior Analytics*, II, 3 (90b 31).
4. Aristotle, *Metaphysics*, I*a*, 1 (993b 9).
5. Aristotle, *Physics*, VII, 3 (247b 9).
6. Although St Thomas does not name Maimonides or his *Guide for the Perplexed* (*Dux neutrorum*), there are evident points of contact between the Catholic and the Jewish theologian. On the reasons for revelation given here, on our knowledge of God, on creation and the eternity of the world, and on Aristotelianism in general, St Thomas has Maimonides in mind both to agree and to disagree with him. By way of background for *SCG*, I, the reader can usefully consult the references to Maimonides in E. Gilson, *History of Christian Philosophy in the Middle Ages* (New York, 1955), pp. 649–651.
7. St Augustine, *De genesi ad litteram*, II, c. 18 (*PL*, 34, col. 280).
8. St Hilary, *De Trinitate*, II, 10, ii (*PL*, 10, coll. 58–59).

Stephen Pattison, 'Some Straw for the Bricks: A Basic Introduction to Theological Reflection'
Contact, No. 99, 1989, pp. 2–3, 4–6, 7–8.

This extract represents a seminal piece of British practical theology over the past 20 years, and reflects the turn to 'theological reflection' as the central activity of practical theology. It sets out one of the methods, namely that of critical correlation, which is still widely used, as well as highlighting some of the strengths and weaknesses of such a model.

Pattison is anxious to avoid the assumption that theology is necessarily to be equated with its more academic manifestations, or that there are privileged groups better qualified to be theological scholars than others. All this is to establish two important qualities of theological reflection: that it is practical, a kind of problem-based know-

ledge, emerging in response to particular needs; and that there is no prescribed style or register in which theological reflection takes shape.

Pattison seeks to render theology as more accessible and responsive to everyday use. He is anxious to shed much of the exclusiveness of theology as it has traditionally been studied, in terms of academic elitism, clerical exclusivity, ecclesial captivity and historical irrelevance. Note the characterization of theology as 'contemporary enquiry' and the language of 'conversation', which has an ease of use about it, denoting something friendly, mutual, flexible and evolutionary. Yet like any conversation, there may be hidden imbalances of power between different participants, or undetected clashes of authority between different sources.

Throughout this extract, therefore, Pattison is insistent upon the practical origins and outcomes of theological reflection. Yet because each practical context or dilemma is novel, and different, then no process of theological reflection will be exactly the same as another. Note, however, that Pattison does not suggest there should be particular models or families of theological reflection, unlike other works which do attempt to trace 'family resemblances' between particular styles of theology. In fact, there is little here to determine how different strands of historical theology might inform current activities of reflection, or how diversity of outcomes might be evaluated. He may also be vulnerable to the question of what makes this model of reflection distinctively 'theological' or even distinctively Christian about this process.

'No straw is provided for your servants and still the cry is, 'Make bricks!' (Exodus 5.16)

Students undertaking placements on pastoral studies courses are bidden with monotonous regularity to indulge in theological reflection. This activity has a mystic flavour to it, for the teachers who demand theological reflection for the most part find it very difficult to say what it is that they are looking for. Hence the quotation from Exodus; students are being asked to make bricks without straw. The purpose of this paper is to provide one particular *entree* to theological reflection which students I have worked with seem to find helpful. I want to suggest that a good starting point for this activity is the model of a *critical conversation* which takes place between the Christian tradition, the student's own faith presuppositions and a particular contemporary situation.

. . .

Theology

The word 'theology' seems to frighten people. One suspects that the images that it brings to their minds are those of serried ranks of learned tomes written by elderly and authoritative men full of incomprehensible profundity which bear no relation to present day reality or to their own situation. Ordinary people (and most theological students are fairly ordinary) fail to see the connection between this kind of theology, which is in fact a very particular kind of theology, and the world in which they live. They most certainly feel unable to compete in the academic theological arena, and if theological reflection means doing this, they feel utterly at a loss. It is this kind of feeling which leads to people either failing to relate theology and reality at all so that belief and practice are kept in separate boxes, or to heroic and pious attempts to 'apply' the wisdom of the tomes to a reality which seems to contradict it at all points. At its worst, this can be an exercise in dull improbability. The word 'theology' must be set free from dusty academic bondage.

The first thing to be proposed, then, is that theology should be seen primarily as *contemporary enquiry*. Judging from the books in libraries, it is easy to come to believe that theology is about restating the verities of the past in ways which make them inaccessible in the present. It is very unfortunate if this impression prevails, for it is a superficial one. Most theology books, however obscure, arise from someone wanting to gain a real understanding of a question which seems to them of contemporary relevance for themselves or others. At the bottom of it all, what unites all theology is its quest for adequate and true responses to the realities of human and religious experience. Good theology is dynamic, searching and open-ended. Some of the most influential theology ever written has been a response to urgent pastoral situations (e.g. that of St Augustine) and it has been characterised by a willingness to really try and listen to and understand present realities rather than to regurgitate the answers of the past. The moral of this is that anyone who in any way tries to understand their situation in the light of faith in the contemporary world is doing theology. You do not have to start doing theological reflection on experience, if you have any questions in your mind at all relating to faith, you are doing theological reflection already! That is not to say, however, that you might not become better at it and find more adequate ways of articulating it.

Theology is active enquiry not just historical research or intellectual gymnastics. But it is probably as well not to talk of theology, but of theolog*ies* in the plural. One thing that worries people when they come to theological reflection is the thought that they might not be approaching it the right way, that they are not conforming to the norm of doing theology. The fact is that there is no formal norm. There are all sorts of ways of doing theology which are so different that it sometimes seems that the only thing that unites them is a common claim to be talking about God and religious experience. Theologies work at many different levels and with very different aims, methods and concerns. In universities, for example, some theologians are mainly devoted to the history of the faith tradition or to studying the theology of the Bible; they use historical and linguistic methods. Others enter into dialogue with philosophy, while some see their activity as the intellectual ordering of the faith experience of the contemporary church at a high level of abstraction. A few study the ethical implications of the Christian faith and others try to explore the theoretical and theological aspects of pastoral care. Even within 'academic' theology, then, there is considerable diversity; often scholars in one academic discipline have only a very hazy understanding of what their colleagues are doing. Within and outside the academic environment a thousand theological flowers blossom. Readers may have heard of process theology, existential theology, fundamentalist theology, black theology, liberation theology, narrative theology and others.[1] The point is that all these theologies have very different features and methods. The moral for the student is that if theologians are so different in their approaches and cannot agree on what theology is, there can be no one right way of doing theology and perhaps one's own way is as good as anyone else's. It has its own validity and usefulness within one's own situation.

. . .

The Method of Critical Conversation

As I said at the beginning, the model I want to commend as a starting point for theological reflection is that of the critical conversation. The basic idea here is that the student should imagine herself as being involved in a three way conversation between a) her own ideas, beliefs, feelings, perceptions and assumptions, b) the beliefs, assumptions and perceptions provided by the Christian tradition (including the Bible) and c) the contemporary situation which is being examined. For the sake of concreteness it may be helpful to personify these elements and imagine them as people who may or may not know each other to a greater or lesser extent who come together in a room to have a verbal conversation. Each participant in the conversation will have questions to ask of the others (I shall come to the specific questions later) and each will need to get to know the others.

This model of conversation has several advantages: –

1) A conversation is a concrete event which is a familiar part of everyday life even if the participants in the conversation of theological reflection are not real people.

2) The personification of participants allows the identification of starting points from different perspectives and allows heuristic clarity.

3) A real conversation is a living thing which evolves and changes.

4) The participants in a conversation are changed, both by what they learn and by the process of conversing with other participants.

5) Participation in a conversation implies a willingness to listen and be attentive to other participants.

6) Conversations allow participants to discover things about their interlocutors which they never knew before; all participants end up seeing themselves and others from new angles and in a different light.

7) The concept of conversation does not necessarily imply that participants end up agreeing at every point or that the identity of one over-rides the character of the others.

8) Conversations are often difficult and demand considerable effort because participants start from very different assumptions and understandings. Considerable energy may have to be expended to try and understand the relevance or importance of another participant's contribution.

9) An important part of conversation may be that of silence, disagreement or lack of communication. This element is very important in theological reflection; many people suppose that if they understand the Christian tradition properly, they can then 'apply' its eternal truths easily to contemporary reality. In practice, such thinking often leads to the creation of dubious connections which tend to have a pious and unrealistic tenor. Much more honest, perhaps, to acknowledge that there are enormous gaps between some situations in the contemporary world and the religious tradition but to maintain the belief that theological reflection understood as active enquiry is as much about exploring and living with gaps as well as with similarities.

10) Lastly, conversations can be conducted at many different levels

from that of preliminary acquaintance to that of longterm dialogue. As participants get to know each other, their views of each other and of relevant factors in relation to each other will change and evolve to become more complex and sophisticated. This does not, however, devalue the perceptions and insights gained on the first and perhaps naive preliminary encounter, though later these may be radically modified and relativised.

If what has been said so far about theological reflection as critical conversation seems to complicate that activity rather than simplifying it, it might make more sense if it were explicated in the following more abstract way. The notion of critical conversation between the student, Christian tradition and the empirical situation endeavours to make students conscious of their own presuppositions, the resources of the Christian tradition and the realities of a practical situation in such a way that each modifies and learns from the others in a dynamic interaction. This dialogical process occurs anyway in everyday life, the conversation model simply shapes and sharpens it.

Questions for Critical Conversation

The critical conversation which constitutes theological reflection is a structured and semi-formal one in that it proceeds via certain questions which the participants might ask of one another. One useful set of questions for opening up theological reflection can be derived from the creeds. Rather than taking the creeds as factual propositions, it is possible to frame questions from their basic shape. Christian creeds implicitly answer the questions, Where did we come from and why are we here? (creation), What is the purpose of human existence? (teleology), What stops us from attaining perfection and what would change that situation? (evil/salvation), In what or whom do we put our trust and what do we hope for? (eschatology). These are profoundly religious questions, but it will be noted that they can be asked of completely secular situations, thus allowing creative comparison and critique. They can also be asked of the individual student participating in reflection on practical situations. Thus they provide an opening for commencing comparison and dialogue which is in tune with the concept of theology as an interrogative and enquiring activity rather than a matter of handing down the truths of the past. Other series of questions derived from different sources might be asked. For example, the question, 'How would Jesus react to this situation or this way of perceiving?' could be posed. Again this would act as a critical starting point against which to assess and compare the relative positions and perceptions of participants in a particular critical conversation. Perhaps it would lead to a situation being seen differently, perhaps to a person seeing his or her faith differently. Another place to start might be with the difficult questions posed by a situation which seemed utterly alien to religious belief and practice. In many ways, the starting point does not matter, the important thing is to find a way into critical conversation which ensures that tradition, contemporary reality and a student's assumptions are all questioned in turn by each other.

. . .

Limitations

I hope I have now said enough to interest students in the value of theological reflection and to show how it might begin to work using one very simple model. It would be wrong, however, to end without saying something about the limitations of this method. These are manifold. First, it could be argued that asking questions and engaging in critical conversation is not an adequate way of conceiving theological reflection. Surely, it might be said, theology is about providing eternally valid answers and applying these to everyday life today. It is certainly true that the mutually interrogative method I have outlined tends to lead to further questions rather than solid answers and so it is something of a *via negativa*, ie. a way of getting at truth indirectly. I would suggest that this is a good way to proceed because it avoids giving slick and unrealistic answers in complex modern situations, it has the advantage of showing up some of the weaknesses and drawbacks of theological and other assumptions, it is in line with the fundamentally exploratory nature of theology and also with the educational presupposition that students need to find their own answers to situations if those answers are to hold any lasting value. This is not to deny the long-term important constructive task of creating and evaluating systematically theological beliefs and systems, but simply to relegate it to a subordinate position for the time being.

A further criticism concerns the depth of the critical conversation. It is all very well to suggest that a dialogue can be entered into between the student, a contemporary situation and the theological tradition at anything from the most superficial level. But it is, of course, true that deepening conversation might demand extensive research of a fairly academic kind into the social sciences or the sources and tools of Christian theology. I do not want to rebut this point. My hope is that those who practise theological reflection will get drawn into the complexities of analysis using the tools and insights of secular and theological disciplines in order to construct a more nuanced critique and world view.

It could also rightly be pointed out that the use of this method could lead to a great deal of superficial analysis and opinion which was then gradiosely dignified by being called theology. This is indeed a real possibility; it is certainly true that most theological reflections will only be able to deal with some aspects of situations, traditions and assumptions rather than being comprehensive. My only real defence here is the pragmatic one of holding that it is a good thing for people to start theological reflection at their own level and then it might be hoped that their analysis will become more sophisticated. I would, however, want to resist strongly the idea that only when people are highly educated in the classical, literary-based theological tradition should they be encouraged to begin theological reflection. My own experience of working with students suggests that a traditional theological education may indeed inoculate students against being able to analyse experience and to explore creatively the gaps and connections between contemporary reality and the Christian tradition. A particular kind of academic orthodoxy stifles theological imagination in many cases.

It must be acknowledged that the perceptions which emerge from the critical conversation of theological reflection will often have only strictly limited validity and relevance. We need to get used to the idea that theologies can be disposable and contextual; the conclusions of any particular theological reflection do not need to be seen as relevant for all people in all places and they may, indeed, be thoroughly idiosyncratic. Anyone who wants to commend their insights to a wider audience will find themselves entering into a wider conversation which will itself modify their perceptions. This is a valuable and automatic corrective to egotism and the sort of situational fundamentalism which holds that just because something is true in one's own experience, it must be true for all people everywhere.

Finally, and connected with the last point, it must be recognised that any theological reflection undertaken by a particular individual may well reveal more about that person and their particular perspective than it does about a secular situation or the Christian theological tradition. It is important to realise the limitations of one's own perspective and preoccupations in approaching theological reflection and thus to be self-critical. Self-criticism can be fostered and insights generally can be deepened by undertaking the critical conversation of theological reflection in a group rather than on one's own. The group setting creates real rather than imaginary interlocutors in critical conversation and maximises resources for knowledge and dialogue.

Conclusion

The purpose of this paper has been to engender interest and enthusiasm for theological reflection and to suggest one very particular and inadequate way of starting on this activity. I hope that anyone using it will soon become profoundly dissatisfied with it and will want to find and refine their own method. In this connection, readers may want to consult some of the more sophisticated methods of theological reflection outlined by authors like Don Browning and Michael Taylor.[2]

For my own part, I shall be very happy if I have given people some clue about where to begin and if I have provided for them some manna in the wilderness rather than demanding of them bricks to be made without straw.

Notes

1. The scope and nature of different types of theology can be assayed by consulting, eg., Alan Richardson and John Bowden, eds., *A New Dictionary of Christian Theology* (London: SCM Press, 1983).

2. For more sophisticated works on theological reflection on practice and the assumptions which lie beneath this paper see Don S. Browning, *Religious Ethics and Pastoral Care* (Philadelphia: Fortress, 1983); ed., *Practical Theology* (San Francisco: Harper and Row, 1983), Laurie Green, *Power to the Powerless* (Basingstoke: Marshall Pickering, 1987), Seward Hiltner, *Preface to Pastoral Theology* (Nashville: Abingdon, 1956), Leslie Houlden, *Connections* (London: SCM Press, 1985), Robert J. Schreiter, *Constructing Local Theologies* (London: SCM Press, 1985), Michael H. Taylor, *Learning to Care* (London: SPCK, 1983), Michael Williams, 'The dichotomy between faith and action; towards a model for "doing theology"' in Paul H. Ballard, ed., *The Foundations of Pastoral Studies and Practical Theology* (Cardiff: Faculty of Theology, 1986). The concept of critical conversation I outline here is a development of an idea presented by Taylor in *Learning to Care* but my thinking has been influenced by all the other works as well.

Enrique Dussel, 'Theology of Liberation and Marxism'

in Jon Sobrino and Ignacio Ellacuria (eds), *Mysterium Liberationis*,
New York: Orbis, 1993, pp. 85–7, 94–7, 98–9.

Liberation theology is generally associated with a 'praxis' model of theological reflection in its commitment to a transformative style of discipleship that seeks God in the practical task of achieving justice. Yet it is also a tradition that adopts a firmly correlative approach in its use of different sources from the human and social sciences in order to make sense of its social context. In particular, it has adopted Marxist social analysis as a means of exposing the true dynamics of the economic, social and political division in Latin America and other parts of the two-thirds world; but liberation theologians would always argue that such 'secular' insights are merely confirmed by their readings of the Christian tradition, and in particular in their recovery of the biblical injunctions to observe God's preferential option for the poor.

Dussell is deliberately placing himself in a tradition he regards as both old and new, therefore he emphasizes the enduring dialogue between theology and scientific reason, represented by figures such as Aquinas; but also stresses the novelty of Marxism in its ability to address the particularity of poverty and dehumanization. This is defended on two grounds: first, that as a 'science' (which is something it claims about itself), Marxism is but the latest in a long tradition of other forms of scientific systems of thought with which theology has engaged. Second, Dussell justifies the significance of Marxism by noting how it enables Catholic theologians to be reminded of the social radicalism of their own tradition of encyclicals.

Nevertheless, in an inversion of the 'apologetic' function of correlative theology as a means of commending Christian faith to the non-Christian world, Dussell is conducting a kind of apologetics on behalf of Marxism to the Roman Catholic Church, both by normalizing the constructive use of 'secular' thought throughout Christian history, and by stressing the affinities between its moral and political stance and that of Christian social thought.

I. Epistemological Dimension: Faith and the Social Sciences

Theology, a reflection arising from praxis, has need of a series of theoretical instruments if it is to pronounce its own discourse. Having explained this first point, we still have three others to address: Which

Marxism are we talking about? Why are Marxist tools used? And –
the most important from a descriptive point of view – why do liberation theologians use Marxism?

1. *Theology and Scientific Discourse*

All theology, through the ages, has used some particular scientific
discourse as a mediation for the construction of its reflection. Faith
is the basic moment of theological discourse. Faith, in turn, is an
aspect of *praxis* – *Christian* praxis. Christian activity or praxis
includes the *light* in which theological thought can be regarded as
Christian. That is to say, the daily praxis of existential faith is the
light that shows whether activity may be seen to be the following of
Jesus of Nazareth. In like manner, praxis, which includes faith as
its Christian foundation, is the constituent antecedent of theology.
Theology is nothing but a theoretical discourse (spiritual, sapiential
and methodical, but likewise always 'practical', according to Thomas
Aquinas) that, from a point of departure in Christian praxis, in the
light of faith, reflects, thinks, supplies with a rational foundation, the
reality, the problems that saw praxis encountered on a daily basis. It
belongs to theology to be a 'methodical' discourse; that is, it follows
the most developed rules or requirements of the most developed
rationality of the epoch in which it is being practiced. In the Babylonian context of the sixth century B.C., the 'Adamic myth' is a
theological construction corresponding to the best of the symbolic
rationality of its time (for example, vis-à-vis the myth of Gilgamesh).
Jesus used the theological tools of his time (those of the rabbinical
and Pharisaic schools, and so forth). From the second century of our
era, with the appearance of the Greek Christian theological schools
(first those of the Apostolic Fathers, then the Apologists, then Alex-
andrinians like Origen), Christian faith built up its theological discourse through the use of the 'science' (*epistēmē*) of its time: Platonic
philosophy (and theology). Platonic 'categories' permitted the construction of a Christian theology through the use of tools that in the
first century had been regarded as intrinsically perverse – part of a
'pagan', anti-Christian culture. In the twelfth century, at a time when
Aristotelianism had been *explicitly condemned*, Albertus Magnus and
Thomas Aquinas used Aristotle, who provided them with a system of
categories in which a theological discourse could unfold that was
destined to hold sway in Catholic theology down to our very day.

In the nineteenth century, the German theologian Johan Moehler
employed the instruments of the philosophy of his time to effect

an in-depth renewal of a German Catholic theology that had fallen hopelessly behind a Protestant theology outfitted with the best philosophy of the Enlightenment and Hegelian thought. It was not until the twentieth century that Karl Rahner, with an existential philosophy in a Heideggerian cast, or a Johannes Baptist Metz, with the philosophy of the Frankfurt 'critical school', brought theology abreast of the thinking of their time.

In other words, theology has always had to seize upon a method (traditionally almost exclusively a philosophical one) in order to construct, from praxis, from faith, a methodical, rational, scientific discourse.

2. Why Are Marxist Analytical Tools Used?

Liberation theology arises from an experience of Christian praxis – a faith praxis. Historically and concretely, theology has always been anticipated by Christian praxis and ecclesial faith – the faith and praxis of Christian groups and theologians-to-be. The concepts that a nascent Latin American theology found itself under the obligation of expounding and justifying in order to meet the needs of militant Christians were the theological reasons accounting for the meaning of the '*political* commitment' of these Christians. But why a political commitment? In order to bring about a social, economic, and political change that would permit the exploited clases (first), the poor (more theologically), and the Latin American people (last) to reach a just, humane, fulfilled life. It is the twofold demand of (1) a theological reflection on the 'political commitment' (2) in order to serve the oppressed, the 'poor', the people, that required this nascent theology to use other analytical, interpretative, tools from those known to previous theological tradition. Faced with the absence of an adequate theology already in existence, theologians had to seize upon the *Latin American critical social sciences* – not only 'social' sciences (such as sociology, economics, and so forth), but 'critical' (concerned with discovering and situating the reality of injustice) and 'Latin American' (because our continent had questions 'of its own' to resolve) social sciences. The decision to use these tools, then, was not an a priori dogmatic or epistemological decision. It was Christian praxis and faith, and criteria fundamentally spiritual and pastoral (the *fact* that Christians were becoming involved in politics in order to fight injustice, together with the social teaching of the church) that made adequate analytical categories necessary.

Thus it came about that an infant Latin American theology began to make use of the tools of Marxist categories (emerging historically from the Marxism of the French tradition, already being used in student and worker groups). Juan Luis Segundo, José Comblin, Gustavo Gutiérrez, and I belonged to the generation that had studied in France or Belgium. That set of instruments – we shall see presently what it was and how it was used – made it possible for the new *theology* that began in 1968 to call itself *liberation* theology (in Rubem Alves's Princeton dissertation[1]) to reach unexpected results in the area of the analysis of historical, social, and political realities (as well as in other areas, once it had discovered its methodology, which was applicable to other levels of reflection, as would soon be the case with a theology of the liberation of women, of the oppressed races, and so on). What was occurring, if we may so speak, was an epistemological revolution in the world history of Christian theology. For the first time, the critical social sciences were being used. Political economics and sociology, which had originated only well into the nineteenth century, had never been consistently used by Christian theology. Just as modernism produced a crisis with its use of *history* in theology (from Renan to Blondel), so also liberation theology generated a crisis by adopting the *social sciences*, and among them, as their critical nucleus, Marxism. The twenty-first century will show how important liberation theology has been in its missionary function in the contemporary world, beginning at the end of our own twentieth century – in the world of the poor, in Latin America, Africa, and Asia, and very particularly, in the nations of 'real socialism', where it is the only intelligible, understandable, and prophetic theology possible.

. . .

III. Paths Now Opening

Thomas Aquinas taught that theology is a science because it practices a *method* – in Thomas's case, the Aristotelian. Liberation theology's habitual use of its scientific tools is in full conformity with the tradition of earlier theologies, from the time of the Apostolic Fathers through the Fathers of the Church and the medieval Latin theologians, down to our present day. It is the *first* theology, of course, to use *Marxism* as a valid mediation – having previously set that Marxism on a level compatible with Christian faith. The Fathers of the Church used Platonism, St Thomas used Aristotelianism, and Rahner's theology, to cite a modern example, used Heidegger. In the nineteenth century, the use of the science of history occasioned the Modernist crisis. And yet today all theology is historical: the crisis has passed. This is what will happen in the twenty-first century with Marxism. What is interesting is that it is a theology of the peripheral countries that has been the first – in virtue of the necessity imposed on it by its practical, liberative option – to attempt the use of Marxism. Thus, that theology has had to suffer criticism, misunderstanding, and even condemnation; but the road it has taken has remained open, and future generations will be able to travel it in safety, orthodoxy, and justice. Let us consider only certain present challenges, which promise a bright future.

1. Reception of Marxist Categories in the Magisterium of the Church

I should like to give only one example here, among the many I could offer, but one that will be strong enough to make it possible to understand the situation. In millions of its members, the church is now experiencing the reality of a noncapitalist world. In that world, Marxism and Marxist categories are part of daily life – what Husserl or Habermas would have called the *Lebenswelt*. In *Laborem Exercens*, the 1981 encyclical, a number of different categories are used; there is a very intelligent understanding *of Marx* in many passages *against* a naive, economistic, Stalinist Marxism. Let us see some instances of this.

The basic structure of the encyclical is that of a description of the relationships obtaining among *work*, *bread*, and *life*.[2] *Life* is the origin; human *persons* are living beings. Because they are alive, these persons consume their lives; they have *needs*. Needs call for the creative activity of work, which produces *bread* (the product par excellence in biblical thought). Then this bread, this product, consumed, *satisfies* need and restores and augments life. This is the life cycle.[3] Marx enunciates this in prototypal fashion:

> I should have objectified my *individuality* and its peculiarity in my production [read 'my bread'], and should therefore have double enjoyment: during the activity, the experience of a *vital individual* expression, and in contemplating the object [the bread], the *individual* joy of knowing that my *personhood* is an objective power. My work would be the expression of free life, to the extent that it partakes of the joy of *life*.[4]

Speaking of the relationship between bread or production and consumption or satisfaction, Marx manifests a frank personalism:

> In the former [production], the producer is objectified as a *thing*. In the latter [consumption], the thing created by [the producer] becomes *person* [*personifiziert*].[5]

And this is repeated in his famous passage: 'Merchandise [read "bread"] is an external object, a thing which, thanks to its properties, *satisfies human needs.*'[6]

Needs, for Marx, are *human*. 'Work is one of the characteristics that distinguish the human being from the rest of creatures,' declares the encyclical.[7]

In conformity with Catholic social teaching, the encyclical declares that the *dignity of the human person* is the foundation of the dignity of work. On this point the agreement with Marx is even literal:

> Some labors realized by the human being may have an objective *value*; . . . nevertheless, . . . they are measured by the yardstick of the *dignity of the actual subject* of the work: the person.[8]

Marx says explicitly:

> Work as *absolute poverty* [*absolute Armut*] . . . exists without mediation, . . . and can only be an objectivity unseparated from the *person* [*Person*]: only an objectivity that coincides with its immediate *bodiliness* [*Leiblichkeit*].[9]
>
> Work . . . is the nonobjectified, that is, unobjective, that is, *subjective* existence of work itself: work not as object, but as activity, . . . as living source of value.[10]
>
> By . . . capacity for work we understand the ensemble of physical and mental faculties existing in *bodiliness*, in the *living personhood* [*lebendige Personlichkeit*] of a human being.[11]

The author of certain pages of the encyclical knows Marx's work very well. He speaks of 'capacity for work' (*Arbeitsvermöge*),[12] which Marx uses in the *Grundrisse* (1857–58) and in the *Manuscripts* of 1861–63 and 1863–65, but which he replaces with 'work power' (*Arbeitskraft*) in *Das Kapital* (1867), and which later Marxism therefore no longer uses. For Marx, 'work *itself* has no [economic] value'; only 'capacity for work' does,[13] since it is the 'creative source of value'[14] because it has worth or dignity (it is an *end*) and is not a *means* (the *value* of merchandise). And for Marx, as for the encyclical, the person, the subjectivity, the dignity of work ('living work')[15] is the source of the value of all *things* – even of the *thing* called *capital*.[16]

Thus there is complete agreement that the basis of the value of '*objective* work'[17] – a properly Marxist category – is '*subjective* work'[18] – also a Marxist category: work as subject and subjectivity, from the text cited from the *Grundrisse* and many others. The encyclical (with its primacy of the human being in the *process of production*,[19] the primacy of the human being over things)[20] asserts 'the principle of the priority of labor over capital',[21] inasmuch as capital is only objectified, accumulated work.

Finally, the encyclical criticizes the isolation of persons in capitalist society, from the viewpoint of the existence or 'sign of the active person amidst a community of persons',[22] which recalls a text from the *Grundrisse*:

> A free *individuality*, based on the universal development of *individuals*, subordinating their *community* [*gemeinschaftliche*] productivity . . . as social legacy constitutes the third stage. *Community* production is subordinated to *individuals* and *controlled in community fashion* by them as their own legacy . . . It is the *free* exchange *among individuals* associated on the basis of appropriation and *community control* of the means of production.[23]

For Marx, as for the encyclical, human toil ('living work', or the 'subjectivity of work'), as individuality in community – that is, the human person of the worker – is the point of departure for an ethical critique. Categories like 'means of production',[24] 'objective' work in the form of technology,[25] or the statement that 'capital cannot be *separated* from labor, and that in no wise can labor be set over against capital,'[26] refer to categories or distinctions *strictly* of Marx himself, which the encyclical uses to criticize, and rightly so, Stalinist, dogmatic, and economistic Marxism. The encyclical, like liberation theology, makes a certain categorical use of Marx, just as St Thomas used Aristotle.

. . .

Conclusions

The theology of liberation springs from, and learns in a disciplined manner from, the praxis of the Latin American people, the base Christian communities, the poor and oppressed. It justifies, first, the political commitment of militant Christians, thereupon to do the same with the entire praxis of the impoverished Latin American people. It is a critical theological discourse, then, which situates the traditional questions (sin, salvation, church, christology, sacraments, and so on) on a *concrete*, pertinent level. It does not reject the *abstract* (sin *in itself*, for example), but it situates it in *concrete* historical reality (the sin of *dependency*, for example).

It was on the basis of a need for a concrete critical theological reflection from a point of departure in the poor and oppressed that the use of the toolbox of the human sciences, especially Marxism, became necessary. The theology of liberation is the first theology in history to use these analytical instruments, and it takes them up on the strength of the demands of faith, avoiding economicism, a naive dialectical materialism, and an abstract dogmatism. Thus it can criticize as sin capital, dependency, and so forth. It fixes no political alternatives. That is not the function of theology. But it is careful not to fall into the trap of a 'third way': neither capitalism nor socialism, but a Christian political solution. It does not thereby cease to be an orthodox (arising from orthopraxis), traditional (in the strong sense of the word) theology. In a missionary spirit, it enters into a dialogue with Marxism (that of Latin American political parties or movements, and even the Marxism of the countries of actual socialism, where its discourse is likewise understandable).

During certain decades, the prophetical positions of liberation theology were referred to as 'the usual' by the perennial 'wise'. Like a Jeremiah jailed in his own Jerusalem, the theology of liberation will have to repeat the experience of criticism and persecution that the prophets had to undergo. 'O Jerusalem, Jerusalem, you slay the prophets and stone those who are sent to you!' (Luke 13:34).[27]

– Translated by Robert R. Barr

Notes

1. Rubem Alves, *Toward a Theology of Liberation*, published under the title of *Theology of Human Hope* (Washington, D.C., 1969).

2. 'With his *work* man must gain his daily *bread*' (first line of the encyclical, and nos. 1, 9, etc.). On the 'maintenance of life', see foreword, nos. 1, 2, 3, 8, 10, 14, 18, etc.

3. Cf. Dussel, *Filosofía de la producción*, on the 'pragmatic circle' and the 'poietic [productive] circle'. The first 'circulates' between need and consumption; the second, from need to production to product to consumption.

4. Karl Marx, *Paris Notebook* (1844): *Cuaderno de Paris* (1844) (Mexico City, 1974), pp. 155–56; *MEGA*, sect. 1, vol. 3 (1932), pp. 546–47.

5. Karl Marx, *Grundrisse*, Span. ed., 1: 11.

6. Karl Marx, *Das Kapital*, I, 1.

7. *Laborem Exercens*, foreword. In *Manuscript 1* of 1844, Marx clearly explains the difference between human work, which has awareness and freedom, and mere animal activity.

8. *Laborem Exercens*, no. 6

9. Marx, *Grundrisse*, Span. ed., 1: 235–36. Cf. Dussel, *Producción teórica*, chap. 7, pp. 139ff.

10. Marx, *Grundrisse*. The same text is found in *Manuscripts of 1861–1863* (*MEGA*, II, 3, p. 147; see Dussel, *Hacía un Marx desconocido*, chap. 3, sect. 1).

11. *Das Kapital* (1873), 1, 4, 3 (Span. ed., p. 203; *MEGA*, II, 5, p. 120, of 1866). We shall explain this question in a work in preparation, in which we shall expound *Das Kapital* by way of a scientific commentary.

12. For example, 'as capacity for work or aptitude for work' (*Laborem Exercens*, no. 5); 'the capacity for work' (*Laborem Exercens*, no. 12).

13. 'The only opposite to objectified work is nonobjectified work, *living work. . . .* The one is value of incorporated use, the other occurs as human activity in process; the one is value, the other is *creator of value*. A given value will be exchanged for activity *creative of value*' (*Manuscripts of 1861–1863*, notebook 1: *MEGA*, II, 3, p. 30). Cf. Dussel, *Hacía un Marx desconocido*, chap. 3, sect 1.

14. For Marx, 'creation' of value is 'from the nothing' of capital: 'How can a greater value emerge from production than that that has entered into it, unless *something be created from nothing [aus Nichts]*?' (*Das Kapital*, III, chap. 1: *MEW* 25:48).

15. See Dussel, *Hacía un Marx desconocido*, chap. 14, sect. 2. Marx writes a critique of the reified objectivity of capital from a point of departure in the *personal subjectivity* of the worker.

16. The 'fetishism' is only an inversion: the *person* of the worker becomes a thing; and the thing of capital, a person. Cf. Dussel, 'El concepto de fetichismo en el pensamiento de Marx', *Cristianismo y Sociedad* 85 (1985): 7–60.

17. Marx speaks of 'objectified' work, or the objective meaning of work.

18. Marx's 'living work' is work as act, activity, subjectivity/subject – the individual's self, the person of the worker, poor, stripped. This is the ongoing reference of all of Marx's critical thought. His entire work is an *ethics*: 'Were we *animals*, we could naturally turn our backs on the *sufferings of humanity*, and just concern ourselves with our own skins. But I should have regarded myself as rather impractical to *have died* without at least having completed the manuscript of my book *Das Kapital*' (Letter of April 30, 1867: *MEW*, 30, p. 542).

19. For Marx, the 'living work' subsumed in capital is used, consumed as 'work process' within capital (in the *Grundrisse*, in the *Manuscripts of 1861–63 and 1863–65*, and in *Das Kapital*).

20. *Laborem Exercens*, no. 11.

21. Ibid.

22. Ibid, foreword.

23. Marx, *Grundrisse* Span. ed., 1: 86; Germ. ed., pp. 75–77.

24. *Laborem Exercens*, nos. 12, 13, 14, etc.

25. Ibid., no. 5.

26. Ibid., no. 13. At the beginning of his *Paris Notebook* (1844), Marx notes that work cannot be 'separated' from capital as if they were two autonomous 'things', because the whole of capital is only objectified work. They are not two *things*. There is only one 'subjectivity' (work), and capital is only this same subjectivity, *objectified*. Thus the 'trinity' is transcended (the three factors, work, capital, land) that is criticized by Marx in *Das Kapital*, III (chap. 7 of the 1865 *Manuscript*, original folios 528ff., in the Amsterdam archive). For all of this see my forthcoming book on the 1863–65 *Manuscripts* (third redaction of *Das Kapital*).

27. The present contribution was prepared before the events in Eastern Europe or the elections in Nicaragua: hence no reflection on these phenomena is included here.

Rosemary R. Ruether, 'Feminist Theology: Methodology, Sources, and Norms'

in *Sexism and God-Talk*, Boston: Beacon Press, 3rd edition, 1993, pp. 12–15, 16–19, 20–26, 45.

In this well-known extract from a seminal text in Christian feminist theology, Rosemary Ruether sets out some basic precepts of her position, which may be characterized as a 'reformist' rather than 'radical' stance. That is, Ruether believes that the tradition, while responsible for the marginalization of women in the Church, can be revised in a more inclusive and constructive direction.

Essentially, Ruether argues that the history of theology has privileged the experiences, perspectives and achievements of some groups at the expense of others. In particular, women's experiences have been unrepresented; and the extant tradition needs to be expanded and renewed by the reintegration of such marginalized sources. Thus, for Ruether, the development of the theological tradition proceeds by a constant process of assimilation of new sources – but significantly, too, the recovery of lost or hidden voices as well.

It is interesting to note that while this method of theological development is a broadly correlationist one – in that canonical 'tradition' is placed in dialogue with other additional or marginal authorities – Ruether speaks of all her sources as comprising 'usable tradition' even though in reality they include both theological and non-theological material. So for Ruether, 'tradition' is always a synthesis of heterogeneous sources in creative tension.

Yet what criteria should guide the basis by which the tradition evolves, and a new synthesis emerges? For Ruether, what marks the tradition as flawed also guides its imperative to reconstruction: its capacity to promote 'the full humanity of women' by embracing and reflecting 'women's experience'. While the coherence of this term has been hotly contested in feminist circles, Ruether's dual approach of critique and reconstruction continues to exert an enduring influence over feminist theological methodology.

Women's Experience and Historical Tradition

It has frequently been said that feminist theology draws on women's experience as a basic source of content as well as a criterion of truth.[1] There has been a tendency to treat this principle of 'experience' as unique to feminist theology (or, perhaps, to liberation theologies) and to see it as distant from 'objective' sources of truth of classical theologies. This seems to be a misunderstanding of the experimental base of all theological reflection. What have been called the objective sources of theology; Scripture and tradition, are themselves codified collective human experience.

Human experience is the starting point and the ending point of the hermeneutical circle. Codified tradition both reaches back to roots in experience and is constantly renewed or discarded through the test of experience. 'Experience' includes experience of the divine, experience of oneself, and experience of the community and the world, in an interacting dialectic. Received symbols, formulas, and laws are either authenticated or not through their ability to illuminate and interpret experience. Systems of authority try to reverse this relation and make received symbols dictate what can be experienced as well as the interpretation of that which is experienced. In reality, the relation is the opposite. If a symbol does not speak authentically to experience, it becomes dead or must be altered to provide a new meaning.

The uniqueness of feminist theology lies not in its use of the criterion of experience but rather in its use of *women's* experience, which has been almost entirely shut out of theological reflection in the past. The use of women's experience in feminist theology, therefore, explodes as a critical force, exposing classical theology, including its codified traditions, as based on *male* experience rather than on universal human experience. Feminist theology makes the sociology of theological knowledge visible, no longer hidden behind mystifications of objectified divine and universal authority.[2]

The Hermeneutical Circle of Past and Present Experience

A simplified model of the Western theological tradition can illustrate this hermeneutical circle of past and present experience. We must postulate that every great religious idea begins in the revelatory experience. By *revelatory* we mean breakthrough experiences beyond ordinary fragmented consciousness that provide interpretive symbols illuminating the means of the *whole* of life. Since consciousness is ultimately individual, we postulate that revelation always starts with an individual. In earlier societies in which there was much less sense of individualism, this breakthrough experience may have been so immediately mediated through a group of interpreters to the social collective that the name of the individual is lost. Later, the creative individual stands out as Prophet, Teacher, Revealer, Savior, or Founder of the religious tradition.

However much the individual teacher is magnified, in fact, the revelatory experience becomes socially meaningful only when translated into communal consciousness. This means, first, that the revelatory experience must be collectively appropriated by a formative group, which in turn promulgates and teaches a historical community. Second, the formative group mediates what is unique in the revelatory experience through past cultural symbols and traditions. As far back as human memory stretches, and certainly within the history of Biblical traditions, no new prophetic tradition ever is interpreted in a cultural vacuum. However startling and original the vision, it must always be communicated and made meaningful through some transformation of ideas and symbols already current. The hand of the divine does not write on a cultural *tabula rasa*. Thus the Hebrew prophets interpreted in new ways symbols from Canaanite and Near Eastern religions. Christianity, in successive stages, appropriated a great variety of both Jewish and Hellenistic religious symbols to interpret Jesus. The uniqueness of the vision is expressed by its ability to combine and transform earlier symbolic patterns to illuminate and disclose meaning in new, unexpected ways that speak to new experiential needs as the old patterns ceased to do.

The formative community that has appropriated the revelatory experience in turn gathers a historical community around its interpretation of the vision. This process goes through various stages during which oral and written teachings are developed. At a certain point a group consisting of teacher and leaders emerges that seeks to channel and control the process, to weed out what it regards as deviant communities and interpretations, and to impose a series of criteria to determine the correct interpretive line. The group can do this by defining an authoritative body of writings that is then canonized as the correct interpretation of the original divine revelation and distinguished from other writings, which are regarded either as heretical or of secondary authority. In the process the controlling group marginalizes and suppresses other branches of the community, with their own texts and lines of interpretation. The winning group declares itself the privileged line of true (orthodox) interpretation. Thus a canon of Scripture is established.

Once a canon of Scripture is defined, one can then regard subsequent tradition as reflection upon Scripture and always corrected by Scripture as the controlling authority. In Catholicism and Orthodoxy the notion of the other equally authoritative 'apostolic' traditions flowing from early times and existing alongside canonical Scripture does not quite disappear. Creeds, liturgical customs, and oral tradition passed down through apostolic sees also provide access to the original faith of the 'primitive community'. However much the community, both leaders and led, seek to clothe themselves in past codified tradition that provides secure access to divinely revealed truth, in reality the experience of the present community cannot be ignored.

. . .

Crises of Tradition

Religious traditions fall into crisis when the received interpretations of the redemptive paradigms contradict experience in significant ways. The crisis may be perceived at various levels of radicalness. Exegetical criticism of received theological and Scriptural traditions can bring forth new interpretations that speak to new experiences. This kind of reform goes on in minor and major ways all the time, from individuals making their own private adaptations to teachers founding new schools of interpretation. So long as this is accommodated within the community's methods of transmitting tradition, no major break occurs.

A more radical break takes place when the institutional structures that transmit tradition are perceived to have become corrupt. They are perceived not as teaching truth but as teaching falsehood dictated by their own self-interest and will to power. The revelatory paradigms, the original founder, and even the early stages of the formulation of tradition are still seen as authentic. It seems necessary to go behind later historical tradition and institutionalized authorities and 'return to' the original revelation. In the literal sense of the word, there is no possibility of return to some period of the tradition that predates the intervening history. So the myth of return to origins is a way of making a more radical interpretation of the revelatory paradigm to encompass contemporary experiences, while discarding institutions and traditions that contradict meaningful, just, and truthful life. Usable interpretative patterns are taken from Scripture and early community documents to set the original tradition against its later corruption. The original revelation itself, and the foundational stages of its formulation, are not challenged but held as all the more authoritative to set them as normative against later traditions. The Reformation followed this pattern of change.[3]

A still more radical crisis of tradition occurs when the total religious heritage appears to be corrupt. This kind of radical questioning of the meaningfulness of the Christian religion began to occur in Western Europe during the Enlightenment. Marxism carried the Enlightenment critique of religion still further. Marxism teaches that all religion is an instrument the ruling class uses to justify its own power and to pacify the oppressed.[4] This makes religion not the means of redemption but the means of enslavement. The very nature of religious knowledge is seen as promoting alienation rather than integration of the human person. This kind of ideological critique throws the truth content of religion into radical ethical disrepute. Such an attack on religion is considered 'true' by a growing minority of people when they perceive the dominant religious traditions as contradictory to the contemporary experience of meaning, truth, and justice.

Ideological criticism of the truthfulness of the religion may still allow for some residue of genuine insight into the original religious experiences and foundational teachers. The prophets of Jesus may be said to have had truthful insights into just and meaningful life, but this became corrupted and turned into its opposite by later teachers, even within Scripture. Discarding even the truthfulness of foundational teachers, the critic may turn to alternative sources of truth: to recent critical schools of thought against the religious traditions; to suppressed traditions condemned as heretical by the dominant tradition; or to pre-Christian patterns of thought. Modern rationalist, Marxist, and romantic criticism of religion have followed such alternatives in the last two hundred years.

Why seek alternative traditions at all? Why not just start with contemporary experience? Doesn't the very search for foundational tradition reveal a need for authority outside contemporary experience? It is true that the received patterns of authority create a strong need, even in those seeking radical change, to find an authoritative base of revealed truth 'in the beginning' as well as a need to justify the new by reference to recognized authority. These needs reveal a still deeper need: to situate oneself meaningfully in history.

The effort to express contemporary experience in a cultural and historical vacuum is both self-deluding and unsatisfying. It is self-deluding because to communicate at all to oneself and others, one makes use of patterns of thought, however transformed by new experience, that have a history. It is unsatisfying because, however much one discards large historical periods of dominant traditions, one still seeks to encompass this 'fallen history' within a larger context of authentic and truthful life. To look back to some original base of meaning and truth before corruption is to know that truth is more basic than falsehood and hence able, ultimately, to root out falsehood in a new future that is dawning in contemporary experience. To find glimmers of this truth in submerged and alternative traditions through history is to assure oneself that one is not mad or duped. Only by finding an alternative historical community and tradition more deeply rooted than those that have become corrupted can one feel sure that in criticizing the dominant tradition one is not just subjectively criticizing the dominant tradition but is, rather, touching a deeper bedrock of authentic Being upon which to ground the self. One cannot wield the lever of criticism without a place to stand.

The Critical Principle of Feminist Theology

The critical principle of feminist theology is the promotion of the full humanity of women. Whatever denies, diminishes, or distorts the full humanity of women is, therefore, appraised as not redemptive. Theologically speaking, whatever diminishes or denies the full humanity of women must be presumed not to reflect the divine or an authentic relation to the divine, or to reflect the authentic nature of things, or to be the message or work of an authentic redeemer or a community of redemption.

This negative principle also implies the positive principle: what does promote the full humanity of women is of the Holy, it does reflect true relation to the divine, it is the true nature of things, the authentic message of redemption and the mission of redemptive community. But the meaning of this positive principle – namely, the full humanity of women – is not fully known. It has not existed in history. What we have known is the negative principle of the denigration and marginalization of women's humanity. Still, the humanity of women, although diminished, has not been destroyed. It has constantly affirmed itself, often in only limited and subversive ways, and it has been touchstone against which we test and criticize all that diminishes us. In the process we experience our larger potential that allows us to begin to imagine a world without sexism.

. . .

Is There a Historical Tradition for Feminist Theology?

First we must say that there is no final and definitive feminist theology, no final synthesis that encompasses all human experience, criticizes what is sexist, and appropriates what is usable in all historical traditions. This book, therefore, represents not *the* feminist theology but *a* feminist theology. However wide its historical sweep, back to Biblical traditions, forward toward a post-Christian world, encompassing minority as well as majority tradition, it is nevertheless an exercise in feminist theology with a particular selection of human experience. This selection is and can only be from the historical tradition, in its broadest sense, that has defined my identity. If I seek out the minority as well as the majority traditions of that community, its repressed pre-Christian side as well as its dominant tradition, I still operate within a particular historical tradition.

Many other traditions are not considered: Asian, African, Hindu, Buddhist, and so on. An Asian Buddhist or an Iranian Muslim, or even Christians from these backgrounds, would bring together a cultural synthesis different from the one I present here. This is not a 'fault'; it is simply necessary recognition of historical particularity and limits. What I seek here is a working paradigm of the human situation drawn from a sufficiently large sample of experience that can eventually stimulate dialogue and lead to yet a further synthesis. Other feminist theologians must create other paradigms and make different syntheses of various cultural-religious traditions.

While particularity is affirmed, exclusivism is rejected. God is not a Christian or Jew rather than a pagan, not white rather than Asian or African. Theological reflections drawn from Judeo-Christian or even the Near-Eastern-Mediterranean-European traditions do not have a privileged relation to God, to truth, to authentic humanity over those that arise from Judaism, Islam, and Buddhism. Nor are they presumed to be the same. Exactly how a feminist theology drawn from other cultural syntheses would differ is not yet known. But we affirm at the outset the possibility of equivalence, or equal value, of different feminist theologies drawn from different cultural syntheses.

Having clarified the particularity but nonexclusivism of the historical traditions considered in this work, we can ask where within those traditions we can find usable foundations for feminism. I draw 'usable tradition' from five areas of cultural tradition: (1) Scripture, both Hebrew and Christian (Old and New Testaments); (2) marginalized or 'heretical' Christian traditions, such as Gnosticism, Montanism, Quakerism, Shakerism; (3) the primary theological themes of the dominant stream of classical Christian theology – Orthodox, Catholic, and Protestant; (4) non-Christian Near Eastern and Greco-Roman religion and philosophy; and (5) critical post-Christian world views such as liberalism, romanticism, and Marxism.

All of these traditions are sexist. All provide intimations of alternatives: equivalence and mutuality between men and women, between classes and races, between humanity and nature. All suggest concepts of God that would affirm such alternative relationships. Yet even these alternatives exist in forms distorted by sexism. Their potential for aiding us in imagining a new humanity can be disclosed by subjecting each to feminist critique and bringing them together in a new relationship. By allowing Canaanite religion to criticize Hebrew religion rather than only the reverse, by allowing minority Biblical and Christian traditions to criticize dominant traditions, one begins to discover lost critical principles. One senses suppressed human potential lurking beneath the dominant traditions and, in many cases, providing a lost key to the meaning of dominant traditions.

. . .

Conclusions

The feminist theology proposed here is based on a historical culture that includes the pre-Christian religions suppressed by Judaism and Christianity; Biblical prophetism; Christian theology, in both its majority and minority cultures; and, finally, the critical cultures through which modern Western consciousness has reflected on this heritage. It seeks, in effect, to recapitulate from a feminist, critical perspective this journey of Western consciousness. To be sure, it would be pretentious to assume that one can really embrace the whole experience in all its aspects. There are many avenues of Christian and non-Christian culture that will not be given 'equal time' in this account. What is sought here is not the inclusion of limitless possibilities, but a working paradigm of some main trends of our consciousness, both its dominant side and its underside. Thereby we can begin to glimpse both what has been lost to humanity through the subjugation of women and what new humanity might emerge through the affirmation of the full personhood of women.

Notes

1. See Judith Plaskow, *Sex, Sin and Grace: Women's Experience and the Theologies of Reinhold Niebuhr and Paul Tillich* (Washington, D.C.: University Press of America, 1980), pp. 29–50.

2. Sallie McFague, *Metaphorical Theology: Models of God in Religious Language* (Philadelphia: Fortress, 1982), chap. 5.

3. Robert L. Wilken, *The Myth of Christian Beginnings: History's Impact on Belief* (Garden City, N.Y.: Doubleday, 1971).

4. For the classic texts of Marxist critique of religion, see *Marx and Engels on Religion*, introd. Reinhold Niebuhr (New York: Schocken, 1964).

Wendy M. Wright, 'Babette's Feast: a Religious Film'

Journal of Religion and Film, Vol. 1, No. 2, October 1997, available online at http://www.unomaha.edu/jrf/Babetteww.htm

In an early contribution to the emergent study of religion and film, the British theologian Clive Marsh used a revised version of H. Richard Niebuhr's typology of 'Christ' and 'Culture' (1997). He argued that just as Niebuhr characterized a range of relationships between the sources and norms of 'culture' and 'Christian tradition', so too could the relationship between film and theology be understood as existing on a continuum, ranging from incompatibility, identity or tension between their respective world-views.

Wright's analysis of the 1987 film Babette's Feast *adopts the second of Marsh's categories, and takes a broadly 'correlative' approach in which 'secular' knowledge or activity is seen as affirming the core elements of the Christian message. She maintains that the film may be considered religious in a number of ways: most obviously, its subject-matter and key characters deal with religious characters and settings. Yet on another, deeper level, she argues that it relates a story unmistakably shaped by Christian dynamics, in that it charts a journey from loss to recovery, despair to hope, death to new life. Furthermore, argues Wright, the film abounds in a sacramental cele-*

bration of the power of the material world to disclose God at work in creation, and the power of acts of hospitality, generosity and love to effect healing.

Critics of the 'identity' model of Christ and culture argue that too close an assimilation between theological sources and secular values risks attenuating the scope of the gospel, by associating themes of transcendence and mystery too closely with one particular human expression. Similarly, it may gloss over elements in the film that call into question received theological understandings drawn from the more standard 'texts' of tradition and Scripture. Nevertheless, it enables viewers to see how theological motifs are inescapably inter-twined with wider cultural forms and how the creative arts return constantly to Christian motifs and metaphors for inspiration.

. . . Director and writer Gabriel Axel based his 1987 film, *Babette's Feast*, on a short story of the same name by Danish writer Isak Dinesen. With some exceptions, especially of emphasis, the film is a close rendering of the original tale. The story treats of a sectarian group of persons whose entire lives have been shaped by their religious convictions. In accord with many viewers' common-sense notion of what makes a film religious, *Babette's Feast* would qualify because religious people and institutions are its overt subject matter. The characters pray, worship and conduct their affairs within the context of their faith. Moreover, the narrative is concerned with the inner-dynamics of the religious group over a period of years and takes a perspective on their manner of being religious. But let me offer here a summary of that basic story.

Jutland, Denmark. The later part of the nineteenth century. Two elderly maiden sisters, Martine and Filippa, the daughters of a long-deceased prophet-founder of an austere Christian sect, maintain a simple life of piety and charitable works and carry on their father's memory by presiding over his small band of remaining disciples . . .

[T]he sisters content themselves with lives of piety. Their untiring work among the poor has . . . been made possible with the help of a maid, Babette, who one stormy night fourteen years earlier had arrived on their doorstep, a refugee from the terrors of the French civil war whose husband and son had perished . . .

The prophet's sect by this time has lost most of its early vitality. The few remaining members, all of whom are advanced in years, have fallen into the habit of quarrelling. Old disagreements have reawakened, and past sins cast a heavy pallor over the congregation.

Their hymns – 'Jerusalem, my heart's true home', 'never would you give a stone if a child begged for food' – recall the pastor's eschatological vision of a world transformed but fail to kindle the former devotion and zeal. Hoping to heal some of the community's wounds, Martine and Filippa plan a simple celebration in honor of their father on what would have been his one-hundredth birthday. As the date approaches, Babette receives word that she has won one hundred francs in the French lottery thanks to a ticket an old friend of hers had renewed each year.

Babette reflects on what to do with her winnings and requests of the sisters that they allow her to prepare, just once, a real French meal, and serve it for the pastor's celebration. Reluctantly they agree. Babette proceeds to order from the continent supplies the likes of which the sisters have never dreamed: wines, live quail and turtle. Martine and Filippa begin to fear that something akin to a witches' Sabbath is about to take place and they fearfully alert the rest of the disciples. All agree that they will attend the dinner with their minds on higher things, as if they had no sense of taste.

The evening of the celebration arrives and one of the disciples, the aunt of Lowenhielm [a former admirer of Martine] announces that her visiting nephew, now a general, will join them for dinner. Babette is immersed in the astonishing, sensuous and elaborate preparations for her meal. The guests arrive, their somber, otherworldly dress and demeanor in high contrast to the sumptuous table set before them. General Lowenhielm alone, unaware of the group's strategy to remain disengaged, is overwhelmed by the exquisite fare which unfolds in magnificence before them, course by course and liquor by liquor . . .

Gradually, warmed by the fine wines and the general's example, the guests begin to respond, not only to the feast itself, but to one another. Old quarrels are healed, past sins genuinely forgiven. The general rises and, echoing the deceased pastor's words, acknowledges the reality of a world illuminated by love. When he departs he tenderly acknowledges to Martine that during the intervening years he had always been with her in love and friendship and that during this evening he had learned that with God all things are possible. The dinner comes to a close as the disciples leave and, illuminated by moonlight in the village square, they spontaneously join hands in a circle and dance . . .

. . . On the fundamental level of subject matter and narrative interest, *Babette's Feast* must certainly qualify as a film in which religion features prominently. The film-makers take a distinct perspective on their religious characters and their world. But there is much,

much more to the religious vision of *Babette's Feast* than is evident in this common sense matter of subject matter, plot, character and dialogue.

Any viewer could enjoy *Babette's Feast* as a simple narrative in which religious characters come to some sort of awakening. It could be experienced as a story about a group of rather stuffy, old-fashioned folks with a glum otherworldly view of things who, in a wondrous meal, are initiated into the delights of enjoying the pleasures of life. In this vein it could be viewed as a critique of religion itself. But one doesn't have to scratch the surface of the film very deeply to find this a limited view. For *Babette's Feast* is saturated with religious symbolism of the most specifically Christian kind and read through the lens of that symbolism the film is simultaneously an exploration of the foundational Christian myth of death and resurrection, a study of competing Christian views of reality, and an affirmation of the ultimate sacramentality of the created order.

Within the first minutes of the film, the viewer is treated to a vision of the sect at worship, voices raised in song: 'Jerusalem, my heart's true home . . .' Already the most fundamental Christian symbolism comes into play. Jerusalem, the image of a transfigured world where, at the end of time, all the deepest human hopes and longings will be fulfilled. There, according to Christian understanding, the eschatological banquet will be served. All that is partial will be completed, all sorrow turned to joy, all that is estranged be reconciled, all that is lost, found. The blind will see, the deaf will hear, the lame will leap for joy. All will be reconciled. The disciples live in anticipation of that other-worldly end-time in the new Jerusalem.

And food, that pivotal Christian symbol, is introduced explicitly at the end of the congregation's first stanza. 'Never will you give a stone to the child who begs for bread,' they sing, echoing scripture. Already the irony is set up. These earnest believers, inhabiting a stony, barren land where their meager fare is unappetizing ale-bread and split cod (which has been visually presented to us hanging up to dry in the opening shots), beg to be fed at a banquet table of unsurpassed bounty. *Babette's Feast* is thus a thoroughly religious film in the sense that it plays with foundational Christian themes and imagery. The heavenly banquet. The redemption of the world.

In fact, *Babette's Feast* is structured to recapitulate the central dynamic of the foundational Christian myth. It visually presents a movement from death to resurrection. And it does so by introducing a salvific figure who transfigures the main characters' world through a loving act of self-giving.

. . . It is the final segments of *Babette's Feast* that are most saturated with Christian symbolism. The pastor's memorial banquet becomes a recapitulation of the Last Supper and, by extension, of the Christian liturgy and the eschatological banquet. With the general added to the remnant, they are twelve at table. With Babette in the kitchen preparing the food, they are thirteen. Even the progress of the supper mirrors the rhythm of the liturgical rite. The general's private examination of conscience serves as the anamnesis, the wiping away of past mistakes, a remembering in a new way. The gathered band then proceeds to recall the days of their early inspiration, when their prophet was with them and life was filled with promise and miracle. Then the banquet begins in earnest with Babette in the background, supplying a meal her guests scarcely have eyes to see or tongues to taste. But gradually as they are fed, they awaken to the miracle taking place in their midst. That miracle resides not only in the food itself but becomes embodied in the community gathered there. Not only are the sins of their past mutually forgiven, these past lapses are seen in a new transfigured light.

. . . Babette herself is clearly a Christ-image, coming mysteriously and humbly to live with the community, taking on the role of a servant, finally giving all she has to provide a banquet in which the most profound longings of the heart are answered and hungers filled. Wine is poured out in excess. Bread quite literally mirrors manna in the desert . . .

In the manner of all fine art, *Babette's Feast* is neither slavish nor overly literal in its exploration of Christian symbols. There is not one simple reading of the film to make one point. Multiple interpretations emerge and the richness of the imagery takes on a life of its own, opening out to the ongoing interpretations of multiple viewers. Nevertheless, the film's symbolic matrix is clearly Christian. Whether one sees a critique of a Christianity which over-stresses moral rectitude or a vision of a universe that is essentially sacramental or the reconciliation of the world and spirit or the movement from death to resurrection, *Babette's Feast* is clearly a film that takes its life from the exploration of religious symbolism . . .

John W. de Gruchy, 'Art in the Life of the Church'

in *Christianity, Art and Transformation*, Cambridge: Cambridge University Press, 2001, pp. 239–40, 242–4, 245, 246–7, 248.

De Gruchy draws parallels between artistic endeavour and religion. Both seek to articulate the meaning of life and to give tangible form or expression to the human spiritual quest. Artistic achievement is not only a sign of human creative gifts but a vehicle of divine epiphany.

Creativity, in its potential to break through the barriers of the mundane and awaken the imagination, can contribute to the transformation of the world. Reminiscent of Ellen Charry's characterization of the 'aretegenic' nature of theology – or that which is conducive to the cultivation of virtue – de Gruchy argues for a conception of religious art that exists to inspire ethical responsibility and to help shape an appropriately directed moral life. Art cultivates an aesthetics or sense of 'holy beauty' of God that translates into an antipathy towards all that is ugly or unjust.

As with other examples of theological reflection, de Gruchy considers the dilemma of using human and culturally bound forms of representation to depict the transcendent or divine. Yet still, the arts contribute to the life of faith by sharpening the sense of the triune God, present in creation, affirming the material world in all its brokenness and glory. De Gruchy's theological reflection is Trinitarian: God's creative activity is a source of human wonder and worship, but is matched by the dynamics of incarnation and fellowship, an imperative to realize God's beauty in human affairs.

Note, finally, how de Gruchy uses these staple theological themes to elaborate a normative vision for the use of the creative arts in religion. So while art is judged to be a valid and necessary medium for theological reflection, its appropriation is nevertheless to be conducted within certain parameters of orthodoxy.

Artistic Creativity and Christian Conviction

Great art, like authentic religion, seeks to express awe and wonder, and to overcome the superficiality of life by exploring its depths. It is concerned about personal integrity in its endeavour to communicate the truth as it is perceived; and it evokes deep emotion, whether of sadness or joy, dread or elation.[1] So it is no surprise that many of the most distinguished artists of the twentieth century irrespective of their cultural context have been people of deep spiritual perception, and

some have been committed Christians. Paul Cézanne, in some ways
the father of modern painting, was a devout Catholic who confessed
to a friend that he could not paint if he did not believe.[2] But many
others have been alienated from the church either because they have
felt rejected or else because it has been lacking in aesthetic richness
and depth. Experiencing an absence of the aesthetic in the church,
they have found sanctuary in art.

. . .

In restoring the creative arts to their rightful and necessary place in
the life of the church the issue at stake is, then, not the decoration of
the sanctuary in ways that are pleasing to the senses, 'art for art's
sake in the church', but something more profound. We are concerned
with the recovery of a genuinely theological aesthetics which, as [. . .]
is rooted in the triune life of God, and the *cantus firmus* of the cross,
and related to the transformation of the world. And, in agreement
with Bonhoeffer, we are concerned about rebirth of the creative spirit
through the recovery of aesthetic existence in the life of the church.
Without the *cantus firmus* the enriching polyphony that follows creative imagination is impossible. But the *cantus firmus* rightly understood creates space for the expression of the creative imagination
with freedom and integrity. With this in mind we turn to consider
some criteria for evaluating the place of art in the life of the church
which may help us discern what is appropriate, whether in worship,
formation or witness.

Art in the sanctuary is not primarily for the sake of contemplation
apart from the world (as in Platonism), but a way of enabling responsible action in the world. So faithful creativity also has to do with the
way in which art in the sanctuary engenders Christian involvement
in society. For the church to acquiesce in tasteless shoddiness will not
inspire its members to creative expressions of response to the gospel
in the world. There are undoubtedly remarkable exceptions to this
rule. But it is self-evident that the environment within which people
are nourished normally affects their development and their perspective on life. The same is true when it comes to the life of the church.
Christian formation takes place not only through teaching (truth) or
example (goodness), but also through the cultivation of a sense of
taste for what is genuinely beautiful in a world of competing images
and ugliness. This is not to reduce art to didactic purposes, yet it has
a similar concern.

In recovering the links between aesthetics and social ethics in the
life of the church, 'holy beauty' provides a fundamental criterion for

evaluating art from a Christian perspective in determining whether it is liturgically appropriate. The category of 'beauty' links the Christian approach to art to the traditionally aesthetic touchstones of value and taste, while 'holiness' indicates that the Christian understanding of 'beauty' is also distinct, that it is theologically derived. 'Holy beauty' is the Old Testament foundation for a Christian aesthetic when it comes to determining what art may be appropriate within the sanctuary. It speaks of a God whose transcendent mystery cannot be captured through artistic representation, for that is idolatry. Following our earlier discussion on idolatry and political power, 'holy beauty' demands the exclusion not only of representations of God as such, but of all signs and symbols of human pretension, hubris and absolutist claims. We must neither compromise the hiddenness and mystery of God ('the holy of holies') nor confuse the glory and power of God with images that invariably reflect or reinforce our own interests, whether personal, national, ethnic or class. Iconoclasm in this regard is a necessary outworking of the prophetic trajectory in the biblical tradition.

Yet the God who is holy is also present in the sanctuary and, as Isaiah and many others testify, can be experienced. 'I have looked upon you in the sanctuary, beholding your power and glory', declares the psalmist (Psalm 63:2 NRSV). For the Christian this other side of the dialectic of 'holy beauty' is especially affirmed in the incarnation and experienced through the Holy Spirit. The hidden God is the revealed God; the mystery of God has been made known in Jesus Christ and is present for us through the Spirit. So the awesome holiness of sacred space, which is common to many religions, must not override the sense of God's presence 'where two or three are gathered together' in the name of Jesus Christ, who makes himself known through the Spirit in word and 'the breaking of bread'.

This trinitarian confession lies at the heart of the Christian faith and is the basis of genuinely Christian worship, as can be seen in all classic liturgies and great eucharistic prayers of thanksgiving. The latter begin by acknowledging God's creative power, love and holiness, (Isaiah's trisagion 'Holy, holy, holy'), then they affirm Christ's incarnation, crucifixion, resurrection and second advent, and conclude by invoking the presence and action of the Holy Spirit. So it is that in the 'breaking of bread' (nothing could be more materialist and available to the senses) and the proclamation of the word, God is known in Christ through the Spirit evoking our response of praise, confession, thankfulness and service. It is in this way that the beauty of God revealed in Christ makes its appeal to us, drawing all humanity into the life of the triune God in anticipation of the fulfilment of all things. Art in the sanctuary is appropriate when it is consonant with this triune confession of faith. That is when it contributes to a sense of the presence of this God who seeks to draw us into the divine life, and send us into the world to bear witness to God's love, grace and justice. As such, art in the sanctuary is not crassly didactic but eminently liturgical and formative for Christian life and witness.

There are various corollaries that can be drawn from this triune confession of faith with regard to visual art in the sanctuary, though the same would apply to other forms of art. The first refers to the connection that is made between God as creator, redeemer and sanctifier. If God as creator of the world is the supreme artist, then the natural world provides the point of departure for artistic response to God. The Bible 'exults in the artistry of God, in the beauty of the created order, culminating in a response of amazement and astonishment'.[3] We have already noted [. . .] how this was embodied in the tabernacle and temple in ancient Israel, where many of the works of art were representations of nature. This is something often lost sight of in considering what is appropriate art for the Christian sanctuary because we tend to start with redemption and quite literally lose sight of creation. Flower arrangements in the sanctuary are important, for this reason if no other, and are often the only way in which something so fundamental to biblical faith is represented. This may explain why too often Christians have failed to recognise the integral connection between their faith and the environment. There is an urgent need to bring back into the sanctuary appropriate representations of God's creation.

. . .

The crucifixion uncovers the depths of human depravity and the extent of human fallenness. In so doing it evokes an artistic response that explores the brokenness of creation, the dehumanising powers at work in the world, the alienation of people from God, from each other and from nature, indeed the demonic nihilistic force that continually erupts in human history and experience. Any romanticising of art that denies the reality of evil, the pervasive suffering of creation, the human will-to-power and the experience of the absence of God runs counter to the Christian confession. But the crucifixion also reveals, even more so, the extent of God's solidarity with creation and humanity in its suffering, and the quality of God's redemptive grace and love. Therefore, any idealising of art or notion of beauty that removes God from involvement in the struggles of human history and denies God's pathos or redemptive purpose runs counter to the Christian confession. The alien yet redemptive beauty of the cross is the heart of the Christological *cantus firmus*. The cross is the supreme icon of the transformation of ugliness into beauty, as many paintings of the crucifixion themselves demonstrate.

. . .

The fact that I have stressed the 'alien beauty of the cross' is not meant to detract from the need for art that celebrates life in all its fullness: quite the contrary, for that is what aesthetic existence is about. But just as we cannot really appreciate the transforming power and beauty of the transfiguration or the resurrection except from the perspective of the horrors of crucifixion, so redemptive beauty can only be fully appreciated when we, with Dostoyevsky and many others, have some sense of the ugliness from which we are redeemed.

The resurrection proclaims God's triumph in Christ over the ugly power of sin, evil and death; it speaks of a 'hope which is against hope' and the promise of the fulfilment (recapitulation) of all things in Christ. Art in the sanctuary must express the victory of Christ over that which dehumanises people and destroys creation, and affirms hope for a transformed world. But such art must not perpetuate the triumphalism of so much in Christian history and tradition. Any art that glorifies the church must be excluded from the sanctuary. So too must art that denies the possibility of the redemption and transformation of human beings and the world. Art may well depict the human descent into hell, but given that every Christian act of worship is premised on the resurrection of Christ and anticipates the transfiguration of reality, art in the sanctuary should speak above all of the transfiguration of life.

Obviously not all art in the sanctuary can capture the whole of the Christian confession of faith any more than one sermon can do so. Moreover, the sanctuary should not become an art gallery, cluttered up with 'works of art' trying to express the sum of Christian faith. That is why art, even within the canon of appropriateness, needs to be carefully selected and even changed from time to time, in order to represent the drama of creation and redemption. Dillenberger thus poses an important question when he asks whether the work of individual artists 'without a consistent iconographic scheme, provide a religious ambience, susceptible to and encouraging of, the life of faith'.[4] Works of art in the sanctuary should represent and recall our interconnectedness with nature, keep us aware of injustice and human suffering, open us up to the healing power of God's grace and beauty and, making us sensitive to God's surprising incursions into human history, keep hope alive. Sometimes the 'grand narrative' of redemption will be powerfully represented, but art in the sanctuary should also reflect the many and varied narrative by-paths of the Bible and Christian tradition whose rich and diverse wisdom provides guidance and meaning to our fragmentary lives.

The gift of the Holy Spirit is an article of faith that connects our themes of faithfulness and creativity, art and transformation, in a remarkable way. The Spirit is, from a Christian perspective, both the source of artistic creativity and the source of empowerment in the struggle for justice and transformation. The Spirit of creativity is the Spirit of Mission. As we have noted several times, theologians through the centuries have insisted that all artistic creativity is inspired by the Spirit, whether the artists are Christian or not.

. . .

Doing Theological Aesthetics in Context

Throughout our discussion we have been mindful of the importance of context and culture for understanding the relationship between Christianity and art, and especially for the role of art in social transformation. Art as integral to culture must always be contextually rooted, no matter how universal its appeal. But this also means that art is historically situated, so that the relationship between Christianity and art has to be constantly renegotiated and freshly understood. As Pattison puts it: 'the relationship between art and religion does not stand outside history and cannot be fixed definitively once and for all. Instead that relationship is constantly acquiring a new shape as each continues on its separate – yet related – way.'[5] As culture changes, so also will the way in which Christianity expresses itself in art change. That is one reason why the task of doing theological aesthetics has to be engaged in in every context and generation.

Notes

1. See B. Watson, 'The Arts as a Dimension of Religion' in *Religion and the Arts in Education* ed. Dennis Starkings (London: Hodder & Stoughton, 1993), pp. 95ff.

2. Alexander Liberman, *The Artist and his Studio* (London: Thames and Hudson, 1988), p. 6.

3. Walter Brueggemann, *Theology of the Old Testament* (Minneapolis: Fortress Press, 1997), p. 339.

4. J. Dillenberger, 'Artists and Church Commissions', (New York: Continuum, 1996).

5. George Pattison, *Art, Modernity, and Faith* (London: SCM Press, 1998), p. 9.

Tim Gorringe, 'The Long Revolution'

in *Furthering Humanity*, Aldershot: Ashgate, 2003, pp. 12–16.

Tim Gorringe's commentary on H. R. Niebuhr's famous typology of 'Christ' and 'Culture' takes place in the context of a wider discussion of the significance of human cultural activity for Christian theology. In his critique, embodied in this short extract, we can see both Gorringe's appraisal of the use of 'ideal types' as a form of analysis, as well as his evaluation of the various alternative stances of 'oppositional, conformist, synthetic, dualist and conversionist modes' (p. 313).

What emerges is that all five types represent, to some degree, a kind of correlational model, in that none of the alternatives can escape the influence of culture, especially if culture is understood as the sum total of human achievement – a definition Gorringe himself favours in a memorable phrase as 'what we make of the world' (Gorringe, 2004: 3). In other words, it encompasses both the interpretive processes of intellect and high culture, as well as the material aspects of human fabrication and labour. Given such a comprehensive definition, it is hard to see how we can be human and not participate in culture, however 'counter-cultural' a particular group may wish to be.

Returning to Niebuhr's typology as a whole, however, it is clear that there are still major differences in the way in which the various claims of what perhaps might better be described as the universal experience of being human (inhabiting and making culture) and the specific calling of faith (as in being a Christian or the identity of the Body of Christ) are seen to interact with each other. As Gorringe observes, however, Niebuhr has somewhat been superseded by at least two trends: first, a greater awareness by the late twentieth and early twenty-first centuries of the 'global' nature of culture and its diversity of cultural expressions; and secondly, the emergence of interest in popular culture – often, as an environment of lived experience and meaning which corresponds to Gorringe's anthropological understanding – which further alerts us to the complexity of the term.

Christ and Culture

Richard Niebuhr provided a famous, if rather ahistorical, typology for understanding the interaction of Christianity and culture in *Christ and Culture*, published in 1951. Within a few years of the book's appearance, notes John Howard Yoder, 'the terms suggested, and the classification of various typical positions which it proposed, had become the common coin of contemporary thought, not only among specialists in Christian ethics, but in many other circles as well'.[1] For this reason we have to give it particular attention.

The lectures which gave rise to the book were delivered in 1949, near the beginning of the emergence of the world order, or disorder, in which we presently live. The Berlin airlift was under way, and the world lay frozen into two polarized political ideologies. The position of a significant part of the Church with regard to this development was made clear when the Vatican, which had been able to make a Concordat with German fascism, announced excommunication for anyone practising or preaching communism. Senator McCarthy began his hearings the next year. President Truman announced his plan to bring 'underdeveloped' nations up to the level of the developed, initiating the so-called 'development decade'. All over the world former colonies were claiming their independence. There was, then, a strong sense of world reconstruction. In this context Niebuhr was concerned with the values which would underpin such reconstruction, values which he found in the Christian gospel.

In his understanding of culture he drew on the work of American social anthropology, and defined culture, or civilization – for he does not want to distinguish between the two – as the 'total process of human activity' and the total result of that activity.[2] We cannot define its essence, but we recognize that it is social, a form of human achievement, and constitutive of values which articulate the human good. The idea of the kingdom of God is just one amongst many such values. Because 'culture' describes everything we do as humans it is irreducibly plural and 'lays its claim and authority' on every person. The question Niebuhr posed was how the Christian should respond to this authority and claim. The criterion was provided by 'the Jesus Christ of the New Testament' who defines the gospel, and who, in turn, exercises authority over Christians.[3] There are, then, two authorities and the task is to map their relationship. To this end he proposed a fivefold typology which, despite extensive discussion and critique, has survived the fifty years since its first airing. Niebuhr's work has survived as well as it has partly because it is well nuanced, and therefore resists crude caricature. He recognizes that he is proposing 'ideal' types, which no historical individual perfectly exemplifies, and further that the positions shade into one another. Nevertheless he wants to suggest that Christian responses to culture fall into oppositional, conformist, synthetic, dualist and conversionist modes.

The first letter of John in the New Testament with its warnings against 'the world' and 'the lust of the flesh, the lust of the eyes, and the pride of life', and Tertullian and Tolstoy in the later tradition, illustrate a stance of 'Christ against culture', where the gospel calls into being what is later called an *oppositional* culture. This stance, Niebuhr felt, was necessary but inadequate. Though we recognize the contribution of monasticism and Protestant sectarianism, instantiations of this view, the real reform of culture was accomplished by more moderate voices. The historical record is, therefore, against the antagonistic response to the wider world. Methodologically it is impossible because human beings cannot exist outside culture. Radical Christians are caught in a double bind, making use of the culture they ostensibly reject. Theologically this type of position supposes that revelation stands outside culture, which is impossible, and it tends to suggest that sin is found in culture and not amongst the elect, generating thereby a sectarian Church which exists for itself rather than for the world. It is also inadequately Trinitarian, failing to establish a proper relation between Christ and Creator, and therefore tending to Manichaeism.

The polar opposite stance is that of Christ understood as fulfiller of culture. No biblical support for this view is suggested, but Niebuhr might, perhaps, have turned to Wisdom. In the tradition Ritschl and Harnack, but also the Christian socialists Shailer Matthews and Ragaz, exemplify this view. Niebuhr is noticeably as hard on those who are attracted by Marxism or socialism as on those who identify the gospel with bourgeois society. The strength of the *conformist* stance is that it makes the universal meaning of the gospel clear and does justice to all those aspects of Christ's work which affirmed the body, or the culture, of his day. Its weakness is a tendency to appeal to cultural elites, to overvalue 'reason', to underestimate sin, and therefore to end up with some kind of self-reliant humanism. It too fails to give an adequate account of the relation of Christ and Creator.

Niebuhr's third category, 'Christ above culture', describes the attempt to take the middle view, what he calls the *synthetic* position. Thomas Aquinas is the main exemplar, a monk who served a Church which was the principal guardian of high culture in its day. (This is one of numerous occasions when Niebuhr slips between the anthropological sense of 'culture' and the notion of 'high culture'.) Aquinas' idea that God is the law in Godself; that creation manifests 'natural' law; and that good positive law aspires to echo this, is the perfect example of the middle way. In the classical formulation, grace does not destroy nature but perfects it. The danger is that this view tends to absolutize the relative and reduce the infinite to a finite form. What was manifestly 'natural' for Thomas is not for us, and it now seems that agreement as to what is natural cannot be reached. There is also an endemic tendency for the middle way to graduate towards cultural conservatism and to institutionalization.

Luther and Kierkegaard are taken to illustrate a fourth position, of Christ and culture in paradox. Where the Christ against culture paradigm takes its stand against culture in general, this position is more concerned with the question of the divide between God and human beings. The Church is corrupt as well as culture; piety may be as sinful as passion. The *dualist* recognizes that she or he, too, belongs to a culture which is corrupt. The danger with this position is that the relativization of all human works can lead to antinomianism on the one hand, and to cultural conservatism on the other. There is no necessary link between law and grace.

The final category is that of Christ as the 'transformer of culture', exemplified by the rather unlikely combination of Augustine and F. D. Maurice, and this position is clearly Niebuhr's preferred option, despite his disavowal of any one 'right' answer to the problem. It is the only one of the types to which the objections are not stated. The *conversionist*, so called, takes creation seriously, as well as atonement, and has a more sanguine view of its possible redemption here and now. The position has, in Niebuhr's view, a more positive understanding of history as the story of God's 'mighty deeds'. History is read as the story of the dramatic interaction between God and human beings. It underlies a practice of responsible engagement which nevertheless recognizes that the kingdom is quite different from anything we create. Augustine, read, like the Augustine of Radical Orthodoxy, without the anti-Pelagian treatises, is seen not to reject the cultural tradition he has inherited, but to transvalue it, to redirect, reinvigorate and regenerate it.

For all its popularity, this typology is nevertheless full of problems. I have noted that Niebuhr tends to elide the anthropological notion of culture with that of 'high culture'. As soon as you do that the typology starts to fracture. Tertullian, for example, was the most brilliant Latinist of the Western tradition, and we simply need to mention Tolstoy's name in this connection to indicate the problem. Those who come from the 'counter cultural' tradition very often do so precisely in view of their knowledge of, and even commitment to, the high culture tradition. Conversely, those representing the 'Christ of Culture' position may sometimes avow a populism which finds the high tradition profoundly problematic. In short, as soon as we nuance the idea of culture we find the need to develop a richer understanding of the engagement of Church and culture than Niebuhr's typology allows. As Yoder puts it, every morally accountable affirmation of culture discriminates:

> The cultural stance of the Christian church according to the New Testament will . . . not be a matter of seeking for a strategy to be applied uniformly, either accepting or rejecting . . . all of 'culture' in the same way . . . Some elements of culture the church categorically rejects (pornography, tyranny, cultic idolatry). Other dimensions of culture it accepts within clear limits (economic production, commerce, the graphic arts, paying taxes for peacetime civil government). To still other dimensions of culture Christian faith gives a new motivation and coherence (agriculture, family life, literacy, conflict resolution, empowerment). Still others it strips of their claims to possess autonomous truth and value, and uses them as vehicles of communication (philosophy, language, Old Testament ritual, music). Still other forms of culture are created by the Christian churches (hospitals, service of the poor, generalized education, egalitarianism, abolitionism, feminism). Some have been created by the Peace Churches (prison reform, war sufferers' relief, international conciliation).[4]

Such discrimination makes Niebuhr's global use of the category of culture impossible. At any given point any Christian might want to invoke all of Niebuhr's categories to describe their relation to the dominant culture.

A further problem relates to the broad brush nature of Niebuhr's examples. He notes that probably all fail to exemplify their case exclusively. This is indeed the case, and some, like the Gnostics, or Augustine, perhaps hardly exemplify it at all. So vague is his typology that it cannot be falsified.[5] He makes his case modestly but all this does is to underline the view that any conviction that truth can be known and can lay upon us definite claims which we must unequivocally obey is naïve.[6] To say that there is no one right answer is to canonize pluralism. His preferred 'conversionist' paradigm by 'being inclusive and pluralistic, fitting to the Ivy League graduate school culture, makes it precisely the best view after all'.[7]

Niebuhr consistently points out that the positions he critiques are inadequately Trinitarian, but, given his starting point in the Jesus of history, this is true for his own work. His central preoccupation is with discipleship to the historical Jesus, and with avoiding any implicit or explicit Manichaeism, any failure to honour creation.

However, given the need to understand culture through the categories of Wisdom, Logos or Spirit, exemplified equally by the Wisdom tradition, Justin, Hegel, and the missionary theologians (!), a satisfactory theology of culture must be more full-bloodedly Trinitarian than that. The absence of a Trinitarian perspective perhaps accounts for his individualistic understanding of the Church which, again, has failed to learn from Herder's insistence that everything, and everyone, is related, and that culture has to be understood in terms of those relations. The Church as a body has almost no place in the argument for Niebuhr. The 'conversionist' paradigm which he favours has what Yoder calls a 'vacuity about moral substance' which follows on from the failure to define criteria or lines of direction for change.[8] What is meant by transformation is so inadequately defined that it is virtually indistinguishable from the Western doctrine of progress.[9]

For all of these reasons this immensely influential typology has to be dropped, to be replaced not with an alternative typology, but with a more complex mapping of the interrelation of gospel and culture.

Notes

1. Yoder says of *Christ and Culture*: 'Few single works of contemporary theology could compare [to it] for popularity going beyond theological circles, for enormous formative impact upon the way other people think, and for great "holding power".' J. H. Yoder, 'How H. Richard Niebuhr Reasoned: A Critique of Christ and Culture' in G. Stassen et al. (eds) *Authentic Transformation*, Nashville: Abingdon, 1996, p. 31

2. H. R. Niebuhr, *Christ and Culture*, New York: Harper and Row, 1951, p. 32.

3. Niebuhr, *Christ and Culture*, p. 12.

4. Yoder, 'How Niebuhr Reasoned', p. 69.

5. Yoder, 'How Niebuhr Reasoned', p. 51.

6. Yoder, 'How Niebuhr Reasoned', p. 52.

7. Yoder, 'How Niebuhr Reasoned', p. 82.

8. Yoder, 'How Niebuhr Reasoned', p. 43.

9. Yoder, 'How Niebuhr Reasoned', p. 53.

'Speaking of God in Public': References and Further Reading

Aquinas, Thomas (1999), *Selected Writings (Penguin Classics)*, ed. R. McInerny, Harmondsworth: Penguin.

Foerst, A. (1996), 'Artificial Intelligence: Walking the Boundary' *Zygon*, Vol. 31, No. 4, 681–92.

Gorringe, Tim (2003), *Furthering Humanity*, Aldershot: Ashgate.

Marsh, C. (1997), 'Film and Theologies of Culture' in C. Marsh & Gaye Ortiz (eds), *Explorations in Theology and Film*, Oxford: Blackwell, pp. 21–34. See also

Marsh, C. (1998), 'Religion, Theology and Film in a Postmodern Age: A Response to John Lyden', *Journal of Religion and Film* Vol. 2, No. 1, available online at: http://www.unomaha.edu/jrf/marshrel.htm

Niebuhr, H. R. (1951), *Christ and Culture*, San Francisco: Harper & Row.

Rahner, K. (1982), *The Practice of Faith: A Handbook of Contemporary Spirituality*, eds K. Lehmann and A. Raffelt, London: SCM Press.

Tillich, P. (1959), *Theology of Culture*, ed. Robert Kimball, New York: Oxford University Press.

Williams, Delores S. (1989), 'Womanist Theology: Black Women's Voices' in Carol S. Christ and Judith Plaskow (eds), *Weaving the Visions: New Patterns in Feminist Spirituality*, San Francisco: Harper & Row, pp. 179–86.

6

'Theology-in-Action': Praxis

Introduction

This method of reflection is perhaps best associated with the so-called theologies of liberation that emerged out of the two-thirds world at the end of the 1960s. Yet when contemporary liberation theologians speak of the biblical injunction to keep faith with God's 'preferential option for the poor' they stand in a long tradition that insists that true faith is expressed in integrity of action that seeks to fulfil God's reign on earth as in heaven. Thus, it is possible to identify a deeper historical continuity within praxis: an insistence that the *believing* of 'right religion' is identical with the *making* of 'right relationships', especially in situations of poverty, disempowerment or oppression. Such a privileging of faith as *practice* can be traced as having decisive roots in a biblical tradition of prophetic denunciation of outward observance of religious rules at the expense of true integrity, equated with the works of compassion and solidarity with the poor. It is also manifest in traditions that number among the most blessed of God's people those who recognize the suffering presence of Christ in the faces of the poor, the excluded – 'the little ones of history' as Gustavo Gutiérrez puts it.

Similarly, this model of theological reflection is exemplified by many of those whose insistence on freedom of belief, action and worship has led them into conflict with institutional or establishment religion, and for whom faith is not to be mediated via external authority or circumscribed by creeds or doctrines, but is necessarily open to the promptings of the Holy Spirit, often in the form of personal religious experiences. The Society of Friends, or Quakers, bears witness to this tendency. Out of a context of religious radicalism in post-Civil War England, the Quakers insisted that every person possessed an 'inner light' or spark of spiritual discernment. This faith in 'that of God in Everyone' translated into a religious and social egalitarianism. Since all individuals were, potentially, vessels of the Holy Spirit, it bestowed an irreducible dignity upon everyone that could not be abused by exploitation, disrespect, poverty or discrimination; yet equally, since all were possessed of the potential to bear testimony to one another, regardless of social rank, then no institution or creedal formulation could be elevated above the promptings of the Holy Spirit in the hearts of all people.

The praxis method of theological reflection has also recast practical theology itself as what has been termed a 'performative' discipline: that the practices of faith, corporate and individual, embody their own core principles. Theology is a form of *phronēsis* or practical wisdom, in which the convictions of the Christian faith are evident within the purposeful and goal-directed practices of the community. In her postmodern practical theology, for example, Elaine Graham reverses the direction of much conventional theological reflection, so that far from practice being the application or outworking of philosophical or metaphysical truths, theological truth-claims are *primarily* expressed and enacted in practical contexts. Theological reflection, or articulation of Christian doctrine, is then a secondary activity, a systematization of what is always already enacted and proclaimed in faithful practice.

Didache, Chapters VII–XVI

in Clayton N. Jefford (ed.), *The Didache in Context*, Leiden: Brill, 1995, pp. 9–14.

The Didache, or 'Teachings of the Twelve Apostles', is one of the earliest extant Christian texts and reflects a period (the first 200 years of the Common Era) when patterns of worship, ministry and discipline were still evolving. The Didache is a document concerned with the regulation of the Christian life and features sections on practices such as fasting, baptismal and eucharistic rites, as well as guidance on the conduct of ministry. Scholars agree that it contains fragments drawn from other sources – readers will find echoes from many other early Christian writings, including many epistles – and is a mixture of moral exhortation, a primer in ministry and instruction in conduct of ritual practices. Yet it is concerned to undergird all its practical advice with theological principles; and even if the references are somewhat eclectic, they perhaps reflect concern by the authors or editors to reinforce their practical guidance with familiar texts and teachings from other sources.

The Didache demonstrates how the corporate life of the earliest Christians was focused around specific practices of fasting, prayer, baptism and the eucharistic meal, not simply as optional obligations but as defining signs of a common way of life. It spells out how the practices of following the example of the earthly Jesus on the part of the community were intended to be performative identifications with the risen Christ. It is of interest within a discussion of theology-in-action, therefore, given that it demonstrates the origins of much Christian doctrine in the context of communal worship and how the tasks of individual nurture and formation, and concerns about the regulation of the corporate community, gave rise to some of Christianity's earliest formularies and creeds.

VII

1   As for baptism, baptize this way.[1]
Having said all this beforehand [i.e., all that is written above], baptize in the name of the Father and of the Son and of the Holy Spirit, in running water.
2   If you [sing. through verses 2–4] do not have running water, however, baptize in another kind of water; if you cannot [do so] in cold [water], then [do so] in warm [water].   3   But if you have neither, pour water on the head thrice in the name of Father and Son and Holy Spirit.
4   Before the baptism, let the person baptizing and the person being baptized – and others who are able – fast; tell the one being baptized to fast one or two [days] before.

VIII

1   Let your fasts not [coincide] with [those of] the hypocrites. They fast on Monday and Thursday; you, though, should fast on Wednesday and Friday.   2   And do not pray as the hypocrites [do]; pray instead this way, as the Lord directed in his gospel:

'Our Father in heaven,
May your name be acclaimed as holy,
May your kingdom come,
May your will come to pass on earth as it does in heaven.
Give us today our bread for the morrow,
And cancel for us our debt [owed for sin],
As we cancel [debts] for those who are indebted to us,
And do not bring us into temptation,

But preserve us from evil [or, from the evil one].
For power and glory are yours forever.'

3   Pray this way thrice daily.

IX

1   As for thanksgiving, give thanks this way.
  2   First, with regard to the cup:
     We thank you, our Father,
     For the holy vine of David your servant
       which you made known to us
       through Jesus your servant.
     To you be glory forever.
  3   And with regard to the fragment:
     We thank you, our Father,
     For the life and knowledge
       which you made known to us
       through Jesus your servant.
     To you be glory forever.
    4   As this fragment lay scattered upon the mountains
      and became a single [fragment] when it had been
      gathered,
    May your church be gathered into your kingdom
      from the ends of the earth.
    For glory and power are yours,
      through Jesus Christ, forever.
  5   Let no one eat or drink of your thanksgiving [meal; i.e., the eucharistic meal] save those who have been baptized in the name of the Lord, since the Lord has said, 'Do not give to dogs what is holy.'

X

1   When you have had your fill, give thanks this way:
    2   We thank you, holy Father,
    For your holy name,
      which you made dwell in our hearts,
    And for the knowledge and faith and immortality,
      which you made known to us
      through Jesus your servant.
    To you be glory forever.

3 You, almighty Lord, created all things for the sake of your name, and you gave food and drink to human beings for enjoyment, so that they would thank you;
But you graced us with spiritual food and drink and
  eternal life through <Jesus>[2] your servant.
4 Above all, we thank you, Lord, because you are
  powerful.
To you be glory forever.
5 Be mindful, Lord, of your church,
    to preserve it from all evil [or, from every evil being]
    and to perfect it in your love.
And, once it is sanctified, gather it from the four winds,
  into the kingdom which you have prepared for it.
For power and glory are yours forever.
6 May favor [or, grace] come, and may this world pass by.
Hosanna to the God of David!
If anyone is holy, let him come.
If anyone is not, let him repent.
Our Lord, come! Amen.
7 Allow the prophets, though, to give thanks as much as they like.

XI

1 Accordingly, receive anyone who comes and teaches you all that has been said above. 2 If the teacher himself turns to teaching another doctrine [which will lead] to destruction, do not listen to him, but [if it will lead] to an increase of justice and knowledge of the Lord, receive him as the Lord.

3 In the matter of apostles and prophets, act this way, according to the ordinance of the gospel. 4 Let every apostle who comes to you be received as the Lord. 5 He shall stay <only>[3] one day, or, if need be, another day too. If he stays three days, he is a false prophet. 6 When the apostle leaves, let him receive nothing but [enough] bread [to see him through] until he finds lodging. If he asks for money, he is a false prophet. 7 Do not test any prophet who speaks in spirit, and do not judge him, for every [other] sin will be forgiven, but this sin will not be forgiven. 8 Not everyone who speaks in spirit is a prophet but only the one whose behavior is the Lord's. So the false prophet and the prophet will be recognized by their behavior. 9 Any prophet who gives orders for a table [i.e., a meal] in spirit shall not eat of it; if he does, he is a false prophet. 10 If

any prophet teaching the truth does not do what he teaches, he is a false prophet.   11   No prophet, examined and found true, who acts for the earthly mystery of the church but does not teach [others] to do everything that he himself does, shall be judged by you, for his judgment is with God. The ancient prophets acted in the same way.   12   You shall not listen to anyone who says in spirit, 'Give me money, or something,' but if he is asking that something be given for others who are in need, let no one judge him.

XII

1   Let everyone who comes in the name of the Lord be received, and then, when you have taken stock of him, you will know [what he is like], for you will have right and left perception [i.e., perception of what is good and bad about him].   2   If the person who comes is just passing through on the way to some other place, help him as much as you can, but he shall not stay with you more than two or three days – if that is necessary.   3   If he wants to settle in with you, though, and he is a craftsman, let him work and [thus] eat.   4   If he has no craft, you shall use your insight to provide a good way for him to avoid living with you as a Christian with nothing to do.   5   If he is unwilling to do what that way calls for, he is using Christ to make a living. Be on your guard against people like this.

XIII

1   Every true prophet who wants to settle in with you deserves his food.   2   In the same way, a true teacher, too, deserves his food, just as a worker does.   3   So when you [sing.] take any firstfruits of what is produced by the wine press and the threshing floor, by cows and by sheep, you [sing.] shall give the firstfruits to the prophets, for they are your [pl.] high priests.   4   If, however, you [pl. through verse 4] have no prophet, give [them] to the poor.   5   If you [sing. through verses 5–7] make bread, take the firstfruits and give them according to the commandment.   6   Likewise, when you open a jar of wine or oil, take the firstfruits and give them to the prophets.   7   Take the firstfruits of money and clothing and what-ever [else] you own as you think best and give them according to the commandment.

XIV

1 Assembling on every Sunday of the Lord, break bread and give thanks, confessing your faults besides so that your sacrifice may be clean. 2 Let no one engaged in a dispute with his comrade join you until they have been reconciled, lest your sacrifice be profaned. 3 This is [the sacrifice] of which the Lord has said: '"to offer me a clean sacrifice in every place and time, because I am a great king," says the Lord, "and my name is held in wonder among the nations."'

XV

1 Select, then, for yourselves bishops and deacons worthy of the Lord, mild tempered men who are not greedy, who are honest and have proved themselves, for they too perform the functions of prophets and teachers for you. 2 So do not disregard them, for they are the persons who hold a place of honor among you, together with the prophets and the teachers.

3 Correct one another not in anger but in peace, as you have it [written] in the gospel; and let no one speak to anyone who wrongs another – let him not hear [a word] from you – until he has repented. 4 Perform your prayers and your almsgiving and all that you undertake as you have it [written] in the gospel of our Lord.

XVI

1 Keep vigil over your life. Let your lamps not go out and let your waists not be ungirded but be ready, for you do not know the hour at which our Lord is coming. 2 You shall assemble frequently, seeking what pertains to your souls, for the whole time of your belief will be of no profit to you unless you are perfected at the final hour. 3 For in the final days false prophets and corruptors will be multiplied, and the sheep will turn into wolves, and love will turn into hate. 4 As lawlessness increases, they will hate and persecute and betray one another, and at that time the one who leads the world astray will appear as a son of God and will work signs and wonders, and the earth will be given into his hands, and he will do godless things which have never been done since the beginning of time. 5 Then human creation will pass into the testing fire and many will fall away and perish, but those who persevere in their belief will be saved by the curse itself [or, by the very one who is (under?) a curse?]. 6 And then the signs of truth will appear, first, the sign

of extension [of the cross?] in heaven, next, the signal of the trumpet call, and third, resurrection of the dead – 7 not of all, however, but, as it has been said, 'The Lord will come and all the holy ones with him.' 8 Then the world will see the Lord coming upon the clouds of heaven . . .[4]

Notes

1. Here and throughout the following chapters to the end of the work, the second person *plural* form is used when the audience is addressed.

2. Read 'Iηοοῦ with the Coptic version. The reading is consistent with parallel phrases in the Greek text; see 9.2, 3; 10.2.

3. The negated particle εἰ μή is found in a similar sentence at 12.2, and it is supported by the Ethiopic version. Without it, the Greek sentence means 'he shall not stay one day', which does not fit the context.

4. The text probably had a few more lines which have been lost in the direct line of transmission.

Joe Holland, 'Roots of the Pastoral Circle'

in Frans Wijsen, Peter Henriot and Rodrigo Mejia (eds), *The Pastoral Circle Revisited: A Critical Quest for Truth and Transformation*, New York: Orbis, pp. 5–12.

Holland's text locates the roots of this particular method of theological reflection in Latin American liberation theology, in progressive Roman Catholic social action movements and in the philosophical tradition of phronēsis, *or practical wisdom. All converge around a shared emphasis on the indivisibility of reflection and action, and on the need to find interpretative or hermeneutical means by which the two dimensions of* praxis *(as value-directed action) can be mutually instructive. They all share a conviction, also, that human consciousness is always already embedded in social reality; hence Holland's equivocation about the initial phase of reflection as 'insertion', as if individuals and communities needed in some way to 'arrive' in the temporal world from somewhere else. Similarly, no act of 'seeing' is independent of evaluation and judgement, and the moment of 'action' is always informed by the pre-commitments of observation and social analysis.*

Holland is arguing that the fundamental triangular shape of 'see, judge, act' runs deep not only within progressive Roman Catholic thought in the shape of movements such as Catholic Action and liberation theology, but has long been a staple framework for papal social encyclicals. The reason for this commonality of approach, he argues, lies in a deeper philosophical wellspring of Aristotelian thought, as mediated by Thomas Aquinas. This rejected a Platonic form of disengaged, rationalist intuitive method in favour of a more contextual, empiricist way of knowing. Thus, the introduction of phronēsis, *or practical wisdom, was intended to a large extent as an alternative to a more 'applied' model, in which 'axioms' or general principles were applied into practical cases. For practical reasoning, empirical engagement* with *the facts of the matter – and thus by implication, practical immersion* in *the facts of the matter – precede all other forms of knowledge, judgement or action. Theological reflection thus begins and ends in practice; and the task of the pastoral triangulation of see–judge–act is to equip the practitioner with the kind of knowledge that will facilitate prudential judgement.*

The Catholic Social Tradition

In tracing the historical roots of the pastoral circle we can discern three historical levels of sources for the method. The first and most obvious level is, of course, Latin American liberation theology. The second level is the older 'see, judge, act' tradition of modern lay Catholic Action movements, originally European in character, and growing out of the deep tradition of Catholic social teaching. The third level is the praxis model *(phronesis)* of Aristotelian thought, which entered the Catholic tradition through medieval Scholasticism. I speak at more length of the first level and only briefly of the second and third.

Roots in Latin American Liberation Theology

The pastoral circle comes to us most immediately, of course, from Latin American liberation theology, a rich and still developing theological movement. In addressing this root I first offer some reflections on the historical context of liberation theology and then reflect briefly on each of its three steps.

I do not include here the 'insertion' phase of the pastoral circle as found in *Social Analysis*, because it was not found explicitly in the original model of liberation theology or in the earlier 'see, judge, act' model. When drafting the manuscript, Peter Henriot and I had a friendly and even humorous disagreement about whether or not to include it, with Peter Henriot in favor and myself opposed. My viewpoint was that the term *insertion* reflected the old Platonic consciousness of dualistic spirituality that saw the religious reality as outside the temporal world. Instead, I argued that everyone was already and always a part of the very fabric of the social reality and, therefore, could not be 'inserted' into it. Nonetheless, being self-consciously explicit about our social location is a helpful exercise, so I certainly do not object to its presence in the book.

Clearly Latin American liberation theology arose as a movement linked to the post-World War II revolutionary spirit of overthrowing formal European industrial-capitalist colonialism in Africa and Asia, a form of colonialism that had been implanted following the birth of the second stage of industrial capitalism (the machine revolution) in the second half of the nineteenth century. Latin America had been originally colonized in the form of European mercantile-capitalist colonialism two hundred years earlier, but in the industrial-capitalist era it had come under the control of US neocolonialism.

Also, one might argue that the new theological movement was a response to the profound social dislocations caused in Latin America by the earliest phase of the global stage of modern industrial capitalism, in turn precipitated by the postmodern electronic revolution. During the years of President John F. Kennedy's Alliance for Progress, international networks of transportation and communication were becoming more sophisticated and US businesses were developing a more active presence within Latin America. Two key results were the growing urban middle classes and the exploding numbers of rural peasants migrating to the expanding urban-industrial centers. Both of these developments undermined the old power of the Latin American landed aristocracies, which had been traditionally allied with the Catholic higher clergy.

Latin American liberation theology, with roots also in the 'see, judge, act' methodology of Catholic Action, added richer specificity and deeper prophetic critique to this method (which I address more below). So let us now address each of the three steps of this method.

Radically Prophetic Social Analysis. To the moment of 'see' (when one studies the surrounding society) the new theology brought to theological method – for the first time in an integrally and formally theological way – the contribution of the social sciences. It was perhaps no coincidence that Gustavo Gutiérrez had studied at the Catholic University of Louvain in Belgium, the home of the great radical Catholic priest-sociologist François Houtart. At the same time, many church workers in Latin America were turning to the social sciences to understand the vast social and demographic changes shaking the Latin American world. Of course, not all turned radical, for we might recall the case of Roger Veckemanns, SJ, who became a bitter enemy of liberation theology. In contrast to Veckemanns, Latin American liberation theology turned to dialogue with Marxian social analyses (though it did not accept Marxian philosophical assumptions or Marxian strategies).

It also turned, at least in the Brazilian case, back beyond Marx to his precursor in the use of the dialectic, namely, the extraordinary German philosopher G. W. F. Hegel. In many ways the Brazilian 'conscientization' movement was a shift from Marx back to Hegel and, I propose, one highly helpful for dealing with the increasing hegemony of the neo-liberal cultural ideology. (While in Chile, I was blessed to be able to study with Paulo Freire's exiled master-teacher and friend from the Catholic University in São Paulo, Ernani María Fiori, himself a neo-Hegelian philosopher.)

Certainly today some criticize early liberation theology for its confinement within the analytical categories of class and colonialism, that is, for not stressing strongly the equally important dimensions of race-ethnicity and gender, as well as ecology. But its radical analysis of the dimensions of class and colonialism was an important development in Catholic social thought, and one that is being richly supplemented by more recent contributions of liberation theology stressing race-ethnicity, gender, and ecology. Others perhaps criticize the original tendency by some to limit the social-scientific perspective to authors heavily influenced by the Marxian tradition. But the integration of a Marxian critique of capitalism was also an important development (and one that John Paul II himself used in his encyclical on human work, *Laborem exercens*). It is hard to imagine how the genius-filled insights of Marx could be left out of any comprehensive social analysis, provided that the insights of other social-analytical traditions are also included, and provided that the mechanistic-materialist foundations of Marxist ideology are not accepted.[1]

Mosaic Turn in Theological Reflection. To the moment of 'judge' (reflecting on what has been 'seen' and doing so in the light of reason and faith, including the resources of the Bible, the church's tradition, and the *sensus fidelium*), liberation theology proposed a radical shift to the dominant classical heritage of the Catholic theological perspective.

In the Hebrew scriptures we may discern two major poles, a prophetic one centered in the figure of Moses, and a kingly one centered in the figure of the David. Though the two represent polar opposites, there is a historically organic dialectic between them. Moses was a liberator of oppressed Jewish slaves, and David was an anointed warrior-king whose establishment of a hierarchical 'Zionist' kingdom of Israel represented the fulfillment of God's liberation of the slaves from Egypt under Moses' leadership. The Jewish priesthood with its Temple ultimately came to symbolize religious leadership for the Davidic perspective, while the Jewish rabbinate, created in the Babylonian Exile, came to provide leadership for the Mosaic perspective in later periods of Judaism.

In his life Jesus had presented himself more in terms of the Mosaic pole. Indeed, he defined himself as a rabbi (again, the religious leader of the post-exilic Mosaic pole) and not as a priest (the religious leader of the Davidic pole). Further, his Jewish name, Joshua or Yeshuah (with Jesus being Greek version) is the biblical name of the one who continued the mission of Moses.

With the Christianization of the Roman Empire under Constantine, and with seminal roots in pro-Roman Pauline theology, the imperial Christian understanding shifted away from the socially prophetic Mosaic pole to the socially legitimating Davidic one, as reflected in the Pauline emphasis on Jesus' title of Christos, that is, the anointed king like David. In the Davidic pole the social structure is seen as legitimate and not open to fundamental or systemic prophetic critique (while in the Mosaic pole the whole social structure is prophetically called into question). And so it was with classical and modern Catholic Christianity's Davidic legitimating of the original Roman Empire, of the later Holy Roman Empire, and of the still later mercantile-capitalist European empires of the sixteenth-century conquest of the Americas, as well as of the industrial-capitalist European empires of the nineteenth-century conquest of Africa and Asia.

Through its turn to the symbol of the Exodus, grounding symbolically its prophetic critique of the structural captivity of the poor and oppressed, liberation theology proposed a radical shift for the grounding historical symbolism of Catholic Christianity. It was, however, not the first modern Christian tradition to make this turn, for at the birth of modernity African American slaves in the English colonies of what is today the United States had pioneered the way. Where the English Puritan John Winthrop had looked out at the 'new land' and proclaimed it in Davidic terms a 'New Jerusalem', the oppressed slaves captive in the same land lamented in their soul songs that they were held in a Mosaic 'New Egypt'.

Call for Transformative Strategy. To the moment of 'act' (the point at which the faith-filled reflection on the social reality strategizes how to transform the world), liberation theology added two important contributions, one at the macro level and another at the micro level, with both aimed at systemic transformation.

At the macro level liberation theology sought to change the entire social system of the industrial-capitalist periphery of Latin America. Implicitly, it appears from the literature, the desired transformation would be some revisionist form of socialism, presumably democratic and open to religion, and decentralist and communitarian in orientation – in contrast to the reigning state-centered models of nationalization required in the secular socialist and communist traditions.

Today, with hindsight, we might say that liberation theology's optimistic hopes for dramatic transformations proved naive, especially in the wake of the tens of thousands, perhaps hundreds of thousands, of Latin American victims of repression during the last three decades of the twentieth century. But naive optimism does not invalidate the mission of seeking fundamental systemic transformation; indeed, the need for fundamental transformation seems now more urgent than ever, though not as originally imagined in the framework of the early liberation theology movement.

At the micro level, liberation theology called socially committed disciples of Jesus to form basic Christian communities as a way of supporting themselves spiritually in the resistance against the system's interwoven economic exploitation, political repression, and cultural seduction, and also as a way of participating in the process of transformation. Here again the contribution met an obstacle, for the modern professionalized and clericalized form of the Catholic presbyterate was not able to provide adequate grassroots pastoral leadership for the proliferation of small Christian communities. As a result, postmodern recruitment to the small community model yielded more to the advances of evangelical and pentecostal churches, which did not hesitate to set up radically decentralized, deprofessionalized, and declericalized models of pastoral leadership. This was not the fault of liberation theologians but rather of the rigid ecclesial imagination of the Catholic church's episcopal leadership.

Roots in the lay Catholic Action Movement. Latin American liberation theology also grew out of the earlier and originally European lay Catholic Action movement by rendering it intellectually more sophisticated and prophetic and by radicalizing its famous 'see, judge, act' methodology.

As is widely known, the 'see, judge, act' methodology had been publicly articulated by the late Belgian Cardinal Joseph Cardijn, founder of the Young Christian Workers (YCW) movement, better known in the Romance languages as the JOC movement. Interestingly, Cardijn was always close to the international Pax Romana lay movement of Catholic Action, both before and after the 1925 foundation of YCW.

In this same vein Gustavo Gutiérrez, the acknowledged father of liberation theology, had been a chaplain for Pax Romana in Peru and still remains the official Pax Romana chaplain for Latin America. Similarly, Paulo Freire and the Basic Education movement in Brazil, out of which the first shoots of the basic Christian communities movement emerged, were all rooted in the Brazilian Catholic Action movement. One might even propose that the Brazilian Workers Party and the World Social Forum, also rooted in Brazil, were further developments of this energy, though no longer in confessionally Catholic form.

While the formula of 'see, judge, act' has generally been seen as an ingenious invention of Cardijn, Stefan Gignacz, a native Australian and now Malaysian-based YCW alumnus and lay canon lawyer, points out that Cardijn himself suggested that it had earlier roots but for some reason was always reticent about these roots. Gignacz, whose doctoral thesis at Louvain focused on this very area, argues that Cardijn's 'see, judge, act' method was actually a continuation of the work of the French lay Catholic democratic movement known as Le Sillon (the furrow), founded by Marc Sagnier, with even earlier roots in often marginalized Catholic lay movements and going back to the inspiration of prophetic lay figures like Fréderic Ozanam and also to the visionary but excommunicated French diocesan priest of the mid-nineteenth century Felicité de Lamennais.[2] It is interesting that Lamennais, perhaps the first person to use the phrase 'Christian democracy', also spoke of 'Christian socialism', albeit in a pre-Marxist sense of a general Christian commitment to the impoverished and exploited working class of early industrial capitalism.

Cardijn's reticence, Gignacz continues, was due to the fact that the Vatican had condemned Le Sillon, so Cardijn carefully and intentionally provided camouflage for continuation of its spirit within a new container. Cardijn's 'see, judge, act' formula was, according to Gignacz, his shorthand way of referring to methods of democratic education pioneered by Le Sillon in its campaign to promote study circles. Even Cardijn's notion of forming elite leaders drawn from the worker masses was based on the methods of Le Sillon. Apparently what was blocked in earlier generations finally succeeded under Cardijn's shrewd clerical leadership.

Roots in Catholic Social Teaching from 1740. But the three-step model of the pastoral circle seems also to have still older roots. Much to my surprise, in doing research for two volumes on the historical, philosophical, and theological development of Catholic social teaching in the papal encyclicals, I found the three-step method employed by the popes from the beginning of this tradition in 1740.[3]

Without spending any more time on this point, suffice it to note that the structure of papal social encyclicals from 1740 forward generally follows a three-step model quite similar to Cardijn's 'see, judge, act' method and to liberation theology's three moments of social analysis, theological reflection, and pastoral planning. These encyclicals typically begin with a diagnosis of the social problems confronting society and the church within it; they next move to retrieve from the faith tradition appropriate biblical and theological wisdom to evaluate these problems (generally viewed in negative terms); and finally, in light of this wisdom, they propose pastoral lines of strategy. The actual content of these three steps differs during different periods of the tradition, but the underlying methodology is constant.

Why, we might ask, do we find such commonality of method – albeit with differing contents; differing levels of sophistication; and differing sociological, theological, and pastoral orientations – across such a wide historical span of the Catholic tradition? In the next section I propose a response to that important question.

Catholic Appropriation of Aristotle's Phronesis

In a deeper philosophical sense the third and oldest source of the pastoral circle comes to Catholicism, I propose, from the African Islamic Aristotelian tradition in southern Spain, appropriated by Thomas Aquinas at the University of Paris in the thirteenth century. Up to that point the dominant philosophical tradition in Western Christian civilization had been Platonism or neo-Platonism, with Augustine of Hippo, of course, as the outstanding neo-Platonic theologian of the Christian tradition.

For Plato (at least for the traditional account of his texts[4]), truth was not discovered through investigation of the sensate material world, but rather through the rationalist intuition ('remembering' from a prior life of the soul outside the body) of abstract intellectual ideas, usually translated in English as 'forms'. The truth of these forms could then be ethically 'applied' from higher rational heights to the lower and limited material world of the particularities of time and space. Thus, for the Platonic tradition, ethics implicitly involves two methodological moments: (1) the articulation of moral 'axioms' (abstract 'values' or 'ideals') based on the intelligible forms; and (2) the application from above of these ideals to the less real world.

By contrast, for Aristotle the material world, known through the senses, was the only source of our knowledge, and so the search for abstract truth grew only out of concrete knowledge of the real world. In the realm of ethics Aristotle made a further distinction, not found in Plato, between theoretical reason and practical reason *(phronesis)*, with the latter involving less certitude and requiring prudential judgment. Thus, for the Aristotelian tradition, ethics implicitly involves three methodological moments: (1) rational-empirical study of reality; (2) articulation of general moral principles of right reason developed from knowledge of the reality; and (3) prudential recommendations on how to proceed in action according to right reason within reality.

There are many more dimensions of contrast between Platonic and Aristotelian ethics that could also be mentioned. For example, Aristotle proposed a communitarian understanding of the human person, claimed that the state is a natural institution rooted in the family and charged with developing virtuous citizens and with seeking the common good, and grounded ethics in the ways of nature (akin to the later Stoic tradition of natural law and today to the return to natural ecological wisdom) – all of which are found in the Catholic social-ethical tradition. By contrast, for Plato the human person was an autonomous individual who formed voluntary but rational social contacts, the state was the most powerful of these contracts and had as its purpose to enhance the economic division of labor and to restrain political evil, and the institution of the family was a concession to the masses but something elites should escape.

While the Platonic approach to social ethics is still found through Kantian variants in much of liberal Protestantism, and while in some ways the cultural project of the modern world may be seen in part as an outgrowth of a pervasive Platonic revival during the European Renaissance, the Aristotelian approach to social ethics has been dominant in Catholicism to some degree since the time of Aquinas and almost universally since the time of the Council of Trent.

Intriguing further developments in the Catholic social-ethical appropriation of Aristotle were achieved by early modern Spanish Scholastic theologians and activists as a critique of the Spanish *Conquista*. Those late Scholastics who took up the defense of the original peoples of the Americas (Native Americans) may well have planted key philosophical foundations for the subsequent legal justification of participatory democracy and for the defense of human rights. This historical period and these figures remain an important area for future research. But, to confirm the link back to liberation theology, let us at least note here that Gustavo Gutiérrez was so attracted to the greatest among the activists of this late Scholastic coalition, Bartolomé de Las Casas, that he produced a major study of his life and, like Las Casas, himself became a Dominican friar.

Conclusion

While it may have proven stimulating to reflect on the personal and historical roots of the pastoral circle, that stimulation itself grants us no fertility unless we set it against the horizon of fresh challenges in our emerging future. Elsewhere I have written more about the present global historical context and about my interpretation of the emerging postmodern era.[5] It is my sincere hope that other authors in this volume will address the issue of postmodernity, as well as other challenges for the future use of the pastoral circle, such as ethnicity, gender, and ecology.

Notes

1. It is important to note that while Catholic social teaching has been and remains deeply critical of capitalism, it is not thereby anti-business. Capitalism as a formal system is an experiment of only a few hundred years within the modern era of the human journey, and due to its undermining of ecological, societal, and spiritual sustainability, it increasingly appears to be a failed experiment. Business, by contrast, is thousands of years old and will continue, I propose, in the post-capitalist era to flourish, albeit in a more communitarian and ecological form.

2. Stefan Gignacz has summarized his analysis in ENEWS, the electronic journal of Pax Romana's Australian Catholic Movement for Intellectual and Cultural Affairs. Available at www.acmica.org.

3. Only the first in this two-part series has been published: Joe Holland, *Modern Catholic Social Teaching: The Popes Confront the Industrial Era, 1740–1958* (Mahwah, NJ: Paulist Press, 2003). It is important to note that papal social encyclicals do not begin in 1891 with *Rerum novarum*, though it provides the foundation for the strategic papal response to the second stage of industrial capitalism. Rather, they begin in 1740 with the popes' first strategic responses to the European Enlightenment with its new ideology of liberalism, and then later to its embodiment in liberal democracy and liberal capitalism.

4. There are current postmodernist readings of Plato that claim his apparent doctrines were actually the opposite of what he held and were sketched in a playful sense of paradox and irony. Whether or not these are accurate readings, and I myself have deep doubts about them, what is at stake is not Plato's actual

intentions but rather the dominant appropriation of Plato within classical Christian civilization. In that appropriation Plato's words were clearly taken at face value.

5. See Joe Holland, *The Regeneration of Ecological, Societal, and Spiritual Life: The Challenge to Humanity in the Emerging Postmodern Planetary Civilization* (Miami: Pax Romana Center for International Study of Catholic Social Teaching, 2003).

Ken Leech, 'Liturgy and Liberation'
in *The Sky is Red*, London: Darton, Longman & Todd, 2003, pp. 183–6.

Kenneth Leech, a British writer on spirituality and social justice, articulates the connections between a biblical call for justice and the corporate witness of the Church in the world as enacted in its liturgy, especially in the rites of Eucharist and Baptism. Liturgy is always rooted in everyday life and in the basic human needs of 'birth and death, washing and feeding' (p. 337), thereby reminding us of our physical and temporal existence. It must therefore avoid accusations of 'preciousness' or sanitization, and be contextual, risky and engaged, since its very embeddedness in such human activities is a part of its transformative power, because liturgy adopts such mundane routines and places them in a sacramental context, thereby rehearsing in ritual form what needs to be achieved in wider society.

Liturgy is a disciplined re-enactment of the drama of salvation, and becomes a ritual representation of God's redemptive activity in the world, a microcosm both of humanity in its broken (and 'messy') condition as well as humanity transformed in Christ. Far from being an other-worldly escape from the realities of social justice, Christian liturgy is an enactment in real time and real social relationships of God's alternative vision of the kingdom. Similarly, the enactment of the liturgy is an embodiment of a community's hope for a transformed world, in which its vision of God's love for creation and commitment to the equality and dignity of all persons is realized, however imperfectly.

The liturgy is something which is done. It has a life independent of the subjective states of those involved. Frederick Hastings Smyth even compared it to a laboratory experiment, and, while this aspect can be distorted and exaggerated, it is important to stress the objectivity of the liturgical action. This is not to equate liturgy with magic. Magic

locates divine efficacy outside the historical order. The Christian liturgy is a manifestation within historical time of the redemptive and
sanctifying power of God to transform human communities. However, it is vital to create conditions which make the performance of
the rite more authentic. Liturgical spirituality is rooted in human life.
The liturgy draws its central symbolism from human life – birth and
death, washing and feeding. It draws on impure materials and soiled
language. It has been said that the best liturgies are messy, indeed
that liturgical spirituality is only possible for those who are willing
to let life be messy, language impure and God dangerously close.[1]
Excessive tidiness, and the quest for purity and clarity, are alien to
symbolic and sacramental action.

At the present time, partly because of the one-dimensional nature
of much mainstream worship, there is a particular danger of the cult
of the powerful leader, be he (and it usually is a 'he') preacher, healer
or cultic guru. The saga of the Nine O'Clock Service in Sheffield,
which led to serious cases of sexual misconduct and exploitation,
brings out some central issues in the nature of worship: the danger of
reliance on a 'charismatic' leader, the likelihood of disintegration
and collapse if liturgy is disconnected from tradition, and yet paradoxically the importance and necessity of wildness and ecstasy in
worship. It is unwise to panic in the face of such serious abuses, or
to withdraw into a liturgical form which is safe and dull. (Sexual
abuse by the clergy is not exactly unknown among liturgical conserva-
tives!) How can these needs be reconciled? I believe only through
ascetical discipline, personal holiness, and a structured liturgical ethos.

One of the most ancient images in Christian spirituality is that of
'sober intoxication' – a phrase made memorable by St Ambrose in
one of his office hymns.

> *Laeti bibamus sobriam*
> *Ebrietatem Spiritus.*

'Let us joyfully drink of the sober inebriation of the Spirit.' In commenting on this, Stanley Evans described the Christian as a controlled
drunk, purposively intoxicated by the Holy Spirit.[2] The expression of
this in worship is really important, and, although it is filled with risks,
it is preferable to its opposite – the repressive boredom of the dull
and lifeless.

Christian liturgy is not an occasion for performance by some ego-
centric individual or for the experimentation in the latest trendy fad.
It is a social act, the expression of the faith and commitment of a

dedicated community. It is essentially a social act. This is something which has been particularly stressed by Anglican thinkers, and which is now being rediscovered elsewhere in the Christian world. The late John Robinson, when he was Dean of Clare College, Cambridge, pointed out how central was the liturgy to all Christian action in the world. The eucharistic action was the pattern of all Christian action, the germ of all society redeemed in Christ.[3] In the Eucharist we assert and enact our solidarity in Christ, our *koinonia* and common life in him. The eucharistic action undermines all pretentions of class and privilege – indeed, it is a powerful way of creating the kind of social unit which can resist them and destroy them.

The struggle against injustice in the Church has to be incorporated at the very heart of the liturgical life of the body. For example, I do not see how we can witness effectively against racism and social injustice by seeing these things simply as matters for justice sub-committees and boards for social responsibility. As long as this atti-tude prevails, they will always be tangential and peripheral to the central Christian task. The resistance to racism has to be located where it belongs: at the very heart of the liturgy, and specifically in the baptismal covenant. The degree of this commitment comes out best in liturgies from outside England – for example, in the American Book of Common Prayer. Here, during the rite of baptism, the candidate is asked:

> Do you renounce Satan and all the spiritual forces of wickedness that rebel against God?
> Do you renounce the evil powers of this world which corrupt and destroy the creatures of God?

A few minutes later the following questions are asked:

> Will you persevere in resisting evil, and, whenever you fall into sin, repent and return to the Lord?
> Will you seek and serve Christ in all persons, loving your neighbour as yourself?
> Will you strive for justice and peace among people, and respect the dignity of every human being?

In this baptismal renunciation and commitment, the Christian com-munity is formed, and regularly renewed, as a community of resist-ance. Just as the worship of ancient Israel was an act of 'doxology against idolatry and ideology',[4] so our witness is rooted in the adoration of the one true God who demands total obedience and who undermines the powers of this world. The liturgy is the heart of the protest against the disorder of the world.

References

1. Nathan Mitchell, 'The spirituality of Christian worship', *Spirituality Today* 34:1 (March 1982), pp. 5–17.
2. Stanley G. Evans, *The Social Hope of the Christian Church*, Hodder and Stoughton, 1965.
3. J. A. T. Robinson, *On Being the Church in the World*, SCM Press, 1964 edn, Chapter 3, 'Matter, power and liturgy'.
4. Walter Brueggemann, *Israel's Praise: Doxology against Idolatry and Ideology*, Minneapolis: Fortress Press, 1988.

Marjorie Procter-Smith, 'Feminist Ritual Strategies: the *Ekklesia Gynaikon* at Work'

in Fernando F. Segovia (ed.), *Toward a New Heaven and a New Earth: Essays in Honor of Elisabeth Schussler Fiorenza*, New York: Orbis, 2003, pp. 500–5, 511–12.

This extract continues the theme addressed in Ken Leech's text, of the role of liturgy in expressing and prefiguring social change. Here, it is concerned with the creation of liturgies and rituals as part of a wider Christian feminist strategy. Procter-Smith considers the relative neglect of the feminist liturgical movement, both within the wider Church and on the part of scholars. Yet even among practitioners, there is confusion over what makes a liturgy 'feminist', which crystallizes some important questions about the praxis model of theological reflection: if liturgy is seen as a means of transformation, then how is this actually achieved? Similarly, if its theological values are considered to be 'performative' then what criteria are used to judge its efficacy, both theological and strategic? What, then, constitutes a 'genuinely emancipatory' liturgy?

Procter-Smith's essay originally appeared in a book of essays dedicated to the feminist biblical scholar Elisabeth Schüssler-Fiorenza, and so it makes use of Fiorenza's concept of ekklesia gynaikon, often translated as 'woman-church'. Its vision of a renewed community of women and men refuses simply to invert or reproduce existing relationships of hierarchy. Instead, it works actively to articulate practices that will function to challenge patterns of exclusion. The liturgical and ritual practices of worship must connect with wider social realities, so that liturgy is not a refuge from social injustice but a vanguard for change. Feminist rituals thus become sites of 'feminist emancipatory strategies' (Procter-Smith, 2003, p. 511), by embodying within the ekklesia gynaikon *the kinds of relationships and values that will enable true and lasting transformation to take place: the relegation of women into a 'private' or domestic sphere; the authority of the sole voice rather than multiple perspectives; the development of practices of dissent; and, last but not least, strategies that 'embody equality'. In the practical context of such transformative liturgy is planted the seeds of change. Ritual is not an evasion of problematic relationships therefore, but a necessary part of overcoming them by creating alternative spaces for imagining new kinds of arrangements.*

The Feminist Liturgical Movement

For some thirty years now, feminists have been engaged in the process of creating religious rituals and liturgies.[1] This represents a substantial amount of work, reflected in the publication of collections of feminist prayers, hymns, and other liturgical and ritual materials as well as the beginnings of descriptive and analytical assessments of this work. Beginning in the early 1970s, Jewish and Christian feminists challenged the liturgical hegemony of ecclesiastical power structures and claimed their own liturgical authority. Born out of the struggles of the women's liberation movement, the feminist liturgical movement has as its aim the emancipation of women from the constraints placed on them in church and in society. Although the liturgical work of feminists in biblical religions is generated in diverse settings and among groups of women claiming differing identities, common trends in practice have been readily identified.

This considerable body of work as well as the liturgical innovations it represents, however, continues to go largely unregarded by scholars of contemporary religious movements and trends, whether those scholars approach the subject of contemporary worship practices from the perspective of social analysis or of liturgical developments. Studies of new religious movements fail to note the existence of feminist liturgy groups. Liturgical researchers address issues of cultural context or the needs of contemporary worshipers with scarcely a glance at the feminist critique of traditional worship.[2] And those concerned with analyzing and prescribing cures for the drop in numbers of mainline Protestant churchgoers pay not the slightest

attention to the withdrawal of full support by women and their formation of groups that exist on the periphery or even entirely outside the
bounds of institutional churches. This withdrawal of women from
full support of mainline churches in North America has been well
researched – and by feminist researchers, I hardly need add.[3] Yet, far
from addressing the issues being raised by feminist liturgical groups,
many mainline churches have taken a retrograde position of
attempting to resolve the decline in membership by reiterating or in
some cases attempting to return to conservative or even fundamentalist positions, especially regarding women's roles.

While such silence and disregard are at least in part indicative of
the continuing marginalization of women and women's concerns in
the church and academy generally, they also suggest that feminist
ritualizing has not yet achieved the 'claiming the center' that is necessary to effect substantive change.[4] Until very recently, the feminist
liturgical movement within Christianity and Judaism has proceeded
on a pragmatic and exploratory basis. Earlier work – including most
of my own – has engaged in constructive creation of feminist ritual
practices, in the summarizing of those practices, or in proposals for
the creation of yet more feminist ritual practices. This is probably a
necessary sequence of approaches to feminist ritualizing in general
and to Christian and Jewish feminist liturgy in particular. Feminist
liturgical construction has developed as part of a social movement as
well as in response to the changes in religious women's consciousness
as a result of the feminist movement. Thus, its roots lie in a matrix
of social practice rather than theoretical speculation.

It is also appropriate, thirty years into the feminist liturgical movement, to step back and examine the implications of these processes
of ritual construction, summary, and proposal, to discover what has
been learned about ritual process as well as to discover what remains
to be done. It is time to address theoretical questions: What is feminist
liturgy? What makes a ritual feminist? What does such a ritual aim
to accomplish, and how does it accomplish it?

Descriptions of common characteristics of feminist liturgy abound.
Although these descriptions differ in the arrangement or categoriz-
ation of the practices observed, a surprising degree of consistency
emerges.[5] To date, most of the data have been collected from experiences of North American and northern European feminist groups.
Although these are variously named 'principles', 'marks', 'starting
points', or 'characteristics', they are always understood to derive from
observation of or participation in the practice of creating and performing feminist liturgies. We can summarize them as follows:

1. Shared, egalitarian leadership and relationships preferred over hierarchical forms
2. Circular and horizontal patterns (in spatial arrangements, movement, etc.) preferred over vertical patterns
3. Interconnections with the natural world valued over human mastery or demonization of nonhuman nature
4. Emphasis on women's experiences, lives, relationships, empowerment, and liberation
5. Critique (explicit or implicit) of patriarchal liturgical practices that marginalize, omit, silence, or limit women

These characteristics beg the question of the student in my feminist liturgy class, 'What makes them feminist?' If we understand them to reflect 'woman-identification', why are these characteristics or principles associated with women? In part, these ritual practices reflect a form of resistance against patriarchal religious and liturgical practices. Such resistance is central to feminist Christian commitment. However, resistance against certain forms of oppression or suppression can have the apparently paradoxical effect of reinforcing the very patterns one intends to resist. Thus, Teresa Berger argues, 'The Women's Liturgical Movement embodies practices of resistance to traditional liturgical genderization, not by abdicating the category gender, but by making gender a crucial determinant of new liturgical practices'.[6] While not convinced that gender is as necessarily central to feminist liturgical practices as Berger suggests, I do agree that the patterns chosen for feminist ritualizing often replicate patriarchal gendered dichotomies. Patriarchal dichotomies associate women with nature, relationships, and mutual sharing. Moreover, such dichotomizing tendencies have the effect of strengthening their appearance of inevitability; as Elisabeth Schüssler Fiorenza puts it, 'Insofar as Euro-American feminist discourses have tended to valorize women and femininity over against men and masculinity, they have reproduced this androcentric symbolic construction of male-female gender polarity and compulsory heterosexuality that are constitutive of the patriarchal order'.[7]

Ritual theorist Catherine Bell argues that ritualization involves the creation and maintenance of oppositional, hierarchical structures that demand a process of resistance and accommodation: 'Any ideology is always in dialogue with, and thus shaped and constrained by, the voices it is suppressing, manipulating, echoing'.[8] Thus, it can be argued that feminist liturgies often employ ritual strategies that have the effect of reinforcing the ideology they intend to resist, much in the same way that my students found themselves unable to conceive of a way of ritualizing that did not involve investing in cultural stereotypical assumptions about women. This does not seem to be so much paradoxical, as Berger argues, as ultimately self-defeating. Berger argues for the 'destabilization of the subject "woman".'[9] But it is difficult to see how the emancipation of an oppressed group can be brought about by the 'destabilization' of the group itself. Berger rightly points out that, within Western patriarchal ordering, 'woman' as a category has not always included all women. This suggests not a destabilization of the term but an expansion of it, to include women who have not been included in the patriarchal category of women. Any feminist framework must take this demand into account if it claims to have as its objective the emancipation of women.

How then is it possible to create feminist ritual practices, within a Christian context with a long history of restrictions of women's liturgical practice, that not only disrupt patriarchal ideologies but replace them with emancipatory and egalitarian practices? Clearly, a feminist framework that moves beyond sex-gender dualism is required in order to found feminist ritual strategies that are genuinely emancipatory. For such a framework, we may turn to the critical feminist theology of liberation of Elisabeth Schüssler Fiorenza.

Toward a Critical Feminist Emancipatory Theology of Liturgy[10]

To date, liturgical theology in general has taken little notice of the substantial work of liberation theologians.[11] On the other hand, feminist liturgical practices are often indebted to the work of feminist theologians, especially in biblical studies and constructive theology.[12] However, there is considerable diversity within feminist theology; indeed, it is more accurate to refer to feminist theologies, in the plural. In order to address the issues already raised, however, I will draw substantially from Schüssler Fiorenza's approach.

A critical feminist theology of liberation, as set out by Schüssler Fiorenza, is best understood as part of the feminist movement for the political and social emancipation of women. Likewise, the feminist liturgical movement is also best understood as an aspect of the feminist movement, directed toward the emancipation of women in Christian (and Jewish) worship. Thus, a feminist emancipatory liturgical theology first must take seriously the social and political as well as religious contexts in which women live their lives, and second must engage in critical assessment of those conditions. It cannot concern itself with questions of language, access to ordination, reconstruction of religious symbols, and so forth, apart from attention to the wider social, political, educational, and cultural dimensions of women's struggles. A feminist emancipatory liturgical theology points beyond the immediate liturgical context. It is naturally focused on issues of language, symbol, and leadership in the same way that feminist biblical scholarship concerns itself with biblical texts. As a critical feminist liberation approach to biblical texts demands attention to the uses of the texts and their potential for harm or for good in human lives, especially the lives of women, so also a critical emancipatory liturgical theology attends to the consequences of liturgical forms and practices with a view to their potential for creating and sustaining the liberation and well-being of all people. This primary commitment to social change distinguishes feminist liturgical theology from other forms of liturgical theology.

Commitment to social change demands critical attention to and assessment of oppressive social contexts. Feminist theory and analysis have identified the social structures of patriarchy as central to this critique. Yet definitions of patriarchy differ. An understanding of patriarchy that sees it as a social system in which all women are dominated by all men takes into account only the sex/gender dualism basic to patriarchal structures. It fails to account for complex social contexts in which some women exercise domination over some men, or other women. It erases the interplay of other complicating factors such as race, ethnicity, age, sexual identity, class, ability, and other oppressive relationships. By limiting the focus of the critique to sex-gender relationships, such theories render women of color and other oppressed groups invisible. Furthermore, such an approach to patriarchal structures, even while attempting to critique them, in fact reinforces them. Schüssler Fiorenza sums this up succinctly, drawing attention also to the way in which this interpretation naturalizes gender dualism:

> Oppositional discourses, such as feminist theory or theology, are never independent of their dominant discourses and patriarchal societies and institutions. On the contrary, they are inextricably and inevitably intertwined with them as long as they labor under the terms of those dominant discursive formations . . . In collusion with dominant patriarchal ideology, such oppositional discourses on the feminine make us think that, like race, sex is a 'natural category'. Thus both gender and race differences become 'common sense' and they 'feel real' for most people.[13]

Instead of this sex-gender model of patriarchal structures, Schüssler Fiorenza proposes the term 'kyriarchy', 'rule of the master', in order to draw attention to patriarchy as a 'pyramid of multiplicative oppressions', rather than simply the rule of men over women. Schüssler Fiorenza argues that this is best understood by drawing on the logic of classical patriarchy 'as a complex pyramidal political structure of dominance and subordination, stratified by gender, race, class, religious and cultural taxonomies and other historical formations of domination'.[14] Thus patriarchy, or more accurately kyriarchy, establishes and supports not only male domination but also white supremacy, class privilege, and religious intolerance. In light of this analysis, a critical feminist theology must articulate a vision of community in which the kyriarchal structures that divide women are not ignored or minimized, but are taken seriously. It must also be able to articulate a vision of feminist community that enables political and religious collaborations across these divisions, with the common aim of creating a just world that is safe for women and all oppressed people.

A feminist emancipatory liturgical theology that is built on this foundation must understand its task as creating and sustaining the real (not theoretical) communities in which these difficult conversations and hopeful collaborations can take place. It must recognize that taking up an oppositional position relative to patriarchal religious groups and practices inevitably engages it in sustaining the system it opposes. Feminist liturgical practices that resist patriarchal sex-gender dichotomies by attempting to valorize the feminine side of the dichotomy can only replicate kyriarchal domination, in part because these practices reinforce the dichotomy, in part because engagement in the dichotomous structure erases women of color and anyone who suffers from oppression that cannot be defined by the sex-gender system. Thus, these practices can function only to reinforce race and class privilege by offering white, educated women spiritualized support that does not challenge that privileged world. Feminist emancipatory liturgical theology requires that we avoid reinforcing kyriarchal structures by taking a critical stance toward our own feminist liturgical traditions and practices as well as the practices of the patriarchal church. We must take seriously our commitment to 'sisterhood', not in the abstract but in reality, by recognizing the community of all women, especially the women absent from our feminist gatherings and from whose oppression women of privilege benefit. If feminist liturgical practices are to disrupt patriarchal dichotomies, we must be willing also to disrupt those that benefit some women at the expense of others. It must be admitted that the feminist liturgical movement has not always been willing or able to make room for this theological self-understanding. A new approach to feminist ritualizing is needed.

. . .

The Ekklēsia Gynaikōn at Work

The creation of what Chandra Talpadi Mohanti calls 'imagined community' or the theorizing of the *ekklēsia gynaikōn* 'as a site of feminist struggles for transforming societal and religious institutions' requires moving from the imagination to the body, from theorizing to actualizing.[15] For this, feminist emancipatory strategies of ritual practice are required. Although the contextual character of ritual practice in general and the intentional contextuality of feminist liturgical practice in particular prevent the production of fixed forms or even abstract principles, it is possible to identify strategies that can be understood to be the *leitourgia* of the *ekklēsia gynaikōn*.

Perhaps the most significant and difficult strategy suggested by the foregoing exploration is to make visible the arbitrary oppositional and oppressive kyriarchal structures that otherwise appear to be inevitable and 'natural'. The development of specific strategies to make oppressive structures visible and to expose the arbitrary nature of 'commonsense' assumptions will depend on context. An essential place to begin is the development of strategies that overcome the public/private dichotomy that assigns the private sphere to women and thus to women's ritualizing practices.

A second necessity is the development of ritual strategies that make room for multiple voices rather than the imposition of the single voice. Liturgically, this means developing ritual strategies that do not depend on the single or the unison voice but allow for heteroglossia.[16] Not until all voices can be heard, all social locations and cultural experiences included, can the *ekklēsia gynaikōn* be realized. Strategies that enable this employment of many voices make up its *leitourgia*.

A related strategy is the development of liturgical practices of dissent. Traditional and even some feminist liturgical practices make no allowance for expressing dissent, assuming unanimity of perspective. Yet, within the *ekklēsia gynaikōn*, understood as the space for the struggle toward radical democracy within the multiplicative oppressions of kyriarchy, dissent is inevitable. It is important that this be understood precisely as dissent, and not difference, since the notion of dissent draws attention to power differentials, whereas the language of difference obscures them. Liturgical practices that make room for dissent make explicit the otherwise hidden power relationships and give voice to the struggle against disempowerment.

Strategies that embody equality are also necessary. This is especially important not only for the disruption of hierarchical dichotomies common in culture and sanctified in religion but also because of the oppositional character of ritual itself. Liturgical practices of equality are not possible without liturgical practices that allow for dissent. Suppression of dissent renders equality impossible. Strategies of radical democratic equality make room for competing visions of the truth that can be articulated and embodied in the process of creating *ekklēsia gynaikōn*.

Development of such strategies will, for Christian communities, necessitate engaging practices of feminist ritualizing in conversation with Christian symbols, images, and traditional practices, subjecting them not only to critique but also constantly evaluating them in light of the struggles of women against patriarchy in its many guises. This process in turn demands the development of feminist spiritual discernment. By this term I do not have in mind a practice limited to an elite group or individual but a process of prayerful attention by the *ekklēsia gynaikōn* to the accumulated and conflicting experiences of Christian ritual practice. Especially, a process of feminist spiritual discernment must include attentiveness to what the ritualized body knows as well as what it does not know.

Notes

1. The earliest publication of feminist liturgies was A. Swidler, *Sistercelebrations* (Philadelphia: Fortress Press, 1974). For a review of some of the early history of the feminist liturgical movement, see Procter-Smith, *In Her Own Rite: Constructing Feminist Liturgical Tradition* (Nashville: Abingdon Press, 1990): 18–25; 2nd edition (Akron, OH: OSL Press, 2000), pp. 6–13. For more recent developments within the movement, see the Preface to the second edition, *In Her Own Rite*, 2000, pp. ii–x.

2. A significant exception to this is Robert F. Taft ('A Generation of Liturgy within the Academy', *Worship* 75 [2001], p. 51), who includes the work of feminist studies in theology in his review of the field of liturgical studies. However, he does not note the lack of integration between feminist liturgical studies and the rest of the field.

3. For early evidence of this phenomenon, see R. Radford Ruether, *Women-Church: Theology and Practice of Feminist Liturgical Communities* (San Francisco: Harper & Row, 1985). For recent research on the strained relationship between women and mainline Christianity in North America, see A. T. Lummis,

A. Stokes, and M. T. Winter, *Defecting in Place: Women Claiming Responsibility for Their Own Spiritual Lives* (New York: Crossroad, 1995).

4. For an early working out of this approach, see Procter-Smith, *In Her Own Rite*, 1990, pp. 147–48 (2000, pp. 134–35).

5. For discussion and other ways of listing characteristics, see T. Berger, *Women's Ways of Worship: Gender Analysis and Liturgical History* (New York: Pueblo Press, 1999), pp. 122–43; M. Collins, 'Principles of Feminist Liturgy,' in *Women at Worship*, ed. Procter-Smith and Walton, pp. 17–24; M. Procter-Smith, 'Marks of Feminist Liturgy,' *Proceedings of the North American Academy of Liturgy* (1992): 69–75; L. Northup, *Ritualizing Women: Patterns of Spirituality* (Cleveland: Pilgrim Press, 1997), pp. 28–52; G. Catalano Mitchell and G. Anderson Ricciuti, *Birthings and Blessings: Liberating Worship Services for the Inclusive Church* (New York: Crossroad, 1991), pp. 13–15.

6. Berger, *Women's Ways of Worship*, p. 144.

7. E. Schüssler Fiorenza, 'Spiritual Movements of Transformation?' in *Defecting in Place*, p. 222.

8. C. Bell, *Ritual Theory, Ritual Practice* (New York/Oxford: Oxford University Press, 1992), p. 191.

9. Berger, *Women's Ways of Worship*, p. 147.

10. This section is deeply indebted to the work of Elisabeth Schüssler Fiorenza, especially the exposition of her theology as laid out in *But She Said: Feminist Practices of Biblical Interpretation* (Boston: Beacon Press, 1992). The ideas I take up here, however, are found in many places throughout Schüssler Fiorenza's publications.

11. A notable exception is B. T. Morrill, *Anamnesis as Dangerous Memory: Political and Liturgical Theology in Dialogue* (New York: Pueblo Press, 2000).

12. The work of Elizabeth J. Smith (*Bearing Fruit in Due Season: Feminist Hermeneutics and the Bible in Worship* [New York: Pueblo Press, 1999]) is a particularly good example of this influence.

13. Schüssler Fiorenza, *But She Said*, p. 113.

14. Ibid., p. 115.

15. Schüssler Fiorenza, *But She Said*, p. 130.

16. For a more complete development of this idea, see Procter-Smith, *Praying with Our Eyes Open*, pp. 30–39.

Eden Grace, 'An Introduction to Quaker Business Practice'

World Council of Churches, available online at
http://www.wcc-coe.org/wcc/who/damascuspost-03-e.html and
http://www.edengrace.org/quakerbusiness.html

Eden Grace's discussion of standard Quaker practice occurs within the context of an ecumenical discussion of the World Council of Churches about the nature of church governance, and may be read as something of an apologia on behalf of the Society of Friends. Grace is acting as an advocate of her tradition's approach to decision-making, and its potential for other Christian traditions, by stressing its essentially theological identity. As Eden Grace says, 'To ask a Quaker to describe the Meeting for Business is to ask for a testimony of the core of our faith': all activities, no matter how routine or bureaucratic, are forms of theology-in-action, or living testaments to their core principles.

It is no surprise that Quakers therefore refuse the distinction between 'worship' and 'business' (or, by inference, spirituality and politics, sacred and secular) since everything is governed by the same principles. In particular, Quaker meetings for worship do not represent a withdrawal from worldly matters, but are a form of performative act of witness to the way in which all aspects of life are imbued with, and transformed by, the presence of the divine.

These principles are above all experiential and democratic: just as the activity of shared worship is one of attending to the movement of the Spirit within all people, regardless of worldly status, so too business is conducted according to the conviction that Truth is to be discovered through careful attendance to that of the divine within everyone. Yet, as Grace acknowledges, this has been developed in dialogue with a process of distilling these core principles into a guiding discipline by which proper discernment might be judged. But right conduct, both in devotion and business, is regarded as an essential and authentic mark of godly community.

This paper is intended as an introduction to how Quakers make decisions, and why we do it that way. The hope is that this perspective might be helpful to the Special Commission as it asks these questions of the WCC's own process. In offering this introduction, I speak, as is the custom among Friends, from my own experience of the Divine truth as I have received it and without any authority to speak officially for the Religious Society of Friends. My experience is as an American Friend, and I offer here a reflection on the practice used by American and European Friends. Friends all over the world have discovered the ways that Quaker practice speaks to their condition. I hope that my contribution can be supplemented in the future by contributions from non-western Quakers, and that a richer picture might thus emerge which could be of even greater use to the World Council of Churches.

The first comment to make about Quaker business practice is that it is of central importance to Friends. It is rooted in our deepest theological affirmations, and is one of our highest spiritual experiences. To ask a Quaker to describe the Meeting for Business is to ask for a testimony of the core of our faith. Therefore I will need to start here with some basic theological affirmations, and then proceed to draw their implications for decision-making.

The primary theological doctrine and spiritual experience of Friends is that the living Christ is present to teach us Himself. No priestly intermediary is necessary for Divine access, for 'there is One, Christ Jesus, who can speak to thy condition.'[1] Rooted in such texts as John's prologue, Quakers believe that the Light of Christ is given in some measure to all people. This experience of the immediate presence of Christ, both personally and corporately, implies that we may be led by the Inward Teacher. Since Christ is not divided, the nearer we come to Him, the nearer we will be to one another. Thus the sense of being led into Unity with one another becomes a fundamental mark of the Divine work in the world.

Based on this theology, Friends commit themselves to discovering and implementing the will of God. This is the purpose of the Quaker Meeting for Business. 'Since our method of transacting business presumes that in a given matter there is a way that is in harmony with God's plan, our search is for that right way, and not simply for a way which is either victory for some faction, or an expedient compromise.'[2] What we call 'the Sense of the Meeting' is not the collected wisdom of those present, but the collective discernment of God's will. There is no place for activities such as motions, seconds, amendments and votes in our process of collective discernment. Our bold affirmation is that God does indeed have a will for us, that God is actively trying to communicate that will, and that we are capable, through corporate prayer, to discover that will. A sign that we have achieved our goal of discerning God's will is the experience of Unity which is recognized and affirmed by those gathered.

Quakers profess a theocratic understanding of authority. 'The primary authority is that of God, as the God whose will is sought, as Christ who presides, and as the Holy Spirit who inspires and empowers. Thus the task of the meeting is to listen in worship, putting itself under that authority, to discern the right way forward on any piece of business.'[3] All human leadership is subordinated to the authority of Christ, the true shepherd of any gathering of Christians. All participants in the Meeting are equally capable of being used by the Holy Spirit, and those who moderate the Meeting are seen as servants of the gathering discernment process.

A Quaker Meeting for Business is conducted in the context of worship, and with the same expectant waiting upon the Spirit as in the Meeting for Worship. The Business Meeting begins and ends with periods of open worship, and an atmosphere of reverence and devotion is maintained throughout the Meeting. Each contribution to the discussion is heard in a spirit of prayer. As the spiritual momentum grows and the movement of Christ is felt among us, we experience the Gathered Meeting, in which we are gathered into Unity with Christ and become of one heart and mind.

Quakers do not practise the outward ritual of Eucharist in our worship, but seek rather to experience and celebrate the inward spiritual participation in Christ's death and resurrection which comes from being raised up together into Unity in God. 'We believe that a corporate practice of the presence of God, a corporate knowledge of Christ in our midst, a common experience of the work of the Spirit, constitute the supremely real sacrament of a Holy Communion.'[4] In the experience of Quakers, the Meeting for Business is one of the deepest occasions for this 'eucharistic' event. Thus the spiritual depth of the Meeting is cherished and upheld throughout. 'The right conduct of Business Meetings, even in routine matters, is important to the spiritual life of all. Care must be taken that the enduring value of a spiritual community is not sacrificed to the immediate goal of action.'[5]

'Consensus' is a word sometimes used to describe a Quaker-like process. Yet Quakers would insist that this is not the most suitable term. Consensus (or unanimous consent, or general agreement) are [sic] based on the work of human wisdom and reason, whereas 'the Sense of the Meeting' is based on the prompting of the Spirit. Consensus is commonly understood to require mutual compromise – shaving away at positions until we find a core which is objectionable to none. The Quaker approach tries instead to reach toward a higher and greater Truth that speaks to all concerns in ways that could not have been foreseen. We discover what God wants for us, as opposed to what we thought we wanted. 'Consensus is the product of an intellectual process. Sense of the Meeting is a commitment of faith.'[6] This difference is more than semantic. In resisting the word 'consensus' we refuse to allow our Sacrament to become secularized. Preferred terms would be 'Unity' or 'Sense of the Meeting'. The latter emphasizes the goal for the Gathered Meeting, and the former evokes the core theological affirmation of God's will for humanity.

I will freely admit that a Quaker Meeting for Business is vulnerable to abuse. Those who do not enter the process in a right spirit can seriously jeopardize the Meeting. In order for the Meeting to function, the members must share a commitment to a spiritual discipline. This discipline is cultivated rather than regulated, and it takes time to acquire. There is no official list of rules, although each Yearly Meeting (autonomous Quaker church) has a book of discipline which gives guidance on the spirit and practice of the Meeting for Business. Some elements of the discipline are:

- attitude toward God: We enter into the Business Meeting with hearts and minds prepared to be led by the Holy Spirit. We renew our commitment to Divine authority and our belief that the living Christ is present this day to teach and lead us. We submit to Divine will and seek to lay our own strong feelings and desires before God.
- attitude toward the other members: Our process places a high value on the strength of the community. A Sense of the Meeting is only achieved when those participating respect and care for one another. It requires a humble and loving spirit, imputing purity of motive to all participants and offering our highest selves in return. We seek to create a safe space for sharing. We pray that we might listen carefully, respectfully, lovingly. We listen always for the presence of God through what someone is saying, knowing that each of us is endowed with some measure of Divine Light. The creation of the blessed community is both a necessary prerequisite and an inevitable by-product of corporate discernment. While this is most easily accomplished at the local level, where members are already known to each other, it has been our experience that, when we ask the Lord's help, deep Christian community can form even among strangers.
- attitude toward the process: We value process over product, action or outcome. We respect each other's thoughts, feelings and insights more than expedient action. The process of reaching a decision yields more 'results' than the decisions themselves. Attention to the Divine movement in the community is, in fact, the source of decision and action, so that process and outcome are ideally two sides of the same Sacramental experience. Through that experience of the Unity of the Meeting, we are prepared for faithful discipleship in the church and world. A decision which is made without that experience is of little value.
- attitude toward potential outcomes: We know that none of us is likely to enter the Meeting with a fully-formed understanding of the will of God, and so we expect that a new way will emerge which is not necessarily identified with the position of any person or faction. '. . . a group, meeting in the right spirit, may be given greater insight than any single person.'[7] 'A gathered meeting under the authority of God is often able to find unity in creative ways which were not considered before the meeting but which become

apparent during its course. Though the process of Quaker business may take some time, at the end it can find a united meeting able to act swiftly because the action has been widely agreed.'[8]

- commitment to the authority of the meeting: All authority rests in God. Once the Meeting has discerned God's will as best it can at that moment in time, the decision of the Meeting is vested with a measure of Divine authority. Decisions are not 'revisited' by staff, clerks or committees. Those who were not present accept the decision of the Meeting. This is not to say that the Meeting's decisions have ultimate authority, since our discernment is never free of human imperfection. The Meeting itself can always revisit decisions, and new light may be found.

- role of human leadership: The Meeting is served by a Presiding Clerk, and often also a Recording Clerk. Friends are appointed for a limited time, and these roles are widely shared among the membership. The Clerks have no formal authority of their own and can not speak for the Meeting. Their task is to focus and enable the discernment of the Meeting by laying business before it in an orderly way, managing the pace and discipline of the discussion, listening for the Sense of the Meeting to emerge, restating that Sense in clear language and asking for approval, and recording the business in written minutes. The Clerks develop the agenda and discern whether an issue is ripe for consideration by the Meeting or needs further seasoning by a committee. The Clerks are responsible for judging the 'weight' of each comment by discerning the movement of the Spirit in the Meeting, rather than developing a tally of opinions pro and con. The Clerks are servants of the Meeting and not participants in the discussion. On rare occasion, when a Clerk finds that he or she must speak to an item of business, a replacement Clerk must be found until that item is concluded. Thus we avoid the temptation to assign any authority to human figures which would obscure our utter dependence on the authority of God.

- role of written minutes: The Clerk makes sure the Meeting understands what is being approved by stating it in clear language which is written down, read back, discussed and approved by the Meeting at the time the decision is made. The minutes, once approved, become authoritative. They are kept and referred to indefinitely. Thus minutes and minute-taking are crucial to the process, and are seen as a weighty spiritual practice rather than clerical function.

- preparing an item of business: Generally, the Business Meeting benefits from having items seasoned beforehand by a committee. The committee usually brings the item with a recommendation, but even if it does not, it should have done some work on preparing the item and anticipating various questions and concerns.

- personal conduct: We usually only speak once to each item. We only speak when recognized by the Clerk. We don't plan messages ahead of time, but listen instead to the movement of the Spirit and pray for guidance as to whether we are being led to speak. We fully expect that our message may not be needed, as God may have empowered another individual to offer the same insight. We do not offer redundant messages, since the Sense of the Meeting is not discerned by a tally of opinions. We pray continuously for the Meeting and its Clerks. Friends often find the Meeting for Business to be a purgative, humbling and awe-inspiring experience as we let go of our own self and personal agenda. Although the Meeting is a solemn event, humor is sometimes appropriate and helpful. We refrain from comments which suggest argument, debate or an attempt to convince, and rather give testimony to our experience of the leading of the Spirit in this matter. We listen thoughtfully and respectfully, observing a pause between messages for deeper listening. Each person present has a responsibility to participate and not hold back if they are led to speak. Every member of the church has the responsibility to attend the Business Meeting to the extent they are able.
- on dissent: 'If an individual differs from what appears to be the general sense of the Meeting, it may be taken as a sign that the Divine will has not quite been grasped.'[9] The Meeting should be especially sensitive to sincere expressions of difference from the growing Unity. These may indicate that the Meeting has not truly listened to God's prompting among us. When a Friend feels he or she must 'stand in the way' of Unity, the Meeting and the Friend will patiently labor together in hopes of coming to a truer understanding of God's will. However, individuals do not hold a power of veto, and should be ready to recognize the validity of corporate leadings and to submit to them if conscience allows, being recorded in the minutes as 'standing aside'. While we boldly profess a spirituality of unmediated relationship with the Divine, we are always mindful of how the human person is, in fact, already a mediating force. Our own past experience, our fears, our sin, and the influence of our cultural context, can all obscure our discernment of God's will. The presence of dissent and discord in the Meeting is therefore

always an occasion for prayer, repentance and conversion by the whole Meeting.

- on time: Quaker decision making takes time. We can not allow ourselves to be hurried. A sense of urgency or pressure can quickly erode a process of deep seeking. We don't impose a deadline for making any decision. If Unity is not reached in one Meeting, the matter is laid over.

- on not finding the sense of the meeting: We take no action until there is Unity on taking action. Thus the Quaker process is essentially a conservative process in that respect. Things stay the same until we are in Unity on changing them.

Friends would not claim to have perfected this process, or that we always practice it with complete faithfulness. What I've described in this paper is Quaker process in its ideal form. Most Friends are painfully aware of how humans falls short of the spiritual ideal, and of how fragile our process can seem. Corporate discernment of the will of God is a risky and imperfect proposition. In relying so extensively on the Holy Spirit, we make ourselves vulnerable to pitfalls and failures. However, far from being a weakness, such vulnerability is central to our understanding of the power of worship (and business) 'in spirit and in truth'. To fall into the hands of the living God requires leaping, laying ourselves open to risk. Our commitment to this process, and our assurance of its outcomes, can only be proven in the eschaton, but still we give testimony to the truth we have been given, and are able to say that we have tested this method and found it that it does indeed bring us into Unity with the will of God.

More could certainly be said about how Quakers make decisions, and I hope others will supplement this paper with their own contributions. It is exciting to Friends that the World Council of Churches is looking at models of decision making in hopes of developing one which is less conflict-based and more spiritually grounded. Quakers believe that we hold our process in trust for the whole Church, and now may be a time to share it. I hope that my contribution here has been faithful to the gift I have been given, and that it will prove helpful to the Special Commission as it continues to discern God's will for the future of the World Council of Churches.

Sources

- Brinton, Howard, *Guide to Quaker Practice*, Pendle Hill Pamphlet 20, Wallingford, PA: Pendle Hill Publications, 1955.
- *Faith and Practice of New England Yearly Meeting of Friends* [NEYM F&P], Worcester MA: New England Yearly Meeting, 1985.
- Morley, Barry, *Beyond Consensus: Salvaging Sense of the Meeting*, Pendle Hill Pamphlet 307, Wallingford PA: Pendle Hill Publications, 1993.
- Nuhn, Ferner, *Friends and the Ecumenical Movement*, Philadelphia PA: Friends General Conference, 1970.
- Sheeran SJ, Michael J., *Beyond Majority Rule: Voteless Decisions in the Religious Society of Friends*, Philadelphia: Philadelphia Yearly Meeting, 1983.
- Scott, Janet, 'Worship in the Religious Society of Friends (Quakers)', manuscript submitted as a study document for the Faith & Order Commission of the WCC, 1998.
- Scott, Janet, 'Business Meetings' manuscript submitted for inclusion in the forthcoming Dictionary of the Religious Society of Friends, 1999.

Notes

1. George Fox, founder of the Religious Society of Friends in the 1650s.

2. Thomas Brown, *Faith and Practice of New England Yearly Meeting of Friends* (hereafter NEYM F&P), p. 117.

3. Janet Scott, 'Business Meetings' manuscript.

4. From a Quaker position paper written and offered by the three Quaker delegates to the Lausanne Conference on Faith and Order in 1927. This paper, which tried to explain the Quaker position on sacraments and the non-use of outward elements, became the center of a heated debate on whether Quakers could be considered Christian, and more broadly on the matter of religious liberty. The question was finally determined by Bishop Charles Gore of the Church of England with his statement 'God is not limited by His sacraments', see Ferner Nuhn, *Friends and the Ecumenical Movement*, Philadelphia PA: Friends General Conference, 1970, p. 19–22.

5. NEYM F&P, p. 222.

6. Barry Morley, PHP, p. 5.

7. George Selleck, NEYM F&P, p. 116.

8. Janet Scott, 'Business Meetings' manuscript.

9. George Selleck, NEYM F&P, p. 116.

Elaine Graham, 'Pastoral Theology as Transforming Practice'

in S. Pattison and J. W. Woodward (eds), *Blackwell Reader in Practical and Pastoral Theology*, Oxford: Blackwell, 2000, pp. 106–10, 111–13.

This summary of the main arguments of Transforming Practice *represents one of the most influential examples of the 'turn to performativity' within contemporary practical theology. Graham argues that the discipline has been over-preoccupied with therapeutic or ministerial activity at the expense of articulating the core theological principles at the heart of faithful practice.*

The position spelled out at the start of Transforming Practice *is summarized here, as follows: Western culture lives in an age that has become aware that categories of being and knowing, which once seemed certain, solid and ontological, have been shaken. A comforting sense of the world undergirded by a consensus of axiomatic values is shattered by a proliferation of religious and secular belief systems.*

Postmodernity may have unveiled the illusion of unmediated revelation of truth, but there is still a need to trace how sources and norms of knowledge rise up in concrete ways from human practice. Hence Graham's use of notions such as practice, performativity and habitus: *the self, society and moral values are all constructed by and through the actions of everyday life. The past – what we might call tradition – acts as the container or residuum of past action, a deposit or convention of past knowledge that provides working material for creative agency or 'regulated improvisations' within the context of the story. New situations interact with the story, and engagement in new practices gives rise to new moral knowledge. Practice in response to new situations is disclosive, engendering new realities. Embodied practices have meaning, but the meaning is ultimately inseparable from the practices themselves. The purposeful activities of the Christian faith community in response to moral questions, drawing upon revelation as contained in the collective tradition, constitutes the performative* habitus *of Christian truth: theology is enacted and embodied in practice.*

Age of Uncertainty

The historical and sociological epoch known as modernity is displaced by the signs of the times of 'postmodernity' and with it comes a host of voices to destabilize Enlightenment concepts of truth, human nature, knowledge, power, selfhood and language that have informed Western thought for two hundred years (Gay 1973; Kearney 1994; Reader 1997).

However, my anatomy of postmodernity does not merely conceive of intellectual debate independent of social, political and economic factors. The 'crisis' of postmodernity is not simply one of believing, but of revolutions in patterns of work and leisure, use of technology, the exercise of civic power, participation and citizenship, access to resources, relationships to the environment, and the use and abuse of scientific innovations (Hall et al. 1992). We might also include in our analysis the growth of religious pluralism and the decline of organized religion, especially in Western Europe, as signs that patterns of believing and belonging are changing. The pre-eminence of the Christian way of life can no longer be taken for granted (Davie 1994).

A frequent topic of debate concerns whether postmodernity is a successor epoch of modernity, or a critical corrective to it. My preference is for the latter analysis: as Richard Bernstein has it, the mood of postmodernity is a 'rage against humanism and the Enlightenment legacy' (Bernstein 1985: x). Postmodernity exposes the *hubris* of Enlightenment optimism, tempers the excesses of literalism, objectivism and humanism, and retrieves from the margins the repressed and hidden 'Others' of Western modernity. The postmodern is where modernity is called to account, where its confident assertions are put to the test:

> Postmodernism reminds us that we are already too determined ourselves; we can never exhaustively account for the conditions which make the world, time, knowledge, the human animal, language, possible ... Postmodernism reminds modernity of its own constructed nature; the arbitrariness and instability of its own constructions. (Ward 1997: xxvi)

Feminist thought, whilst in many respects a child of the Enlightenment, also exhibits a postmodern scepticism towards many of the precepts of modernity. Feminists have argued that dominant views of human nature, self, knowledge, action and value are constructed *androcentrically*: that is, they assume that maleness and masculinity are the norm for adequate accounts of what it means to be human, how I achieve a sense of self, what counts as verifiable and reliable knowledge, the relationship between thought, will and action, and the sources and norms of ultimate value, truth and beauty. Once we introduce the notion of these concepts as 'gendered', however, we gain a clearer sense of some of the ways in which Enlightenment views must necessarily be revised. The challenge of feminism thus illustrates the crisis of conventional values and the necessity of accommodating diverse and heterogeneous experiences (Flax 1990).

Transforming Pastoral Theology

Christian thought and practice has, inevitably, been touched by the intellectual and social currents of postmodernity. Despite lively debate within philosophical theology, however (Ward 1997), much of this has ignited little interest on the part of pastoral, or practical, theology. Yet the practical question of the sources and norms that might inform 'Christian faithful witness in the Church and the world is as fundamental and problematic an issue as the purely philosophical implications of postmodernity. In the face of the collapse of the 'grand narrative' of modernity, what values of hope and obligation may now inform purposeful Christian action and vision?

One of the symptoms of postmodernity, it is said, is a resurgence of the sacred; and this opens up possibilities that go beyond either a reversion to premodern fideism or a drift into New Age eclecticism. My paramount concern is thus to remain true to the continuity of Christian witness whilst responding anew to the challenges of the present age. A necessary part of the critical reclamation of the 'boundaries' and 'horizons' (Oliver 1991) of Christian identity will therefore be a robust engagement with the ambiguities of a post-secular age:

> Set free from the compulsion to talk about God, there is a new and deeper freedom to talk about God and *not* to talk about God . . . In its engagement with the secular psychotherapies, neither does pastoral counselling need to lose its Christian identity as care offered in the community of faith. Set free from the compulsion to be 'religious', it has a genuine freedom to point beyond the secular to the One who is the source of all healing. (Lyall 1995: 107)

For most of the twentieth century, the predominant model of pastoral theology has been that of the theory and practice of individual care, prominently informed by the therapeutic models of the modern psychologies. The tasks of pastoral ministry – worship, preaching, social action, personal care, Christian formation and community-building – have traditionally been regarded as the exclusive province of the ordained clergy. However, as sociological changes have precipitated a greater demand for active participation in church life by the laity, and feminist critiques have questioned the invisibility of women's pastoral role as agents and clients of care, intensive scrutiny has been generated into the identity and aims of the pastoral task and the self-understanding of the Christian community (Graham and Halsey 1993; Lyall 1995).

Schleiermacher's original vision for Practical Theology designated the discipline as the 'crown' of theological enquiry, derivative of the higher forms of philosophical and historical theology (Schleiermacher 1966; Burkhart 1983). The burden of theological understanding and formulation was therefore directed towards the entirety of Christian practice, albeit within the service of ecclesial ministry, although it did effectively reduce practical theology to a deductive, or 'applied' theology. However, we may see a timely corrective to this within contemporary theologies of liberation which effectively turn Schleiermacher's system on its head. In their emphasis on *praxis* and context as hermeneutically primary, experience is thus envisaged as the origin, not the application, of theological formulation:

> [T]he permanent self-identity of the Christian faith cannot be pre-supposed ... There is no purely theoretical centre of reference which can serve in an abstract, speculative way as a norm of identity. Truth does not yet exist; it cannot be reached by interpretation, but it has to be produced by change. (Davis 1994: 90–1)

According to this view, therefore, pastoral theology breaks out of the 'clerical paradigm' (Farley 1983a) and locates itself as the 'critical inquiry into the validity of Christian witness' (Wheeler and Farley 1991: 15). The proper object of the discipline is not the moral reasoning of the congregation (Browning 1991) or the activities of the pastor (Hiltner 1958) or 'applied theology', but the practice of intentional communities. Pastoral theology studies the whole mission of the faith-community, as expressed in its diverse practices of ordering the faithful, engaging in social justice, communicating the faith, and administering Word and Sacrament. Pastoral theology is reconceived, therefore, as the critical discipline interrogating the norms that guide all corporate activity by which the community enacts its identity.

Practical Wisdom

Looked at from other perspectives, my proposal to reconstitute pastoral theology as the theorization of Christian practice looks promising. Contemporary feminist theories regard gender identity, relations and representations as generated by performative practices of 'gendering' (Flax 1993), rather than derived from an ontological or biological dualism. Gender is a self-reflexive phenomenon: we experience ourselves as simultaneously the creators and creations of gendered culture. There are no transhistorical essences of gender, but only *practices* that realize or reinforce difference (Connell 1987; Butler 1990; Graham 1995).

Such a model presents identity and culture as 'performative'. Pierre Bourdieu's concept of *habitus* – a kind of practical knowledge within which human social action enacts and constructs culture – is a synthesis of structure and agency: a 'system of structured, structuring dispositions ... constituted in practice and ... always oriented towards practical functions' (Bourdieu 1992: 52). Such a *habitus* is also, I contend, necessarily embodied. Social structures are inscribed on bodily activity; embodied action creates tangible institutions.

As a working definition, we might therefore characterize practice as 'purposeful activity performed by embodied persons in space and time as the subjects of agency and objects of history' (Graham 1996: 110). Purposeful practices are the bearers of value: cultural norms are reproduced and handed down but there is also scope for creative re-rendering. Pastoral practice constitutes the *habitus* of faith; it is both inherited and indwelt but also infinitely creative: a performative practical wisdom (*phronêsis*) which we inhabit and re-enact.

Thus, the core values of communities or cultures are not to be conceived as transcendent eternal realities, but as provisional – yet binding – strategies of normative action and community within which shared commitments might be negotiated and put to work. Ethics and politics therefore become processes and practices, rather than applications of metaphysical ideals.

. . .

Transforming Practice

Nancy Eisland's recent work *The Disabled God* (1994) claims to advance a 'liberation theology of disability' that models many of the criteria for pastoral theology outlined above. Eisland draws upon conventional resources of personal experience, cultural factors and Christian tradition (Tracy 1981), although the parameters of each of these categories are subtly revised within a hermeneutic in which *alterity*, difference and the retrieval of 'stories seldom heard' (Milhaven 1991) are privileged as having theologically disclosive authority. The validity of theological truth-claims are 'acted out' (Eisland 1994: 95) and will be tested by their ability to animate a renewed practical wisdom for the Church: 'The struggle for wholeness and justice begins with the practices and habits of the church itself' (1994: 111).

Speaking of difference

In drawing on the *narrative experience* of two women with disabilities, Eisland refuses to render disability as if it were an ontological category. Rather, the stories bear witness to a plurality of definitions of mobility, impairment and body image. These accounts do not pathologize or victimize their narrators, but nor do they suppress the distinctive experiences of those with disabilities: 'It encompasses the recognition that disability does not mean incomplete and that difference is not dangerous' (Eisland 1994: 47).

Hermeneutics of suspicion

Christian teaching on disability, healing and illness is critically examined, and elements of *tradition* that portray disability as the result of sin, or suffering as a visitation from God to test the afflicted, or an opportunity for the 'able-bodied' to exercise charity, are found wanting. Instead, Eisland's criterion for theological authenticity within the tradition is one which empowers those with disabilities as theological subjects. They are affirmed as the authors of their own narratives of Divine disclosure:

> A liberatory theology sustains our difficult but ordinary lives, empowers and collaborates with individuals and groups of people with disabilities who struggle for justice in concrete situations, creates new ways of resisting the theological symbols that exclude and devalue us, and reclaims our hidden history in the presence of God on earth. (1994: 86)

The symbols of faith around disability therefore have a performative power to 'create normative standards for human interaction' (1994:

91); Eisland advances a contextualized Christology of the 'disabled God . . . in a sip-puff wheelchair' (1994: 89).

Transforming communities

The truth-claims of the Gospel are thus incarnated in the worshipping community that seeks to embody the suffering but transfigured presence of the 'disabled God'. Eisland focuses on the significance for such communities of the Eucharist, a sacrament, not of exclusion, but a sign of the 'body broken for a people broken' (1994: 114). In the figure of the transfigured Christ – who retains his wounds even in a risen state – God's solidarity with suffering is realized. A vision of God embedded in human encounter and renewal animates genuinely disclosive practical wisdom: words made flesh in a community which fosters a generosity to others. Such transformative practice facilitates and encourages the exercise of the qualities of solidarity, wholeness and reconciliation, practices by which divine disclosure can be effected.

New Horizons

The process of going *beyond* the situated and concrete towards the encounter with the Other may also serve as a metaphor for the human experience of God. It speaks of authentic faith occurring at the very point of loss of certainty and self-possession: divine activity and presence are offered in the mystery of *alterity*. Thus, Eisland's thoroughly Christian incarnational theology understands the human and immediate as a 'sacrament' of the transcendent and divine: 'Our bodies participate in the imago Dei, not in spite of our impairments and contingencies, but through them' (Eisland 1994: 101).

Just as identity in the postmodern condition is contingent, performative and provisional, so theological truth-claims are to be seen as forms of *phronêsis*, or practical knowledge: faith and truth cannot be separated from practical action, which is the very vehicle and embodiment of the Word made flesh:

> Where is God? we ask. Look to the underside of history and the emancipatory struggles of oppressed peoples everywhere. Or look to the ecological quest for the wholeness and integrity of life. Or to the dialogical creation of common though shaky ground in the midst of cultural and religious differences . . . My thesis is that the

answer to the challenge of postmodernity – how to speak meaning-fully of God's presence and action in the world – is already implicit in these practices. (Hodgson 1994: 65–6)

Can we regard authentic pastoral practice, therefore, as that which draws us into encounter with the 'Other', towards a deeper under-standing of our own identity-in-relation? Pastoral theology is an interpretative discipline enabling faith-communities to give a public and critical account of their performative truth-claims. It attempts to capture glimpses of Divine activity amidst human practice. Pastoral theology aims to put to the test the conviction that the imperatives of hope and obligation are enshrined in transformative practice that seeks to realize a larger vision yet to come.

Bibliography

Bernstein, R. J. (1985), *Habermas and Modernity*, Cambridge: Cambridge University Press.

Bourdieu, P. (1992), *The Logic of Practice*, Cambridge: Polity Press.

Browning, D. S. (1991), *A Fundamental Practical Theology: Descriptive and Strategic Proposals*, Minneapolis: Fortress Press.

Burkhart, J. E. (1983), 'Schleiermacher's vision for theology' in D. S. Browning (ed.), *Practical Theology: The Emerging Field in Theology, Church, and World*, San Francisco: Harper and Row, pp. 42–60.

Butler, J. (1990), *Gender Trouble: Feminism and the Subversion of Identity*, London: Routledge.

Connell, R. W. (1987), *Gender and Power*, Cambridge: Polity Press.

Davie, G. (1994), *Religion in Britain since 1945: Believing without Belonging*, Oxford: Blackwell.

Davis, C. (1994), *Religion and the Making of Society*, Cambridge: Cambridge University Press.

Eisland, N. (1994), *The Disabled God*, Nashville, Tenn.: Abingdon.

Farley, E. (1983a), 'Theology and practice outside the clerical paradigm' in D. S. Browning (ed.), *Practical Theology: The Emerging Field in Theology, Church, and World*, San Francisco: Harper and Row. pp. 21–41.

Flax, J. (1990), *Thinking Fragments: Psychoanalysis, Feminism, and Postmodernism in the Contemporary West*, Berkeley: University of California Press.

Flax, J. (1993), *Disputed Subjects: Essays on Psychoanalysis, Politics and Philosophy*, London: Routledge.

Gay, P. (1973), *The Enlightenment: An Interpretation. Volume I: The Rise of Modern Paganism*, London: Wildwood House.

Graham, E. L. (1995), *Making the Difference: Gender, Personhood and Theology*, London: Mowbray.

Graham, E. L. (1996), *Transforming Practice*, London: Mowbray.

Graham, E. L., and Halsey, M. (1993), *Life-Cycles: Women and Pastoral Care*, London: SPCK.

Hall, S., Held, D., and McGrew, T. (eds) (1992), *Modernity and its Futures*, Cambridge: Polity Press.

Hiltner, S. (1958), *Preface to Pastoral Theology*, Nashville: Abingdon.

Hodgson, P. C. (1994), *Winds of the Spirit: A Constructive Christian Theology*, London: SCM Press.

Kearney, R. (1994), *Modern Movements in European Philosophy: Phenomenology, Critical Theory, Structuralism*, 2nd edn, Manchester: Manchester University Press.

Lyall, D. (1995), *Counselling in the Pastoral and Spiritual Context*, Buckingham: Open University Press.

Milhaven, A. L. (ed.) (1991), *Sermons Seldom Heard: Women Proclaim Their Lives*, New York: Crossroad.

Oliver, G. (1991), *Counselling, Anarchy and the Kingdom of God*, Lingdale Papers 16, Oxford: Clinical Theology Association.

Reader, J. (1997), *Beyond all Reason: The Limits of Post-Modern Theology*, Cardiff: Aureus.

Schleiermacher, E. F. (1966), *Brief Outline on the Study of Theology*, trans. T. N. Tice, Richmond, VA: John Knox Press.

Tracy, D. (1981), *The Analogical Imagination: Christian Theology and the Culture of Pluralism*, London: SCM Press.

Ward, G. (1997), *The Postmodern God*, Oxford: Blackwell Publishers.

Wheeler, B. G., and Farley, E. (eds) (1991), *Shifting Boundaries: Contextual Approaches to the Structure of Theological Education*, Louisville, KY: Westminster/John Knox Press.

Oscar Romero, *The Violence of Love: the words of Oscar Romero*

translated by James R. Brockman, London: Fount, pp. 11, 28, 29.

In these simple verses, Romero communicates the power of the Christian life as a witness for peace and justice amidst a world of violence and conflict. The consistent theme is that the Church will be judged – by God and by the world – by its uncompromising identification with the poor and oppressed, and by its willingness to take up the cross of Christ. In other words, it is in the quality of its deeds rather than its words that the gospel will fully be realized. The exercise of discipleship in the context of lived experience is a primary form of 'speaking of God' in the world. This is also a world-affirming creed, in that Romero sees no contradiction between a relationship focused on God and a concern for social justice and a ministry alongside those who are hungry or dispossessed; the Gospel is proclaimed, and God is revealed, when people of faith take up such causes.

Romero implicitly answers some of the critics of liberation theology who claim that it reduces salvation to a political or economic creed, by identifying true liberation as reconciliation with God. This is thus a thoroughly theological understanding insofar as Romero reminds his readers that it is God who is to be proclaimed as the source of justice, love and human rights, and that more temporal considerations will fall short of this ultimate vision.

How I would like to engrave this great idea
on each one's heart:
Christianity is not a collection
of truths to be believed,
of laws to be obeyed,
of prohibitions.
That makes it very distasteful.
Christianity is a person,
one who loved us so much,
one who calls for our love.
Christianity is Christ.

November 6, 1977

Do you want to know if your Christianity is genuine?
Here is the touchstone:
Whom do you get along with?
Who are those who criticize you?
Who are those who do not accept you?
Who are those who flatter you?
Know from that what Christ said once:
'I have come not to bring peace, but division.'*
There will be division even in the same family,
because some want to live more comfortably
by the world's principles,
those of power and money.
But others have embraced the call of Christ
and must reject all that cannot be just in the world.

November 13, 1977

* Luke 12:51.

. . .

When we struggle for human rights,
for freedom,
for dignity,
when we feel that it is a ministry of the church
to concern itself for those who are hungry,
for those who have no schools,
for those who are deprived,
we are not departing from God's promise.
He comes to free us from sin,
and the church knows that sin's consequences
are all such injustices and abuses.
The church knows it is saving the world
when it undertakes to speak also of such things.

December 18, 1977

. . .

Let us not measure the church
by the number of its members
or by its material buildings.
The church has built many houses of worship,
many seminaries,
many buildings that have then been taken from her.
They have been stolen
and turned into libraries
and barracks
and markets
and other things.
That doesn't matter.
The material walls here will be left behind in history.
What matters is you,
the people,
your hearts,
God's grace giving you God's truth and life.
Don't measure yourselves by your numbers.
Measure yourselves by the sincerity of heart
with which you follow the truth and light
of our divine Redeemer.

December 19, 1977

'Theology-in-Action': References and Further Reading

Boff, C. (1996), 'Methodology of the Theology of Liberation' in Jon Sobrino and Ignacío Ellacuría, (eds.), *Systematic Theology: Perspectives from Liberation Theology*, Maryknoll, NY: Orbis, pp. 1–21.

Gutiérrez, Gustavo (1996), 'Theology: A Critical Reflection' in James B. Nickoloff (ed.), *Gustavo Gutiérrez: Essential Writings*, London: SCM Press, pp. 30–4.

Procter-Smith, Marjorie (2003), 'Feminist Ritual Strategies: the *Ekklesia Gynaikon* at Work' in Fernando F. Segovia (ed.), *Toward New Heaven and a New Earth: Essays in Honor of Elisabeth Schussler Fiorenza*, New York: Orbis, 2003, pp. 498–515.

Religious Society of Friends (1994), *Quaker Faith and Practice*, Warwick: Warwick Printing Co.

7

'Theology in the Vernacular': Local Theology

Introduction

This method of theological reflection is based upon the conviction that the Christian gospel does not exist in abstract form but is most authentically encountered when it is incarnated within specific cultural contexts. This being the case, it will assume diverse shapes according to the local environment in which it is embodied, and speak in the vernacular using the idioms, symbols and narrative forms employed in everyday life. Those who advocate this understanding of theology see the work of theological reflection as being akin to that of learning a language. Painstaking attention must be given to learning a vocabulary, mastering grammatical rules and learning when it is appropriate to speak. However, when a language is fully grasped something more is achieved than technical proficiency. The speaker also gains access to a world-view which comes to shape their own understanding at a very deep level. Similarly, when theologians seek to communicate in a way that is relevant within a particular cultural context, they will find their own understanding of the gospel challenged, enriched and transformed through this process.

Some of the very earliest stories of Christian missionary activity show believers wrestling with the challenge to express the Christian message in ways that were appropriate to the heterogeneous cultural context of the Roman Empire. The Pentecost narrative (Acts 2) can be read as endorsing the insight that God speaks to people in their own language rather than in a special sacred tongue. While there have been periods in the Church's history when theologians have assumed a natural affinity between the gospel and a particular cultural form (from Constantinian imperialism to liberal democracy) this perspective has always been challenged, particularly by those who attempt to speak with strangers and those who find their identity in contradiction to the dominant cultural norms. Indeed, periods of renewal and heightened spiritual awareness often take place when a dominant Christian tradition receives the stimulus of insights that come from outside its own familiar territory. For example, the flowering of Christian mystical theology in medieval Spain cannot be understood without acknowledging that the innovative spiritual thinkers whom the Church now honours, such as Teresa of Avila and St John of the Cross, were deeply influenced by both their Jewish roots and the Islamic traditions of Iberian culture.

In recent times some of the most important developments to have taken place within local theology have been as a result of awareness that an affirmation of the universal nature of the Church must be balanced by acknowledgement of the importance of local cultures. Vatican II was an important milestone in this process in that it celebrated a 'plurality' of cultures and named this diversity the fruit of divinely inspired human creativity. That this understanding was achieved during a period in which national liberation movements were struggling for autonomy and independence is no coincidence. Resistance to colonialism, racism and globalizing capital continues to be a source of inspiration for local theology. Yet it is not only in situations of dramatic conflict that it exercises powerful appeal.

Theology in the vernacular has received many important insights from anthropology, a discipline that provides tools to analyse the ways in which cultures transmit meaning and values through material practices, symbols, narratives and rituals. The work of the anthropologist Clifford Geertz, who described culture as the web of meaning that sustains human life, has been particularly important. It is now widely recognized that cultural diversity is not a simply a geographical phenomenon. Our complex postmodern societies are ones in which webs of meaning are spun by local communities of identification (such as congregations), tightly knit subcultures and those who use the resources of popular culture to generate and sustain their identity. There is a work of theological reflection to be done in all such contexts, discerning what of spiritual worth and value is being expressed in the vernacular tongues and varied dialects that constitute local speech. Local theologians believe that God is present and active in generating these insights. They possess the potential to renew Christian understanding and enable us to discover and claim previously unrecognized or unregarded aspects of God's embodied revelation in Christ.

Stephen Bevans, 'Contextual Theology as Theological Imperative'

in *Models of Contextual Theology*, Maryknoll, NY: Orbis Books, 1992, pp. 1–4.

The following extract presents a very clear introduction to our selection of readings on local theology. Stephen Bevans sets out the reasons why an increasing number of scholars and pastoral practitioners from different traditions and contexts have come to believe that the construction of appropriate forms of contextual theology is 'imperative' for them. Bevans argues that these 'local theologians' have developed a contemporary understanding of theological reflection and also rediscovered some of the most traditional and fundamental truths concerning theological method.

Among the new insights into theological reflection that have been achieved is the recognition that theology can helpfully employ ephemeral, experiential and culturally conditioned knowledge in conjunction with the more established and authoritative resources of reason, Scripture and tradition. This volatile mixture ensures that theological discourse is never static, objective or permanent. The best theological thinking is no longer viewed as standing somehow beyond our everyday world but as located, responsive and useful for Christians living within it. A new honesty about the provisionality of Christian thinking returns us to the traditional sources of theological insight and we come to recognize that scripture and tradition are themselves the product of contextual reflection. Bevans argues that this is an invigorating perspective that should generate renewed creativity in Christian thinking.

Contextual theology can be defined as a way of doing theology in which one takes into account: the spirit and message of the gospel;[1] the tradition of the Christian people; the culture in which one is theologizing; and social change in that culture, whether brought about by western technological process or the grass-roots struggle for equality, justice, and liberation.[2] Doing theology contextually is not an option, nor is it something that should only interest people from the Third World or missionaries who work there.[3] The contextualization of theology – the attempt to understand Christian faith in terms of a particular context – is really a theological imperative. As we understand theology today, contextualization is part of the very nature of theology itself.

In this first chapter I will explore this thesis by first pointing to the discontinuity and continuity of a contextual approach to theology in comparison with traditional or classical theology. Then I will reflect on several factors, both external and internal, that make the contextualization of theology necessary in today's world and today's understanding of Christian faith.

Contextualization as both New and Traditional

A contextual approach to theology is a departure from the notion of traditional theology, but at the same time it is very much in continuity with it. To understand theology as contextual is to assert something both new and traditional.

First of all, contextual theology understands the nature of theology in a new way. Classical theology conceived theology as a kind of objective science of faith. It was understood as a reflection in faith on the two *loci theologici*[4] (theological sources) of scripture and tradition, the content of which has not and never will be changed, and is above culture and historically conditioned expression. But what makes contextual theology precisely contextual is the recognition of the validity of another locus theologicus: present human experience. Theology that is contextual realizes that culture, history, contemporary thought forms, and so forth are to be considered, along with scripture and tradition, as valid sources for theological expression.

While classical theology understood theology as objective, contextual theology understands theology as unabashedly subjective. By *subjective*, however, I do not mean relative or private or anything like that. When I say that contextual theology is subjective, I mean it is a result of the modern appropriation of the 'turn to the subjective at the beginning of modern times'[5] and points to the fact that the human person or human society, culturally and historically bound as it is, is the source of reality, not a supposed value- and culture-free objectivity 'already out there now real.'[6]

As Charles Kraft puts it,

> there is always a difference between reality and human culturally conditioned understandings (models) of that reality. We assume that there is a reality 'out there' but it is the mental constructs (models) of that reality inside our heads that are the most real to

us. God, the author of reality, exists outside any culture. Human beings, on the other hand, are always bound by cultural, subcultural (including disciplinary), and psychological conditioning to perceive and interpret what they see of reality in ways appropriate to these conditionings. Neither the absolute God nor the reality [God] created is perceived absolutely by culture-bound human beings.[7]

Reality is not just 'out there'; reality is mediated by meaning,[8] a meaning we give it in the context of our culture or our historical period, interpreted from our own particular horizon and in our own particular thought forms. For example, whether it is just about to be harvested, drying in the sun, or cooked and on the table, United States Americans call rice *rice*; Filipinos and other Asians have distinct names for each of these forms of rice. Similarly, Eskimos have various names for what most North Americans or Europeans see as *snow*. Asian languages reflect a view of the world that is strongly hierarchical and reflective of the respect that Asians hold for people in authority. Our world is not just *there*; we are involved in its construction. We do not simply see, as Ian Barbour points out; we only 'see as'.[9]

As our cultural and historical context plays a part in the construction of the reality in which we live, so our context influences our understanding of God and the expression of our faith. The time is past when we can speak of one right, unchanging theology, a *theologia perennis*. We can only speak about a theology that makes sense at a certain place and in a certain time. We can certainly learn from others (synchronically from other cultures and diachronically from history), but the theology of others can never be our own. Henri Bouillard said that a theology that is not up-to-date (*actuelle*) is a false theology. We can paraphrase Bouillard by saying that a theology that is not somehow reflective of our times, our culture, and our current concerns – and therefore contextual – is also a false theology. Charles Kraft says practically the same thing when he says that theology, when it is perceived as irrelevant, *is in fact* irrelevant.[10]

So the enterprise of contextualization is a departure from the traditional way of doing theology; it is something new. But at the same time, contextualization is also very traditional. While we can say that the doing of theology by taking culture and social change in culture into account is a departure from the traditional or classical way of doing theology, a study of the history of theology will reveal that every authentic theology has been very much rooted in a particular context in some implicit or real way. 'Contextualization . . . is the sine qua non of all genuine theological thought, and always has been.'[11]

Contemporary scripture studies, for example, have revealed that there is no one theology of the Hebrew or Christian scriptures, much less of the Bible as a whole. The Bible literally means 'books' (*biblia*), and the Bible is a library, a collection of books and consequently of theologies. The Hebrew scriptures are made up of Yahwist theology, Elohist theology, Priestly theology, Deuteronomic theology, and Wisdom theologies – to name but a few. These theologies are all different, sometimes even contradictory of one another. They reflect different times, different concerns, and even different cultures as Israel moved from an agrarian society to a monarchy, from an independent state to a vassal of Assyria, Greece, and Rome. In the Christian scriptures, we know that every gospel is different because of the different circumstances in which they were written, each reflecting the concerns of quite different communities. Paul is different from James, and the deutero-Pauline pastoral epistles reflect quite different concerns from the genuine Pauline letters. Indeed, British theologian (now bishop) Stephen Sykes has argued that the Christian message itself contains a basic ambiguity that makes pluralism and controversy part of the identity or essence of Christianity itself.[12]

If we turn to the church's early theologians after the New Testament era, we see them trying to make sense out of the faith in terms of the dominant and all-pervasive Hellenistic culture. Clement of Alexandria, for instance, made use of the insights of the Stoics; Origen made use of Plato; Augustine was strongly influenced both by Plato and the neo-Platonists of his time.[13] The whole structure of the post-Constantinian church reflected imperial structures. Bishops were treated like members of the imperial court, wore vestments that rivaled those of the emperor, and presided over imperial political divisions called dioceses. The early councils of the church made use of Greek words (albeit stretching their meanings sometimes) to express points of Christian doctrine. One of the most significant moments in theology was when, at Nicea, a philosophical term (*homoousios*, or consubstantial) was used to express what was meant by the scriptures regarding the identity of the Logos or incarnate Word.[14] As Virginia Fabella points out, the true significance of Nicea, and later of Chalcedon, is 'the underlying challenge they pose to us to have our own contemporary culturally-based christological formulations'.[15]

It is also well known that Thomas Aquinas used the newly discovered works of Aristotle as a vehicle for a new synthesis of Christian doctrine. Aquinas now is regarded as the paragon of orthodoxy, but he was as controversial in his day as Hans Küng or Charles Curran is in ours – his books were even burned by the bishop of Paris soon after his death!

In his important study *Corpus Mysticum*, Henri de Lubac presents additional evidence of the contextuality of medieval theological thinking. Within the more symbolic mentality of the patristic era, de Lubac points out that the Eucharist was referred to clearly as the *corpus mysticum*, or mystical body of Christ; the church, on the other hand, was referred to as the *corpus verum*, or real body of Christ. However, as Christian thinking began to be dominated by a more Teutonic realistic mentality, the two terms began to be used in exactly the opposite way, to refer to exactly the opposite realities. By the time of Berengarius, who spoke of the symbolic presence of Christ in the Eucharist, the Eucharist was spoken of as the real body of Christ (*Ave, Verum Corpus, natum ex Maria Virgine!*) and the church began to be spoken of as Christ's mystical body.[16]

One of the aspects of Martin Luther's greatness as a theologian is that he articulated the whole new consciousness of the individual as it emerged in the West at the dawn of modernity. His struggle to find a personal relationship with God was very much in tune with the tenor of the times and was a major reason why his call for the reformation of the church was heard by so many people. The theology of the Catholic Counter-Reformation was forged in the context of opposition to the Protestant challenge. Theology of the sixteenth and seventeenth centuries, both Protestant and Catholic, was nothing if not contextual!

Many more examples from the history of theology could be given – for instance, Schleiermacher's monumental attempt to root theology in experience in response to the romanticism of his age, and the Catholic Tübingen's school's efforts to align Catholic theology with post-Kantian philosophy (particularly that of Schelling).[17] We could mention as well Paul Tillich's conviction that theology needs to be done as a correlation of human 'existential questions and theological answers in mutual interdependence',[18] and Karl Barth's highly contextual theology of the Word of God.[19] What becomes clear, in any case, is that even a cursory glance at the history of theology reveals that there has never been a genuine theology that was articulated in an ivory tower with no reference to or dependence on the events, the thought forms, or the culture of its particular place and time.[20]

Notes

1. The term *gospel*, of course, is quite ambiguous, and, as G. Arbuckle says, its meaning will differ within the various Christian traditions. G. Arbuckle, *Earthing the Gospel* (Maryknoll, N.Y.: Orbis Books, 1990), pp. 3–4.

2. I speak of contextual theology involving *four* elements – gospel, tradition, culture, and social change; other writers limit the elements to three, fusing culture and culture change into one element (cf. Arbuckle, *Earthing the Gospel*, p. 4). While I acknowledge that culture is never a static reality and change is part and parcel of what a culture is, the distinction of social change from the social web that is human culture is important for the methodological perspective I want to develop in this book. Methodologically speaking, the anthropological model I will develop focuses mainly on the traditional elements in a culture (kinship, funeral practices, language, etc.) while not totally ignoring the phenomenon of change that is taking place due to contemporary secularization or movements of liberation. On the other hand, the praxis model does not exclude traditional elements in a culture, but its emphasis is on the possibilities of change within it. I would *distinguish* culture from social change without claiming that the two are totally separable from each other.

3. The term *Third World* is admittedly a controversial one. W. J. Grimm points out that while the term originally had a positive meaning, analogous to the emerging power of the Third Estate during the French Revolution, its meaning has subsequently shifted: 'it no longer referred to the aspirations of nations hoping to develop independent governments and economies. It became a term of comparison. The third world was now defined in terms of the first.' W. J. Grimm, 'The "Third" World', *America* (May 5, 1990): 449. Because of this, Grimm suggests that the term be abandoned. On the other hand, the Ecumenical Association of Third World Theologians (EATWOT) – a group that would be very sensitive to any term that would demean their cultures – uses the term quite unapologetically. See K. C. Abraham, ed., *Third World Theologies: Commonalities and Convergences* (Maryknoll, N.Y.: Orbis Books, 1990). It is because these theologians use the term that I have chosen to use it here.

4. My use of the term *loci theologici* reflects the traditional Roman Catholic usage, especially developed by M. Cano in his *De Locis Theologicis* (Salamanca, 1563). Cf. J. Wicks, 'Luoghi Teologici', *Dizionario di Teologia Fondamentale* (Assisi: Editrice Citadella, 1990), pp. 645–47; J. Thornhill, 'Loci Theologici', *New Catholic Encyclopedia*, 8 (New York: McGraw-Hill, 1967), p. 950. *Loci* in some Protestant circles is used to designate the various classical themes of theology, e.g., God, Trinity, Grace, Christ, etc. This use is based on Melanchthon's work *Loci communes rerum theologicarum* (1521), revised as *Loci praecipui theologici* in 1559. For a contemporary example of this use of *locus* or *loci*, see C. Braaten and R. Jenson, eds., *Christian Dogmatics* (Philadelphia: Fortress Press, 1984), pp. v–xv and xix.

5. K. Rahner uses this phrase in several of his essays. See 'The Hermeneutics of Eschatological Assertions', in *Theological Investigations* IV (Baltimore: Helicon Press, 1966), p. 324.

6. This phrase is one used often by B. Lonergan. See *Insight: A Study in*

Human Understanding (New York: Philosophical Library, 1957), pp. 251–52; and *Method in Theology* (London: Darton, Longman and Todd, 1972), pp. 251–52. Lonergan's underlying epistemology might be referred to as a 'critical realism'. For a discussion of the importance of a shift from 'naive realism' or 'naive idealism' to critical realism, see P. Hiebert, 'Epistemological Foundations for Science and Theology', *TSF Bulletin* (March–April, 1985): 5–10 and 'The Missiological Implications of an Epistemological Shift', *TSF Bulletin* (May–June, 1985): 12–18.

7. C. H. Kraft, *Christianity in Culture* (Maryknoll, N.Y.: Orbis Books, 1979), p. 300.

8. Cf. Lonergan, *Method in Theology*, pp. 28, 76–77, 238.

9. I. G. Barbour, *Myths, Models and Paradigms: A Comparative Study in Science and Religion* (New York: Harper and Row, 1974), pp. 120–21. Cf. P. Berger and T. Luckmann, *The Social Construction of Reality: A Treatise on the Sociology of Knowledge* (New York: Doubleday, 1967) and A. J. Gittins, *Gifts and Strangers: Meeting the Challenge of Inculturation* (Mahwah, N.J.: Paulist Press, 1989), pp. 1–28. See also J. B. Miller, 'The Emerging Postmodern World', in F. B. Burnham, ed., *Postmodern Theology: Christian Faith in a Pluralist World* (San Francisco: Harper and Row, 1989), p. 11. For a striking illustration of the 'social construction of reality', see M. Eliade, *No Souvenirs: Journal, 1957–1969* (San Francisco: Harper and Row, 1967), pp. 213–14.

10. Kraft, *Christianity in Culture*, p. 296.

11. D. J. Hall, *Thinking the Faith: Christian Theology in a North American Context* (Minneapolis, Minn.: Augsburg, 1989), p. 21.

12. S. Sykes, *The Identity of Christianity* (London: SPCK, 1984), p. 23. The entire argument is laid out on pp. 11–34.

13. On the strong contextual nature of early Christian theology, see D. Bosch, *Transforming Mission: Paradigm Shifts in Theology of Mission* (Maryknoll, N.Y.: Orbis Books, 1991), pp. 190–213; cf. J. González, *Christian Thought Revisited: Three Types of Theology* (Nashville, Tenn.: Abingdon Press, 1989).

14. See J. C. Murray, *The Problem of God, Yesterday and Today* (New Haven, Conn.: Yale University Press, 1964), pp. 45–53; and B. J. F. Lonergan, *The Way to Nicea: The Dialectical Development of Trinitarian Theology* (London: Darton, Longman and Todd, 1976), pp. 136–37.

15. V. Fabella, 'Christology from an Asian Woman's Perspective', in V. Fabella and S. Ai Lee Park, eds., *We Dare to Dream: Doing Theology as Asian Women* (Maryknoll, N.Y.: Orbis Books, 1989), p. 9.

16. H. de Lubac, *Corpus Mysticum: l'eucharistie et l'Eglise au Moyen Age*, 2d ed. (Paris: Aubier, 1949).

17. See B. Gerrish, 'Continuity and Change: Friedrich Schleiermacher on the Task of Theology', in *Tradition and the Modern World: Reformed Theology in the Nineteenth Century* (Chicago: University of Chicago Press, 1978) and *A Prince of the Church: Schleiermacher and the Beginnings of Modern Theology* (Philadelphia: Fortress Press, 1984). On the Catholic Tübingen school, see T. F. O'Meara, *Romantic Idealism and Roman Catholicism: Schelling and the Theologians* (Notre Dame, Ind.: University of Notre Dame Press, 1982).

18. P. Tillich, *Systematic Theology* (Chicago: University of Chicago Press; New York: Harper and Row, 1967), Vol. I, p. 60.

19. See D. Tracy, *Blessed Rage for Order: The New Pluralism in Theology* (New York: Seabury, 1975), p. 27; D. J. Hall, *Thinking the Faith*, p. 355.

20. See F. George, 'Ecclesiological Presuppositions in Inculturating the Faith: Three Examples from Mission History', *Neue Zeitschrift fur Missionswissenschaft*, 45 (1989/4): 256–64.

Robert Schreiter, 'Religious Identity: Synthesis and Syncretism'

in *The New Catholicity: Theology between the Global and the Local*, Maryknoll, NY: Orbis Books, 1997, pp. 73–9.

In The New Catholicity, *Robert Schreiter, a member of the religious order Missionaries of the Precious Blood, returns to themes explored in his famous earlier work,* Constructing Local Theologies *(1985). This book considered the legacies of colonial, imperial and missionary encounters and the need to develop ways of communicating the gospel that respected local cultures rather than imposing alien religious systems upon them. In this earlier work he was careful to register the impact of a dominant capitalist system upon local contexts. In this later text, he offers a more detailed and systematic response to globalization – both economic and cultural – and postmodern pluralism. These are taken as challenges that are no longer encountered somewhere 'out there' but affect life in every local social context. Schreiter believes that their impact must be considered in all contemporary engagements, in both mission and apologetics.*

The passage extracted here focuses upon questions relating to religious identity: a crucial area of concern in recent times. He discusses three potential responses to cultural encounter. The first is resistance: upon encountering alien religious ideas, particularly if presented by a dominant group, people may refuse to participate in the new structures and find creative ways of employing indigenous traditions as a means of subverting their claims. In this frame old ideas are translated into the present and achieve new currency. This can have liberating potential but should also cause us to reflect upon how much questions of power are implicated in our allegiance to traditional religious symbols and practices. The second response, to which Schreiter devotes more attention, is hybridity. He claims that this is a concept which has gained significantly in importance as all local cultural contexts begin to display the signs of unprecedented cultural couplings that could not have been predicted in more stable times. Hybridity can be celebrated as the creative conjunction of diverse cultures or mourned as the breakdown of traditional boundaries. Whatever the case, the syncretistic religious practices that are a feature of hybrid cultures pose a challenge for theology. The last response is hierarchical, in which religious authorities may attempt to divert the mix of cultures and religions in a particular direction. Such efforts have had mixed results in the past. Schreiter believes that the Church must now reflect upon the outcomes of its previous interventions in order to discern appropriate ways to 'inculturate' the gospel today.

Resistance

Because power plays such a strong role in cultural encounter, and because that encounter is often intrusive, unequal, and violent, the reaction to the encounter is not infrequently resistance. Resistance can take the form of utter refusal to participate, or, if participation is forced, of withdrawal as soon as possible. One sees such resistance among the Pueblo peoples in response to their forced Christianization in the sixteenth century. An uprising effectively drove out the Spanish conquerors for nearly forty years. In some places churches were destroyed and *kivas* (the sacred assembly sites) were built on the same sites. Eventually the Spanish reconquered the area, but the Pueblo peoples to this day engage in a range of double belongings.[1] Often, however, such direct resistance is not possible. Then more selective forms of resistance are undertaken. The old religious ways go underground and are maintained in secret. Sometimes selective forms of resistance are possible in public. On the Santo Domingo Pueblo, for example, there are no Christian funerals, since all burials are done according to the 'old ways'. Christian clergy are not informed of deaths until all the rites have already taken place. In other instances Christian religious performance is followed, as in the veneration of the saints or the celebration of fiestas, but devotion is directed to other spirits as well. This is well documented in Afro-Brazilian and some Afro-Caribbean forms of Christianity.[2]

Among the native peoples of the Americas, and among those Africans transported there as slaves, a dense variety of forms of resistance and of survival can be found. These result in religious identities that continue to reshape themselves in new moments of conflict. It is not simply a return to the 'old ways'. The old ways are reinterpreted in light of the present. Richard Wilson has traced how the Q'eqchi' of Guatemala have moved from traditional Catholicism, to its leaders embracing liberation theology, to a reinterpretation of their Mayan heritage that sometimes entails the abandonment of Christianity altogether. Because many of the Q'eqchi' were displaced by the army, their relations with the mountain spirits (the *tzuultaq'as*), who are specific to a given mountain, were sundered. Those relations had to be recontextualized under new conditions in the Maya resurgence. As a result of this complex process, the *tzuultaq'as* continue to take on forms appropriate to their new contexts. In the nineteenth century they appeared to the Q'eqchi' dressed as German *finqueros* (plantation owners), and more recently they have appeared in military garb. Power is the common denominator. Wilson sums up the significance of this: 'indeed identity should not be seen as a bounded Aristotelian concept but as an assortment of paradoxes that interact dynamically without ever being reconciled.'[3]

Hybridities

A second set of identity formations might be called hybridities. Defined simply, a hybridity results from an erasure of a boundary between two (cultural or religious) entities and a redrawing of a new boundary. This has also been called 'creolization', a hybrid of African slave and European New World language and culture. It is celebrated in contemporary Hispanic theology in the United States as *mestizaje*, the mixing of Native American and Spanish peoples.[4]

In the nineteenth century, cultural and racial hybridity was much debated, with many holding that such mixing would lead to a diminishment of the strengths of the races, with the inferior race (i.e., African or Native American) overwhelming the superior one (i.e., the European).[5] This prompted advocacy for cultural and racial 'purity', evidenced in the rise of miscegenation legislation, although a few remarked that even a superficial knowledge of European history showed that much mixing had already taken place, and that there was no 'pure' white or European race. With the advance in knowledge of plant genetics by the end of the nineteenth century, hybrids could be seen as not just different, but potentially superior to unmixed varieties. But such knowledge had a hard time penetrating the prevailing racialist and cultural discourse.[6]

In my discussion of the varieties of syncretism and dual religious systems in *Constructing Local Theologies*, I described six types of mixing which now would be called hybridities. Regarding syncretistic phenomena:

> (1) where Christianity and another tradition come together to form a new reality, with the other tradition providing the basic framework; (2) where Christianity provides the framework for the syncretistic system, but is reinterpreted and reshaped substantially, independent of any dialogue with established Christianity; (3) where selected elements of Christianity are incorporated into another system.

Regarding dual religious systems:

> In the first set, Christianity and the other tradition are perceived as two distinct religious traditions, with both being practiced side by side. In the second set, Christianity is primary, with some selection of elements from a second tradition, which is nonetheless practiced separately from Christianity. In the third set, what constitutes religion in each of the systems becomes problematic as Christians try to remain faithful both to Christianity and to their national identity.[7]

While spoken of separately at that time, in terms of elements and religious systems, these six types can now be spoken of together in the contemporary discourse of hybridities. Most of the phenomena were looked at then in terms of the results of colonialism, where Christianity had initially been imposed on peoples or where its superiority and integrity had been stressed to the detriment of local religious forms. Those phenomena and those situations persist. But globalization, and the tensions between the global and the local, have become a seedbed for new varieties of hybridities, from New Age varieties that combine elements of Asian religions, Christianity, and native traditions of North America and pre-Christian Europe to African Independent Churches and the third generation of New Religions in Japan.

Hybridity is part of life in globalized cultures – either as an act of survival among the poor or as an act of choice in fashioning the self among the wealthy. From one perspective it can be seen as the latest stage of detraditionalization brought about by Enlightenment rationality, leading at best to an ever new 'invention of tradition'. But surveyed more carefully, there is at the same time a retraditionalization taking place in which elements of traditions are affirmed by their very inclusion in the scheme.[8] Traditions are often seen, especially by their guardians, as being more cohesive than they in fact might be. There are elements of indeterminacy in every tradition that make innovation possible.

Two final things need to be said regarding hybridities and religious identities. It was noted above that some people experience life as being in 'tiempos mixtos', a combination of premodern, modern and postmodern existences. This experience can give rise to what Nestor Garcia Canclini has called 'hybrid cultures', that provide strategies for moving between these different times.[9] As was noted in chapter 1, time was the primary metaphor of modernity, while space seems to be the metaphor of the postmodern. Because these three 'times' are now coeval, hybrid cultures are constructions that allow pathways for moving between all three.

Hybrid cultures, these new constructions out of fragments of other cultures that serve as strategies for negotiating life in a globalized society, require religious identity construction commensurate with their situations. The more positive affirmation of popular religion in recent years as a legitimate way of experiencing God has been a step in that direction. The incorporation of indigenous religious traditions into Christian performance, especially in the Americas, has been another. One of the things that has become more and more apparent, at least from a cultural point of view, is that the reforms of the Second Vatican Council were addressed particularly to the challenges of modernity as experienced in secularized societies. Other cultural settings, while not ignored, were certainly not given the same kind of emphasis. This is not surprising, since introducing the language of culture into Church documents was still at an early stage. The ability to allow a number of religious forms to coexist, even when they cannot be completely reconciled, is providing for a hybrid religious identity appropriate to the times. The tensions are not resolved – centralization and inculturation within the Roman Catholic Church remain – but this should be viewed not as a problem to be solved, but as a source of a deeper life in Christ. It is an asymmetrical source for the development of new forms for carrying an ancient message.

The second thing to be said relates to the emerging discussion about 'third cultures', that is, newly constructed cultures that mediate between two cultures.[10] The concept came first from programs for translation used by computers, where one language is translated into another language by passing through a third language which serves as a common basis for all translations. Perhaps what will be needed in a world of hybridities is such a third culture, which, while preserving difference in each of the cultures encountered, can serve as a kind of translation box through which communication can pass. This is an idea that still needs to be developed. Does, for example, the Vatican see itself as that kind of third culture for the Roman Catholic Church, mediating between local churches in terms of communication and practice? This is something to which we shall return in the final chapter.

Hybridity may be a fact of the globalized world, celebrating the diversity it creates. But all are not sure that this celebration of hybridity should be done uncritically. Robert J. C. Young, for instance, fears that hybridization will erase the discriminations of difference, leading us to take difference less seriously.[11] Ella Shohat reminds us that celebrating hybridity will legitimate the colonial violence that created it.[12] Both of these questions deserve further attention. If boundaries of difference now mark the globalized terrain as did boundaries of territory at an earlier time, what legitimacy and durability should they be accorded? While it is all well and good to point out how communications technologies, such as the Internet, are constantly erasing boundaries, all of this presumes a relatively peaceful and equitable environment. What serves to guarantee and secure that environment? Second, boundaries also serve in the formation of identity. Those boundaries can be quite permeable, but they nonetheless help orient and situate people in the world. One can talk about the construction of the self in postmodernity, but one must also find ways of articulating life in community, since belonging is one of humanity's strongest needs.

That colonial hybridities were born of violence is something that must not be forgotten. Many contemporary hybridities into which people are thrown are of the same nature, where local social ecologies are disrupted by market forces, where members of different generations in a family of migrants are torn by loyalties to conflicting values. One must be careful, however, to distinguish critique of hybridities because they besmirch imagined purities from critique that addresses violence. Here once again the development of an ontology of peace may be central to engaging in an appropriate critique.

Hierarchical Formations

The third formation of religious identity might be called hierarchical. By this is meant that church leadership or its intellectual elite try to move the cultural and religious mixing in a certain direction. At least three strategies are used to form religious identities in this way.[13] The first is a policy of tolerance, permitting a variety of possibilities to flourish within a circumscribed space. This can produce an easy or 'soft' pluralism with an agreement that many things may flourish as long as they do not produce conflict. While superior to outright warfare, which is becoming more and more common again, it may also lead to a lack of commitment to any specific tradition.

A second strategy for identity formation is hierarchic encompassment, whereby church leadership moves to incorporate outside practices and ideas. The choice of the date December 25 to celebrate the Nativity of Christ was such an encompassment of the Roman Saturnalia, as was the introduction of evergreen trees into Christmas celebrations in northern Europe. Encompassment is a recontextualizing of signs and performances that may make identification with Christianity easier for members of the culture, even as it brings change into Christianity as well.

Finally, new identities may be formed through legislation. Official church reforms by church or political leadership are intended to foster new identities. Such was the case in the sixteenth century Reformation in Europe. Official promotion of certain saints or special devotions have functioned to shape religious identities in Catholicism. For example, Our Lady of Fatima was clearly connected to anticommunism. With communism's demise, she is now directed especially against accommodation to Western-style consumerism. Legislation may work to make inculturation more possible (as in the vernacularization of the Roman Catholic liturgy after Vatican II). In those church bodies where legislation of this nature is possible, it can be a powerful force for expediting inculturation – or postponing it.

This review of different ways of forming religious identity is neither exhaustive nor taxative. Each represents a different way of approaching the issue of how identity takes shape. Knowing something of such processes is important for understanding their outcomes in the intercultural dialogue about syncretism and identity. If identities have been shaped as acts of resistance, dialogues with interlocutors perceived as oppressors will not go very far. The mixes in identities often need to be sorted out, but the mixing must first be accepted as a process by which genuine identity is formed. Hierarchical models can be used both to promote and to block inculturation. An ability to conceptualize how religious identities might be formed is an important part of entering the dialogue on syncretism and synthesis.

Notes

1. For some of this history, see Ramon Gutiérrez, *When Jesus Came, the Corn Mothers Went Away: Marriage, Sexuality, and Power in New Mexico, 1500–1846* (Stanford: Stanford University Press, 1991).

2. On the latter, see Burton Sankeralli (ed.), *At the Crossroads: African Caribbean Religion and Christianity* (St James, Trinidad and Tobago: Caribbean Council of Churches, 1995).

3. Richard Wilson, *Maya Resurgence in Guatemala* (Norman, OK: Oklahoma University Press, 1995), p. 305.

4. On creolization, see Ulrich Hannerz, 'The World in Creolization,' *Africa* 57 (1987): 546–59. For *mestizaje* see Virgil P. Elizondo, *The Future is Mestizo: Life Where Cultures Meet* (New York: Meyer-Stone, 1988).

5. As Robert Young, *Colonal Desire* (London: Routledge, 1995), 4, points out, much of the discourse of 'race' in the nineteenth century is equivalent to the discourse on 'culture' in the late twentieth century.

6. Ibid.

7. Schreiter, *Constructing Local Theologies*, (London: SCM Press, 1985), pp. 147–49.

8. See Paul Heelas, Scott Lash and Paul Morris (eds.), *Detraditionalization: Critical Reflections on Authority and Identity* (Oxford: Basil Blackwell, 1996), which is as much about retraditionalization as it is about detraditionalization. See especially the essay of Timothy W. Luke, 'Identity, Meaning and Globalization: Detraditionalization in Postmodern Space-time Compression', pp. 109–33.

9. Nestor Garcia Canclini, *Hybrid Cultures: Strategies for Entering and Leaving Modernity* (Minneapolis: University of Minnesota Press, 1995). First published in Mexico in 1989.

10. See, for example, Featherstone, *Undoing Modernity*, (London: Sage, 1995), p. 114. Homi Bhabha speaks of a 'third space.'

11. Young, op. cit., p. 17.

12. Ella Shohat, 'Notes on the "Post-Colonial"', *Social Text* 31/32 (1992): 99–113.

13. Following Rosalind Shaw and Charles Stewart, 'Introduction: Problematizing Syncretism,' in *Syncretism/anti-syncretism: the politics of religious synthesis*, ed. Charles Stewart and Rosalind Shaw (London: Routledge, 1994), p. 22.

Chung Hyun Kyung, 'Following Naked Dancing and Long Dreaming'

in Letty Russell (ed.), *Inheriting Our Mothers' Gardens: Feminist Theology in Third World Perspective*, Louisville, KY: Westminster Press, 1998, pp. 53–70.

Chung Hyung Kyung is a Korean theologian who is best known for her radical affirmation of the mixed roots of her own religious identity. She believes authentic Christianity is a resilient and adaptable religion that should not fear the consequences of encounters with other traditions. There is no pure kernel to belief. Faith must grow out of the native soil of the people who profess it and carry the authentic marks of their sufferings, ancestral memories and traditions. However, Chung does not believe that this entails a nostalgic or uncritical attitude to the past. Cultures carry profoundly conservative practices into contemporary contexts and these must always be challenged. Women, and others who are disenfranchised by hierarchical systems, can use their own narratives, experiences and survival strategies to help mutate ambivalent traditions into liberating and life giving forms.

In the essay printed here, Chung narrates the moving story of her 'two mothers'. This encapsulates, in an especially vivid form, her thinking on the themes of hybridity, resilience and liberation: topics she explores in more conventional terms in her other theological writing (see, for example, Chung 1990). As well as communicating some very challenging ideas this passage is also a personal testimony to the spiritual strength and wisdom of women who are seeking to find ways of engaging with traditional religious ideas and new religious thinking in order to pass on a precious inheritance to their daughters.

'Mom, stop it!'

I screamed at her, but she did not look at me. She continued her dance, moving nearly naked in the forest. I felt ashamed of her; I wished she were not my mother. There was nothing to hide the scene before me. There was a deathly silence around us, except for Mother's singing and the sound of the river.

Under the hot sun of August, the forest seemed to be taking a nap. There were no villagers moving about, only Mother and I. She looked like a person who did not belong to this world. I saw real happiness in her face while she was singing and dancing. I could see her breasts, the lines of her body – large, like a whale's – through her wet underwear. I did not want anybody in the world to see that shape, my mother's body that had worked and lived. I finally started to cry out of extreme embarrassment. I wanted to hide from her. She did not look anymore like the noble mother of whom I was always proud. But in spite of my crying, she continued singing and dancing, twirling in the forest as a child might, twirling and dancing in a space of her own.

This happened twenty-four years ago, when I was seven. My mother and I were traveling together to visit her older sister, who lived in a small, remote village in a southern province in Korea. My father was deeply involved with his business and had remained at home in Seoul. I had been raised in a big city, and traveling to a remote village was not easy for me. No bus or train service was available. We had to go over the mountain and cross the river. I was exhausted from walking so long on the dusty road under a hot summer sun. Mom had been telling me stories from her childhood as we were walking – how she had played in the river and climbed the mountain with her sisters. So when we came to the river, Mother's memories came to life and she took off her clothes and started to bathe in the water. She encouraged me to bathe with her. I was shocked. How could she do this? I looked to see whether there were any other people around. No one was there. I did not approve of my mother's behavior at all. I hoped she would finish her bathing as soon as possible. I sat on the riverbank and waited.

At last she got out of the water, but the situation only grew worse. She began singing a song I had never heard before. She danced while she was singing. I thought my mother had gone crazy; otherwise she would never have acted like that. Humiliation and confusion made me cry. 'Mom, stop it, *stop it!*' I screamed, but she continued to dance and sing, her body flopping and straining against the dampened clothes. I could not stop the tears from coming, and we stayed like that – me crying and her dancing – for some time. After a while, because of my continuous crying, she stopped her dance and put on her clothes and we took up our journey again.

One Mother's Story

Most of the time my mother behaved like a typical Korean housewife. She took care of us very well. She saved all the best parts of food for my father and me, eating the leftovers herself. She appeared to be submissive to my father and made many sacrifices on behalf of both of us. But there was a contradiction in her life. From time to time, her behavior showed a wild, raw, extreme passion for freedom that was not characteristic of the model Korean woman. The contradiction that she lived she also taught me. The manner in which she raised me was very different from other Korean mothers. Even though she kept telling me to be a 'nice' likable girl, she never asked me to cook for family gatherings or feasts, which is the Korean girl's family duty. Rather, she would give me a small amount of money and tell me to go to the library to study whenever the big feasts came. She always told me that I could learn how to cook any time I wanted, but I could not learn how to study once I became older. Sometimes she scolded me because she thought I was too tomboyish. She frequently told me that if I was not feminine, I would not get married because no man would want me. But at other times, she seriously told me not to get married. She said I could not live a full life in marriage because marriage, for a Korean woman, meant giving up freedom.

I still vividly remember the night I had a serious fight with my college boyfriend over the issue of marriage. I loved him very much, but I could not jump into the marriage, as he was insisting, because I had strong doubts about the limitations it would place on my freedom. I could not live without freedom. He accused me of being a selfish woman. I came home crying after a bitter argument with him and had a long conversation with Mother. After listening to my story, she leaned toward me in utter seriousness and offered her advice.

'Hyun Kyung,' she said, 'do not get married. I have been married for more than forty years. Marriage works for the man, but not for the woman. Forget about your boyfriend. Korean men don't understand women. Live fully. If you want to do something very much – from your heart, from your gut – then do it. Don't hesitate. If you don't have money, then make money, even if it means selling your used underwear. Discipline yourself to be a good scholar when you are young, since you always have loved to learn.' And she added, with ambivalence, 'Go abroad to study. And if, while you are studying, you find a good *Western* man who can understand *you*, your inner life, then get married. *Western* men seem more generous to women than Korean men.'

I was very surprised by my mother's response. I could not believe what she had said. Her advice to me contradicted my image of her as a model Korean woman, someone who worried that I might not get married, who scolded me for my 'unfemininity'.

My mother passed away one year after I arrived in the United States to begin my theological studies. I cried in my bed every night for more than six months after she died, missing her – missing her like a little motherless child. I felt as if I were standing by myself in the middle of a wilderness, struggling with a powerful storm. My mother had gone; it was the loneliest time in my life.

The Other Mother's Story

Three years after my mother's death, I returned to Korea. There I heard about the existence of my other mother from my cousin-sister. She told me that I had a birth mother besides my late mother. I could not believe it.

If it were true, how could it be that I had never heard about her? If it were true, it would mean that my late parents had totally deceived me. Even in their last words, my father and mother did not mention her to me. If I really did have another mother, a birth mother, then this woman had been erased from my family history, totally erased for the entire thirty years of my life.

My cousin-sister took me to meet my other mother. With confused emotions, I silently followed her until we came to the door of my other mother's home just outside the city of Seoul. I had brought a dozen red roses with me to give to my other mother. I stood at her doorway, holding the roses, and timidly reached for the doorbell.

An old woman opened the door. When she saw me her eyes filled with tears. She took my hands in her own and asked, 'Is this Hyun Kyung?' I said, 'Yes.' Then she began to sob. She told me, 'Finally I have met you! I thought I would die without seeing you. Now I can leave this world without holding my *han*.'[1]

I did not even know how I felt. I felt numb. Without knowing how to respond, I listened to her story.

My mother was a Korean version of a surrogate mother. In Korea, we call these women *ci-baji*. *Ci* means seed, *baji* means receiver. Therefore, the literal meaning of *ci-baji* is 'seed receiver'.[2] According to my birth mother, my late mother could not conceive a child even after twenty years of marriage. My father became very anxious. He wanted to have *his* own child in order to continue *his* family line. So he asked my late mother to search for a *ci-baji* woman for him. My late mother found a woman from the countryside who was a *yu-mo*[3] for a child in our neighbourhood. My father, however, did not like her at all; he thought she was not bright and beautiful enough to be a *ci-baji* for *his* future child. He sent her away and began to look for a *ci-baji* himself. He found a woman he liked, a woman who had lost her husband during the Korean War. She lived with her mother. My father followed her for a few months and finally persuaded her to conceive a baby for him. She and my father had posed for a picture when they knew that she had become pregnant, and she showed that picture to me. She was a good, healthy-looking woman. She gave birth to me and raised me until my first birthday.

The day after my first birthday, my parents came to my birth mother's house and took me from her. She did not want to let me go, but she could not challenge my parents. They were economically and politically powerful in her city. So she had to give me up, and I, of course, soon forget her.

She became mentally disordered for a while because of her intense feelings of helplessness and sadness. Even when she recovered from the mental disorder, she could not regain her physical strength for a long time. She said she spent more than a year crying and missing her child. My parents had commanded her not to see me until I had married and borne my first child.

My father was kind to her, but my mother was not. Once my birth mother visited my parents' home because she missed me so much, but my mother did not even allow her to enter the house. My birth mother kept a record of the days of my life. She showed me an old photo album. Surprisingly enough, there I was, first as an infant, a student, and at other stages of my life. She said my father had sent her photos of me, and she kept them carefully. She had watched me and prayed for me for thirty years. They were prayers offered from the shadow of history.

She had inquired after my well-being in various ways. She knew what happened to me in my primary school, high school, and college years. She asked people who had gone to school with me about my activities, but always without revealing her relationship to me. She deliberately did not make herself known to me in order not to hurt my feelings or jeopardize my future. In Korean tradition, children who are born by a *ci-baji* woman are not considered legitimate; they are like second-class children. In the Yi Dynasty, which lasted until the dawn of the twentieth century in Korea, those who were born of a surrogate mother could not take exams to hold governmental offices.[4] This tradition still thrives in Korean society today, although in a subtle way. That is why she did not want to reveal herself to me. She remained hidden for my sake.

I stayed with her for two days before returning to the United States. When she fell asleep, I looked into her face. White hair and many wrinkles told me of her hard life's journey. In her face, I met all Korean women who had been erased into the underside of 'he-story'. I held her hand and cried.

Marriage and Motherhood

These are the stories of two women. One had the privilege of being a 'legitimate' wife and mother but continuously wondered about the meaning of marriage. She had the safety of assured food, clothing, and shelter because she was a legitimate wife, but she also had to accept her husband's affair – also 'legitimate' – because she was barren. She wanted freedom badly, but she could not go beyond the rules of Korean society.

The other woman was denied the privilege of being a legitimate wife and mother because she was not officially married to my father. This 'illegitimacy' put her on the underside of history. She became a 'no-name' woman, who was nearly erased from my family history. Even though she was productive, she was unable to claim her right and space as mother of the child to whom she had given life. She was threatened continuously by poverty because she did not have a legitimate husband, whose duty, according to Korean tradition, would have been to take care of his wife.

My mothers hated each other. The one who raised me resented the one who gave birth to me because she thought this woman took her husband's love away. She might better have hated her husband, but she could not; he was the one who gave her security within the structure of society. All her anger and frustration were projected onto my birth mother, the safest target to attack. For her part, my birth mother hated the mother who raised me, because she took her baby and thus became the 'legitimate' mother of her child. And of course my birth mother missed me even more because the mother who raised me did not allow her to see me.

Both mothers loved their child. I really believe the mother who raised me loved me as a birth mother would have. In many ways, she totally devoted herself to me, always being there when I needed her. I still remember vividly the way she treated me, taking me everywhere she went, decorating my hair with many colorful ribbons. She often told me I was the most beautiful girl in the world, even though I was not a pretty girl at all in the ordinary sense.

When I prepared for the junior high school and senior high school entrance exams, she brought warm lunches, freshly cooked, to my school every day in order to encourage my studies. My success in school was very important to her. Once I was almost forced to drop out of college because I could not afford the tuition. At that time my father was bankrupt. We had moved to a very poor neighborhood and hardly had enough money to cover everyday expenses. I decided to give up my studies, but she would not let me. She promised to borrow some money from her close friends. On the day she was to bring the money, I sat in the registrar's office, waiting for her. Hours passed, but she did not come. I almost gave up. Then, near closing time, I saw her: my elderly mother running to the registrar's office in my college. She was sweating. I could see she was exhausted, but also relieved. Very gently, she placed the money in my hand. I broke into tears. Sobbing, I asked her, 'Mother, where did you get this money? I know you have been worried about buying even the basic things.'

Her eyes filled with tears too. 'Don't worry about that. God provided the money. You just study hard.' I loved her from the deepest part of my heart. Even though I was confused by her ambivalent remarks concerning marriage and femininity, she provided me with the space I needed to explore my own daring ideas. In the ways that matter, I was her 'own' child.

My birth mother loved me too. She wanted me to be the legitimate child of a good family. She did not want to ruin my social image, to make me subject to the scornful strictures that Confucian culture in the Korean tradition sets for those born outside of marriage. That was why she spent thirty years following my life from the shadows. She showed her love for me by waiting and erasing herself totally from my personal history. She told me how much she wanted to come for my college graduation and marriage ceremony. I was *her* 'own' child too.

When I met my birth mother in Korea last summer, she talked about my late mother with both anger and gratitude. She was angry because my late mother despised her, yet she was thankful that I had been raised to be a healthy and strong woman.

Both my mothers were victims of a male-defined family system. My father benefited from both women. He received everyday nurturing from my late mother and a child from my birth mother. Since a child is necessary to continue a man's family lineage in Korean culture, he did not feel any social pressure against having a relationship with another woman outside of wedlock. It seemed little more than the natural order of things. But both of my mothers suffered from this social system. For them, it was not a small thing.

The only person who could bring about reconciliation between these two women was their child. Their child was the only connecting factor that could ease the bitterness between them. The love they felt for me enabled them to accept each other in spite of the chasm between them, a chasm caused by the action of a man who held so much power over them.

These are the stories, then, of two mothers who shared a child, the lives of three women bound together by love and embittered by a tradition that honors only men.

Choosing Life: My Mothers' Spirituality

Sometimes I wonder how my mothers could sustain their sanity. My late mother struggled with the burden of being a noble woman within a strenuous marriage that did not acknowledge her humanity, and my birth mother struggled to retain her dignity in the context of continuous poverty and social ostracism. As I now reflect on both mothers' histories, I realize that they used all the life-giving resources they could find around them in order to keep their lives going.

My late mother was officially a Christian. She was a member of a big church in Seoul, where she participated in a strong women's mission group. She played the role of a nice Christian lady in that church. The mission group program gave her an opportunity to express herself in a public area, providing a legitimate excuse to go out of the house. Through that program she found her self-worth as a 'public' person.

However, her Christian faith was not dogmatic. She changed Christian doctrine to suit her own convenience. For example, she had a very interesting view of our ancestor spirit and developed her own religious system. Since my father was a Confucianist, my mother's duty as his wife was to prepare big feast meals for ancestor worship two or three times a month, despite the fact that many Christian churches in Korea still taught that ancestor worship contradicted the Christian faith. One day when I was six years old, one of my friends told me something she had learned in Sunday school: 'You will go to hell if you continue to worship your ancestors!' This was a real shock to me, because I wanted to go to heaven. So on the next ancestor worship day, I asked my mother about the relationship between the Christian God and my ancestors. My mother answered that my ancestors were secretaries of Jesus Christ, who was a god to my mother. 'Because Jesus Christ is so busy in heaven,' she said, 'he can't take care of every detail of our lives. That's why Jesus Christ uses our ancestors as his secretaries to get things done.' My mother's answer relieved me of the fear of going to hell.

Mother seemed to have created a peace for herself between Christian faith and Confucian practice. Both figured prominently in her religious life. She also drew spiritual strength from other strains of traditional Korean religiosity. For example, she often went to female fortune-tellers[5] when she really had a life crisis. She did not go to see Christian ministers[6] – males – to solve her personal problems, even though she was officially a Christian.

My mother also went to a Buddhist temple from time to time, whenever she wanted to meet her women friends and play or dance with them. Korean Buddhism did not prohibit women from drinking, smoking, or dancing during Buddhist festivals – very different from the teaching of Christian missionaries.[7] When Buddha's birthday came, she went to the temple and celebrated with her women friends, drinking and dancing. Some orthodox Christians would say my mother was a heretic because she mixed religions and did not know the real essence of Christianity. Maybe she did not know what was orthodoxy and what was heresy, but she *did* know which things offered life-giving power. And she grasped them with both hands.

My birth mother went through a spiritual journey similar to my late mother's, even though she was extremely underprivileged by comparison. She said she was a Buddhist when she was young, and she had two dreams about my arrival into the world while she was pregnant.

In her first dream, she was inside the temple, holding me piggyback while bowing down to the Buddha. When she finished her bow, the big bell suspended at the temple ceiling began to ring. She immediately knew that my arrival was Buddha's blessing. In a second dream, she saw my father sitting on a small pagoda on Mudeng Mountain in Kwang-Ju.[8] He was wearing a rainbow outfit. Then an amazing thing happened. When she approached my father, Mudeng Mountain suddenly changed to salt. It became Salt Mountain. Salt is a positive symbol in the Korean shamanistic tradition.[9] Korean people believe that salt has the power to exorcise evil spirits. My birth mother received an affirmation of her pregnancy from the Buddha and indigenous Korean spirits. We Koreans call dreams that are connected with a pregnancy *tae-mong*[10] – dreams that show the future of the baby.

My birth mother believed in her dreams. Even though Korean society did not approve of her pregnancy, she knew that the baby came through Buddha's compassion and protection from evil spirits. I was so grateful to her for remembering the details of her *tae-mong*. I felt connected to the ocean of Asian traditions and to the revolutionary spirit of Kwang-Ju, a small city that has been the city of freedom fighters in Korean tradition. She said I was born there; I did not know that. My parents had changed my birthplace on the official governmental records in order to hide my real origin.

My birth mother also visited fortune-tellers in order to check on my well-being. They told her that I would be a great scholar, and she believed them. She said to me she *knew* that I would be very good at school and finally would actually become a scholar. There were no doubts in her mind.

Now she is a deacon in a pentecostal church in Korea. I know the church very well. I hated that church so much as a theological student; I used to think it was dispensing otherworldly, ahistorical religious opium to the people. But after hearing my birth mother's painful life story, I came to understand why she chose that church. Maybe that church was the only place where she felt comfortable, where her spirit was lifted out of this painful world and given a place to dream. This kind of religion can easily become an opiate for people who have no options, no routes out of their personal impasses.[11] Opium is like a magician, for those who have no access to change; it enables them to endure intolerable pain.

My two mothers mixed and matched all the spiritual resources they found around them and established their own comfortable religious cosmos in their hearts. Their center of spirituality was not Jesus, Buddha, Confucius, or any of the various fortune-tellers. All these religious personalities and spirits helped my mothers in various stages of their life journeys, but none dominated their inner life. The real center for their spirituality was life itself. They consciously and uncon-sciously – mostly the latter – selected the life-giving aspects of each religion and rejected the death-giving ones. As Alice Walker said of her great-grandmother's spirituality, my mothers 'knew, even without "knowing" it'.[12] It was a matter of the epistemology of the body. Maybe their conscious selves could not catch up with what their body said because their conscious selves were not ready for the 'new paradigm'. Orthodoxy and heresy debates were meaningless to them, since the words themselves were unfamiliar. Most Korean women of my mothers' age could not go beyond a primary-school education. Their fathers did not send them to school. Higher education was for boys. Boys, therefore, learned how to fight against heresies, how to safeguard their narrow, privileged circles for orthodoxy. Girls did not learn the fancy words in their primary schools.

My mothers made 'chemical changes' in traditional religions by infusing them with the liberative thrusts of already existing religions. Since women were excluded from the public process of determining the meaning of religion, they were free to carve out a religion on their own, without the constraints of orthodoxy. Their 'imposed freedom' allowed them to develop in private a religious organic whole that enabled them to survive and liberated them in the midst of their struggle for full humanity. I want to name my mothers' distinctive spirituality as 'survival-liberation-centered syncretism'. The heart of their spirituality was the life power that sustained and liberated them. 'Life-giving power' is the final criterion by which the validity of any religion is judged.

Inheriting My Mothers' Gardens Through Naked Dancing and Dreaming

Inheriting my mothers' gardens is a dangerous business because I inherited not only their flowers and fruits but also their insects. If I am not a good gardener, the insects will destroy my mothers' gardens. I have to look very closely at the flowers and fruits in order to pick out the insects.

I found some insects in my late mother's garden. They may be called classism, the caste system, and cultural imperialism. Since her husband had money and she was his first and only legitimate wife, my mother used her privilege against another woman, my birth mother. Still, my late mother wanted to get out of her suffocating Korean housewife's role. The problem was that she could not find many channels for her liberation.

Under the patriarchal system, which is defined by the interests of men only, women are separated among themselves according to men's needs. Because women are not the subject of their destiny and relationships but are the object of men's desire and pleasure, women are not raised to make active life-affirming relationships with other women. They are trained only to develop intimate relationships with men, and then only at the men's convenience. Under this patriarchal system, women cannot love each other. They have to be competitive and become enemies to each other because their human worth can only be affirmed by men. In my mothers' hatred for each other, I can see the most dangerous insect: patriarchy.

My late mother thought about the Western world as a model for the liberated world; she judged it by what she saw in the movies and magazines. She knew Western men opened doors for women and gave flowers to them and said 'Ladies first.' Therefore, my late mother assumed that Western men respected women. That was why she told me to marry one. Oh, dear Mom, I'll tell you: Even in the Western world, women are not respected and understood as you thought.

I am glad my father went bankrupt when I was eleven years old. We became very poor after that, and I learned how the majority of Korean people lived. Through the experience of poverty after my father's bankruptcy, I could see the class privilege of our family and the role we played in Korean society. This experience prepared me for the student movement and Minjung theology and finally enabled me to welcome my birth mother without feeling ashamed of her.[13]

In my birth mother's garden, I can find some insects too. Her internalized defeat took away all her power for fighting even before she started her battle against my late parents. She could not fight in this world; her consciousness told her so. She retreated to her own interior mental world, had bitter fighting there, and became mentally disordered. Mom, I am not going to run away into my inner world. I'll fight in this world, in this history, to claim my land and my power!

However, in spite of all these insects, I love my mothers' gardens. In view of the legacies of these gardens, the fruits and insects, what does it mean for me to be a theologian? It means that I must use the fruits they bequeathed to me to help create a perspective on religion that is liberating for women, a perspective that will enable us to claim our life-giving power. No longer will I accept a male-dominated religion or society but will fight until freedom comes for all women. My understanding of God is not primarily defined by the doctrines and ritualistic practices of Christian churches, Buddhist temples, or any other religion. God is found in the life experiences of poor people, the majority of them women and children, and She is giving them power not only to survive amid wretched conditions but also to overcome those conditions. The beauty of the flowers in my mothers' gardens makes me cry with joy; the bittersweetness of their fruits makes me refreshed and nourished.

Dear Moms!

Today is a beautiful day. I invite both of you to my garden. My garden is not fancy, but I am growing some strong, healthy flowers, vegetables, and fruit trees. I named them Eve, Mother of All; Mary, Mother of Jesus; Kwan-In, goddess of compassion; Pārvatī, goddess of cosmic dance; Sarah; Hagar; Du-Ran;[14] Kwang-Myung;[15] and many other women I like.

Here you can dance the naked dance again. I'll join you this time, not crying but laughing. Mary will sing the Magnificat for your dance. Sarah and Hagar will teach you the circle dance. They're a great team. You'll like them.

You would be surprised if you knew how similar your life experiences are to theirs. Pārvatī is a great dancer too. We'll have a spirit-lifting dance festival. If we become tired after joyful dancing, we can take a rest under Eve's apple tree. We can share her apples when we become hungry. Then we can take a nice nap under Kwan-In's Boddi tree. She'll lead us to a fantastic dream world. You'll meet many wise people in your dream.

How does it sound? Exciting, isn't it? Next year, I want to invite many other sisters from various parts of the world to my garden. We'll have a great time together.

Then, maybe next-next-next year, when my plants and trees become stronger, I will invite my fathers and brothers too, if they promise not to play war games in my garden. Then we'll have a family reunion.

Moms, thank you! I am so glad you taught me how to be a gardener. I am so proud of both of you.

Shalom!

Much love,
Your daughter, *Hyun Kyung*

27 September 1987

Notes

1. *Han* is the typical, most prevailing feeling of the Korean people. Korean theologian Hyun Young-Hak described our deep, shared feeling of *han* vividly: 'Han is a sense of unresolved resentment against injustice suffered, a sense of helplessness because of the overwhelming odds against a feeling of total abandonment ("Why hast thou forsaken me?"), a feeling of acute pain, of sorrow in one's guts and bowels making the whole body writhe and wiggle, and an obstinate urge to take revenge and to right the wrong, all these combined.' From Hyun Young-Hak's unpublished lecture at James Memorial Chapel, Union Theological Seminary, New York, April 13, 1982, p. 7.

2. In Korean tradition, *ci-baji* women have been considered baby machines, giving birth to babies out of wedlock for privileged families. Most of them come from underprivileged political, economic, and social backgrounds. Although they take an active role in giving birth to a baby, they are considered little more than a body that produces a baby and do not have the right to keep their children.

3. The literal meaning of 'yu-mo' is 'milk-mother'. These are women who breast-feed children who are not their own: wet nurses in English. These women come from underprivileged backgrounds too.

4. For the resource for women's life under Confucianism, see Lee Ock-Kyung, 'A Study on Formational Condition and Settlement Mechanism of Jeong Juel (Faithfulness to Husband by Wife) Ideology of Yi Dynasty', M.A. thesis from Ewha Women's University, Seoul, Korea, 1985.

5. Fortune-tellers in Korea analyze people's destinies and tell their futures by looking at palm lines, face, etc. Their basic philosophy comes from a Korean-style mixture of Taoism, Shamanism, and Buddhism.

6. Ordained ministry has been a man's job in Korean Christian history. There are very few women ministers, and most of them are single. The majority of the

denominations in Korea consider it illegal to ordain a married woman. Very few accept the ordination of married women.

7. Many Korean churches teach that drinking and smoking are serious sins. Korean society, as a whole, does not consider smoking and drinking acceptable behaviors for women.

8. Kwang-Ju was the site of many demonstrations against Japanese colonialism and dictatorship. It became a symbol of resistance in Korea, especially after the 1980 massacre, in which 2,000 civilians fighting for freedom and democracy were killed by the military.

9. Shamanism is a woman-centered popular religiosity in Korea. It has many gods but no creeds or dogmas or church buildings. Through shamanistic rituals, Koreans exorcise evil spirits, heal the sick, and console those who are oppressed.

10. In Korea, *tae-mong* plays an important role in determining the meaning of one's life. People believe that *tae-mong* is God's prophecy for the baby. Most autobiographies or biographies begin with a description of the *tae-mong*. A baby is connected with all of the past and the future through *tae-mong*.

11. This impasse causes the feeling of *han* in oppressed people. For more information about the relationship between impasse and *han*, see Suh Nan-Dong, 'Towards a Theology of Han', *Minjung Theology* (Singapore: Christian Council of Asia, 1981), pp. 51–69.

12. Alice Walker, *In Search of Our Mothers' Gardens* (San Diego, Calif.: Harcourt Brace Jovanovich, 1983), p. 237.

13. *Minjung* means 'grassroot people' in Korea. Minjung theology arose out of the Korean people's experience of suffering and liberation under the political dictatorship and economic exploitation of the 1970s.

14. My late mother's name.

15. My birth mother's name.

Robert Beckford, 'Jah would never give power to a baldhead: Bob Marley as a Black liberation theologian'

in *Jesus is Dread: Black Theology and Black Culture in* Britain, London: Darton, Longman & Todd, 1998, pp. 117–29.

One of the most challenging questions for local theologians is, in what spirit they should respond to the insights they encounter in other religious and cultural movements. This is not only an academic question concerning the legitimacy of inter-religious dialogue. Nor is it principally a practical question concerning the ways in which Christian rituals might 'borrow' elements that have been important within indigenous cultures. For many, this is also a political issue that entails affirming cultural integrity in the struggle against oppression. In other words it is a question of discovering resources that will sustain faith and generate hope among those who have experienced forms of

Christianity that have denied the worth and value of their spiritual traditions.

This is a subject that is tackled directly in Robert Beckford's important book Jesus is Dread *(1998). In this he demonstrates the significance of music in empowering Black people to resist racism and assert the significance of their religious inheritance. In the extract below he focuses on the Jamaican Rastafarian musician Bob Marley. He asks his readers to examine the theological content of Marley's work and discover what Christians might learn from a serious engagement with his music. There is no suggestion here that Marley should be 'baptized' as a Christian theologian. Nor is it implied that we should uncritically accept all that Marley stands for and has come to represent. However, Beckford does suggest that we might discover more authentic and liberating forms of Christianity through listening to what Marley has to say and concludes that Marley points us towards a God, 'in tune with the rhythms of Black life'.*

Marley's method

What then is Marley's theological method? I want to suggest two significant focuses: the first concerns the way he validates truth (that is, his system of knowing); the second concerns the way in which he interprets the Bible. We begin with his system of knowing.

Marley's knowledge-system

Naturally, Marley does not use the traditional theological methods found in your average systematic theology textbook. Instead, he draws upon three Jamaican traditions. The first is the use of experience; the second is a commitment to radical social change; and the third is the nature of the discourse, reggae music. Let us begin with experience.

For Bob Marley, experience is the basis for interpreting the social world. Consequently, he rejects the knowledge-validation processes used in the classrooms of traditional education. For Marley, traditional education is a false consciousness which maintains the subservient position of Black people. Explicit reference is made to education as false consciousness in the song *Four Hundred Years* from the *Catch a Fire* album, where The Wailers (vocals by Peter Tosh) causally link four hundred years of Black oppression with a corrupt educational system:

> Four hundred years and it's the same philosophy,
> Four hundred years and the people they still cannot see . . .
> Four hundred years, four hundred years
> Head-decay-shun and the same philosophy.

Marley's rejection of the educational system is symbolically expressed in his changing the English word 'education' to form 'head-decay-shun'. Head-decay-shun is oppression.

'Real' knowledge for Marley must be validated by experience. Experience is a filter which enables us to find meaning in the world. For instance, experience as the criterion of meaning is demonstrated in the title-song from the *Natty Dread* album. On the surface, the song describes a Rasta walking the Jamaican streets; as he walks, he hears children calling to him, sees the buildings and eventually, through these experiences, realises that Jamaica is not the home of the Rasta:

> I walked up the first street,
> And I walked up the second street to see.
> Then I trod on through third street,
> And then I call to some Dread on fourth street.
> Natty dread locks in a fifth street.
> And I skip one place to sixth street.
> I've got to reach seventh street . . .
> Oh, Oh, Natty, Natty,
> Natty twenty-one thousand miles away from home
> Oh Natty, Natty
> And that's a long way
> For Natty to be from home.

On another level, we can interpret the song as the Rasta's inner journey, the streets representing stages of consciousness. This journey entails the growing knowledge of ethnic identity and historical belonging. So the first aspect of Marley's method is a system of knowing built on personal experience. But the problem with experience is that it does not offer a more accurate means of assessing truth-claims: experience is simply a more democratic way of approaching the analysis of a given situation. Its primary benefit is that it allows insight from subjugated perspectives.

The second aspect of Marley's method is commitment to radical social change. There are two areas of concern in his music: first, the destruction of Babylon, and second, the liberation of the poor.

The existing social order – or 'Babylon' – must be destroyed. As Carolyn Cooper has shown,[1] Marley advocates both militant and psychological revolution. Regarding the former, on several occasions Marley advocates violent change. For example, in *Crazy Baldheads* from the album *Rastaman Vibration*, he advocates noncooperation with the system (the penal, educational and religious institutions). In addition, 'Baldheads' – those who defend the system – must be dealt with:

> Build your penitentiary; we build your schools
> Brain-wash education to make us the fools.
> Hate-rage you reward for our love
> Telling us of your God above.
> We gonna chase those crazy,
> Chase those crazy bunkheads,
> Chase those crazy Baldheads out of the town.

On other occasions, Marley advocates a more philosophical, less aggressive, approach to radical social transformation. Cooper shows that, whereas *Crazy Baldheads* talked of militant social action, *Redemption Song* on the *Uprising* album develops the subject of psychological liberation. This song tells Black people to free themselves from psychological oppression, referred to as 'mental slavery':

> Emancipate yourselves from mental slavery
> none but ourselves can free our minds.
> Have no fear for atomic energy
> Cause none of them can stop the time.
> How long shall they kill our prophets
> While we stand aside and look?
> Some say, 'It's just a part of it,
> We've go to fulfil the book.'
> Won't you help to sing
> These songs of freedom?
> Cause all I ever had,
> Redemption songs.

It is Marley's belief that emancipation from mental slavery is integral to liberation from social and political oppression. For example, the third line of the song, 'Have no fear for atomic energy', was written to give psychological empowerment to the African National Congress (ANC) after White apartheid South Africa had become a nuclear power. In this song, Marley wants the ANC to know that not even White nuclear power can 'stop the time' – that is, prevent the inevitability of their victory.

The second facet of Marley's commitment to radical social change is the emancipation of the poor. Marley's canon contains much creative insight into the plight of the poor, not only in Jamaica but also in Africa. He speaks with conviction of the systematic brutalisation of the weak by the powerful. However, as mentioned in the song *slave driver*, 'the table is turned'. The poor must now rise up. For example, in the song *Big Tree*, Marley proclaims that the weak and the poor, inspired by Jah, will put a halt to the work of the wicked. Marley's quest for radical social change was not realised in his lifetime – but this was not necessarily his aim. Far more important was his desire to raise the awareness of the Black masses. In this task, his contribution to Black consciousness was immense – the reason for Marley (along with several tons of amplification equipment) being the star attraction at Zimbabwe's Independence Day celebrations.

The third aspect of Marley's method is the nature of his discourse – that is, reggae music. Reggae music emerges from the urban proletariat in Jamaica. It is the descendant of slave music, containing the survivals of slave rhythms and songs. Reggae reveals how the medium in which theology is expressed is itself significant for communicating the meaning of God. In Black churches, song is a valid means of communicating divine truth – indeed, Black Pentecostalists believe that God is present in certain types of song or music. When the presence of God's Spirit is felt in a song, Black Pentecostalists talk about the music and song being 'anointed'. In a similar fashion, I am suggesting that God (Jah) may be present in the rhythms of reggae music, which expresses the aspirations of oppressed people. However, it is important to note that not all reggae is Rastafarian worship music. But our primary concern here is with 'churchical' or worship music in Rastafari.

In summary, Marley's system of knowing consists of three tools: experience, a commitment to radical social change and reggae music. Our next task is to show how this theological method interacts with the Bible. We turn to Marley's method of interpretation.

Marley's biblical interpretation

Marley's interpretive method is best understood as a process. It begins with inner revelation – truth which emerges from personal experience. In other words, when Marley says, 'So Jah seh', he refers to revelation which has come directly from Jah. Once revelation emerges, the Bible must confirm it. Guidance means finding correspondence between revelation and a biblical event, symbol or word. This exploration of the text might take place individually or communally. Reasoning with Jah is sometimes assisted by burning incense in the temple of God – that is, smoking 'ganja' (cannabis).

This hermeneutic is witnessed in the development of key doctrines. For example, the founding fathers of Rastafari believed in the deity of Haile Selassie (1892–1975 – former Emperor of Ethiopia), in Black repatriation to Africa, and that the Western world, including Jamaica, was evil. They found support for these beliefs in the Bible, and used biblical images to signify a range of correspondences with these revelations. Hence in the lyrics of Marley we discover that Selassie signifies Jah Rastafari, Africa corresponds to the Promised Land, or Zion, and Jamaica is synonymous with evil or Babylon. Marley uses this hermeneutic to interpret the contents of the Bible. I would like to demonstrate this by focusing on two of his theological hallmarks: the Second Advent of the Messiah, and Africa as the land of liberation.

The arrival of the Second Advent is declared in *Get Up, Stand Up*, on the *Burnin'* album. Marley and the Wailers confess, 'We know and we understand, the Mighty God is a living man'. Here, the 'Mighty God' is Haile Selassie. He is the Black God who has returned to save Black people. The proof of his divinity lies in Rasta's personal revelation and also biblical proof: for instance, in *Blackman Redemption*, on the *Confrontation* album, Selassie's genealogy is used as proof of his divinity: as Emperor of Ethiopia, Selassie (like Christ) is 'from the root of David, through the line of Solomon'. So just as Christians declare Jesus divine because of revelation and biblical confirmation, Marley, as a Rasta, declares Selassie divine. However, this interpretation is problematic for two reasons: first, it reveals an uncritical approach to the text; second, it relies heavily upon an idealised and romanticised view of African history.

The second theological hallmark of Bob Marley's songs is the belief that Africa – in particular, Ethiopia – is the land of liberation for Blacks. Old Testament references to Ethiopia, such as, 'Let bronze be brought from Egypt; let Ethiopia hasten to stretch out her hands to God' (Ps. 68:31), are Rastafarian proof texts which support the belief that Africa plays a central role in God's plan for Black redemption. Moreover, repatriation to Africa is seen as part of God's act of deliverance. In the title-track from the *Exodus* album, repatriation to Ethiopia is expressed as the flight of 'Jah people' to Africa. Marley asks each person to search themselves, recognise who they are and consequently leave Babylon:

> Open your eyes and look within
> Are you satisfied with the life you're living?
> We know where we're going
> We know where we're from.
> We're leaving Babylon
> We're going to our father's land.
> Exodus!
> Movement of Jah people.

Here, the personal revelation of the importance of Africa, reaffirmed in Scripture, results in a new practice: the return of Black people to Africa, psychologically as well as physically.

Is Marley a Black liberation theologian?

First, we must answer a more general question: is Marley a theologian at all? As we have seen above, Bob Marley has a theological method and applies it to the Christian Scriptures in order to produce a theology. In my opinion, Marley is a theologian – not necessarily a traditional Christian theologian but definitely a Rastafarian theologian. However, despite speaking on behalf of the marginalised and being of working-class origins, on another level, Marley must be seen and heard as a wealthy musician who maintained physical and political links with the Jamaican proletariat. In short, his perspectives, as a Rastafarian theologian, emerge from a position of relative privilege in the Jamaican context.

Second, I would contend that Marley is a Black liberation theologian, because his theology is totally concerned with the liberation of the oppressed. Nowhere is this more clearly articulated than in the final track from the *Kaya* album, entitled, *Jah would never Give Power to a Baldhead*. Here, Marley states that the work of Jah in the world is the liberation of the marginalised and downtrodden. Such is Marley's belief in God's bias towards the poor that he states categorically:

> Jah would never give power to a Baldhead
> Run come crucify the Dread
> Time alone, oh time will tell
> Think you're in heaven but you're living in hell.

Here, it is impossible for God to bless those who oppress. It is only a matter of time before divine retribution is meted out to the misguided oppressors: their heaven will become hell.

What can we learn from Marley the theologian?

We turn to our next question: if we take Marley seriously as a Black liberation theologian, what can we learn from him? I would like to outline three areas in which Marley's theology speaks to our contemporary context in Britain.

Theology and ideology

First, he informs us that theology is an ideological project – is never neutral or value-free. Like Marx, Marley believes that religion reflects human interests. In this case, Marley's ideology bespeaks local and global resistance against racialised oppression. As far as Marley is concerned, to refuse to stand up for the rights of the disenfranchised is to show a flagrant disregard for the value of human life. For example, in *Get Up, Stand Up*, on the *Burnin'* album, Marley declares to Christian people: 'If you knew what life was worth, you would fight for yours on earth'. Importantly, Marley formulates his understanding of God in the oppressed community, seeing God in the faces of the Black dispossessed.

However, we must recognise the negative ideologies in Marley's canon. Black feminist Patricia Hill Collins encourages Black thinkers to look at the lives of those people whom we deem important figures in Black communities, in order to see if their personal lives match up to their ideas. Marley's personal life raises questions for Black women, suggesting that he did not have a lot of respect for them. His promiscuous lifestyle, and his general failure to honour Black women in his music, reminds those of us concerned with using Marley as a source for our theology that any theological enterprise concerned with Black liberation in Britain must take seriously the multidimensional nature of oppression. That is, we must be not only concerned with racism but also with sexism. Given the race, class and gender exploitation of Black British women, any theology of liberation must be a theology that empowers Black women.

The African heritage

Despite Marley's highly romanticised and uncritical appropriation of Africa, there is much to gain from his focus on Africa as an area of biblical significance. Marley's Afrocentrism challenges the thrust of any Black British theology. His method suggests that our religious and cultural African roots are as important as the historical and cultural routes that make many Black people a diasporan people. This point is vitally important, especially when we consider the cultural, social, political and religious ignorance of many Black Christians in Britain concerning their African heritage. Furthermore, Marley's orientation inspires a healthy political suspicion of all theological studies and approaches which are patronising and negatively biased against Africa and Africans, both continental and diasporan. This is a real issue in theological education, where Africa and Africans are ignored in biblical studies. Only in recent years, through the efforts of Afrocentric biblical scholars and popularist writers, have Black biblical studies crept on to the syllabus of a few British theological institutions which have the vision and courage to take Black perspectives seriously. It has been interesting to note those biblical scholars who go out of their way to denigrate Black approaches to the text, despite not having read work by Afrocentric biblical scholars.[2]

Music as theology

Marley reminds us of the importance of church music as a medium for doing theology. We live at a time when many Black churches continue to borrow songs from a variety of Christian traditions, both Eurocentric and Afrocentric. It is not uncommon to go into Black churches and hear songs from traditional English hymn books, the Moody and Sankey hymnal, and Graham Kendrick. However, Marley's theology encourages us to develop a hermeneutic of suspicion towards all songs and their lyrics, because genres are political. For example, Sunday after Sunday Black Christians sing about 'lilies of the valley' and 'deer panting after water'. There is little, if any, awareness of the political and theological implications of singing about spaces and places which have very little correspondence with the real-life social spaces and places occupied by many Black and non-Black urban people. Marley encourages us to question where our songs come from, and whose world-view they articulate and validate. Another way of looking at this is to ask what kind of theology would be communicated if the images used in songs emerged from Black life-settings. Marley is an example of this process: his songs tell of his world in Jamaica, its concrete social and political realities. This is why I often say to the song-leaders at my church in Handsworth, 'Why don't you write a song about God in the high-rise flats, maisonettes and housing association properties, rather than always referring to God in hills, valleys and mansions? Surely God belongs in our neighbourhood too?' What I am suggesting is a relocation of songs and lyrics to facilitate a more vivid expression of God's presence among us.

Marley's theology and Christianity

Possibly the most challenging aspect of Marley's theology is its diametric opposition to traditional Christianity. By proclaiming that 'Jah would never give power to a Baldhead', on the *Kaya* album, Marley rejects the authority of Baldhead religion, that is, Christianity.[3] Marley experiences European Christianity as an integral part of the *rhaatid* (English-raging)[4] Babylon system. Furthermore, the European-Christian collusion in slavery, colonialism, imperialism and neo-colonialism in Jamaica is proof of its inherent anti-Blackness. Hence, for Marley, Black people cannot achieve their God-given humanity within the Christian religion. To do so, they must become Rastafarian.

However, this is a contradiction. Although Rastafari claims to be qualitatively different from European theology, in reality Rastafari is bound to the traditional English–Christian religion, because it uses the same manuscript traditions and sources. Despite this aberration, Marley challenges us to question the usefulness of the Christian religion for Black disaporan subjects – namely, how can we reconstruct the Baldhead religion so that it has relevance in contemporary Black Britain? As mentioned above, when reconstructing Baldhead religion, we must take seriously Black women's (womanist) concerns about patriarchy in Black Christianity.

Marley's theology continues to live in the appropriations of Black diasporan music; it is highly significant that, for many weeks in the charts recently, the Number 1 song was *Killing Me Softly* by the versatile, highly politicised US hard-core hip-hop trio The Fugees, who claim Bob Marley as their primary musical influence.[5] In tribute, like many musicians worldwide, they rework his social and political critique and religious orientation. Hence, through The Fugees, another generation of listeners and consumers are exposed to Marley, whose theology points us to a God of rhythm, in tune with the rhythms of Black life.

References

1. Carolyn Cooper, *Noises in the Blood: Gender, Orality and the Vulgar Body of Jamaican Popular Culture* (Durham, NC: Duke University Press, 1995).
2. I have had numerous discussions with Black students who have told of their biblical studies lecturers' attitudes to Black and liberationist approaches to the text.
3. Bob Marley and the Wailers, *Time Will Tell, Kaya* (Island Records, 1978).
4. See Michio Ogata (ed.), *Rasta/Patois Dictionary*, updated 1995 (African Studies Web Site, 1996).
5. See *True Magazine* (May 1996).

Gordon Lynch, 'Why Should Theologians and Scholars of Religion Study Popular Culture?'

in *Understanding Theology and Popular Culture*, Oxford: Blackwell, 2005, pp. 36–40.

Gordon Lynch's book Understanding Theology and Popular Culture *(2005) is a very helpful exploration of the connections between 'seeking normative answers to questions of truth, goodness, evil and beauty' in religious/spiritual terms and the way people use the resources of popular culture to give their lives meaning, depth and coherence. In the extract below he takes as a working example the way film has become an important resource for theological reflection. While there are still some theologians who do not see popular culture as a medium that is able to carry the profound understandings of human life that theology seeks to engage with, many more are coming to recognize that film is one of the most important vehicles for the shared communication of spiritual values we currently possess.*

Recognizing the significance of film for theology does not lead to a consensus concerning how an authentic conversation between theology and popular culture should take place (see also the extract by W. Wright in Chapter 5 of this volume). Some theologians restrict their engagement to films with an explicit religious content or a biblical plot. Still others would look for 'Christ figures' within cinema. Lynch favours a more radical approach. A dialogue with film will enable theology to reflect upon its own values and commitments. The resources of popular culture offer a 'nitty gritty' picture of the realities of life outside the academic study or the parish setting. They also provoke reflection upon new visions of healing, power and redemption that are stirring in specific local contexts and are able to generate fresh and creative theological thinking.

Using the Texts and Practices of Popular Culture as Material for Theological Reflection

Defining theology can be as complex a task as defining 'religion' or 'popular culture', and the emergence of a range of contextual, liberation, and post-Christian theologies since the latter part of the twentieth century has further demonstrated the wide range of forms that this discipline can take (see, e.g., Ford, 2004). In this book, I will work with a broad definition of theology as the process of seeking normative answers to questions of truth, goodness, evil, suffering, redemption, and beauty in the context of particular social and cultural situations. The breadth of this definition [. . .] is aimed at including the wide range of people who find themselves involved in the study of academic theology today, a group that includes not only people with particular religious commitments (such as Christians, Jews, and Muslims) but also increasing numbers of people working from post-Christian or humanist perspectives. Whilst the way in which I talk about theology as a discipline in this book is intended to be as inclusive as possible, it is also realistic to recognize that 'theology' is still primarily conducted by people with religious (most often Christian) commitments or who are living and working in the context of particular church or faith communities. In practice, then, theology tends to be a discipline concerned with how particular religious traditions can be related issues of truth, goodness, evil, suffering, redemption, and beauty in the contemporary world.

If we understand theology as the exploration of these kinds of questions in relation to particular religious beliefs and traditions, then it is clear that a growing number of writers are using texts and practices from popular culture as a focus for such reflection. This approach to theological reflection typically involves a critical dialogue between a particular religious text or theological concept and a specific aspect of popular culture. Through this process of critical conversation between popular culture and theological texts and concepts, writers have thus sought to use popular culture as a means of exploring issues including the nature of God, the possibility of meaning in life, the nature of sin and evil, and the nature of redemption.

There is a particularly well-established literature of this style of theological reflection in relation to film (see, e.g., Marsh and Ortiz, 1997). Indeed Margaret Miles (1996) suggests that film is an important focus for theological reflection precisely because films are an important cultural medium through which contemporary issues and concerns are explored. Some writers, notably David Jasper (1997), have questioned whether popular film is simply too formulaic and superficial to serve as a serious focus for theological reflection. But the wider trend is for theologians to focus on popular Hollywood films rather than art-house movies as the focus for their work.

Within this approach to the theological study of popular culture, the notion of dialogue is a very important one. This concept implies that the popular cultural text or practice needs to be taken seriously on its own terms (i.e., its own 'voice' needs to be heard) in order for a proper conversation between theology and popular culture to take place. As Robert Johnston puts it in relation to film:

> the danger of theological imperialism is high enough in practice that I would argue that [Christian] moviegoers should first view a movie on its own terms before entering into theological dialogue with it . . . To give movie viewing this epistemological priority in the dialogue between film and theology – to judge it advisable to first look at a movie on its own terms and let the images themselves suggest meaning and direction – is not to make theology of second-ary importance . . . But such theologizing should follow, not precede, the aesthetic experience. (Johnston, 2000, p. 49)

An adequate dialogue between theology and popular culture thus requires what Michael Dyson (2001, p. 118) has referred to as an 'ethical patience', in which the theologian does not make hasty judg-ments about what they find tasteful or distasteful, or try to impose their pre-existing concepts on to popular culture. One example of the latter are books and articles that attempt to identify 'Christ-figures' in contemporary film (see, e.g., Malone, 1997; Bergeson and Greeley, 2000). To suggest, however, that Edward Scissorhands or the Preacher in *Pale Rider* are 'Christ-figures', though, is to impose Chris-tian symbolism on to these movies in a way that fails to hear what those movies are saying on their own terms. Serious theological reflection on popular culture goes beyond the superficial identification of religious themes and symbolism within it to a more substantial dialogue between cultural texts and practices and wider theological questions and resources.

Within the more substantial literature offering theological reflec-tion on popular culture, three particular approaches have so far emerged.

Firstly, there are writers who *explore popular culture in relation to biblical texts*. Robert Jewett (1993, 1999) has sought, for example, to relate Pauline letters from the New Testament to contemporary film. Jewett describes his work as an attempt to establish an 'interpretative arch' between film and biblical text in which a mutual dialogue can take place between the questions and concerns of contemporary culture and the questions and concerns of the first-century Church. Whilst Jewett recognizes the importance of listening seriously to the perspectives offered within contemporary film, he is also clear that he ultimately gives priority to insights that emerge out of the biblical text. This enables him, for example, to argue that the film *Amadeus* exemplifies Pauline notions of sin (Jewett, 1993, pp.31ff.) or to critique the notion of vengeance offered within the film *Pale Rider* (Jewett, 2000).

A different approach to studying popular culture in relation to the biblical text has been developed by Larry Kreitzer (1993, 1994, 2002). Rather than reading contemporary film in the light of biblical texts (as Jewett does), Kreitzer seeks to 'reverse the hermeneutical flow' and to read the Bible in the light of contemporary film. Kreitzer thus suggests that a sensitive engagement with the images and meanings of contemporary films can help to stimulate our imaginative and critical engagement with the Bible. For example, Kreitzer (2002, pp. 105ff.) notes recent debates amongst biblical scholars about the Synoptic Gospels' account of the crucifixion of Jesus, which began 'at the third hour' (i.e., 9 a.m.) and was marked by darkness suddenly falling 'on the sixth hour' (i.e., noon). These debates have encompassed discussion about the meaning of this claim about darkness falling. Is it, for example, meant to be a historical claim (for which there is no clear corroborating evidence) or is it meant to be a metaphorical statement about the unfolding struggle between Jesus and the forces of darkness? Kreitzer suggests that attention to a twentieth-century film such as *High Noon* can make us more aware of how narratives can use of images of time, light and darkness to heighten a sense of dramatic tension about an imminent conflict between good and evil. The implication is that through studying the film *High Noon*, we might be better equipped to engage imaginatively with the accounts of Jesus' crucifixion and might avoid getting into relatively fruitless debates about the historicity of specific claims of the Gospel text.

A second approach involves *exploring popular culture in relation to particular theological questions and concepts.* A good example of this approach is Christopher Deacy's (2001) book *Screen Christologies.*[1] A central concern for Deacy is the way in which contemporary films explore issues of redemption. Deacy claims, theologically, that redemption is only possible on the basis of a full and accurate recognition of the nature of the human condition. In the book of Ecclesiastes, for example, the narrator (Qoheleth) offers a detailed account of the arbitrary and apparently meaningless nature of human life. Yet is precisely out of a recognition of the bleak horizons within which we live that some kind of hope or redemption can be found. As Deacy (2001) puts it:

> Indeed, far from suggesting *rejection* of life, let alone self-destruction, Qoheleth affirms that *within* the limits of our knowledge, ability and circumstances . . . once we accept the actuality of death and the finitude of human existence without the illusions which the fear of death so easily generates, then the mind can be redeemed and set free from what amounts to a major source of crippling activity. We can subsequently learn to live authentically within the prescribed limitations and boundaries of our existence. (Deacy, 2001, p.61)

On the basis of this theological understanding of redemption, Deacy offers a critique of a range of contemporary films. He is critical of films such as Frank Capra's classic *It's a Wonderful Life*, which Deacy sees as offering an idealized, inauthentic vision of what human life is really like. By contrast, Deacy identifies the tradition of *film noir* as offering far more adequate, and ultimately redemptive, images of human existence. The *film noir* style (popularized by films such as *The Big Sleep, The Maltese Falcon,* and *Double Indemnity*) depicted characters who were morally ambiguous, and who were essentially powerless in the face of the arbitrary and meaningless nature of existence. At their conclusion, such films rarely offered neat resolutions of the dilemmas with which the characters had struggled. Such visions of human life are, argues Deacy, a far more authentic basis on which to begin to build genuinely redemptive responses rather than the escapist fantasies of the more traditional 'Hollywood ending'. Theological questions about the nature of redemption therefore provide Deacy with a framework for critically evaluating images of life offered through contemporary cinema.

A third style of theological reflection in relation to popular culture is to *explore popular culture as a source of methods for doing theology*. Anthony Pinn (1995, pp.113ff., 2000) has, for example, suggested that in the black musical traditions of blues and rap it is possible to identify a theological method of 'nitty gritty hermeneutics'. By this, Pinn means that it is possible within these musical genres to identity an approach to interpreting life which is committed to 'telling it like it is' in the face of a hostile world. Furthermore, this 'nitty gritty hermeneutics' is concerned with developing a full and honest insight of the world, even though this might mean challenging more romanticized images or unsettling existing social conventions. Such an approach to thinking about life remains important in the lives of black communities in America which continue to be blighted by racist and unjust social structures. Whilst Pinn acknowledges that rap music has not always offered the constructive social and cultural criticism that a 'nitty gritty hermeneutics' should aim for, he argues that rappers still provide a number of examples of a commitment to 'telling it like it is'. As such, Pinn argues, theologians may have useful lessons to learn about how to engage in their own work from such examples.

Robert Beckford (1998, pp. 115ff.) has also developed a similar argument in relation to the music of Bob Marley, in which he proposes that Marley's work offers important insights into what it means to undertake black liberation theology. Marley's music demonstrated his commitment to using his own experience of oppression to interpret the world, his commitment to social and psychological liberation, and his commitment to a particular discourse and cultural form (reggae music) to develop liberatory ideas and images. Marley's interpretation of the Bible was also fundamentally guided by his experience of oppression and commitment to liberation. Whilst Marley was clearly not a Christian theologian in any orthodox sense, Beckford argues that the commitments that shaped his music offer a useful guide for those who want to undertake black liberation theology. Again, popular culture can be read as providing models and methods for how theologians might conduct their own work.

Note

1. For other examples of this kind of study see Miles, 1996; Stone, 2000; Beckford, 2001, pp.98ff.

Bibliography

Beckford, R. (1998) *Jesus is Dread: Black Theology and Black Culture in Britain*, London: Darton, Longman and Todd.

Beckford, R. (2001) *God of the Rahtid: Redeeming Rage*. London: Darton Longman and Todd.

Bergeson, A. and Greeley, A. (2000) *God in the Movies*. New Brunswick: Transaction Publishers.

Deacy, C. (2001) *Screen Christologies: Redemption and the Medium of Film*, Cardiff: University of Wales Press.

Dyson, M. (2001) *Holler if You Hear Me: Searching for Tupac Shakur*, London: Plexus.

Ford, D. (ed.) (2004) *The Modern Theologians* (3rd edition), Oxford: Blackwell.

Jasper, D. (1997) 'On systematizing the unsystematic: a response,' in (eds.) C. Marsh and G. Ortiz, *Explorations in Theology and Film*, Oxford: Blackwell, pp. 235–44.

Jewett, R. (1993) *St Paul at the Movies: The Apostle's Dialogue with American Culture*, Louisville: Westminster John Knox.

Jewett, R. (1999) *St Paul Returns to the Movies: Triumph Over Shame*, Grand Rapids: Eerdmans.

Jewett, R. (2000) 'The disguise of vengeance in *Pale Rider*,' in (eds.) B. Forbes and J. Mahan, *Religion and Popular Culture in America*, Berkeley: University of California Press, pp. 243–57.

Johnston, R. (2000) *Reel Spirituality*, Grand Rapids, MI: Baker.

Kreitzer, L. (1993) *The New Testament in Fiction and Film: On Reversing the Hermeneutical Flow*, Sheffield: Sheffield Academic Press.

Kreitzer, L. (1994) *The Old Testament in Fiction and Film: On Reversing the Hermeneutical Flow*, Sheffield: Sheffield Academic Press.

Kreitzer, L. (2002) *Gospel Images in Fiction and Film: On Reversing the Hermeneutical Flow*, London: Continuum.

Malone, P. (1997) 'Edward Scissorhands: Christology from an urban fairy-tale,' in (eds.) C. Marsh and G. Ortiz, *Explorations in Theology and Film*, Oxford: Blackwell, pp. 73–86.

Marsh, C. and Ortiz, G. (eds.) (1997) *Explorations in Theology and Film*. Oxford: Blackwell.

Miles, M. (1996) *Seeing and Believing: Religion and Values in the Movies*, Boston, MA: Beacon.

Pinn, A. (1995) *Why Lord? Suffering and Evil in Black Theology*, New York: Continuum.

Pinn, A. (2000) 'Rap music and its message: on interpreting the contact between religion and popular culture,' in (eds.) B. Forbes and J. Mahan, *Religion and Popular Culture in America*, Berkeley: University of California Press, pp. 258–75.

Stone, B, (2000) *Faith and Film: Theological Themes at the Cinema*, St Louis: Chalice Press.

Philip Sheldrake, 'Space and the Sacred: Cathedrals and Cities'

Contact, No. 147, 2005, pp. 8–17.

This rich and multilayered article by Philip Sheldrake explores how cathedrals have functioned as symbols of transcendence from the 'great age' of their construction in the Middle Ages to the present day. We have located it in this section on local theology for two important reasons. First, Sheldrake considers the importance of cathedrals as 'spiritual texts'. Experts in church architecture will point out that every aspect of the construction of a cathedral has theological meaning. Sheldrake affirms this but points out that the sacred text of a Cathedral is like a palimpsest – an etched tablet upon which new meanings are continually overscored upon what has already been written. The disorderly inscription of new meanings in these 'memory palaces' occurs organically as successive generations deposit their own material symbols (whether these be in the shape of architectural innovations, memorials, inscriptions or ephemeral objects) in a place where they expect they will be honoured and respected.

Second, cathedrals become emblems of the sacred in the city. It has become commonplace to talk of the importance of 'sacred space' in the functional urban environments in which the majority of people live. Sheldrake does not deny the importance of an inspiring building. However, his interpretation of sacred space is much broader. The space of a cathedral must be genuinely inclusive, welcoming the many casual visitors who bring their own spiritual aspirations to shelter within its walls. It must also be means of hallowing the space around, pointing to the sacredness of all space rather than demarcating the boundaries of divine presence.

Both of these functions attributed to cathedrals are of great significance for local theology. All buildings used for worship can be read as sacred texts and palaces of memory. Looking carefully at a local church with its architecture, furniture and everyday objects can help us to understand the spiritual aspirations of the congregation which inhabits it and the community in which it is set. Recognizing the significance of sacred space within a local environment can also help Christians reorientate their lives towards the communities in which they are set and 'seek again the sacred even in the ambiguity of the streets'.

Summary

The article explores the historic and contemporary meaning of cathedrals as sacred spaces. It suggests that cathedrals should be understood as 'spiritual texts' and offers a theory of interpretation. The first part of the article also briefly discusses the original role of cathedrals in cities as expressions of an understanding of the world and of human existence. The second part of the article explores the theological problem of conceiving cathedrals as emblems of the sacred in the city and the practical problem of how to handle such emblematic places in our late-modern or postmodern culture.

Setting the Scene

Since childhood I have been exploring cathedrals of various traditions and have also had close associations with several. As a historian as well as theologian I not only have a long-standing interest in religious architecture but have also been concerned to extend what we understand by theological-spiritual 'sources' beyond a disproportionate emphasis on *written texts*. When I worked in Cambridge, the display that introduced visitors to King's College Chapel began, 'We exist not only in the world but in an image or picture of the world'. In other words, we exist within general systems of signs by which we identify ourselves and develop a worldview. Specifically, great medieval churches such as King's College Chapel and cathedrals express in their architecture and decoration a quite specific image of the cosmos. Cathedrals are 'texts' in the sense that we can 'read' their sign systems and thus seek to interpret their meaning. Because cathedrals were intended to be acts of worship in themselves, as well as a space for liturgy, it is not unreasonable to say that their architecture is directly at the service of theology and spirituality. Religious architecture is a bearer of specific ideas and symbols – not least images of God and God's relationship to humankind.

Christianity did not begin as a religion of buildings. Even after it parted company with Judaism towards the end of the first century CE, it remained for a long time a network of small cells of initiates who did not need large buildings. The *Ekklesia* was the gathering of believers long before it ever came to mean a building. In this context, the crucial period was the fourth century when official cultic approval was given to Christianity. The achievement of a public face for the Church brought with it the need for public architecture. With the legalization of Christianity under the Emperor Constantine came the building of basilicas, the expansion of public liturgy and the growth of artistic decoration. The sites of major churches were often associated with the tombs of holy people. It is also worth recalling that churches were built first and foremost for rituals, such as baptism and the Eucharist. These symbolized the incorporation of the believer into the death and resurrection of Jesus Christ. Thus the sacredness of church buildings cannot be separated from their role in facilitating the union between the Christian and Jesus Christ.

A major feature of Christian buildings as 'spiritual texts' is that they are physical containers for the Body of Christ, the Church. A church building is not meant to be fundamentally either a theatre or a classroom – *essentially* concerned with ritual performance or didactic teaching. Churches have been traditionally oriented towards the East – towards the rising sun that symbolizes the divine Son of God, the glorified Christ. Placing the main altar at the east end had the purpose of lifting the eyes of the community to Christ who sat at the right hand of God. At a deeper level, it pushed believers onwards on a journey of following Christ in discipleship. This notion of cathedrals facilitating a 'movement beyond' is something I will return to later.

It is now widely recognized that there was a diverse aesthetics and theological symbolism during the great age of medieval cathedrals (see Eco, 1986). Gothic 'space' has been characterized as dematerialized and spiritualized. It expressed the limitless quality of God through the soaring verticality of arches and vaults – a deliberate antithesis to human scale. The medieval fascination with the symbolism of numbers cannot be ignored. The basic three-storey elevation of medieval Gothic (main arcade, triforium and clerestory) cannot be explained purely by progress in engineering but involved Trinitarian symbolism. Later Gothic buildings, such as King's College, are notable for another characteristic. The stone walls that support the chapel have been reduced to a minimum and replaced by expanses of glass. The biblical stories portrayed in the windows might teach the worshipper much about the doctrine of God's salvation but the glass also expressed what has been called 'a metaphysics of light'. God was increasingly proclaimed as the one who dwelt in inaccessible light yet whose salvific light illuminated the world.

In the vision of Abbot Suger, the great twelfth century proponent of Gothic architecture, St Augustine's aesthetics played at least as important a part as the theology of light of the sixth-century theologian known as Pseudo-Dionysius (see McGinn, 1995). Hence an Augustinian *harmonia*, or fitting order established by God, is a central theme in theorizing about cathedrals. This order refers both to the building and to the worshipping community it contains. Suger referred to 'perspicacious order' as the key to his vision for the Abbey of St-Denis – and 'order' is the characteristic word in Augustine for the harmonious beauty of the cosmos (1979: 100–101). A religious building in the mind of Suger should evoke wonder, be adequate to its purpose of worship and point beyond itself to the eternal 'house of God'. The religious building is an access point to the transcendent and its harmony is represented not simply by geometry or architectural coherence but by the degree to which it fulfils this spiritual function.

Part of the intellectual formation of Abbot Suger that lay behind his 'reading' of a church building was medieval sacramental theology. What integrated the building was Christian *practice*. As physical places, churches were locations of liturgical assembly. This is not merely a mechanical or practical issue. One of the key features of the sacramental theology of Suger and implicitly the understanding of cathedral buildings as a kind of sacrament of God's presence and action is that materiality is *necessary* in order to draw humanity upwards to the heavenly realms. It is also important to add that medieval people had an integrated worldview rather than a differentiated one. They believed in an ultimate unity in the universe. The conception of the cathedral is a good example. Every detail in the building recapitulated the architectonic design of the structure as a whole. This reflects an approach to life in which the whole (macrocosm) is somehow reflected in each part (microcosm).

Medieval architectural theory was undoubtedly also influenced by a theology of light. God was spoken of especially as light. 'Light comes from the Good, and light is an image of this archetypal Good' (Pseudo-Dionysius, 1987: 74). Everything created stems from that initial uncreated light. The cosmos was a kind of explosion of light and the divine light united everything. There was, therefore, an overarching coherence. A gradual movement back towards God, the source of all light, complemented an outward movement of the divine into the cosmos. Everything returned to God by means of the visible; from the created to the uncreated (see Sheldrake, 1995: 200–201).

Cathedral portrayals of God, after the time of Suger, focused on the ultimate mystery of God yet also on the joining of God with human nature. As a result, one of the greatest symbols of the doctrine of the incarnation, the Virgin Mother, was the heart of the iconography of cathedral glass and the decoration of high altars. This was not just Marian devotionalism. The Christianity embodied in medieval cathedrals was built on a theology of God as almighty and unknowable yet incarnate and revealed.

Cathedrals and Cities

In social terms, the development of the great cathedrals was an urban phenomenon. It also represented a shift in understanding 'the sacred' (see McDannell & Lang, 1988: 70–80). In the early Middle Ages 'the sacred' was represented most radically by ascetics or monastic communities living in rural areas. From about 1150–1250 the first urban renewal since the end of the Western Roman Empire took place. This had a major impact on social and theological perspectives even though urban expansion still embraced only 5% of the European population. In terms of biblical imagery for the sacred, there was a gradual move from the Book of Genesis to the Book of Revelation, from a Garden of Eden restored to a New Jerusalem. At the heart of the new cities grew up the cathedrals and the Gothic style.

In the urban cathedral, heaven was invoked symbolically in the spirit of Revelation, chapter 21. To enter the great cathedrals was to be transported into heaven on earth by the vast space, the progressive dematerialization of walls with glass and floods of light and the increasingly elaborate liturgies. For Suger church buildings had to be more impressive than other city buildings. The treasures should evoke the splendour of heaven and the clergy, mimicking the blessed in heaven, would conduct liturgy in silks and gold.

The architecture of the cathedrals attempted to portray, evoke and invoke a peaceable oneness between Creator and creation. This was a utopian space where an idealized heavenly harmony was anticipated in the here and now. But it was *idealized*. As Georges Duby, the French medievalist, suggests, 'it would be a mistake to assume that the thirteenth century wore the beaming face of the crowned Virgin or the smiling angels. The times were hard, tense, and very wild, and it is important that we recognize all that was tumultuous and rending about them' (1981: 95). The social symbolism of cathedrals was also ambiguous. While they portrayed a divine-human unity they also manifested a this-worldly reality of social hierarchies and values (see Bedos-Rozak, 1995: 243–44).

Cities reflect and affect the quality of human relationships. In urban environments we cannot separate functional, ethical and spiritual questions. If a place is to be sacred, it must affirm the sacredness of people and the human capacity for transcendence. I suggest that in an earlier age the cathedral, for all its limitations, fulfilled that function in Western cities. It was at the same time an image of God and a symbol of the ideals of the citizens set in the heart of the city. The American philosopher Arnold Berleant suggests that the cathedral was a guide to an 'urban ecology' that contrasts with the monotony of the modern city 'thus helping transform it from a place where one's humanity is constantly threatened into a place where it is continually achieved and enlarged' (1992: 62). At best, the cathedral promotes more than a two-dimensional, static urban 'map'. It offers communion with something that lies deeper than the need for an ordered public life.

This kind of centre is not purely functional but evocative. If we leave for a moment the theological language that we must inevitably use of an explicitly *Christian* symbol, it is possible to speak more generally of a cathedral deliberately speaking of 'the condition of the world'. It both expresses the history of human experience and yet transcends an easy understanding of it. Perhaps most important of all, cathedrals are repositories for the cumulative memory and the constantly renewed hopes of the community. Even today, to enter such a building is to engage with generations of human pain, achievements and ideals. This 'memory palace' is a constant reminder that in itself *remembering* is vital to a healthy sense of identity. The moment a building like a cathedral becomes *fixed* rather than continually changing it is a dead space, not a living symbol of the city.

Sadly, contemporary urban places too frequently lack this centred quality because we have built nothing into them that is precious to us. It is not unusual to regard the modern city as a purely functional environment. Yet even 'function' involves more than simply practical organization. The issue of space is more than an impersonal problem of engineering. The question of urban space has a great deal to do with the creation of perceptions. The high-rise office block is not the same elevating moral and spiritual presence as a cathedral. It tends to speak of the forces of size, economics and impersonal power. The cathedral is a kind of paradigm. It points to the fact that, at its best, our sense of place is a sense of the sacred – what is sacred to oneself, to the city community and sacred in relation to the higher order of things, however that is understood.

Space and the Sacred: The Problematic

In the second part of this essay, I want to turn my attention to the problems both of *conceiving* cathedrals as emblems of the sacred in the city and of *handling* such emblematic places. There are two broad issues. First, what are the implications of treating cathedrals as texts? Second, what happens when we seek to accumulate and protect 'the sacred' in places like cathedrals?

1. Interpreting Cathedrals as Texts

Historic religious buildings such as European cathedrals are a type of 'spiritual classic' on a par with great written texts. A theory of interpretation is clearly important in relation to all texts. While texts are historically conditioned, some cross the boundaries of time or place and retain their importance in contexts very different from their own. In the words of the American theologian, David Tracy, these are 'classics'. As he puts it, they disclose something that remains compelling. They continue to challenge readers and bring them into transforming contact with what is enduring and vital in the Christian tradition. In general, the strength of classics is that they do not merely teach but are capable of persuading and moving people to a response (1991: chapter 3). As Tracy notes, there is a qualitative difference between a classic and a period piece. Interestingly, Tracy extends the idea of a 'religious classic' beyond written texts to embrace artefacts and people.

Modern theories of interpretation assume that the meaning of 'classics' is not limited by the intentions of the original creator. This is what enables a classic to come alive in other times and places. Thus a classic such as a religious building is not a timeless artefact but demands constant reinterpretation by people who approach it from within their own historical circumstances. To treat a cathedral as 'a work of art', to be preserved in essentially constant form, raises all kinds of difficulties for those (liturgists and theologians) who suggest that the 'meaning' of cathedrals is only arrived at by interpretation-through-use (Bedos-Rezak, 1995b).

A theory of interpretation that allows for the continual unfolding of 'meaning' raises the difficulty of whether every architectural change over time can be justified as an appropriate 'rewriting' of a 'building-as-text'. In English medieval cathedrals with a subsequent post-Reformation history, this is no easy question. The 'integrity' of such buildings is a spiritual and theological issue as much as an architectural one. Because English cathedrals went through the Reformation and then a period of iconoclasm during the seventeenth-century there are particularly painful issues associated with various periods of major deconstruction. With the substantial dilution of the medieval sacramental system and the replacement of a great deal of ritual performance by the proclamation of the Bible, hearing and speech rather than sight and movement were for a long time given primary importance. A reformed Church of England with a new liturgy needed a different kind of building. If buildings should resonate with the lives of those who use them, there was integrity in reforms to the medieval cathedrals and arguably also in the sometimes heavy-handed recovery of an idealized medievalism in much Victorian restoration. My point is that neither change was purely artistic but expressed shifts in liturgical practice as well as in theology.

In the case of Salisbury Cathedral, in many respects the worst destruction of the medieval layout took place not at the Reformation but in the eighteenth century. This was inspired by an Enlightenment aesthetic – separated from any concept of use – that suggested that buildings should be freed from clutter as well as be light and bright. Medieval glass was replaced by plain windows, traces of medieval painting were whitewashed, tombs were repositioned in the nave in tidy lines, and medieval screens and other divisions were removed. I would argue that James Wyatt's mandate in 1785 to 'restore and beautify' the cathedral served the integrity of the building less well than Reformation changes. This was not merely because the changes were disrespectful of the building's fundamental logic but also because they happened when liturgy and theology were at low ebb (see Spring, 1991: 71–83).

Recent scholarship on medieval cathedrals has moved away from the idea that buildings are simply monuments of pure architecture. It is critical to their interpretation that cathedrals are places of social connection and of community definition. To put it another way, a building without performance is merely an item of abstract styling and that can never be the case with cathedrals. This raises a further question: *who* are the valid 'interpreters'? The community of 'capable readers' changes over time. Even if the regular worshippers and staff have a privileged role, I want to suggest that a wider community of interpretation exists which also contributes to reading the cathedral text. These people are not merely passive recipients of a meaning determined by others. This view will be problematic for those who believe that cathedrals *only* exist for Christian worshippers. Today's visitor may as likely be a tourist as a worshipper and may have no sense of what the cathedral originally expressed or how cathedrals are used liturgically.

The editors in a collection of essays on the role of cathedrals in contemporary English society refer sympathetically to the 'odd', 'unusual' or 'disadvantaged' people who regularly enter cathedrals from the city streets in order to find physical warmth or mental solace (Platten & Lewis, 1998: 123–24, 135–36, 148). There is still a tendency, however, to speak in terms of 'visitors' (whether the 'odd' or the tourists) being responded to in ways that maintain the fundamental 'integrity' of the building *as a place of Christian liturgy*. Worship *is* central but there is a danger of a purified notion of integrity that does not embrace spiritually or socially different people with varied needs (see Platten & Lewis, 1998: 30–32). Yet, might it be that the marginal, however they are conceived, actually offer a 'rereading' of church buildings that is part of their contemporary 'integrity' rather than a problem for it? For those for whom tradition-as-precedent is important, it is illuminating to recall that our tidy notion of religious buildings is a post-medieval conception. One senses in earlier ages a greater permeability between sacred space and the outside. The 'profane' spilled into the space in the shape of beggars, animals, markets and other gatherings.

My point is that while the majority of people who enter cathedrals these days may have little sense of the original meaning of the buildings, this does not necessarily imply a total abandonment of cathedrals as 'spiritual texts' by a non-Church majority. Indeed, there is plenty of evidence that cathedrals attract far more interest than associated museums or visitors' centres (Davie, 2000: 162–67). A residual sense of the sacred not only draws visitors to such buildings but also makes them uncomfortable with entry charges. They perceive that churches are not the same as museums or other buildings that are merely associated with historical heritage. The fact is that

> sacred space is in some way public space, even if it is not used by most people on a regular basis. If this is the case, the oversight and management of religious buildings must remain a public issue, counteracting growing, perhaps exaggerated, tendencies towards privatization in other aspects of religious life. (Davie 2000, 164)

This raises interesting questions when there are plans to reorder historic churches. Are non-worshipping visitors merely an incidental addition from the tourist-heritage industry? Are they passive targets for new forms of Christian evangelism? Or are they active participants in a new process of interpretation that is exploring previously unanticipated layers of meaning in cathedral buildings? Tourism can be superficial and the 'heritage industry' tends to reduce history to what is diverting. However, this suggests to me that the modern cathedral visitors should neither simply be patronized nor pandered to. A 'conversation' model of interpretation allows both the building and the visitor, with their respective integrities, to be taken seriously.

2. Movement Beyond: Accumulating or Dispersing the Sacred?

Richard Sennett, the American urban sociologist, has argued that Western culture suffers from a division between inner and outer life. 'It is a divide between subjective experience and worldly experience, self and city' (1993: xii). This is based on an unacknowledged fear of self-exposure, viewed as a threat rather than life-enhancing. Apart from consumer spaces, city design has therefore increasingly concentrated on creating safe divisions between different groups of people. Public space becomes bland as its main purpose is to facilitate movement across it rather than encounters within it (1993: xii–xiii).

For Sennett, Augustine's *City of God* is the foundational expression of the triumph of an inner spiritual 'world' searching for eternal fulfilment over the physical city (1993: 6–10). Social places, characterized by difference and diversity, are to be viewed with suspicion. Sennett suggests, therefore, that by denying the value of the outside, Christianity reinforces Western doubts about diversity. Sennett equates 'the sacred' with *sanctuary* which implies protection and *refuge* from a wider world. In the pre-modern city, buildings like cathedrals were 'sanctuaries' in both senses and so promoted withdrawal from outer life.

I agree with much that Sennett says about modernist city planning and the idealization of protected private worlds. However, he misunderstands both Augustine and how 'the sacred' was materialized in the pre-modern city. 'The sacred' was *not* confined to ritual sites like cathedrals but was dispersed into a wider sacred landscape of the streets. The sense that the city as a whole was a sacred landscape was reinforced by processions and blessings. In medieval cities the Eucharist was more obviously a *public drama* that enacted God's reconciling work in the city. This included cathedral liturgy but also embraced street processions on the feast of Corpus Christi. Other processions, the performance of Passion plays in the streets and the many wayside shrines all evoked a sense of urban place that is at odds with the Modernist concept of a city as an impersonal, smoothly-running machine and with the kind of planning that dominated urban reconstruction after World War II. Even today, in Catholic countries, cities frequently retain medieval examples of wayside religious shrines. For example, the rich collection of street shrines in the *città vecchia* of Bari has been the subject of scholarly research (see Cortone & Lavermicocca, 2001–03).

Medieval citizens sometimes made the heavenly Jerusalem of Revelation 21 a model for urban planning. The Statutes of Florence of 1339 emphasised the existence of the sacred number of twelve gates even though, in fact, the city had by then extended to fifteen gates (Frugoni, 1991: 27). Later in the Middle Ages, the development of the great Italian piazzas owed much to the preaching churches of new religious orders. These buildings opened out onto great spaces where crowds gathered to listen to sermons (for example, Santissima

Annunziata in Florence). The colonnaded piazza offered a vision of the city, metaphorically (it engendered a concept of public space for intermingling) and practically (it opened up new urban vistas).

So-called pre-modern society, prior to a post-Reformation, post-Enlightenment tidying up of categories, was more at home with a dialectical vision of life. This could encompass the presence of the holy and the sinful, light and dark, in the same space – markets in the nave and shrines in the streets! The later polarization of sacred and secular spheres – whether or not you attribute it like Sennett to the impact of Reformation theology – led to the retreat of the sacred from public space and life (which became increasingly secularized) into the purified containers of religious buildings and into the private realm.

For all the contemporary fascination with sacred places and pilgrimage, there are alternative voices that speak compellingly of the movement of the sacred beyond the boundaries of religious buildings – the *dispersal* rather than the *protection* of the sacred. These views need to be held in creative tension alongside the notion of cathedrals as sacred spaces. The voices speak as Christians but their vision of the sacred chimes in with the plea of influential contemporary urbanists like Leonie Sandercock for planners to re-embrace the notion of a city as *spiritual* (Sandercock, 2003).

The first voice is Albert Rouet, Bishop of Poitiers, who, in a striking essay on architecture and liturgy, comments, 'Sacred space is that of God's nomads. This itinerancy is an important characteristic of those who seek God, of those who are members of the People of God' (Rouet, 1997: 95). Without ignoring the sacramental symbolism of church buildings or denying their rare power to shape communities of contemplation, Rouet notes that, beginning with an empty tomb, Christ's 'place' is now his Body. 'The Body of Christ is the place where charity becomes visible.' For this reason, church buildings make sense ultimately in relation to the human community that they enable. For this reason,

Ecclesial space also denies itself in a way. The hope which Christ gave to the Church cannot be contained in any limited geographical spot. The Good News drives us beyond. The holiness of the person of Christ is shared, exteriorized, and communicated . . . Christianity is a religion without spatial limits. (1997: 105)

Another voice is the late Michel de Certeau, one of the most significant interdisciplinary French thinkers of the late 20th century and an unconventional Jesuit. In his later years he sought to speak in a Western world where institutional Christianity was no longer treated as the place of definitive meaning. Like Rouet, de Certeau suggested that the primary symbol of discipleship is the empty tomb (2000: 234). Jesus is not finally *here*; he is always going ahead of us into the Galilee of the world. Drawing on his background in Ignatian spirituality, with its emphasis on mobility and the quest for the *magis* (what is greater), de Certeau suggested that spirituality should avoid the temptation to settle for a definitive place but pursue the age-old tension between discipleship (following), and conversion (transformation). Believers are called to follow faithfully in the direction of Jesus' perpetual movement onwards (2000: 226). Christians are to journey with no security apart from the story of Christ that is to be 'practised' rather than merely stated.

> The temptation of the 'spiritual' is to . . . transform . . . conversion into an establishment, to replace the 'poem' [of Christ] which states the hyperbole with the strength to make history or to be the truth which takes history's place, or, lastly, as in evangelical transfiguration . . . to take the 'vision' as a 'tent' and the word as a new land. In its countless writings along many different trajectories, Christian spirituality . . . ceaselessly criticizes this trap . . . (2000: 236)

These voices do not undermine the understanding of cathedrals as 'sacraments' but they remind us that such buildings, like all sacramental symbols, are boundary places and points of departure. 'Boundaries are the place of the Christian work, and their displacements are the result of this work' (de Certeau, 1997: 151).

To bring us full circle, I earlier commented that placing the main altar at the east end lifted the eyes of the community to Christ and pushed believers onwards to follow Christ in discipleship. A theology of sacramentality needs material symbols like cathedrals. However, these do not protect the sacred against an inherently profane 'out there'. Cathedrals are truly themselves if they facilitate a risky 'movement beyond' and outwards to seek again the sacred even in the ambiguities of the streets.

References

Bedos-Rozak, B. (1995) 'From as Social Process' in Virginia Chieffo Raguin, Kathryn Brush & Peter Draper, (eds.), *Artistic Integration in Gothic Buildings*, Toronto: University of Toronto Press, pp. 236–248.

Berleant, A. (1992) *The Aesthetics of Environment*, Philadelphia: Temple University Press.

De Certeau, M. (1997) 'How is Christianity Thinkable Today?', in Graham Ward (ed.), *The Postmodern God*, Oxford: Blackwell, pp. 142–158.

De Certeau, M. (2000) 'The Weakness of Believing: From the Body to Writing, a Christian Transit', in Graham Ward (ed.), *The Certeau Reader*, Oxford: Blackwell Publishers, pp. 214–243.

Cortone, N. & Lavermicocca, N. (2001–2003) *Santi di Strada: Le Edicole Religiose della Cittá Vecchia di Bari*, 5 volumes, Bari: Edizione BA Graphis.

Davie, G. (2000) *Religion in Modern Europe: A Memory Mutates*, Oxford: Oxford University Press.

Duby, G. (1981) *The Age of the Cathedral: Art and Society 980–1420*, Chicago: University of Chicago Press.

Eco, U. (1986) *Art and Beauty in the Middle Ages*, New Haven: Yale University Press.

Frugoni, C. (1991) *A Distant City: Images of Urban Experience in the Medieval World*, Princeton: Princeton University Press.

McDannell, C. & Lang, B. (1988) *Heaven, A History*, New Haven: Yale University Press.

McGinn, B. (1995) 'From Admirable Tabernacle to the House of God: Some Theological Reflections on Medieval Architectural Integration' in Virginia Chieffo Raguin, Kathryn Brush & Peter Draper (eds.), *Artistic Integration in Gothic Buildings*, Toronto: University of Toronto Press, pp. 41–56.

Pseudo-Dionysius (1987) *The Divine Names*, Chapter 4.4, in Colm Luibheid (ed.), *Pseudo-Dionysius: The Complete Works*, London: SPCK.

Platten, S. & Lewis, C. (1998) *Flagships of the Spirit: Cathedrals in Society*, London: Darton Longman & Todd.

Rouet, A. (1997) *Liturgy and the Arts*, ET Collegeville: The Liturgical Press.

Sandercock, L. (2003) *Cosmopolis II: Mongrel Cities in the 21st Century*, London/New York: Continuum.

Sennett, R. (1993) *The Conscience of the Eye: The Design and Social Life of Cities*, London: Faber & Faber.

Sheldrake, P. (1995) *Spirituality and History: Questions of Interpretation and Method*, 2nd edition, London: SPCK.

Spring, R. (1991) *Salisbury Cathedral: A Landmark in England's Heritage*, Salisbury.

Suger (1979) *Libellus Alter De Consecratione Ecclesiae Sancti Dionysii*, IV translated in Erwin Panofsky, *Abbot Suger on the Abbey Church of St Denis and its Art Treasures*, Princeton: Princeton University Press.

Tracy, D. (1991) *The Analogical Imagination: Christian Theology and the Culture of Pluralism*, New York: Crossroad.

Chris Baker, 'The Global and Local Context of the Local Church'

in Helen Cameron, Douglas Davies, Philip Richter and Frances Ward (eds), *Studying Local Churches: A Handbook*, London: SCM Press, 2005, pp. 80–7.

The meaning of space and locality has been the subject of much debate in recent times. In this extract, Chris Baker discusses how postmodern theorists analyse the ways in which communities construct their territorial space as a symbol of value, meaning and memory within a globalized capitalist culture. This positive assessment of the significance of locality is countered by others who argue that such is the pace of change that authentic local communities are being destroyed and people are seeking new forms of identity based upon ethnicity or social affiliation. These lack the inclusivity and coherence of traditional neighbourhood groupings.

If local communities are experiencing the kinds of changes outlined above these are of great significance for local Christian congregations. In poorer areas, where the postmodern challenges of fragmentation, dispersion and loss of traditional roles are most keenly felt, it becomes even more important to discover the charism or gift the local church can offer its community. Baker does not believe that there is one model according to which the local church should function. Rather, through pursuing its distinctive vision and being true to its own character, each local church can bring its own talents and energy to the work of social regeneration.

So What Is the Local Within the Postmodern?

I want now to define the series of values and realities now referred to by the word 'local', and to do so, I will use the socio-economic theories of Manuel Castells and Zygmunt Bauman. Castells, for example, describes one of the results of global capitalism as a shift from conceiving of *space as place* to *space as flows*.

In economic terms, *space as flows* describes how capital investment, the new service economy and advanced technology connect in ways which no longer 'depend on the characteristics of any specific locale for the fulfilment of their fundamental goals' (Castells, 1996). The advanced services which now dominate the wealth-creating agenda of globalization require 'the dynamics of information-generating units, while connecting their different functions to disparate spaces assigned to each task to be performed' (Castells, 1989). In other words, once a product has been designed, its various stages of production can be established anywhere in the world wherever market costs are cheapest, causing increased migratory activity as both middle-managers and workers follow the flows of this investment. Castells notes some of the *social* and *spatial* consequences of his theory:

> The new professional managerial class colonizes exclusive spatial segments that connect with one another across the city, the country and the world; they isolate themselves from the fragments of local societies, which in consequence become destructured in the process of selective reorganization of work and residence. (Castells, 1989)

The rest of the local space not connected to the flows of wealth (populated by the largely unskilled workforce required to engage in routine assembly or auxiliary operations) is subject either to increased segregation and chronic poverty or gentrification, whereby pockets of wealth co-exist, or at least are well-defended, within larger areas of poverty. This leads Castells to suggest that local space can become sites of resistance for those excluded from the new flows of wealth and knowledge.

The communes of resistance defend their spaces, their places, against the placeless logic of the space of flows, characterizing social domination in the Information Age. They claim their historic memory and/or affirm the permanence of their values against the dissolution of history in timeless time, and the celebration of the ephemeral in the culture of real virtuality (Castells, 1997).

A counterbalance to Castells' antagonistic view is provided by the more nuanced perspective of Roland Robertson's theory of *glocalization* (Robertson, 1995). He describes the symbiotic way in which local and global interact with each other as time and space boundaries collapse with advanced telecommunications and cheap air travel. Globalization need not only be seen solely as a threat to local space if the two-way dynamic is recognized where the local shapes the global and benefits from the global in turn. However a more pessimistic view again emerges from Bauman's idea of neo-tribalism. Here the constant fluidity between local and national identities caused by flows of migration leads to disorientation, fear and insecurity. Traditional, locally based communities (with strict membership regulations of inclusion and exclusion) have been largely destroyed. *Neo*-tribes emerge instead to meet the need for distinctive belonging based on ethnic, religious or political affiliations, but also on desire and fear.

The crucial difference is that neo-tribalism relies on individual acts of self-identification and choice. It results in 'concepts' of community, rather than 'integrated social bodies' (Bauman, 1995) and reflects identities created by fashion, leisure, lifestyle or ethnic-religious origin within diasporic or global networks. Bauman's terminology suggests that far from creating greater tolerance and diversity, the processes of postmodern globalization create situations of polarity and segregation.

The Identity and Mission of the Church in the Postmodern World

We now look at four emerging typologies of local church, which in their own ways engage with the dynamics of postmodernity, of 'local' and 'global' outlined above.

Church as Idealized Moral Community

This understanding of the church has a long theological pedigree, but has re-emerged with renewed vigour in recent years. It belongs to a tradition which stresses the christocentric nature of divine revelation and Christian ethics as expressed in the person of Jesus Christ and the biblical tradition. The word of God stands in sharp contradiction and judges 'worldly' sources of revelation based on natural law or human rationality. The church is therefore central as the preferred locus of moral discourse and behaviour.

The tradition has been strongly expressed in recent times by the influential American theologian Stanley Hauerwas. In the 1980s, he constructed a church typology based on a community whose main task is to reflect practically and theologically on its own narrative. *Praxis* is expressed precisely in the shared communal life at the local level: 'the first task of the church is not to supply theories of governmental legitimacy or even to supply strategies for social betterment. The first task of the church is to exhibit in our common life the kind of community where trust, not fear, rules our lives' (Hauerwas, 1981).

A similar self-sufficient Christian response to the wider world is reinforced by the radical orthodoxy writers emerging in the 1990s. John Milbank, for example, argues that Christian revelation undergirds social theory and as such is fundamentally incompatible with 'truth claims and conceptions of morality'. In other words, within a postmodern context of fragmented narratives, the Christian narrative out-narrates other narratives. As Milbank says, 'There is no independently available "real world" against which we must test our Christian convictions, because these convictions are then the most final and at the same time, most basic seeing of what the world is' (Milbank, 1997). Of great importance to him is the way that Christian church embodies this principle of ethical reflection rooted in cross and resurrection. The church is an 'ideal type' in which local members exemplify a life lived in peace and trust, and where alternative economics based on free gift exchange can be practised, both as a response to, and a symbol of, the ultimate reality of God's grace.

This idealized picture of church life can be criticized for its lack of serious dialogue or engagement with the everyday reality of all human beings (including Christians) who struggle with the ambiguities of life this side of the cross. It can also ignore the gap between idealized model and actual reality in churches which can be far from the community of trust and peace envisaged by Hauerwas and Milbank.

Scenario 1

While this idealized church type can be a fantasy easily dismissed, there are some churches that manage to combine a strong ethic based on christocentric revelation with an inclusive engagement with the wider community. The Eden project in Openshaw, Manchester is one of many youth-based projects started in the late 1990s in areas of UK deprivation. The overt evangelism at the heart of Eden's identity, with its stress on discipleship and personal decision-making was controversial in the early days, and is still viewed with suspicion by some local residents and existing community development agencies. But the project in Openshaw has learned from experience and appears more at ease working with a wide variety of partners, both secular and religious, including other churches that have a more liberal approach. They have gained respect for their work with hard-to-reach groups and the sensitivity, openness and accountability with which they engage with vulnerable groups. Its ethos locates it in this church type, but what is new with the Eden project is its willingness to engage with a wide variety of partners. In its alliances, it hints at a new and informal expression of ecumenism that sits lightly to denominational identity (i.e. post-denominational).

Liberation theology model

This typology is modelled on the methodology of liberation theology in South America. It makes the experience of the poor and marginalized the given starting point for theological reflection and mission. Paulo Freire's work was important in fostering and raising people's levels of awareness through adult education, especially within peergroups. This was a prerequisite for social and political transformation. Its greatest strength is its commitment to the social analysis of the wider context in which the church community is placed, an openness to the many influences and power structures that shape cities at both local and global level combined with a firm commitment to be a genuinely local church community incarnated within a local setting.

Usually this model will seek to express this commitment by gathering in local (often eucharistic) worship, which is unconditionally inclusive. This worship setting, sometimes replicated by cell groups meeting in peoples' homes, provides the opportunity for the narratives of peoples' experience to engage with both biblical and symbolic frameworks. In this way, faith comes alive and gives emotional and spiritual resources by which to live a life of dignity in situations that may seem hopeless. Sometimes, the church will also choose to become involved in issues of local concern, joining with other organizations to create better conditions on behalf of the wider community along the lines of Castells' 'communes of resistance' referred to earlier.

The weakness of this model is that, with the analysis of issues facing local communities, can come a pro-poor rhetoric which tends not to do justice to the multicausal nature of poverty and wealth in postmodern communities. There is also evidence to show that both the nature of the poor and the role of the local church can be idealized and romanticized by a nostalgia for a lost narrative of church and community that supposedly existed in perfect harmony (Baker, 2002).

The local/institutional model

The traditional model of church that still exists in most areas, though it is tending to decline in poorer communities, represents at a local level a national institutional church (especially within Anglican and Roman Catholic ecclesiologies). Its strengths are long-term identification with local communities, and a strong association with family histories and local events. The institutional church can be the place where the 'local' community gathers to mark some national event of grief or joy. The sense of being rooted in a local space and carrying its narratives is symbolized by the physical building, often an important local landmark within communities undergoing rapid physical change. Whether in decline numerically or experiencing growth, the institutional type can be the nexus for sets of local relationships which form part of the invisible network of community cohesion. However, there does appear to be a growing trend for successful churches to become less and less 'local' in the geographical sense, as increasing numbers of members come from people travelling from outside the locality.

Scenario 2

A local institutional church in its public worship and rites of passage offers what one East Manchester vicar calls 'the value of a different rhythm and a sense of a quiet, healing space and long-term sustainability'. East Manchester is in the throes of massive regeneration, led by the arrival of the Commonwealth Games stadium and an Asda-Walmart hypermarket. These are expected to attract large numbers of professional singles and couples to settle in the area. His description of what the institutional model of church offers partly relates to the regeneration approach that is concerned with short-term turnarounds and targets, but also speaks to a growing consumerism and freneticism that much investment-led regeneration presupposes: state-of-the-art fitness suites, 24-hour café and dance-club cultures and apartments designed for home-working.

The institutional/local model can be slow to react to rapid change because of its long traditions. This in turn can lead to insularity, and its institutional character can make it harder to introduce the flexibility of worship and approach now required to connect with new patterns of lifestyle and identity.

Network model

The network model is a form that Castells would recognize. It emerges from the 'space as flows' concept and mimics more fluid forms of civil society. The traditional sectors of civil society, welfare associations and charities, the family, churches, political organizations and trade unions are in decline because of, for example, the breaking up of the traditional family structure, the growth of suburban sprawl and the growth in electronic entertainment (Putnam, 2000). Some of these sectors are also becoming more professionalized, thus alienating those people who have traditionally volunteered for its own sake (Centre for Research and Innovation in Social Policy and Practice, 2003). Growth in civil society is in the non-institutional sectors; broad-based organizations (i.e. networks or coalitions of disparate groups formed around single issues such as a living wage), or direct action campaigns focusing on large public demonstrations to change government policy or global trends (for example, Stop the War, Jubilee 2000, The Countryside Alliance).

The identity and role of network church (as far as it has emerged in the few case studies currently available – e.g. Community Pride in Manchester, IMPACT in Sheffield, and TELCO in East London) has mirrored some key characteristics of non-institutional civil society. Individual church members often take the initiative in forming networks of transformation in order to address local or national issues, becoming key members of these networks, and thus accessing more powerful networks and institutions (for example, local councils, national government). As a result of their expertise and grassroots support, these individuals become engaged at the cutting edge issues of process and change.

Scenario 3

Community Pride Initiative is an organization created by the churches, which operates with the network model in Salford and Manchester. It has been at the forefront in creating a unique participatory budgeting experiment with Salford Council, as well as setting up a wide range of networks across the city, designed to inform local communities of government regeneration opportunities, support grassroots responses and offer specialized support (e.g. disability and gender perspectives). It is one of the lead bodies (appointed by the Government Office North West) for the development of the Community Network for Manchester, and is closely linked to Manchester's LSP (Local Strategic Partnership). It has contributed to national evaluation of Government regeneration policy.

This type of 'church' works well with the more 'liquid' forms of civil society and governance and unlike the institutional (or more solid types of church) has a light and flexible structure that makes it able to respond swiftly to change. With no buildings to maintain, minimum bureaucratic structures and autonomy, it can act appropriately at local level.

This model allows the 'church' to interface in the most direct way with issues that affect the wider community, but questions of visibility and identity can be raised. Those engaged in partnership or networking with this type of 'church' may be unaware that it is a church group. Nor is it always clear what the relationship is between a 'networking' church and the more solid forms of 'institutional' church.

Conclusion

These typologies are not an exhaustive list, but indicate current practice that emerges from the postmodern and local context. Some local churches react to plurality, diversity and rapid change by stressing the uniqueness of Christian revelation and seeking a form of identity that removes them from the norms and values of the wider community. Other church communities engage wholeheartedly with plurality and diversity and explore more 'liquid' forms of identity in order to 'go with the flow' of postmodern life. They may not be able to meet the spiritual needs of people for physical buildings and public liturgies at times of crisis or celebration. Within the complexity and ambiguity of postmodern life, there is no one typology that fits all. Each typology has something to offer. For example, networks complement more 'solid' organizations by helping institutions to adapt to changing conditions and to attract more diverse and 'boundary-spanning' contacts (Gilchrist, 2004).

The four typologies are all examples of what we called at the start of this contribution a *new theology of catholicity*. Each has a distinctive *charism* or gift which it offers to the local community, but whose gift needs to be seen not as the definitive or only response to the local context, but one aspect that needs other forms if the wholeness of the church is to be expressed in that local context.

Bibliography

Baker, C. (2002) *Towards the Theology of New Towns: The Implications of the New Town Experience for Urban Theology*, University of Manchester, unpublished PhD Thesis.

Bauman, Z. (1995) *Life in Fragments*, Oxford: Blackwell.

Castells, M. (1989) *The Informational City*, Oxford: Blackwell.

— (1996) *The Rise of the Network Society*, Oxford: Blackwell.

— (1997) *The Power of Identity*, Oxford: Blackwell.

Centre for Research and Innovation in Social Policy and Practice (2003) *Unravelling the Maze – A Survey of Civil Society in the UK*, Newcastle: Centre for Research and Innovation in Social Policy and Practice.

Gilchrist, A. (2004) 'Developing the Well-Connected Community', in H. McCarthy, P. Miller and P. Skidmore (eds), *Network Logic – Essay 11*, London: Demos.

Hauerwas, S. (1981) *A Community of Character*, Notre Dame, Indiana: University of Notre Dame Press.

Milbank, J. (1997) *The Word Made Strange: Theology, Language, Culture*, Oxford: Blackwell.

Putnam, R. D. (2000) *Bowling Alone: The Collapse and Revival of American Community*, New York, NY and London: Simon and Schuster.

Robertson, R. (1995) 'Globalisation: Time-Space and Homogeneity-Heterogeneity', in M. Featherstone et al. (eds) *Global Modernities*, London: Sage.

'Theology in the Vernacular': References and Further Reading

Chung Hyun-Kyung (1990), *Struggle to be the Sun Again: Introducing Asian Women's Theology*, Maryknoll, New York: Orbis.

Geertz, C. (1973), *On The Interpretation of Cultures: Selected Essays*, New York: Basic Books.

Schreiter, R. (1985), *Constructing Local Theologies*, Maryknoll, New York: Orbis.

Sheldrake, P. (2000), *Spaces for the Sacred: Place, Memory, Identity*, London: SCM press.

Acknowledgements

We wish to express our gratitude to the following publishers and authors for permission to reproduce copyright material:

© 'How I Changed My Mind', Kathryn Tanner, in *Shaping a Theological Mind*, Darren C. Marks, 2002, Ashgate.

© 'The Messiness of Studying Congregations Using Ethnographic Methods' in *Congregational Studies in the UK*, Frances Ward; Mathew Guest, Karin Tusting, Linda Woodhead (eds.), 2004, Ashgate.

© *Furthering Humanity*, Tim Gorringe, 2003, Ashgate.

From *Sexism and God-Talk* by Rosemary Radford Ruether. Copyright © 1983, 1993 by Rosemary Radford Ruether. Reprinted by permission of Beacon Press, Boston.

Blackwell, for extracts from pp. 131–5, 142–3, 145, from *On Christian Theology*, Rowan Williams, 2000; for extracts from pp. 106–10, 111–13, from 'Pastoral Theology as Transforming Practice', Elaine Graham, in *Blackwell Reader in Practical and Pastoral Theology*, S. Pattison, J. W. Woodward, (eds), 2000; for extracts from pp. 36–40, from *Understanding Theology and Popular Culture*, Gordon Lynch, 2005, reprinted with kind permission of Blackwell.

Brill Academic Publishers, for extracts from pp. VII–XVI, from *Didache in Context: Essays on its Text, History and Transmission*, Clayton N. Jefford (ed.), 1995. Reprinted with kind permission of Brill Academic Publishers.

Cambridge University Press, for extracts from pp. 239–40, 242–4, 245, 246–7, 248, from *Christianity, Art and Transformation*, John W. de Gruchy, 2001. Reprinted with kind permission of Cambridge University Press.

Chris Baker, for extracts from pp. 5–11, from 'Hybridity and Practical Theology: In Praise of Blurred Encounters', Chris Baker, in *Contact*, No. 149, 2006, reprinted with kind permission of the author.

Darton, Longman and Todd, for extracts from pp. 183–6, from *The Sky is Red*, Kenneth Leech, 2003; for extracts from pp. 150–6, from *Following in the Footsteps of Christ*, C. Arnold Snyder, 2004; for extracts from pp. 117–29, from *Jesus is Dread: Black Theology and Black Culture in Britain*, Robert Beckford, 1998; Reprinted with kind permission of Darton, Longman and Todd.

Ben Edson, for extracts from www.benedson.blogs.com, reprinted with kind permission of the author.

Faber & Faber, for extracts from pp. 16–18; 25–9, from *A Grief Observed*, C. S. Lewis, 1966, reprinted with kind permission of Faber & Faber.

Fortress, for extracts from, pp. xiii–xiv, xvi–xix, xx–xxiii, from *Formation and Reflection*, James N. Poling and Lewis S. Mudge, 1987, reprinted with kind permission of Fortress.

Stanley Hauerwas, for extracts from 'Jesus: The Story of the Kingdom', Stanley Hauerwas, in *Theology Digest*, 26/4, 1978. Reprinted with kind permission of the author.

Gosspad, for extracts from pp. 1–4, 13–16, 18–19, from *The Art of Theological Reflection*, 2nd edition, Patricia O'Connell Killen and John de Beer, 2004. Reprinted with kind permission of Gosspad.

HarperCollins, for extracts from pp. 18–19, 23–5, from *The Pilgrim at Tinker Creek*, Annie Dillard, 1988. Reprinted with kind permission of HarperCollins.

Jossey Bass, for extracts from pp. 9–16, 18–19, from *Mighty Stories, Dangerous Rituals: Weaving Together the Human and the Divine*, Herbert Anderson, Edward Foley, 1998. Reprinted with kind permission of Jossey Bass.

Peter Lang, for extracts from pp. 162–7, from *Exploring Religious Communities Online*, Heidi Campbell, 2005, reprinted with kind permission of Peter Lang.

Lit Verlag, for extracts from 'This Common Road', Heather Walton, in *Pathways to the Public Square*, Elaine Graham, Anna Rowlands (eds), 2005.

Orbis, for extracts from pp. 3–7, 13–18, from *Practical Theology: On Earth As It Is In Heaven*, Terry Veling, 2005; for extracts from pp. 85–7, 94–7, 98–9, from 'Theology of Liberation and Marxism' in *Mysterium Liberationis*, Enrique Dusserl, Jon Sobrino, Ignacio Ellacuria (eds), 1993; for extracts from pp. 5–12, from 'Roots of the Pastoral Circle', in *The Pastoral Circle Revisited: A Critical Quest for Truth and Transformation*, Frans Wijsen, Peter Henriot, Rodrigo Mejia (eds), 2005; for extracts from pp. 500–05, 511–12, from 'Feminist Ritual Strategies: the *Ekklesia Gynaikon* at Work', Marjorie Procter-Smith, in *Toward a New Heaven and a New Earth: Essays in Honor of Elisabeth Schussler Fiorenza*, Fernando F. Segovia (ed.), 2003; for extracts from pp. 11, 28, 29, from *The Violence of Love: The Words of Oscar Romero*, Oscar Romero, James R. Brockman (ed.), 1989; for extracts from pp. 1–4, from *Models of Contextual Theology*, Stephen Bevans, 1992; for extracts from pp. 73–9, from *The New Catholicity: Theology Between the Global and the Local*, Robert J. Schreiter, 1997. Reprinted with kind permission of Orbis.

Alicia Ostriker, for extracts from pp. 5–8, 13–16, from *The Nakedness of the Fathers*, Alicia Ostriker, 1994. Reprinted with kind permission of the author.

Oxford University Press, for extracts from pp. 291–311, from 'The Narrative Quality of Experience', Stephen Crites, in *The Journal of the American*

Academy of Religion, 39, 1971. Reprinted with kind permission of Oxford University Press.

'Some Straw for the Bricks: A Basic Introduction to Theological Reflection' by Stephen Pattison was first published in *Contact* 99, 1982, and is reprinted by permission of the author.

Peeters, for extracts from pp. 75, 93–101, from ' "A Voice Was Heard in Ramah": A Feminist Theology of Praxis for Healing in South Africa', Denise Ackermann, in *Liberation Faith Practices: Feminist Practical Theologies in Context*, Denise Ackermann, Riet Bons-Storm (eds), 1998. Reprinted with kind permission of Peeters.

Penguin, for extracts from pp. 211–13, 215–16, from *Confessions*, Augustine; R. S. Pine-Coffin (trans.), 1961, reprinted with kind permission of Penguin.

For extracts from *Love's Work* by Gillian Rose, copyright © 1995 by Random House, Inc. Used by permission of Random House, Inc.

From *On the Truth of the Catholic Faith* by St Thomas Aquinas, translated by Anton C. Pegis, copyright © 1955 by Doubleday, a division of Random House, Inc. Used by permission of Doubleday, a division of Random House, Inc.

Sage Publications, for extracts from 'How Common Worship Forms Local Character', Samuel Wells, in *Studies in Christian Ethics* 15/1, 2002. Reprinted with kind permission of Sage Publications.

SCM Press, for extracts from pp. 48–52, from *The Poet, The Warrior, The Prophet*, Rubem A. Alves, 2002; for extracts from pp. 133–43, from *Lifelong Learning*, Frances Ward, 2005; for extracts from pp. 7–10, from *Life Together*, Dietrich Bonhoeffer; John W. Doberstein (trans.), 1954; for extracts from pp. 5–9, from *Congregation: Stories and Structures*, James Hopewell, 1987; for extracts from pp. 14–16, 17–19, from *Metaphorical Theology: Models of God in Religious Language*, Sallie McFague, 1982; for extracts from pp. 217–22, from *Church in a Post-Liberal Age*, George Lindbeck; J. Buckley (ed.), 2002; for extracts from pp. 177–81, from 'Perspectives on the Local Church', Will Storrar, in *Studying Local Churches: A Handbook*, Helen Cameron, Philip Richter, Douglas Davies, Frances Ward (eds), 2005. Reprinted with kind permission of SCM Press.

Philip Sheldrake, for extracts from pp. 8–17, from 'Spaces and the Sacred: Cathedrals and Cities', Philip Sheldrake, in *Contact* 147, 2005. Reprinted with kind permission of the author.

SPCK, for extracts from pp. 410–13, 419–23, from *The Seven Storey Mountain*, Thomas Merton, 1948, reprinted with kind permission of SPCK.

Springer, for extracts from pp. 325, 327–30, from 'The Discipline and Habit of Theological Reflection' in *Journal of Religion and Health*, Heather A. Warren, Joan L. Murray and Mildred M. Best, Vol. 41, No. 4, Winter 2002, reprinted with kind permission of Springer.

University of Nebraska at Omaha, for extracts from 'Babette's Feast: a Religious Film', Wendy M. Wright, in *Journal of Religion and Film* [online], Vol. 1, No. 2, October 1997. Reprinted by kind permission of University of Nebraska at Omaha.

Verso, for extracts from pp. 12–19, from *Imagined Communities*, Benedict Anderson, 1983, reprinted with kind permission of the author.

Westminster John Knox Press, for extracts from pp. 42–6, 50–4, from *Doing Body Theology*, James B. Nelson, 1992; for extracts from 'Following Naked Dancing and Long Dreaming', Chung Hyun Kyung, in *Inheriting our Mothers' Gardens: Feminist Theology in Third World Perspective*, Letty M. Russell (ed.), 1988. Reproduced with kind permission of Westminster John Knox Press.

World Council of Churches, for extracts from 'An Introduction to Quaker Business Practice', Eden Grace [online], available at http://www.wcc-coe.org/wcc/who/damascuspost-03-e.html. Reprinted with kind permission of the author.

Subject Index

aesthetics, 307–8, 312, 419 (see also arts, the)

Anabaptist tradition, the, 151–2, **157–63**, 176

Anglican Church, the, 87, 144, 168, 210–11, 256, 258, 339, 434 (see also Church of England, the)

apologetic, 1, 37, 132, 179, 268, 285, 279

applied theology, see theology

architecture, **417–27** (see also aesthetics; arts, the)

arts, the, 40, 268, 303, 307–8, 312n, 429

autobiography, 51, 56, 68, 74, 129, 177, 400 (see also theology by heart)

axiom, 328, 334, 358

baptism, 164, 172–3, 210, 247, 321–2, 337, 339, 418 (see also liturgy)

Bible, the, 17, 37, 119–20, 136, 147, 152, **164–74**, 251, 262, 264, 267, 279, 310, 312, 330, 349, 375, 401, 404–5, 413, 415, 423 (see also biblical studies; scripture)

biblical studies, 1, 89, 253, 344, 408 (see also Bible, the; scripture)

blogging, 86–8 (see also internet; online church)

body, 21, 53–4, 69, 71–4, 78, 84–5, 93–4, 104, 110–11, 116, 123–4, **138–45**, 159, 204, 209–10, 213–5, 218–20, 223–4, 226–7, 242, 253–4, 257, 313, 315, 318, 334, 339, 347–8, 363–4, 376, 387–8, 396, 399n, 419, 427

business, 57, 117, 129, 131, 248, 265, 329, 336n, **349–57**, 387

canonical narrative theology, see theology

capitalism, 38, 173, 176, 224, 228, 233, 245, 292, 329–30, 333, 336n, 430

cathedral, 43, 416–29

Catholic Action (movement), 327–9, 332–3

Christendom, 168, 224–5, 228–9, 231

Christian social thought, 202, 285, 315, 333 (see also social justice)

Church of England, the, 258–9, 357n, 423 (see also Anglican Church, the)

"clash of civilizations", 228, 267n

Name Index